THE PEOPLE MACHINE

THE PEOPLE MACHINE

1817

The Influence of Television on American Politics

by Robert MacNeil

HARPER & ROW, PUBLISHERS

NEW YORK, EVANSTON, AND LONDON

THE PEOPLE MACHINE: *The Influence of Television on American Politics.* Copyright © 1968 by Robert MacNeil. Printed in the United States of America. All rights reserved. No part of this book may be used or reproduced in any manner whatsoever without written permission except in the case of brief quotations embodied in critical articles and reviews. For information address Harper & Row, Publishers, Incorporated, 49 East 33rd Street, New York, N.Y. 10016.

FIRST EDITION

LIBRARY OF CONGRESS CATALOG CARD NUMBER: 68-28209

To Jane

Contents

Preface, ix

Introduction: Television—One Generation Old, xiii

PART I. *"Here Is the News"*
 1. The Audience-Electorate, 3
 2. The Frailties of Television News, 18
 3. Consensus Journalism, 56
 4. Documentaries and Special Events, 75

PART II. *"I Give You the Next . . ."*
 5. Conventions and Election Nights, 95
 6. The Televisible Candidate, 126
 7. Debates, 163
 8. Campaigning by Commercial, 182
 9. The Cost, 228

PART III. *"Speaking to You from Washington . . ."*
 10. The Congressional Image, 243
 11. Government Regulation, 259

12. Presidential Access to Television, 292
13. The Future, 318

Notes, 335

Index, 345

Preface

In 1960, the Democratic Party made the first significant use of electronic computers in the election process. Various alternative campaign strategies were compared by computer with the results of numerous public-opinion surveys. The campaign strategists called the computer "the People Machine."

This faintly ominous phrase, with its overtones of thought control and opinion manipulation, perfectly describes my conception of the political role of American television. Television *is* the Machine through which American people are now reached, persuaded and nominally informed more extensively and homogeneously than ever before. The purpose of this book is to explain how the Machine is used.

The real impact of the medium on the American democratic process is still too sparsely documented or analyzed to justify sweeping conclusions. What evidence I have been able to accumulate disturbs me. It convinces me that there is a pressing need for more public attention to the commercial structure and journalistic independence of television, as well as its relations with government and its exploitation by politicians. In the past, eminent authorities such as V. O. Key have argued that elections *cannot* be controlled by Madison Avenue. Political advertising on television, however, has recently become so sophisticated and extensive as to put that comfortable conclusion in doubt. What goes on behind the screen to produce the political television seen in every American home is something the informed voter should know.

If my critical observations about informational television seem to neglect what is undeniably worth while, it is because someone needs to right the balance. Television's publicity machinery defends the industry so capably—sometimes so excessively—that its virtues are no secret. Perhaps the most self-congratulatory industry in the country, and certainly one of the most powerful lobbies in Washington, television needs no defending.

My observations are based on seven years as a correspondent with NBC News, overseas, in Washington and in New York, and on a year's research pursued after I left NBC to join the British Broadcasting Corporation and the Public Broadcast Laboratory. Naturally, the examples I cite are drawn most often from NBC, but the practices described apply equally, in most cases, to CBS and ABC. During the final writing, circumstances in Vietnam caused something of an upheaval in American television journalism. I would like to think that the sudden access of forthrightness stimulated by the Tet offensive early in 1968 marks an advance for television journalism. I hope this leap out of pusillanimity is permanent.

In addition to my own experiences and research in published materials, much in this book derives from interviews and correspondence I conducted with scores of people in television, government and politics. Many of them are identified in the notes. Some, who so preferred, are not named. I am deeply grateful for the time and thought each of them gave me.

One source upon whom I have leaned heavily is Jack Gould, the television critic of the *New York Times*. His daily columns, which he has graciously made available to me, constitute the most complete account I know of of the evolution of this industry during the past two decades. Gould is easily the most influential critic of the medium. Network executives habitually turn to the second-to-last page of the *Times* every morning for Gould's column before they read the front-page news.

Two other sources require special mention. Theodore H. White has of course provided indispensable accounts of the Presidential elections of this decade. He also happens to be one of the few political writers really sensitive to the impact of television. His vivid observations have been very helpful. Equally important and original in his own field is Herbert E. Alexander, the nation's leading expert on the financing of political campaigns. His many studies, published by the Citizen's Research Foundation of Princeton, New Jersey, are invaluable, and readers hungry for more information about this disturbing aspect of American politics (so intimately bound up with television) are referred to them.

I am grateful to many others who helped in various ways with my research: Maureen Drummy in Washington; Carla Hunt in New York; Neal Pierce, Political Editor of the *Congressional Quarterly,* and his research staff; the ladies in the General Reference Library at NBC; the managements of NBC News, CBS News and ABC News for providing scripts, recordings and other materials; Mr. A. F. Tegen for his generosity with office space in Manhattan; and David Webster, Editor of the BBC-TV program *Panorama,* for his indulgence.

Finally, this book would not have been possible without the dedicated cooperation and, indeed, collaboration, of my editor at Harper & Row, Norbert Slepyan.

R. M.

London
June, 1968

Introduction: Television— One Generation Old

Television has caused a more radical change in political communication than has any other development since our Republic was founded. Nothing before television altered so drastically the techniques of mass persuasion. No other medium has brought the ideal of an informed electorate so close to reality, yet poses so serious a threat of reducing our politics to triviality.

Realizing its enormous power, politicians are rushing to take this exciting new instrument in hand, but they are learning that the medium can both make a candidate and betray him.

The case of Richard M. Nixon is a classic example.

As Republicans gathered before television sets in September, 1960, to watch Nixon debate his Democratic opponent for the presidency, they had every reason to expect an evening of triumph. During the preceding decade, no other political figure seemed to grasp so well the effects of television on the audience-electorate. Astute handling of television, for instance, had kept him on the Eisenhower ticket of 1952 and had thus saved his political career. Other politicians had used TV to advantage in those years, but Nixon was surely the political "star" of the fifties. The Vice-President's supporters thus were satisfied that he would strip away the pretensions of the rich and admittedly handsome Senator John F. Kennedy, shattering the expensively manufactured Kennedy image in a single confrontation.

Instead they saw on the screen a sick, nervous man who appeared haggard and apprehensive as he faced the Massachusetts Senator. There were hollows under Nixon's eyes, and he looked unshaven. Occasionally he wiped perspiration from his face. Nixon seemed a living reproduction of the notorious caricatures cartoonist Herblock had drawn attacking him.

At any other moment in political history, or in Nixon's own life, it would not have mattered much that the Vice-President was not feeling well or even that his makeup had been applied amateurishly, but those accidents, interacting with Nixon's personality, caused an unappealing image of him to reach 70 million Americans, the greatest collection of people ever to witness a single political event.

Nixon still believes that his appearance during the first television debate with Kennedy played a major part in his defeat. Kennedy thought so too.

As the battle of images had gone against Nixon in 1960, so it promised a November defeat for Nelson Rockefeller when, early in April, 1966, the New York Governor called an important meeting in his private Manhattan office. Rockefeller had gathered his closest political advisers to discuss his apparently slim chances for reelection. His eight years in office had been fruitful in the social development of the state, but two tax increases during that period had eroded the Governor's political support. Privately taken polls showed his standing to be so low that his brother Laurence, who was present at the meeting, advised him not to run. Rockefeller decided to run.

Seven months later, Rockefeller won a third term by nearly 400,000 votes. Several factors contributed to his victory, but the principal influence in surmounting his unpopularity was the most adroit and costly use of television ever seen in a political campaign.

Taking politics away from the lawyers

Television has been part of American elections since 1948, but the small number of sets in use and stations operating (by 1952 there were still only 15 million sets and one hundred TV stations) in the early years limited its nationwide effectiveness. So did the uneasy approach of many politicians and the relatively stilted techniques devised by their advisers. In fact, the earnest fireside chats and full-blown speeches that were broadcast tended to weary and even to alienate voters. Today, politicians have all but abandoned such crude tactics, and have appropriated the subtle devices of the Madison Avenue image-makers. As one of the remarkable new breed of campaign directors, Joseph Napolitan, has put it: "We decided it was time to take politics away from the lawyers." The new campaign strategists have made it almost literally true that a politician can be marketed like a bar of soap or a box of corn flakes. They have also alarmingly escalated the costs of political campaigning, thereby imposing severe new strains on the democratic process.

Money spent in buying air time is virtually matched by money spent for expert polling, and for film and videotape production and promotion. In the 1966 Rockefeller campaign, 70 percent of the more than $5 million in campaign expenditures officially recorded was spent on television. Had the Governor's advertising agency, Jack Tinker Associates, had its way, the figure would have been 95 percent.

If politicians are willing to devote so much of their funds to television campaigning, it would be beneficial for the public they are trying to influence to be aware of what they are trying to do and how they are trying to do it. Even voters who are not swayed by television (or who at least think they are not) ought to know what is influencing their fellow voters who are. The demands of political leadership are too great and the pressures of today's political issues are too powerful for the public to allow meaningful political dialogue to diminish by default. Many observers of our political way of life fear that it is already doing so. Murray Levin, for example, has studied closely the campaign techniques of the Kennedy family and believes that television has made campaigns oriented less to issues and more to personality. The medium has also been accused of disrupting the essential cohesiveness of our political parties, and, by its high cost, of leading to a narrowing of the political dialogue because so few can afford to buy into it. Developments during the 1968 Democratic candidates' preconvention campaigns have tended to bear this out.

A golden goose that lays scrambled eggs

If these dangers are real, and if politicians do believe that the way to victory at the polls is through the "boob tube," then important questions are in order.

For instance, what is the source of television's ability to influence elections, to sway large numbers of people in making decisions affecting the future of the country and of the world? Who are these people? Where do they live? How much do they earn? How old are they and how well educated? Most important, how much of their information comes to them via television? For the audience-electorate, is watching replacing reading as the primary window on the world?

While the total circulation of newspapers is still rising (the number of available newspapers is, nevertheless, declining), many newspaper readers are watching television news as well. A large body of Americans who read newspapers infrequently or not at all are exposed to current affairs mainly through television. In 1967, in a survey taken by Burns W. Roper, 64 percent of those asked said they got most of their news about world events by means of television.[1]

In the past ten years, television has reached into virtually every home in the United States. In 1967, 94 percent of the households had at least one TV set. Although the novelty has had twenty years to wear off, television still commands the attention of the average American family for two to three hours every day, more than any other leisure activity.

What are the effects, then, of this day-to-day exposure? What image of the world is the audience-electorate given by television entertainment? What is the intended function of this entertainment, especially with regard to commercials?

More crucial, what about nonentertainment? According to historian Arthur Schlesinger, Jr.: "Probably the greatest influence in shaping political judgment is still the reality of events themselves."[2]

It is inevitable that developments in politics, the economic situation, social conditions, military affairs, science, religion and education have as much to do with the outcome of elections as do the hectic campaign efforts of politicians. How are events reported to the television audience? Is television journalism pursued with the same high standards of accuracy, thoroughness and independence that mark the best of print journalism? Do television entertainment values affect television news? How much respect do television news departments command in the various networks? Under what conditions do TV reporters and commentators work? How forthright are they in covering major issues such as Vietnam and the Negro Revolution? As filters through which the news passes to the audience-electorate, what effects do "stars" like Walter Cronkite, Chet Huntley, David Brinkley, Frank Reynolds and others have on the "shape" of events as the TV viewers see them? Do documentaries and special reports on television serve to increase the political sophistication of the viewer-voter?

Of whatever quality it may be, political information flows to the audience-electorate in a fairly steady stream from day to day, but during campaign years the flow intensifies sharply, and takes varied forms which roughly correspond to more usual television fare. Coverage of conventions and election night voting results involves multimillion-dollar production costs, great blocks of valuable air time and battles for audience and prestige. They are the "spectaculars" of the TV news world.

Day-by-day campaign reports spin on through regular newscasts and special reports. The candidates make their progress through engineered crowds, taking part in manufactured pseudo events, thrusting and parrying charges, projecting as much as they can, with the help of makeup and technology, the qualities of youth, experience, sincerity, popularity, alertness, wisdom and vigor. And television follows them, hungry for material that is new and sensational.

The new campaign strategists also generate films that are like syrupy documentaries: special profiles of candidates, homey, bathed in soft light, resonant with stirring music, creating personality images such as few mortals could emulate.

Analogous to television's ordinary spot commercials are political spot commercials. These are being used more and more frequently, and are directed more and more adroitly at that special, sizable group of voters whom the pollsters have identified as particularly susceptible to televised salesmanship and uncritical in their political judgments. The commercial has long been the cornerstone of television profit; it has also become the cornerstone of campaign success.

In view of the expertise with which politicians seek to reach and "sell" him, the voter may well wonder how it is being done and what television is doing to our political system. What, for instance, is a *televisible* candidate, and how important is it for an aspirant to be one? How is he chosen or created? How can an unknown be made into a "major political figure"? On the other hand, is it true that in spite of all the image-making, the television camera mercilessly separates the false from the true? How serious are programs such as *Meet the Press, Face the Nation* and *Issues and Answers* about penetrating a candidate's image to get to the man beneath? Do television debates reveal or conceal the candidates' true qualities? How are polls and mass advertising combined in commercial campaigns?

Government by television?

Television is but one generation old and is still growing. Among the many problems it has created in that time, none is greater than that of the industry's relationship with government.

At the heart of our system is the understanding that not only will the branches of government limit each other's power, but that the public will keep a close watch on all branches so as to control them. The mechanism for this surveillance is the workings of the press, including television journalism. Given this responsibility, it would follow that television journalists should be exceedingly jealous of their honor in dealing with government, if only because access to their medium is so important to politicians. Unfortunately, television has not guarded its integrity sufficiently well. There is evidence that the television industry, for its own commercial purposes and in unwarranted fear for the safety of its licenses to operate, has at times forced its news departments to adopt a craven and accommodating attitude to Congress and the White House.

At other times, the industry has shown some backbone, but in the words of a White House official who observed the relations of President Johnson and the broadcasting industry: "TV is probably the most powerful mass medium we have, but without a doubt it is more subservient to the establishment than other media. Either it doesn't fully realize its own power or doesn't know how to use it, or is so dependent upon the establishment for survival that it is terrified to antagonize it. It's a giant with a huge club, but with very weak knees."[3]

Richard S. Salant, President of CBS News, regards television as being "more susceptible to Presidential and Congressional pressure than other media. This is simply because television is licensed and because the President, and particularly some legislators, do not regard broadcast journalism as having the right to be independent. Rather they seem to believe that broadcast journalism must somehow or other act as an instrument of their particular version of national policy."[4]

How strong is this tendency of elected officials right up to the President—who are, after all, elected increasingly with the help of television—to treat the medium imperiously? With what obviousness or subtlety do they use it? How do government regulations and the threat of adding more of them affect television policies? How great is the danger that certain powerful officials, especially in the Executive branch, will use television merely as a means of announcing decisions while discouraging discussion, analysis and criticism of what is decided? In other words, are we headed toward an Orwellian world in which television is the voice of a not always visible Big Brother?

If there is much that is exciting and laudable in what television has brought to American public life, there is also much that is disturbing. The beginning of the second generation is a good time to ask questions.

In 1964, Newton Minow wrote: "Through television this nation has moved a long way toward fulfilling an ideal of representative government, with each responsible citizen able to cast a vote with full information and knowledge. We have also stumbled into this electronic evolution with almost no forethought, and we most urgently require a modern map with careful markings on areas that contain quicksand and rockslides."[5]

With these questions as guides, let us now attempt to chart some of the quicksands and rockslides.

PART I

"Here Is the News"

1 The Audience-Electorate

If you are a regular watcher of the *Huntley-Brinkley Report* or the *CBS Evening News with Walter Cronkite,* what are you like? Where do you live? What kind of job do you have? How far did you go in school and how much money do you make? What magazines do you normally read?

Since we are going to look in detail at how politics and news are handled and influenced by American commercial television, we ought first to consider the people who often watch television.

The audience our politicians are trying to reach is an audience that commercial television has built up for other purposes. It is, as Richard S. Salant of CBS has written, "popular *entertainment* which motivated the initial purchase of receivers and which keeps the public in the habit of turning to their radios and television sets for political campaigns."[1] It is also to an extent Chet Huntley, David Brinkley and Walter Cronkite who have created the audience for politicians. What attitudes can the politician expect to find built into this audience by years of exposure to network entertainment, advertising and news? What has a generation of television done to the electorate? First, the news audience. This is what researchers for NBC and CBS have painstakingly discovered:

Perhaps the most remarkable thing about the 36 million Americans who have their television sets tuned to one of the three network news shows each evening is that they are almost a perfect cross section of the nation. By age, household income, education, county size, territory and occupation, they closely follow the national population averages. According to Brand Rating Index, 28.5 percent of American adult men have an education of grade school or less, 43.9 percent went to high school but not beyond, 27.7 percent went to college. In the fall of 1966, adult men who watched the early evening news on CBS, NBC or ABC broke down this way by education: 30.7 percent, grade school or less; 43.7 percent, high school but not beyond; 25.6 percent went to college.[2]

The correspondence between the general American population and that portion of it watching network news is equally close in other categories. One-quarter of the adult women of America (25.8 percent) live in the northeastern part of the country. So do 24 percent of the women who watch network news programs. One-tenth of American men (10.9 percent) work in managerial, office or executive jobs or are proprietors of a business. Those are the occupations of 10.4 percent of the men in the news audience. If these surveys are accurate, the network news departments have been uncanny in hitting a formula for news presentation that induces Americans to sort themselves out with such statistical neatness for the evening ritual. When the magic line is crossed at 7:30 P.M. into the profitable dream world the broadcasters call "prime time," adult America does not fall into the same pattern.

There are places where network news viewers differ slightly from the national population averages. Putting those variations together, one could say that the early-evening news seems to have rather more appeal for men over fifty years and somewhat more for women over fifty than for men of that age group. Proportionately, in their population group, more grade-school-educated Americans are drawn to these programs than are those who went to college or high school. People who earn their living as craftsmen and foremen, or who are students, unemployed or retired, tune in more than people in other professions above or below them. People in smaller towns and rural areas have a stronger habit for Cronkite and for Huntley and Brinkley than do residents of bigger towns and cities, and so do people with household incomes of $8,000 a year or less. These variations are marginal, however, a few percentiles away from the national averages.

So are the variations between the programs themselves. Walter Cronkite attracts a slightly older audience than do Huntley and

Brinkley, while they can attract more women than he can. Over a number of years, the size of their audiences has fluctuated, with CBS doing somewhat better in the summertime, presumably because younger people are outdoors or away on vacation more than are older Americans. On a sample evening, January 11, 1967, the adult audiences were: Huntley and Brinkley (NBC), 16,570,000; Walter Cronkite (CBS), 13,900,000; Peter Jennings (ABC), 5,930,000.[3]

What kind of people these are, and what appetite for information they bring to these programs, is better revealed by describing their reading habits.

Television and the printed word

There are relatively few very heavy readers of magazines or newspapers among the regular TV news audiences. The following table shows how the TV news audience compares with the national average in newspaper and magazine reading.[4] In almost every

	TV-news audience	United States average
Magazine Reading		
Very heavy	17%	16%
Heavy	16	15
Moderate	35	34
Light	13	13
None	19	22
Newspaper Reading		
Very heavy	12	11
Heavy	28	26
Moderate	31	31
Light	10	10
None	19	19

case, the TV news watchers are slightly heavier readers than the population in general. It is fair to say, however, that only the top half of the audience for TV news turns on the television set each evening with any considerable body of knowledge of current affairs. The rest, roughly 18 million people, must be relying heavily on television. Considering that for reasons of status most of us are likely to overstate the amount we read, the dependence on television may be even greater than these figures suggest.

An even clearer picture of the service television journalism provides can be found by looking at which magazines the TV news audience reads. Those most widely read are *Life, Look, Saturday Evening Post* and *TV Guide.* More than a quarter of those watching *Huntley-Brinkley* and *Walter Cronkite* say they read these magazines. When it comes to what the surveys call "general quality" magazines, *Time* and *Newsweek,* there is a much lower percentage of readers in the TV news audience—8 percent of the *Huntley-Brinkley* viewers, 7 percent of *Cronkite*'s.

This is revealing. *Time* and *Newsweek* are undoubtedly the magazines the average American with an interest in staying well informed week by week would turn to. (*U.S. News and World Report* is not included in the survey quoted above.) If 8 percent of the *Huntley-Brinkley* viewers and 7 percent of *Walter Cronkite*'s read these news magazines, then 15 percent of their combined nightly audience of roughly 26 million viewers a night—or 4 million viewers—read *Time* or *Newsweek.* Since the combined adult readership of these two magazines is approximately 25 million,[5] that leaves some 21 million *Time* or *Newsweek* readers not watching the two principal TV news programs. On a weekly basis, NBC claims that *Huntley-Brinkley* has a total audience of 30 million. Supposing it is the same for *Walter Cronkite,* then 60 million people see something of these programs in a week. But 15 percent of that is still only 9 million people, which still leaves 16 million readers of the two news magazines who do not bother to watch network news, although some might be watching ABC. In other words, network television news apparently does not have enough to say to a large body of people who make some positive effort to stay abreast of current affairs.

What do the millions who do depend on television for their knowledge of the world get for their allegiance? To some observers not nearly enough. It was reported in 1967 that three-quarters of a questioned sample of American voters could not properly identify the Vietcong, and when CBS put on a current events test oriented to tenth-grade standards, nearly three-quarters of the sample audience flunked it.[6]

Whatever the failings on specific information, however, many authorities believe that the American public is better informed than it was a generation ago. Some of the credit must go to television, as well as improved and wider education. Herbert J. Gans, the New York University sociologist, believes that the "low culture" group in America (people with lower incomes and less education) "is better informed and more sophisticated today than a generation ago, thanks partly to the mass media, but principally as a result of their increasing urbanization."[7] Elmo Roper, one of the most experienced students of American public opinion, believes that in the last thirty years there has been a revolution in the basic values and commitments of the American people.[8] Roper thinks that people have grown more compassionate about less fortunate members of society, more tolerant about a government role in assuring a decent standard of living to all, and that they accept a wide involvement of their country in international affairs, instead of isolation, as the hope for peace. Professor Gans believes that while the popular culture does reflect more liberal ideas, it is, nevertheless, "still slanted in a conservative direction, and sympathy for the civil rights movement disappears when demonstrations take place outside the Deep South. . . . Even in the lower middle culture some of the changes are only in their infancy."[9]

The lower middle culture is precisely the group, Gans says, who rely on television for their information: "Lower middle culture is the culture of the white collar population, the people with high school diplomas, technical training and increasingly with some years of further education at state universities and small colleges. This taste group is today's mass audience and most of the mass media content and national advertising is aimed at its members, for Hollywood films and for the TV programs with the highest ratings. Huntley and Brinkley speak to them. . . ."[10]

Sufficient research to find out what effect the mass media have on people's thinking is lacking. What has been done, by Professor Gans, for example, does not reveal any dramatic improvement attributable to television. To take one example, television journalism has devoted a substantial amount of time to the civil rights question, from the time of the Little Rock crisis in 1957 to the present. The tone of *network* programming has been emphatically liberal, identifying the advancement of the American Negro toward equality as unquestionably linked to the health of this nation. Doubtless this gave hope to Negroes in the South who had never heard issues involving their rights reported sympathetically. But the report of the President's Commission on Civil Disorders in March, 1968, provided abundant evidence that the education of the lower-middle-class white American has not gone far enough. To the extent it *has* moved, television can claim substantial credit. The three-hour documentary *The American Revolution of 1963,* which NBC mounted in September of that year, was an example of how far television could go, but it is idle to claim, as some people do, that television is more than just another voice crying for reason. People in television so habitually think in millions (of dollars as well as of people) that they assume every word they utter and every picture they show is absorbed with equal intensity by all of their viewers. The audience can, in fact, seem stunningly indifferent.

Professor Gans believes that television and the other mass media "provide more news and controversy than the majority of the audience are willing to accept."[11] In later chapters we shall examine the quality and quantity of information the television news programs give their viewers. For now, let us accept that although millions of people rely on television for information, the amount the medium gives them, the amount they seek or are willing to accept have not brought about any miracle in mass education; a significant number of Americans who want more information turn elsewhere.

A more reliable way of measuring the effect of informational programming on the television audience is to look at the effect on voter turnout. The television industry believes it has significantly raised the proportion of people eligible to vote who actually do so. Authorities outside the industry find no proof that this is so.

Richard Scammon, head of the Election Research Center in Washington, says: "TV has understandably made people more knowledgeable about politics. It certainly has not *decreased* turnout. Perhaps it has made some contribution but it is only one of a number of factors. For example, there is a greater vote in the South due to the abolition of the poll tax."[12]

A thorough study of the effect of TV on voting turnout was made by William A. Glaser of Columbia University. He noted that there had been heavy use of television by get-out-the-vote campaigns sponsored by the American Heritage Foundation, the Advertising Council and other groups. At first glance, television seemed to have superior impact because more people could recall reminders to vote through television than could those through other media. But reminders through the mail and in the press appeared to be more effective in actually getting people to vote. Glaser concluded: " . . . newspaper reading may be more effective than television watching in affecting turnout and in affecting the fulfillment of intention to vote. Or, perhaps a more accurate statement is that newspaper reading and television watching are associated with partly different modes of life with different political patterns. When practiced jointly, newspaper reading and television watching are associated with very high rates of turnout, but television watching may 'add' less to the combination than newspapers."[13]

We have seen, though, that newspaper reading and television watching are "practiced jointly" by only a portion of the television audience, which strengthens the implication that television alone does not raise turnout.

Television made its biggest claim to have increased the vote after the first Eisenhower-Stevenson election in 1952, when the vote increased by 26 percent over 1948. The claim was based on the fact that there were very few television sets in 1948, while more than 15 million homes had them by 1952. But there have been other spectacular leaps in turnout earlier in American history. Between 1836 and 1840, it rose by 100 percent. It rose by 40 percent when Lincoln was first elected President in 1860, compared to the 1856 election. It went up by 30 percent between 1916 and 1920, and by 25 percent between 1924 and 1928.[14] Elmo Roper believes that the biggest barrier to voting is not apathy but restrictive state voting requirements: "Clearly, changes in those voting requirements would do more to 'get out the vote' than any amount of preaching about the virtues of voting by public opinion pollsters or citizens' groups."[15] A study by the Carnegie Institute of Technology of voting behavior in Iowa counties with very high or very low television density in 1952 discovered no television impact on turnout.

If television journalism is not yet able to demonstrate that it has galvanized the sluggish masses into more spirited citizenship, it can properly make other claims.

It is the credo of Reuven Frank, President of NBC News, who created the *Huntley-Brinkley Report,* that "television is a medium for transmitting experience." He says: "It has never covered a national budget and it never will. The reason we don't put the national budget on is that we know people will tune out. We don't consciously put things on that no one will watch."[16]

Television certainly has transmitted experience of the real world over hundreds of millions of viewer hours in the last decade. One can only guess at what effect that dwarf-size, luminous and now colored view of the world has had. People who never travel have seen much of their own country and heard a wide variety of their countrymen talk. People who will never go to the White House have been shown around it by Jacqueline Kennedy and have been able to stare at her as they could never do if they met her. People who will never go to war have now almost "been" there. People who do not have enough to eat have seen the rest of America eating well. People who do not pray hear praying and those who may pray too much have heard others say there is no God to pray to. Bigoted whites have been inside respectable Negro homes. Republicans have heard talks by Democratic politicians. Americans have seen their President's presumed murderer murdered before their eyes.

American television cannot be called a crusader, but it has the modest virtue of having permitted Americans a glimpse of what is real. It may be powerful medicine, although slow-acting.

Idiot box and boob tube

Variety says that "people who were given eyewitness to the Kennedy assassination aftermath and the UN debates on the Arab-

Israel war tend not to think of that as *'television.'* " The reason, the paper says, is that "from its first days, television has been held in the lowest esteem as a cultural force in this country, rapped on all sides for its base commercial motives and lowest common denominator mentality and called names like 'idiot box' and 'boob tube.' "[17] *Variety* is not suggesting that television does not deserve these names.

In 1952, television broadcasters subscribed to a voluntary set of standards known as the Television Code. The preamble to the Code states: "The revenues from advertising support the free, competitive American system of telecasting, and make available to the eyes and ears of the American people the finest programs of information, education, culture and entertainment. By law, the television broadcaster is responsible for the programming of his station. He, however, is obligated to bring his positive responsibility for excellence and good taste in programming to bear upon all who have a hand in the production of programs, including networks, sponsors, producers of film and of live programs, advertising agencies and talent agencies."

It is difficult to know which of those fulsome sentences is most astonishing in the light of what has passed through American television screens since 1952. Few network or local broadcasters seem to have felt an obligation to exercise their "positive responsibility for excellence and good taste." The trouble is that concerned people, including many newspaper critics, have been attacking this neglect for so long, and to such small effect, that they have wearied of the effort. To keep some respectability, they gratefully turn to praising the tidbits of news programming or specials the networks toss out occasionally to placate them. The mornings, afternoons and evenings of rubbish grind on, with a louder and more hysterical fanfare each year for the new season. Sometimes the critics can stand it no longer. This is how *Variety* greeted the 1967–68 season: "They have, with their 1967–68 premieres, brought nothing new to the medium that is a national rage, nothing that is artistically commendable, nothing that advances the medium itself, and nothing to make people—even schoolchildren—talk about or anticipate a single half hour every week."

It is necessary to point out, for those who forget it, that television is not in business primarily to entertain, edify or instruct, whatever the TV Code may say. Those are incidentals. It is in the audience-delivery business, the business of selling time to advertisers. They will buy time when broadcasters can demonstrate that for the price they charge the advertiser will be guaranteed a larger number of viewers in a certain income and age range than another broadcaster can guarantee at the same time of day. To make the system easier to operate and safer for the advertiser, there has been a gradual growth of the "scatter plan," a method by which advertisers are allowed to spread their commercials all over the clock, to appear in any program, so long as the quantity and quality of the audience to be found there suits their purpose. Makers of Geritol, for example, do not want to run their commercials during *Batman* because children do not use Geritol. To make it simpler still, the audience is sorted and arranged by the broadcaster, and offered to the advertiser at a certain "cost per thousand."

Programming is devised (largely in Hollywood) and pretested on audiences to have maximum appeal for groups of viewers advertisers most want to reach. The single group that is most sought after by advertisers are people aged eighteen to thirty-four, for they have most of the buying power in the United States.

Gunsmoke was a popular program on CBS but it was dropped from the 1967–68 schedule despite its high rating because it was attracting too many older people. If a show stays on television too long, its fans get older with it. Fortunately for them, there are still a few businesses around with goods to sell to the old folks. CBS had second thoughts and *Gunsmoke* was granted a late reprieve. It is not much fun getting old in televisionland. You may have stationed yourself dutifully in front of the box for twenty years, helping to make incredible profits for the television industry, but that is forgotten when you pass over the hill at about fifty.

It is this ruthless world that the politician invades at election time, perhaps innocently believing that he is welcome there. It is this world that TV journalists, now and then during the day, are grudgingly permitted to enter with their brief bulletins from outside. It is essential, if either the politician or the journalist is to reach the mind of anyone in this world, that he make himself competitive, that he sufficiently resemble the other goods sold in this market. For the journalist that means mixing show business with his journalism; for the politician it means a willingness to be sold like Geritol.

Reports from never-never land

Television is a machine to manufacture reassurance for troubled Americans. Not confined to commercials, reassurance is part of the entertainment and sometimes even part of the news. The characters in the situation comedies and formula dramas are extensions of the people in the commercials. The object is to disconnect the audience from uncomfortable realities, to lull it on a sea of gentle inconsequence—and then to sell it deodorant.

Few lives are so satisfying or absorbing that people want to live in full-time contact with them. For millions, turning on the television after supper is like the Gemini astronauts cutting the switch that brought in noise from earth and kept them awake. It is snobbish and dishonest to criticize people for wanting to use television to escape, but it is right to criticize the television industry for using this miracle of communications—and the public airwaves—for virtually nothing but escapist fare.

The networks do have their intellectual defenders. Professor Louis L. Jaffe, then a professor of law at Harvard, said in 1961: "These passive sponges are so completely bereft of culture that for them the quality of programs is immaterial."[18] Other academics less cynical have found that habitual exposure to the mass media, which reduce even profound experiences to clichés, "impairs the capacity for meaningful experience . . . inhibits ability to cope with reality."[19]

Broadcasters have become candid in their own defense. Paul Lafferty, the West Coast program head for CBS-TV, made a speech in Hollywood in 1967 in defense of escapism. *Variety* reported: "The public uses TV to escape from the pressures of jobs and marriages, the problems with their kids, their health and their anxieties, he said. Mostly they don't want to be intellectually stimulated and they don't want to be educated; they want to bury their problems in the 23-inch screen. [He] said he doesn't believe anything should be done to change this because all have the right to watch whatever kind of TV they want. And it's because they want escapism in large quantities that the basic programming forms in TV have changed very little since 1950, he noted."[20]

Jack Gould, of the *New York Times,* believes that a major attraction of the medium is its essential simplicity. "The life of the world and the life of the individual are fearfully complicated but the home screen never leaves a problem unresolved beyond the closing commercial. Video, by its very nature, is a cultural barbiturate: in a society beset by leisure time and anxiety, video kills time efficiently and economically."[21]

Perhaps most important for the political consequences, television keeps controversy at bay. Controversy on any level disturbs someone in the audience. Therefore, the day passes on television in almost total blandness. Even the voices, as Michael Arlen of *The New Yorker* has noticed, are "nearly classless, regionless, moderate, well modulated, no sharps, no flats, no tricky chords, no tears, no fits, not even anger."[22]

Television defends itself by saying repeatedly that it *does* operate in the public interest because it gives the public "what it wants." For millions of its viewers that is quite true. Television apologists are as handy with opinion surveys as President Johnson with political polls. Surveys still show that a majority of viewers are satisfied with television fare the way it is, but not as many are satisfied as used to be.

In 1961, Newton Minow made his famous remark that television was a "vast wasteland." The same year Robert Sarnoff, President of NBC, stated his belief that television served the public interest, and was "a balanced blend of light and high-brow entertainment, public affairs and news." Burns W. Roper did surveys in the following years asking people which of these two statements they agreed with. In 1961, 55 percent agreed with Sarnoff and 23 percent with Minow. In 1967, 53 percent still agreed with Sarnoff but 29 percent had come to think, like Minow, that television was a "vast wasteland."[23] Roper commented: "This trend is not healthy from the point of view of television."

While a constant diet of escapist television may be just what millions want (the sale of pulp magazines has shrunk drastically since TV became popular), it is probably denying another important group. The population is not divided into tasteless masses and highly cultured intellectuals. There are many shades of taste and curiosity. It is the marginally curious, especially the young, who may not be strongly motivated by their background or education to improve their taste but who might watch something more stimulating—if it were put there. The passivity television induces in the viewer does not only work for the advertiser; it could as well be used by someone with something fresh or instructive to say. But people on the fringe of those content with escapism will, if fed escapism, happily accept what is offered by an industry ready to exploit their vacant hours and cravings.

The national networks do not like it to be thought that their programs are watched only by low-culture groups. Members of such groups do not get good jobs, and are not good consumers. So it did not please the industry when the respected pollster Louis Harris claimed in January, 1967, that better-educated Americans were abandoning television while it was gaining among the less well-to-do. Harris concluded that "among the most affluent one-fourth of the population, a majority of TV sets are not turned on during most of the evening" and that "a decline in TV viewing among the affluent—people earning more than $10,000 a year—and the college educated continues unabated."[24]

His findings conflicted with information prepared by the A. C. Nielsen Company, the biggest of the firms that supply broadcasters with audience measurement or ratings. Nielsen claimed just the opposite, that viewing by people with incomes over $10,000 had gone up (by 1 percent) from 1965 to 1966 and that low-income viewers had declined (by 3 percent). Nielsen added what advertisers especially liked to hear, that viewing among young adults (eighteen to thirty-four years) had risen substantially.[25]

Whether you believe Nielsen, whose fortunes are wedded to the broadcasting industry, or Harris, whose political polls have had to stand the test of proof in the voting booth, is a matter of personal choice. The fact is that television is not accepted by many intelligent and busy Americans as a necessary or useful part of their lives.

Among the influences at work on the television audience, conditioning it, affecting its attitudes and predisposing it to adopt certain criteria in judging people, the commercials are perhaps the most significant.

Americans are used to a constant barrage of selling. The *Encyclopaedia Britannica 1967 Book of the Year* estimates that the average adult in this country is exposed to more than 650 advertising messages a day, and a study by the advertising industry found that 85 percent of all advertising is not even looked at. Advertising on television, however, is hard not to look at. Even when a viewer tears his eyes from the screen he is pursued by the higher sound volume that, despite the denials of broadcasters, is all too noticeable.

Herbert E. Krugman, who has studied the impact of television advertising, reported that "the public easily lets down its guard to the repetitive commercial use of the TV medium and [that] it easily changes its ways of perceiving products and brands and its purchasing behavior without thinking very much about it at the time of the TV exposure or at any time prior to purchase."[26] Krugman's analysis amounts to a claim that the public can be brainwashed by TV commercials, that levels of the mind below consciousness are played upon and conditioned to produce responses which appear, unbidden, much later. "Furthermore," he adds, "this success seems to be based on a left-handed kind of public trust that sees no great importance in the matter." The political applications of this analysis are obvious. Professor Gans believes that people "accept unquestioningly media content on subject matter of little interest to them."

If incessant hammering with commercial messages thus lowers resistance and disarms the critical faculties, then television has handed the politician willing to use it a vast group of people preconditioned to allow their intellectual privacy to be constantly invaded. They are inured by constant exposure to the subtlest machinery of propaganda, presented in an aura of reassurance which they find comforting. Although the regular audience does not include a high proportion of the upper reaches of American society, in terms of education and wealth, it does comprise a large, influential and highly impressionable mass. It is an audience, as we have seen, that is moderately more sophisticated and somewhat better informed than that of a generation ago, but it is basically conservative and, from its reading habits, passive and incurious about the world. Because it is not particularly interested in many subjects and issues, it will apparently accept what it is told about them more or less trustingly. If it sounds insulting to describe such a large segment of American citizens and voters in these terms, who is to blame for their condition? As a Harvard law professor, Charles L. Black, Jr., put it, one is inclined to "tremble for the sanity of society bombarded with what promoters throw at it . . . forced feeding with trivial fare is not trivial."[27]

2 The Frailties of Television News

In 1958, Edward R. Murrow, the most renowned of electronic journalists, said that broadcast news had grown up "as an incompatible combination of show business, advertising and news."[1] A decade later, although it has grown immensely in power and prestige, television journalism still combines those three ingredients and the combination is still incompatible.

It is pointless to criticize this new journalism for having to share its medium with mass entertainment. William R. McAndrew, late President of NBC News, a man who did much to develop the journalistic potential of TV, has put the situation well: "Our journalism is part of the world of television, which is in great measure a purveyor of entertainment, much of it distinctly lowbrow at that. We are equated with show business and, without belaboring the point, I will only state that this is not an equation that informed, responsible men should rely on."[2]

The equation is not reliable if the bulkheads between news and entertainment TV, with its show business-advertising orientation, are watertight. Unfortunately, they are not. It is not true to say that television journalism *is* show business; it is true that its destiny is ultimately in the hands of men who make their livings in show business and advertising.

For the most part, the men who run the news departments of the three big networks are responsible people with a healthy devotion to the ideals of good journalism. Despite the veneer of cynicism they wear as a defense, most of them are embarrassed by their subservience to other men who are not, or cannot afford to be, devoted to the same ideals. For they know that whatever measure of autonomy and freedom of action the news departments may enjoy at any moment, it is constantly threatened by capricious influences from above. The news people resist what they consider improper influences when they can, and submit when they have to, to survive. They are proud of their victories and rationalize their defeats as tactical withdrawals. They toil with a long view, preferring to think optimistically of a better future, and they confine their disappointments to bitter, private humor over lunch.

Louis Cowan, former President of the CBS-TV network and now a professor at Columbia University, says: "There is an integrity about the news operation which is solid; but not at the network level, at the news department level."[3] Regrettably, it is at the *network* level that the crucial decisions over air time for news, budgets and even the contents of news programs are made. No amount of "integrity" at the news-department level can alter that. The tension rarely produces a big crisis. The news executive may, under unusual provocation, stand by a principle and threaten to resign; he may win a point. Yet control remains beyond his grasp. Dramatic collisions that reach public notice, like Fred Friendly's resignation from CBS in 1966, are rare. Most of the disputes burn out in the thick atmosphere of self-protection and abhorrence of adverse publicity that envelops the television industry.

Cowan continues: "TV is a serious instrument to get and give the news but the time periods are not given. They are not against putting on news but price and audience considerations work against news to the degree that news does not get an audience. Certainly they have not done as much as they might have about news."

The result is that television as a journalistic medium is not highly esteemed by serious print journalists. Many of them would agree with Lester Markel, Associate Editor of the *New York Times,* that "for the large majority, TV is a medium of entertainment." Markel thinks that "anything these viewers acquire by way of information or culture is incidental and almost accidental."[4]

It is this "accidental" factor which is most disturbing when one considers the role of TV journalism today. As we have seen, it is for a great body of Americans the primary source of information. It is a medium increasingly invaded by politicians and under great pressure from powerful officeholders, especially in the White House, to present issues in a manner favorable to them. If TV is thus regarded by politicians as the most powerful medium and at the same time a medium whose journalistic independence is not guaranteed, the results do not serve the American people well. It should not be merely an accident that TV journalists have the time and the money and the autonomy to pursue their craft. But too often it is an accident, and the system of many compromises is simply not good enough, because the product is compromised. That does not disturb people at the network level above the news departments, because they look upon news as another commodity, which sells or does not sell, attracts audience or does not. They believe that, like the other commodities television purveys, news can be shaped, reworked and manipulated, or simply dropped. There is, however, one factor which distinguishes news from almost everything else the networks transmit: it earns prestige.

Prestige for a television network is like the dwindling hoard of gold held by the United States Government. Ever since television became a national medium, the networks have been suffering from a credibility gap between their claims and their performance. Emphasis on news and informational programming is an attempt to close the gap. For broadcast journalism, the need for prestige is the need for health and security. On the surface, then, the arrangement would seem sensible and healthy. To placate the critics, the networks hire keen, thoughtful journalists. Unfortunately, that is not the whole story.

It was quickly discovered by the industry that because prestige was an intangible commodity and the critics who conferred it were fickle, the networks did not always get praise when they thought they had earned it, and they did not always deserve it when it came.

Prestige-earning programs of a cultural or informational nature are expensive. Public service programming may weigh heavily now and then when network executives journey to Washington to tell

Congressional committees once more about their selfless dedication to the public good; but it does not make money. It is easier and cheaper to put on the minimum informational programming that the critics and the competitive situation will accept and then give public relations men the job of inflating the image. The networks do put on a substantial amount of news and current events programming, some of it even profitable, but it remains at the periphery of the industry. The network press departments have the job of making it seem more than it is, so that even within the network news departments, the *appearance* sometimes becomes more important than the *reality;* the news image is often more energetically and expensively pursued than the news itself.

Within the news departments, the activities of the public relations men employed to aggrandize their image are viewed with a mixture of amazement, ridicule and contempt. The network flacks are despised, but they are also feared, because their power derives from the top echelons of the network. Those television journalists who wish to survive and prosper in the system cooperate.

Broadcasting is a business in which it is not only permitted but vital to blow your own horn. It is not sufficient to have performed well. In a medium as evanescent as television that performance will be quickly forgotten. The ambitious man at every level must ensure that everyone who matters in his company and the industry knows what a great job he has done. How to achieve this while affecting a nice modesty among your fellows is one of the subtlest skills in the trade; at the top of the television business (and news departments are no exception), where the stakes are very high, it is useful to have the assistance of professional public relations men. That is just one of the considerations which set the TV journalist apart from his newspaper colleagues.

The first weakness of television journalism is that it suffers from the advertising disease, and is neurotic with self-praise. News programs are required to win maximum audiences just like entertainment programs to enhance their appeal to advertisers. So news programs are promoted as hysterically as are entertainment shows. Working in a network news department is like living behind a ceaseless artillery barrage. The mind at first aches with the constant explosion of superlatives. Eventually, the eyes and ears are numbed. What is particularly debasing to people who are supposed to be dealing in facts is that they are promoted and sold to the public by people with little respect for the truth. Inevitably this infects the news people themselves.

On June 14, 1967, NBC's local station in New York published an advertisement in the *New York Times* to promote the *Eleventh Hour News* and its anchorman, Jim Hartz. The program had earned considerable public following in several years of competent reporting but that wasn't good enough for the PR men.

"Jim and the Eleventh Hour Staff pore over thousands of reports compiled each day by NBC News correspondents in 75 countries to bring you New York's most meaningful late-evening report," the advertisement said. Somewhere between the news department and the man who wrote that copy, there was a considerable separation from the facts.

NBC News employs a large staff in the United States and up to a dozen correspondents overseas. They do not compile "thousands of reports" each day; as we shall see below, they compile very few. As do the other networks, NBC bases the bulk of its news service on the worldwide facilities of the Associated Press, United Press International and Reuters. The networks also have interlocking arrangements to exchange news film made by other broadcasting organizations. On occasion, the services of "stringers" or part-time correspondents employed by a newspaper or wire service are called upon, though more often for radio than for television. At the particular period of the advertisement quoted, in fact, WNBC had introduced an economy wave. The budget of the *Eleventh Hour News* did not permit it to pay for as many fresh reports from around the United States each evening as it had customarily used, so there was less "poring" than usual.

Another example concerned NBC's weekend network news programs. Since 1965 NBC had boasted that it ran seven days of news, treating Saturday and Sunday with the same importance as weekdays. Although both the Saturday and the Sunday news programs found themselves repeatedly pushed off the air by sports programs, that claim had some validity. Then in the spring of 1967, NBC told its affiliate stations that it had contracted to carry ten doubleheader football games that fall, which meant that the *Frank McGee Sunday Report,* one of the better news programs of the week, would disappear for ten weeks. A discussion took place among top executives of the network (not the News Department) as to whether the Sunday news program should be dropped altogether if it was going to be lost for ten weeks. An NBC executive later said the question around which the discussion centered was what the "public relations effect would be of dropping the McGee show," not that a service to the public would be withdrawn. At stake was the loss of prestige the network would suffer for going back on its decision to carry seven days of news. One executive involved was asked how the network would take the loss of prestige if it took the McGee show off the air just when the Public Broadcast Laboratory was inaugurating a series of Sunday evening programs intended to demonstrate the inadequacies of commercial network current affairs programming. The reply was that the *Experiment in Television* series NBC had run for nine weeks in the 1966–67 season had shown how easy it was to get prestige. "We put on nine hours," he said, "and the critics rave over every one."

On May 25, 1967, NBC bought a full-page advertisement in the *New York Times* to ask in bold type: "Did you miss last Saturday's satellite from Europe? Too bad." It referred to a new venture in network journalism, a scheduled news program (the *Frank McGee Saturday Report*) using regular reports from Europe and Asia by space satellite. The idea was to bring the capitals of the world as close as cities in the United States. The advertisement continued: "But you'll get another chance to see and hear Europe *live* this Saturday. And next Saturday. And Saturday after Saturday after that."

The very next Saturday the program did not appear, having been preempted by a baseball game. This frequently happens to the news programs on both Saturday and Sunday evenings during the baseball and football seasons. Sports are more profitable than news and if the two conflict the news gets bounced.

Furthermore, no announcement was made to tell the innocents who tuned in seeking the news that there was not going to be any.

Nor was there an apology. Important affiliate stations in big cities grew angry at trying to find out on which Saturday they could expect a news program and on which the news might disappear in extra innings. Since these programs had an average Nielsen rating of about 6.0, it meant that several million homes were being treated with contempt.

The networks prefer to program "for audience." Advertisers are more easily drawn to sports than to news, not only because the audience is bigger (sometimes it is not), but because it assures, in *Variety*'s words, "an upper economic class male audience" which is lost to the networks in most other TV programs. The value of that audience can be demonstrated by the rates advertisers are willing to pay to reach it. A one-minute spot on the CBS National Football League schedule has sold for as much as $75,000.

Scheduled news programs on weekdays are usually safe from casual preemption because they have developed large enough audiences to be valuable. Weekend news programs, which are newer, have smaller audiences and are more often candidates for preemption. In turn, the more they are preempted or scheduled at different times, the less chance an audience has of developing a viewing habit.

Even weekday programs occasionally get pushed aside by sports.

On June 5, 1967, an announcer on WNBC-TV, New York, came on the air at 5:30 P.M. and said: "Because of the Middle East crisis, the *Sixth Hour News* is beginning half an hour early tonight." In fact, the change in schedule had nothing to do with the Middle East crisis. The NBC network salesmen had persuaded the program schedulers to let a baseball game begin at 7:00 P.M. That meant pushing the *Huntley-Brinkley Report* out of its usual place to a position half an hour earlier, and WNBC's local news program was also pushed back.

The networks are sometimes willing to put *anything* before news if it is profitable enough. Eighteen million people are said to rely on the *Huntley-Brinkley Report* most evenings for their news of the world. For those who did not happen to get home early that night or to turn on their sets sooner than usual, there was no news on that network.

It depends on who is disappointed. The networks are more sensitive to what is said about them by the critics than the despairing television viewer might think. An actress hearing a faint cough during a big scene, a rabbit quivering at the snap of a twig, is not more sensitive than are the corporate bodies of television sniffing the air of critical opinion. When they sense approbation, the network executives trumpet to the world about it. When they hear disapproval, they look for someone to fire or some gimmick to save them.

When Fred Friendly quit as President of CBS News, the network was very concerned about what the much publicized dispute over the failure to carry the Vietnam hearings would do to its corporate image. At that time, CBS was continuing a series of "testing" programs in which viewers at home could compare their own scores on such matters as driving ability and knowledge of the law against a "national average" determined by opinion surveys. Interspersed in the "surveys" taken at that time were a number of disguised questions meant to determine what the public thought about CBS. Among these were such questions as: "Do you know which television network has been involved in a chief executive struggle?"

In this war of corporate image, news programming is the touchstone of prestige. At one point a few years ago, there was heavy competition between NBC and CBS to put on so-called instant specials, hastily mounted thirty-minute or one-hour programs ostensibly designed to throw more light on urgent subjects in the news. Too often the concern was not with what the programs said but merely with the business of putting them on, so that the networks could demonstrate their zeal for public service.

To stimulate good feeling among professional critics the networks turn on a public relations treatment worthy of Hollywood studios. Since news programs are reviewed by the same critics who review entertainment programs, the news departments weigh in with their own stars to flatter the newspapermen. In the summer of 1967, both NBC and CBS took a group of fifty-one TV critics, representing newspapers with a readership of 12 million, on expensive tours of Hollywood to butter them up for the new season of programs, which, in 1968, would include those principal battlegrounds for network prestige the national conventions and election night coverage. Before flying their guests to Hollywood for several days of cocktailing and dining with the stars, CBS took the critics into its news headquarters in New York for a "behind the scenes" briefing in the midst of the Arab-Israeli crisis and a press conference with Walter Cronkite. At the end of the tour, a CBS spokesman said the network was expecting 1,200 published interviews to result from the encounters with the thirty-six network stars and personalities the PR men produced.

It requires an extraordinarily mature and levelheaded individual to resist the tendencies that star treatment encourages, among which are a distaste for contact with people in public; an intellectual laziness developed by having information prepared and predigested by others; and an overweening self-importance. Under the star system, all successful broadcast newsmen are prey to them.

Television journalism also falls into the awards system designed for and controlled by the entertainment side of the industry. The biggest awards are the Emmys, television equivalents of the Hollywood Oscars, awarded by the Academy of Television Arts and Sciences. The plotting and campaigning within the networks to win these awards led Jack Gould to conclude in 1961 that "most of TV's publicized honors are chosen on the basis of pure politics, not merit." CBS News for this reason boycotted the Emmy awards from 1964 to 1967, objecting to the practice of judging news and documentary programs on the basis of votes by members of the TV Academy, who had not seen the programs and who might not be qualified to make a judgment if they had. CBS ended its boycott when the Academy agreed that news entries would be judged by a panel of journalists who would be required to view each entry.

The second important limitation of broadcast journalism is that the network news departments often have no say in decisions about when news programs will be shown, when they will be preempted or killed off, how long they will run and who will appear on them. These decisions are made quite often by men who are not journalists or who have other concerns in mind.

The time segments allotted to journalists on the air and the amount of money they can spend are controlled by the profit considerations of the entertainment, mass advertising end of the industry. The simple rule is more money for news when times are good and short rations when profits go down. The only qualification to that is the prestige consideration. A network may decide as a public relations gesture to increase news programming even when the expense eats slightly into profits.

A good example of how complex a network decision about news programming can be was given by the expansion of the *CBS Evening News* from fifteen to thirty minutes in September, 1963. Newspapers deduced these factors as contributing to the decision: prestige—CBS had won critical acclaim for its coverage of the 1962 off-year elections and wanted to keep up the momentum of being first in news; ratings—to step up the battle for the prime-time-entertainment audience after the news programs; money—more revenue from more commercials; quality—the opportunity to cover the news in more depth. The factors may not have been ranked in that order of importance, but it is unlikely that the only journalistic motive included, a desire to cover the news in more depth, was paramount. NBC immediately made the same decision with the *Huntley-Brinkley Report*.

This expansion in the time the networks devoted to informational programs was more apparent than real. The CBS program *Eyewitness to History* was dropped at the same time, while two valuable weekly series on NBC, *David Brinkley's Journal* and *Chet Huntley Reporting* were both cut back and eventually allowed to wither away.

Network profits mounted without interruption through the prosperity of the 1960's until economic uncertainty in 1967 caused a fall-off. A poorer showing in the second- and third-quarter profits caused immediate repercussions in the news departments. Plans for political coverage in 1968, including the primary elections and the national conventions, suffered budget cuts in all three networks.

In 1961, Newton Minow complained of a "virtual news blackout on television during the prime viewing hours each night." Prime time, in which audiences are bigger and commercial rates higher, runs from 7:30 to 11:00 P.M. "The world goes on during prime evening time," Minow said, "but you wouldn't know it if you were watching television."[5]

That situation still applies, although there are exceptions. CBS has devoted one hour a week of prime time (10–11 P.M. Tuesdays) to news documentaries and NBC one hour every other week (10–11 P.M. Fridays). That amounts to 4 percent of prime time on CBS and 2 percent on NBC. Although it is technically within prime time, NBC's Friday-night spot is usually regarded as a dead period in the week. Other regular news features, such as interview programs like *Meet the Press,* tend to be located at times and on days when there is no danger of causing any fall-off in peak audiences which can be attracted by entertainment programs.

Occasional noble exceptions to this constant deference to profits show what television could be like if the networks would make a habit of the high-mindedness they profess. For four consecutive nights in the summer of 1967, CBS devoted one hour of prime time (10–11 P.M.) to a serialized study of the Warren Commission findings in the Kennedy assassination. It was estimated that 50 percent of all American TV homes saw all or part of the programs, a total audience of 55 million people. Holding an average share of 37 percent of the audience, the CBS programs dominated the ratings in that time segment each night. That may have been in part because the summer audience is smaller and loses millions of younger adult viewers, and also because the summertime schedule of reruns does not offer the same competition as the winter evening schedules. An excellent NBC documentary, *Khrushchev in Exile,* gathered a total audience of 30 million when it was shown twice in prime time in July, 1967.

Such successes show that vast audiences can be tapped for interesting programs of television journalism. Unfortunately, the system regards 10 million people as an unacceptable minority if 15 million people can be attracted to anything else.

Newton Minow put it well in his "vast wasteland" speech in 1961. He told the National Association of Broadcasters: "You know, newspaper publishers take popularity ratings too. The answers are pretty clear; it is almost always the comics, followed by the advice-to-the-lovelorn columns. But, ladies and gentlemen, the news is still on the front page of all newspapers, the editorials are not replaced by more comics, the newspapers have not become one long collection of advice to the lovelorn."[6]

A good deal of the dedication of television to mass tastes is due to the network programming. With a country as vast and diverse as this and with the attitudes of audiences for up to two hundred different affiliated stations to consider, the only way for a network to extract the maximum is to find the lowest common denominator. Yet this may not always be a wise course. Experiments by individual stations around the country have sometimes produced startling results. Station WMAQ-TV, Chicago, which is owned by NBC, puts its evening news program on at 10 P.M., in prime time. In June, 1967, that program had the highest rating in the Chicago market after a campaign was developed to improve and extend its news coverage of the Chicago area.

One difficulty, however, for network program planners is the reluctance of many affiliate stations to carry even those news and documentary programs the network does produce. The ABC News Department has particular trouble not only with its affiliated stations but with those the network owns. NBC and CBS are strong enough corporate entities to tell their O & O's (Owned and Operated stations) generally what programs to carry. At ABC, the O & O's make the decisions, based on sales exigencies; ABC's main evening news program was expanded to half an hour several years after the other networks, and the network had great difficulty obtaining clearance for the program so that it could compete directly with *Huntley-Brinkley* and *Walter Cronkite*. The weekly documentary series *ABC Scope* was run in prime time on the network but the flagship station, WABC-TV in New York, refused to carry it except on Sunday afternoons. Interestingly, the educational station in New York, WNDT, finally offered to carry the documentary on a weekday evening so that a prime-time audience in the country's biggest market could see it. *Variety* commented that the difficulty with *ABC Scope* "reveals a corporate policy that evidently places the O & O's as a major profit source, ahead of the network, regardless of the reduced 'image' impact of ABC News that results." The paper's conclusion was: "At ABC the salesman is king. At NBC and CBS he is merely royalty."

How do you guys know what's going on down there?

In 1963, when Governor George Wallace tried to prevent the integration of Alabama's schools with his "stand in the schoolhouse door," NBC correspondent Tom Pettit, covering the story there, phoned a producer in New York, who started telling Pettit how to handle the story.

"There's a good story in the *New York Times* this morning," he said.

"We don't get the *New York Times* down here," Pettit said.

"Well, the night lead of the AP says—"

"We don't have the AP."

"Never mind. The UP's got a pretty good angle on it—"

"We don't have the UP either," Pettit said.

The producer said, "You don't have the UP?"

"No."

"You don't have the AP?"

"No."

"You don't have the *New York Times?*"

"No."

"Then how do you guys know what's going on down there?"

Television news is not set up to cover or gather the news routinely but to disseminate news that other organizations gather. The greatest proportion of the material is supplied by the wire services. Camera crews and reporters are assigned to cover some headline stories, and there are a handful of reporters on permanent beats like the White House and the State Department. With those exceptions, the network news operation is largely reactive: it goes out to cover the stories which the wires, the newspapers and the magazines have developed through original reporting. Since the United States is too big to have developed truly national newspapers, broadcasting has created the only national journalism. Network journalism commands great resources and employs large staffs, and therefore deserves comparison with newspapers which enjoy national reputations, even if they do not have comprehensive national circulations. Newspapers like the *New York Times* and the *Washington Post* are also dependent upon some wire service and syndicated material, but a high proportion of their material still originates with their staff reporters.

The chief difference between television and newspaper journalism lies in their respective attitudes to the function of the reporter. Television news has not found a central role for the reporter. Preoccupation with the logistical problems of getting "picture" have made the reporter secondary, while show business economics have replaced the reporter in the studio with a "commentator" or front man.

The need for front men derives from the requirement that TV news appeal to a mass audience. Entertainment TV disposes the audience to be attracted by personable stars. Viewing loyalties and habits are developed through identification of particular programs with particular stars. From the beginning, the industry handled news in the same way. Huge audiences for news were developed as star commentators became centerpieces. It has proved so difficult to fit reporters into this pattern that they often have been reduced to a form of window dressing.

The incentives of success are also different from those in print journalism, for the system of rewards belongs to the entertainment industry. During a strike in April, 1967, by the television artists' union (AFTRA), Chet Huntley complained that it was demeaning for journalists to be members of a union of "singers, actors, jugglers, announcers, entertainers and comedians." Demeaning or not, it has a certain logic because TV newsmen are paid in the same manner as singers, actors and comedians—by the appearance. With some recent exceptions, network newsmen make their money from commercial fees paid on top of a basic salary.

The more a newsman appears on sponsored news programs, the more money he earns. Reporters contributing to television news shows receive fees ranging from $25 to $150 for each item used on a program containing commercials. That part of the system discourages sound reportorial activity. A man may spend three or four days quietly digging for facts to support a story, only to find himself receiving a fee of $50 if his story is used—or nothing if the story does not pan out. His colleague, meanwhile, may use the same amount of time rushing to snatch an interview here and put together a few superficial facts there, may place ten separate pieces on the air and may as a result pocket $500. Obviously the system discourages methodical pursuit of information. The object is to get each story on the air and move on to something else.

The scale of compensation paid to the commentator for his work in the studio most effectively separates television from other journalism. The commentator is the pinnacle of a system which glorifies him at the expense of the reporter. Once the broadcast journalist has made the grade and is found to have attributes desirable on the screen, he is rewarded by being taken out of the field. He is given regular commitments as anchorman on one or another regularly scheduled program. The fees for these services are very large. A commentator presenting a five-minute daily television news program on the network receives an additional $360 a week. Preparing and broadcasting a five-minute radio news program once a day for five days a week carries a fee of $250. Fees for longer news programs are negotiable, and because they are paid in the manner of show business personalities, network newsmen find it necessary to hire agents to bargain for them with the employers. Since these fees soon mount up for commentators who are much in demand, annual incomes of $50,000 to $80,000 are common at the network level. For the biggest stars, such as Huntley, Brinkley and Cronkite, the figures are much higher.

Such rewards naturally make the competition for the top two dozen jobs in television journalism keen. And the rewards can be as great, or even greater, in individual stations. Incomes of $40,000 to $50,000 a year are regarded as routine for local-station anchormen in good markets. It has been reported that Jerry Dunphy, anchorman of the news program on KNXT-TV, Los Angeles, receives about $70,000 while Floyd Kalber has been said to have negotiated a contract with WMAQ-TV, Chicago, in 1967, that started at $120,000 a year.

In several ways the money involved acts as a disincentive to reporters. Young men rising in the industry desire to be commentators in the studio, not reporters on the beat. To be taken out of reporting and given a program is considered success; if the program is taken away, that is failure. Moreover, a man cannot easily combine a daily in-studio commitment with the work of a reporter. If he tries, by being absent from the program to do some extended reporting, he loses fees.

The most successful broadcasting journalists are thus largely prevented from going out of the office to do reporting, assuming they are trained journalists and want to go out. Many, especially at the local-station level, are not journalists and do not relish reporting.

To put it in its worst light, the work of the commentator is a form of parasitic journalism. He either rewrites the news from the wire services or, depending on the importance of the program and the magnitude of his stardom, he has a team of writers to do it for him. It is as though the rewrite man on a newspaper were elevated to the salary and prominence of a managing editor, and his byline placed over most of the stories.

Those who remain in the field as reporters, either by professional choice or because the networks did not think them star material, can be frustrated men. They do not file reports as a matter of routine. For example, the NBC London Correspondent may attend a briefing at 10 Downing Street with the Press Secretary of the Prime Minister. Yet it will not be he who tells Americans about it, it will be Chet Huntley. What Huntley says, in all probability, will not even be taken from the notes of the NBC correspondent, but from the notes of the AP or UPI reporter who also covered the briefing with him. Only if the whim strikes the producer of the *Huntley-Brinkley Report* that day will NBC's own correspondent report from London, either very expensively by satellite or, with a day's delay, on film. Unless the *Huntley-Brinkley Report* or some other program is willing to accept a piece from the London man, he does not file the story. Yet every NBC radio and TV news program in that news cycle may be carrying the story from the wires. Even if, on a major story, the NBC correspondent does file a report to a particular program, his view of the story is not routinely circulated to the other programs.

Thus the vast resources and expenditures of the network news departments do not go primarily into providing their own reports of events.

It is difficult even for the most conscientious commentator to handle the news differently. Occasionally, correspondents do go out to cover a story, but their fame often attracts more public attention than do the events themselves. During the 1964 campaign, David Brinkley went to a shopping center in California to watch Nelson Rockefeller on the stump. There was a sizable crowd around Rockefeller but, when Brinkley was spotted, it melted and re-formed around the bigger attraction, the TV commentator. The same thing happened to ABC's Howard K. Smith, traveling with Barry Goldwater in New Hampshire.

Sometimes the stars are prodded by the networks to go out when surveys show that their credibility as newsmen is slipping. The aura of show business infects not only the public but also the news departments. The commentator travels not simply as a working reporter but as a potentate with a retinue. He is scheduled as tightly as a politician so as not to miss too many air commitments in New York. Someone else does the basic digging for facts. No matter how knowledgeable the commentator may be as he travels to the site of the story, he does not have time to see the people involved, to read the materials and to ask the necessary questions to find out what is going on. He has no time to do that essential mulling over which stirs the accumulated facts in a reporter's mind into significance. His time is worth too much money to the network to let him "waste" it. At the worst, on these forays, the stars are like vacationers who briefly stop to be photographed, showing their heads through cut-outs of muscle men and bathing beauties. The alternative is for the star to do his reading and fact-gathering at long distance, carry his prepackaged conclusions with him to the scene, hop off a plane at the scene of the spot news story, deliver his views onto 16-millimeter film and get back on the plane. Although some commentators do acquire the imperiousness of stardom, most of them are embarrassed by the phoniness of such procedures, and therefore go out very seldom.

NBC has recently made a major effort to correct this weakness by adding four permanently featured reporters to the *Huntley-Brinkley Report,* but it still has not significantly increased the material originating with staff reporters. Nor have the networks yet found it economically feasible to employ enough specialists who can cover particular kinds of stories—say, scientific—with expertise.

The reason for this basic shortcoming of TV journalism—its neglect of the true reporting function—is partly economic; but it also stems from a particular view of the news. Walter Scott, the NBC Board Chairman, whose public utterances are remarkably unpretentious for a network executive, has said: "Because television *is* a visual medium, it may scant the background and significance of events to focus on the outward appearance—the comings and goings of statesmen instead of the issue that confronts them."

The comings and goings make easy pictures; the issues usually do not. Obviously, most of the energy and organization of television goes into getting pictures. The logistics of doing that are so formidable (and so expensive) that they overshadow everything else. Consequently, from its inception television news has been criticized for a tendency to let pictures dictate the story. Television newsmen cannot be blamed for wanting to put visual material on a visual medium, but when preoccupation with visual effects overrides news judgment, it encourages emphasis on action rather than on significance and the playing up of trivial or exciting occurrences simply because they can be covered by cameras. That has been the burden of complaint about TV's vivid, and often heroic, coverage of the Vietnam war. The greatest lack is in stimulating public understanding.

Background, analysis and interpretation

For newsmen working for great news organizations, such as Reuters in London, where I have worked, the most elementary principle is to check all new facts coming in against the background to the story. What happens this week is not news until it is seen in the light of what has happened in the weeks and months, and even years, preceding. When selected background is added, many apparently small stories become meaningful and important.

For a number of reasons, broadcast journalism too often ignores the essential background. Part of the fault is the heritage, still unfortunately alive, of the breathless, shouting days of radio, when an announcer intoned a dozen four-line items of news off the wire, heavily seasoned with wrong emphasis and mispronunciations. It was considered better to "hopscotch the world for headlines" (as NBC-TV used to phrase it) than to spend more time on fewer stories. In the worst examples, every event was treated as isolated and shatteringly new. The majority of network radio news programs on the hour and the short daytime TV programs, each about five minutes in length, are still guilty of this passion for headlines with no explanation of what they mean. Commentators preparing these programs are discouraged from lingering too long on any story lest the show drag. It is preferred that they zip along breezily from item to item to keep the sponsors happy.

Even the longer, more serious TV news programs at suppertime are still bedeviled by superficiality. Though the network news departments have raised their standards by hiring trained journalists and introducing professional competence, the network's "front page" programs, expanded to thirty minutes a night, have not escaped the tyranny of show business ideas of pacing. To be dull is worse than being uninformative.

At NBC News, for example, there have been no adequate facilities for backgrounding a story. An index or morgue or clipping service which collects and files information from day to day for instant retrieval is the most elementary part of a news organization. Broadcasters, however, have to rely on their memories, on what recent newspapers they can find, or on what makeshift files they are able to patch together in the midst of very busy lives. NBC's own product is not filed for convenient reference because there is no house respect for it as a source of background information. Consequently there is almost total dependence on the wires, and when *they* do not provide instant background (which they often do not on a fast-breaking story) the news service is left floating and insecure, so that newsmen not only are liable to error but are also discouraged from interpreting the news.

The lack of adequate analysis and interpretation has been remarked frequently by critics of TV news in recent years. The Carnegie Commission, which recommended establishment of a public television corporation, noted that commercial TV news coverage was criticized as "too limited and lacking in depth."[7] Lester Markel of the *New York Times* wrote in 1967 that "the lack of background is especially marked in the evening news programs, which are almost wholly bulletin services."[8]

One obvious way to answer these and similar criticisms would be to allow TV news departments to review the news periodically. James Reston suggests, in his book *The Artillery of the Press,* that "the networks would help if they would set aside an hour each weekend in prime viewing time to review the important news of the week and put it into some historical perspective."[9] There are good commercial reasons why the networks do not produce such programs, but it would be an exciting and valuable undertaking if they did. Ideally, there should be more disciplined effort to interpret the news day by day, plus a periodic review. One of the best news programs on television, for instance, is the monthly *News in Perspective* program produced by National Educational Television. Three *New York Times* journalists, Tom Wicker, Max Frankel and Lester Markel, talk with each other for an hour about the news of the month gone by. The conversation is sometimes quite witty, and is always informative.

Television conspicuously lacks the services of "commentators," in the sense in which that title was used in the heyday of network radio. Television quickly killed off the personalized news commentaries of men such as Elmer Davis, Quincy Howe and Edward R. Murrow. The form still survives on radio in the broadcasts of men like Alexander Kendrick on CBS and the shorter three-minute commentaries that appear in the NBC *Emphasis* and CBS *Dimension* series. Apart from the brief nightly essays of Eric Sevareid on CBS, network television gives no regular commentary on the news.

Again, there are commercial reasons for this. Most network news producers and executives believe that it is too boring to put one man on the screen to talk for longer than about two minutes, and even that is considered likely to bore the audience. The other factor is the fear of alienating the audience. The radio commentators of a generation ago were men of pronounced individual views. Balance was provided by the multiplicity of their voices. If you didn't like Walter Winchell, you could listen to someone else. If you were angered by him, perhaps you would go on listening just because you were mad at him. Television, however, does not want people to be angry. Occasional squirts of opinion do penetrate the pervading blandness; more often there is a gentle leakage—sometimes deliberate—from the mind of the commentator, whose views will seep through the laboriously balanced phraseology. The general rule is that you can be far less forthright on television than you can be on radio. Television does not mind a vacuum; what it abhors is controversy.

All this has a particular relevance to politics. If the nation's chief medium of journalism is suffused with show business values; if it does not regard digging for facts as its primary function and subordinates the reporter's role; if it concentrates on recording action rather than probing significance; if it is afraid to analyze the news for fear of being dull or of dipping into controversy, then television journalism is not fulfilling the traditional journalistic role of putting public men and their activities under the kind of scrutiny that will provide a public check to their actions. This role has given American journalists a prestige that is not usual even in other democratic societies. Of course, it is only one role of journalism. Conveying experience, which television does brilliantly, if fitfully, is another. Entertaining the audience with perceptive or amusing observations on the vagaries of our fellow creatures is another. Television can do that quite well. But is television performing what textbooks on journalism, commentaries on the Constitution and serious journalists expect of their profession? Is it keeping a mature and cynical eye on our governments and politicians?

The TV front page: Chet, David and Walter

A successful businessman in Maine once complained to me that he regularly read the *Wall Street Journal,* the Portland newspapers, *Time* and *Business Week,* but he felt that both *Huntley-Brinkley* and *Cronkite* were "way over the heads" of people like himself. "They don't give enough background; all they do is give a couple of sentences about a story without telling anything that led up to it." If it was over his head, the businessman asked, how was it for the millions in the audience who did not read as widely as he did?

This criticism has validity. Television journalism often can be superficial and over peoples' heads at the same time.

The major effort of the news department in each of the three national networks goes into producing the main evening news programs at suppertime. At NBC, the *Huntley-Brinkley Report* held such a prestigious position in terms of budget, audience and revenue that other members of the staff used to refer to it humorously as the "golden ghetto." Av Westin, a former senior producer with CBS News, and now running the Public Broadcast Laboratory, remarked that "so much of the financial, intellectual and personnel resources go into putting on the half-hour nightly show that it has really tied CBS News into eccentric circles turning around that broadcast."[10] ABC, whose news department operates on shorter rations than the other two, was spending approximately $7.5 million a year out of an annual news budget of $40 million to produce its evening program in 1967. At NBC and CBS, where the news budgets were approximately twice the ABC level, the expenditure on the evening show was correspondingly higher. The fact that these programs earn a considerable profit (the advertising they carry produces revenues which far exceed the cost of the programs) is not relevant since the news departments do not balance their own accounts. The networks set annual budgets for the news departments and the networks collect the advertising revenues. In the case of ABC, for example, the $32.5 million left in the news budget after the evening news show would have to cover all other TV and radio news programs scheduled on the network, all specials and documentaries including space and election coverage, all coverage of unexpected big stories, like the U.N. debates on the Middle East, as well as paying for the overhead of New York headquarters and news bureaus overseas.

The networks claim that on balance the news programming operates at a loss. But the commercial success of the main evening news programs goes a long way toward minimizing that loss by subsidizing unprofitable operations. One source at NBC estimated that the *Huntley-Brinkley Report* brought in revenues amounting to more than five times its cost. Since these programs are so valuable, it is not surprising that they occupy the favored position in the network news departments, and that their ratings are scrutinized minutely.

As a result, the greatest energies and talents of the news departments are channeled into producing a relatively small amount of the total output. Since these programs are really tiny vessels into which to pour the torrent of a day's information, they necessarily contain only a small part of that information. Considerable distillation is necessary to present the essence and all three networks demonstrate great skill in doing so. But it has to be recognized that a great deal must be left out. Although the programs are thirty minutes long, commercials and announcements leave only twenty-four minutes for actual news. At an average reading speed for television that would mean a maximum of 4,600 words in a program if the commentator talked without pause from beginning to end. In practice these programs contain about 3,200 words on average.

Richard Salant once had the text of a typical Cronkite show set in type and dropped into the front page of the *New York Times*. It occupied barely six of the eight columns. On a sample week studied for this book, the three networks' programs each averaged a few hundred words more than the front pages of the *New York Times* and the *Washington Post*. What the television viewer is getting essentially is a headline service. Let us examine more closely what this service provides and how the news judgment of the network news departments compares with two reputable newspapers.

The programs of the three networks were studied for a three-day period, October 2, 3 and 4, 1967.[11] They were analyzed to determine how many words of news each show presented, how many stories, the length of the stories, how many words of the totals were devoted to interpretive or analytic material, how many correspondents participated and how much of the program was carried by the anchorman. With the results averaged for the three days, the programs look very similar.

	NBC (Huntley-Brinkley)	CBS (Walter Cronkite)	ABC (Peter Jennings)
Average total words	3,243	3,351	3,180*
Average number of stories	16	20	22
Average number of stories of 50 words or less	4	5	5
Average number of stories of 100 words or more	8	8	7
Average number of stories of 300 words or more	3	5	3
Average number of words of interpretive material	325	555	(not available)
Proportion of interpretive material	10%	16%	(not available)
Average number of correspondents	7	7	5
Proportion of show carried by anchorman	38%	39%	51%

* The study coincided with a strike against ABC. The scripts provided by ABC News were partially incomplete because videotape had been inadvertently erased during the strike. The missing stories (originating out of New York) were counted by allotting 150 words to each minute.

The differences, such as they are, are interesting. NBC, which had assigned four permanent field reporters to the program two months earlier, had begun to carry fewer stories but to go into them in more depth. Whether more information was conveyed by the method chosen—more or less impromptu chats among the correspondents and Huntley and Brinkley at the end of important stories —was still being debated at NBC, at this writing. The greater length for important stories did not, however, greatly raise the total amount of time given to explaining the news, to providing analysis or interpretation. CBS still devoted more time to this practice, largely because of the nightly commentary by Eric Sevareid which closed the program. Although the ABC performance in this could not be precisely calculated, the impression given was that it explained the news less than the other networks. Obviously the quality of analysis is not in direct proportion to the number of words used, but in a medium which permits so few words to be used at all, it is a fair indicator at least of the intention to give the viewer some guidance. The overall conclusion is that rigid time limitations force the producers to cram as much fresh factual information as they can into the format and that there simply is not time to provide an adequate interpretation. The situation was supposed to improve when the networks expanded these programs to half an hour beginning in 1963 but it did so only slightly. The extra time was used to expand the traditional treatment of stories and to include more features. The same argument is now being heard from those who wish to expand the programs to one hour. That probably will happen eventually, although the problems of getting enough affiliate stations to clear the necessary time will be difficult to solve.

Let us take one of these three days, Monday, October 2, 1967, and compare what each of the networks thought important that evening with the news judgment of the *Washington Post* and the *New York Times,* dealing with the same news cycle the following morning.

LEAD STORY

All three networks agreed with the two newspapers that the close vote in the South Vietnamese Provisional Assembly confirming Messrs. Thieu and Ky as President and Vice-President, respectively, was the day's most important development. Yet each handled it differently. NBC and ABC gave the bare bones of the story in less than 100 words, and then presented filmed reports shot the day before in Saigon of police breaking up hostile demonstrations by Buddhist militants. CBS stayed with the political story, with a filmed report from Charles Collingwood, also shot the day before in Saigon, anticipating the vote and reporting his rather pessimistic conclusions about it. Collingwood said that factionalism in the newly elected assembly had already weakened the moral authority of the new government and that "the prospects of a truly viable government in South Vietnam are as far away as ever." While the filmed demonstrations shown by the other two networks were more exciting to watch, they were not explained in the context of the political situation. On NBC Chet Huntley said the Assembly had no alternative because it was controlled by the military junta and was under American pressure to accept Thieu and Ky. The *Washington Post* and *New York Times* both led with the story but included more detail of the pressure on the deputies to vote the way the junta wanted.

SECOND STORY

NBC ran film acquired from Communist sources and narrated by John Rich in Tokyo showing the efforts of the North Vietnamese to keep the approaches to the Ho Chi Minh Trail in good repair in spite of American bombing raids. CBS said it was protesting to South Vietnamese authorities over the mistreatment of a CBS crew by police during the Saigon demonstrations. ABC summarized the day's fighting in 75 words.

THIRD STORY

NBC devoted 37 words to a report quoting diplomatic sources in London, who said North Vietnam would not commit itself to any scaling down of the war if the U.S. stopped bombing the North. CBS covered the day's war action in 104 words. ABC went to Washington for a filmed press conference with Colonel Robin Olds, the Vietnam jet fighter ace, who emerged from a White House reception saying the air war was useful and effective.

FOURTH STORY

NBC reported briefly that the British Labor Party's annual Conference had opened with strong opposition expected to the Government's support of the American war policy. CBS carried a filmed report by a correspondent in Saigon on the new American Embassy, stressing its fortress-like quality. It was interesting but had only faint connection with the news of that day. The injection of a timeless feature so high up in a news program demonstrates the feeling in the networks that they must keep a good proportion of picture stories throughout the half hour to give variety and pace. NBC and ABC had achieved that with their Buddhist demonstration footage while CBS was running a Collingwood talk piece. Now CBS had to bow to picture, even if it was not up-to-the-minute news. In the same position, ABC moved in a story played prominently on page one in both the *Times* and the *Post,* that Republican Senator John Sherman Cooper of Kentucky had joined those demanding an end to the bombing of North Vietnam. The report was only 68 words long, did not elaborate at all on Cooper's speech and gave the barest recital of where other Senate speakers stood on the question.

FIFTH STORY

On NBC David Brinkley summarized two polls, by Gallup and Harris, showing declining support for President Johnson's handling of the war. He followed that with a slightly fuller account of Cooper's speech than ABC had given and reported an attack on President Johnson by Senator Charles Percy. CBS covered Colonel Olds's press conference outside the White House. ABC had a filmed report from Washington on the swearing in of Thurgood Marshall as the first Negro member of the Supreme Court.

SIXTH STORY

NBC went to Los Angeles for a long report (346 words) on a weekend meeting of the California Democratic Council, which decided to send a peace delegation to the 1968 Democratic National Convention. The reporter, Tom Brocaw, concluded that there was a slim chance of such a delegation reaching the Convention. CBS covered the speech by Senator Cooper in 72 words. It did not mention any other speaker in the debate but gave the fullest account of what Cooper said. ABC carried a long report (560 words) from Cleveland, on the eve of the Democratic primary, in which a Negro, Carl Stokes, was in a close race for the nomination for mayor.

SEVENTH STORY

NBC rounded up Middle East developments in 100 words, including a Jordanian speech at the U.N., an Israeli claim that Egypt had violated the cease-fire and the report that Britain was about to patch up differences with Egypt. CBS covered Thurgood Marshall on film, emphasizing, as had ABC, folksy details of his family's reactions. ABC devoted this space to a brief report on the movements of Hurricane Fern toward Texas.

EIGHTH STORY

NBC's longest story of the evening was an account of a political tour by Ronald Reagan, prefaced with a report by the Associated Press that professional politicians favored Richard Nixon to win three early Republican primaries. It ended with some cross-talk between the reporter, Jack Perkins, and Brinkley and Huntley about Reagan, concluding that the California Governor appealed to Southern conservatives and had impressed his audiences as a statesman, not as an actor. CBS also chose the position just before the middle commercials for its longest piece, on the next day's voting in Cleveland. NBC did not cover Cleveland this evening. ABC took a film report from Omaha on a bus-train crash in Nebraska in which four children died. The story, which made sad but dramatic pictures, was not covered by the other networks on film.

NINTH STORY

NBC dismissed in 63 words a story which was the second lead in both the *Times* and the *Post*—a new test program announced by President Johnson to get private industry to help in creating slum jobs. CBS treated the same story in the same position with even greater brevity (52 words), while ABC did not carry it at all. ABC devoted 92 words to the best human interest story of the day, the discovery by a hunter of a private plane which had crashed six months before in the mountains of northern California with a family of three aboard. All had been injured and in the wreckage was a diary kept by the sixteen-year-old daughter, describing their efforts to stay alive until they died of starvation after two months. CBS covered the story at the same length a little later. NBC did not mention it. Both the *Post* and the *Times* devoted approximately 500 words to the story, the *Post* on its front page, using wire service copy available to the networks.

Tenth story

NBC reported Thurgood Marshall's installation more briefly than did the other networks. CBS gave 90 words to the efforts by Jordan's King Hussein to get arms from Moscow, which NBC did not carry, and followed it with a long filmed feature on the fact that the Middle East war had encouraged young foreigners to go to Israel to work. ABC rounded up the Middle East story at the U.N. and elsewhere in 72 words. The story was front-paged in both the *Times* and the *Post*.

Eleventh story

David Brinkley on NBC gave a brief report (62 words) on the opening of FCC hearings on the question of Pay Television. Roger Mudd, who was substituting for Walter Cronkite on CBS, reported on Hurricane Fern. ABC carried film of Secretary McNamara returning from NATO talks in Ankara and saying he might support a Turkish proposal to defend with atomic mines their frontier with Russia. The *Washington Post* carried the story on an inside page but the story did not appear on the other networks or in the *Times*.

Twelfth story

NBC gave a paragraph to the Nebraska train wreck. CBS reported on the diary of the plane-crash girl. ABC reported that

Robert Seamans, Deputy Administrator of the Space Agency, had resigned to return to private life and mentioned the explanation of James Webb that Seamans had intended to stay only a limited time. NBC did not carry the story.

THIRTEENTH STORY

NBC carried a long filmed report from Charles Quinn in Florida on a drive the day before by teachers to enlist the support of parents in their opposition to education budget cuts by the Republican state administration. The other networks and the newspapers did not carry the story. CBS reported briefly on the train wreck. ABC reported that mediation attempts had begun in the strike by technicians against that network.

FOURTEENTH STORY

NBC reported on Hurricane Fern. CBS mentioned Seamans' resignation. ABC reported that Governor Reagan had sent 200 convicts to pick figs, over union protests. The other networks did not carry this.

FIFTEENTH STORY

Chet Huntley on NBC noted in 33 words that the extreme right-wing National Democratic Party showed unexpected strength in elections in the North German state of Bremen. CBS covered the ninetieth birthday of Arizona Senator Carl Hayden in 43 words. ABC mentioned the Pay Television hearings.

SIXTEENTH STORY

NBC reported that London stock exchange prices rose to their highest level in 22 years, apparently reflecting investors' optimism about Britain's economic outlook. CBS noted the *New York Times* announcement that it would not publish an afternoon newspaper. ABC had a filmed report on Hayden's birthday. NBC did not cover it.

Seventeenth Story

NBC summarized the day's trading on the New York Stock Exchange. CBS did the same. ABC carried a 400-word report with film on the previous day's baseball game in which the Red Sox defeated the Minnesota Twins to win the American League pennant. This was relatively old news by Monday evening—more than twenty-four hours after the game.

Eighteenth Story

The *Huntley-Brinkley Report* ended with a funny closer by Brinkley, drawing humor from an apparently straight statement of who was running and who supported whom in the maneuvering for the 1968 Presidential race. CBS closed with the customary commentary by Eric Sevareid, running 430 words and this evening devoted to South Vietnamese politics. Sevareid's unstartling conclusion was that Vietnam had been in a state of anarchy and that political institutions there were extremely fragile. If the factional quarrels stimulated by the establishment of the first free political institutions were not quieted within a few months, the whole structure would collapse, he said. Sevareid's vestigial optimism in Washington appeared to contradict the pessimism of Collingwood on the spot in Saigon. Sevareid even spoke of "a considerable failure of American journalism" in Vietnam because it could not put "the disparate factors of such a complex country into a coherent pattern." ABC mentioned the New York stock prices.

Nineteenth Story

ABC closed with a commentary which showed signs of yearning to be an editorial but did not dare. It was delivered by Bill Sheehan, who was replacing Peter Jennings. Sheehan said that a "great debate" was shaping up over the Administration's decision to build an antimissile system, with critics questioning McNamara's assertions about its cost and consequences. He then added: "The issues are complicated and a couple of minutes is hardly sufficient time to develop any learned conclusions. But this much is certain. The decision regarding the antiballistic missile system is one that will affect us for many years and maybe even generations to come. It's a subject worthy of prolonged discussion and debate. If you're inclined to be disinterested, you should take another look." One might ask ABC News several questions, notably why it did not make room for even a little "discussion and debate" on that program. If a couple of minutes was too short (actually the commentary ran less than one minute), why didn't they give it the four minutes devoted to a day-old ball game?

The chief impression one is left with after studying these three programs, which are typical in their editorial patterns of daily newscasting, is what a different view of the world the viewers of each program received. The effect was like that of a quick ruffle through a magazine. Each of the programs was informative and each was produced with great skill to avoid dull patches and long periods without interesting pictures. Still, viewers of NBC did not hear about Colonel Olds, the new U.S. Embassy in Saigon, the Cleveland election, the plane-crash diary, the NASA resignation or that Carl Hayden planned to run again for the Senate at age ninety. People loyal to Cronkite were not told about the pollsters' new readings on Johnson's unpopularity, the California peace faction, the AP survey on Nixon, the political travels of Ronald Reagan, the PTV hearings, or right-wing successes in Germany. ABC viewers missed altogether what the newspapers thought was the second most important story of the day, the President's proposals to get private business into the slums to provide jobs. Viewers of the other two networks had the proposal boiled down to twenty seconds of talk. The newspapers thought it was worth more than a column. Of course, it was not a picture story that day. Eventually, when it became one, the networks might have covered it.

There were a number of other stories that day which none of the networks mentioned. To point out but a few, there were serious clashes between French farmers and police which were covered in

500 words in the *Times* and 400 in the *Post*. A former Greek Premier was put under arrest by the military regime (*Times* 400 words, *Post* 200). Both newspapers carried an AP report that the Communists had shelled a hospital and POW camp at Hue, South Vietnam, which the networks did not mention. Both newspapers had wire service reports on Yugoslav police hunting a man also sought by Holland, for being an aide to Adolf Eichmann. Any of those stories was as important as a feature on young people being attracted to postwar Israel, which had the advantage of being "picture."

Herbert Gans, the New York University sociologist, who has studied these news programs, believes that the networks are going on instinct and faith in their emphasis on the visual because there have been no studies to find out what the audience actually would tolerate. "Nobody really knows," Gans says, "whether people really do not want to hear Huntley and Brinkley and Walter Cronkite talk for thirty minutes and not see pictures."[12]

It seems likely that even if these programs were expanded to one hour, the problem would remain. TV journalists have an ingrained fear of straight talk—"talking heads" as they are called in the business. The longer the program, the more film they would have to find to fill it. Since same-day action film with hard news content is often scarce, a greater effort would be made on timeless features. These are not to be scorned, but when time limitations now force the networks to give the world such a quick glance each evening, they occupy too much valuable time. The absence of more penetrating examinations of events would not be felt so acutely in the nightly bulletins, if these programs were supplemented by regular programs of commentary or analysis.

It would be ridiculous, of course, to expect television to provide each evening as much information as is carried in a serious newspaper. Furthermore, newspaper readers often skim to find items which interest them. On television, the viewer has no such freedom of choice, but must sit through the whole program to find something interesting. It can be argued further that skimming the surface of many stories provides the viewer, whose attention must be captured afresh with each item, with too little information to be meaningful. Figures, names and ideas are not easily absorbed by the ear. The networks might provide a more interesting and valuable service if they selected three or four stories each evening and attacked them in depth. There is no reason why each story chosen could not be given several kinds of treatment at once: a simple statement of what is new, an exposition of the background, using whatever film or visual material is available, and a follow-through with informed commentary, not necessarily by a network reporter, if staff men do not have sufficient knowledge to handle it.

Few stories can be made interesting in only twenty or thirty seconds' treatment. The reporter or writer on television thus finds himself pleading and bargaining with the producer for additional segments of ten seconds. Forty-five seconds is considered a long story if there are no pictures to go with it. For example, by no conceivable criterion was the story of the plane-wreckage diary a dull story. Literate and sophisticated viewers would be as moved by it as would uneducated viewers. It is the kind of story people tell each other at home and on the train. Why did CBS and ABC give it only 89 and 92 words, respectively? If Chet Huntley had talked for two minutes about the girl's diary his audience would have hung on every word. Two days later, as it turned out, CBS went back to the story, after it had sent a camera crew and reporter to the crash scene, but, considering Roger Mudd's fine ability to communicate in words alone, the network needn't have waited for pictures.

This passion to be brief when there is no picture is obviously more important in weighty matters of state than in simple human interest stories, although the principle is the same. Let us take a closer look at the three treatments of the Senate debate on Vietnam that Monday.

According to the *New York Times,* which carried 700 words on the debate, starting on page one, Senator Cooper made these points:

- He maintained that the U.S. should unconditionally stop the bombing of North Vietnam as the first step toward negotiations.
- He disagreed with President Johnson's San Antonio speech three days earlier, which held that it was by Hanoi's choice and not

ours that the war continues; the first step lies in American control, Cooper said.
- He pointed out that growing international support for Hanoi's demand indicated there was little hope for a just settlement until the United States took this step.
- He concluded that even if our initiative was unsuccessful, American action should be confined to South Vietnam to "reverse the dangerous expansion of the war" and to test Soviet intentions, in particular whether it would reduce its aid to Hanoi.

Privately, the *Times* said, it was learned that Soviet diplomats had indicated to Senators that military aid to Hanoi would be reduced if the war was confined to South Vietnam.

Cooper was an influential Republican member of the Senate Foreign Relations Committee and former Ambassador to India. His intervention touched off a new debate in which a dozen Senators joined, pushing aside other business. There was a major speech by Senator Charles Percy, who said that President Johnson had failed to pursue every possibility for negotiations and had tried to discredit his critics by suggesting they all demanded unilateral withdrawal.

Obviously the debate was a major extension of Congressional consideration of the war, which many people in and out of Congress believed had been waged too long without adequate legislative discussion.

The networks did it scant justice. ABC carried it as its fourth story, in 68 words:

> In the continuing debate on Vietnam policy, Senator John Sherman Cooper of Kentucky—a Republican—called today for an end to the bombing of the North. Cooper found support from Republican Senator Javits of New York . . . and from Democratic Senators Mansfield of Montana and Fulbright of Arkansas. Administration policy was supported by Senator Gale McGee of Wyoming, a Democrat, and Senator George Murphy of California, a Republican.

ABC did not mention Senator Percy and gave nothing of the substance of the arguments.

NBC gave the story 101 words, in fifth position:

And, today, another Republican Senator, Cooper of Kentucky, joined in what might be called the Republican peace movement and he said the President ought to stop bombing North Vietnam. He said this was the judgment of the world and this country could not ignore it. And Senator Percy of Illinois says the President tries to discredit his critics by saying they advocate immediate withdrawal from the war. Whereas, Percy says, 90 percent of them advocate no such thing. He said the President's failure to understand that suggests there must be something wrong with his policies rather than with his critics.

CBS played it in sixth position, and in 72 words:

The Senate shoved legislative business aside today to engage in a new round of debate on Vietnam, touched off by Kentucky Republican John Sherman Cooper. He called for an end to the bombing of North Vietnam as a first step toward peace talks, and Cooper declared the United States should take this step now before the issue becomes so swept up in the 1968 election that domestic politics might govern the decision.

The last point was an interesting one, which the *Times* omitted, but the CBS version did not convey the substance or spirit of Cooper's remarks. There was nothing to indicate *why* the Senator was taking this stand.

None of these reports attempted to put Cooper's position, or the fresh debate, in the real perspective it required. Three nights before, all three networks had carried, in full, President Johnson's San Antonio speech spelling out his latest conditions for peace talks with North Vietnam.

If the President is worth carrying in full when he talks about Vietnam for a solid half hour, surely the first considered Senate response is due more than twenty-five to forty seconds. Since all the networks did more or less the same thing with the story, one can only assume that that is how the AP and UPI night leads treated it that evening and that none of the networks felt obligated to look further.

Since the networks give such prominence to the President's utterances about the war and to those of his advisers, they owe to the Congressional arm of government adequate coverage of its deliberations.

None of them mentioned Cooper's rebuttal of the President's contention that the choice was Hanoi's, not Washington's. None of them mentioned his other point, which the *Times* saw fit to headline, that confining the war to the South would test Soviet intentions. Only David Brinkley mentioned Percy. None of the reports went into the maneuvering inside the Republican Party for tactical position on Vietnam—looking forward to the 1968 elections—which both newspapers did. In fact, even listening to all three networks, which is impossible in most cities, a viewer would have picked up very little new beyond the impression that another Republican was sounding like a dove. If treatment of the Buddhist discontents in South Vietnam was worth three-hundred-word reports on both NBC and ABC, why was serious American debate about the war not worth at least that much space? The answer, inevitably, was picture. If the Senators had scuffled in the corridors with hostile demonstrators, the networks might have been more interested. Even then, the emphasis would have been on the scuffles and not on the issues.

The major network evening news programs have advanced greatly toward the goal of sound journalism, but they still have some distance to go. They are marvels of organization in the procurement of film from around the world, and they perform wonders of technical competence, but their journalistic achievement is still erratic. Their content demonstrates capricious selection, due not only to lazy news judgment, but to the unshakable belief that picture must come first. When good picture and hard, important news happily coincide, the result is often powerful. When there is important hard news and no relevant picture, then television is in trouble.

The field is wide open for research. The communications department of a large university could help the networks by conducting studies of their programs. It would be useful, for example, to know, over a period of months, what consistent bias, if any, is detected. It would be most interesting to test the television producers' preferences for action over talk on different groups of viewers. It would be fascinating to know whether placement of commercials is a serious impediment to absorption of the news.

And some reliable data on what information viewers really get from the news programs would be invaluable. No one really knows.

Considering the undoubted influence of television news coverage on public thinking about politics, a major effort should be made to find out.

3 Consensus Journalism

Television journalists are by-products of an industry which prefers to have as little to do with reality as possible, and which sees no value as being more important than business expediency in complying with government. Is it, in fact, possible to maintain the better traditions and values of American journalism inside an industry to which consensus and conformity are the foundations of prosperity? Can journalists drink at the same well as businessmen, entertainers and advertising men, and not be infected with their values?

The ambivalence of their role traumatizes many people in network television journalism, and they compensate by becoming cynically complacent. Such adaptation probably does more to damage originality and curiosity than any direct pressure from outside the profession. By *television* standards anywhere in the world, their product is brilliantly professional: slick, exciting and convincing in its aura of authority. Yet how professional is it by journalistic standards?

Mechanics before substance

There is little doubt that regular television news programs like *Huntley-Brinkley* and *Walter Cronkite* must have raised the threshold of public awareness of current events over the past ten years. One can assume that they have conditioned in millions of people who were not avid newspaper readers some appetite for serious news and given them a fleeting familiarity with the world.

For people who have given it some thought, however, electronic journalism cares more about form than content. Leslie Slote, who is Governor Rockefeller's press secretary, and who has been dealing with TV newsmen for years, believes that "people responsible for TV news are fairly unimaginative and seem to be preoccupied with the mechanistic as opposed to the substantive."[1] Slote repeats the frequently uttered criticism that "one of the ingredients lacking in TV news coverage is the *why* factor: it is superficial." His particular concern was with what he thought was the failure of TV journalists in New York State to explain Rockefeller's Medicaid program: "They got so involved in the controversy that they never reported what the program was all about and what it was supposed to do."

In May, 1967, when the late Martin Luther King, Jr., was protesting that the Vietnam war was immoral because it interfered with civil rights progress at home, the *Huntley-Brinkley Report* carried a curious item. It began with Brinkley saying that King had alienated himself from other civil rights leaders and from the Administration by his campaign against the war. He then introduced what was called an "interview" with Hubert Humphrey in which the Vice-President, more in sorrow than in anger, chastised Dr. King. No questioner was ever shown or identified. One only saw Humphrey standing against a wood-paneled background, talking. The circumstances of the interview, or at whose initiative it was given, were never mentioned. It is a fundamental rule of journalism that you must give the circumstances of an interview or statement, for otherwise there is no way of evaluating whether it was inspired or spontaneous. This story left a viewer with the strong impression that the Administration had something to say about Dr. King and that NBC had accommodated it in making a gratuitous attack.

Taken in isolation, such technical matters are perhaps not important. Television news programs are not habitually so careless about journalistic standards. What appears more damaging to television news credibility is the atmosphere of outside pressure in which TV journalists must work, a pressure not always overt but of the sort that suffuses one's thinking so delicately that a person writing a story or broadcasting it may not even be aware of how careful he is being. Buried somewhere in his professional psyche is a feeling of caution put there by years of "politic" judgments by his superiors.

The reassurance syndrome

From time to time, television journalism appears anxious to sell the chief commodity of entertainment TV—reassurance. Apart from the descent to a tone of somewhat deeper unction on occasions of sadness, as during coverage of the Martin Luther King or Robert Kennedy assassinations, the heavily stylized mode of delivery—half sung, half chanted—of many news broadcasters makes most of the stories sound alike and imparts a quality of artificiality to the content. That, coupled with the tendency for newscasters to punctuate their performances with smiles, conveys a false geniality which drains the news of meaning.

Research into audience preferences in New York and Los Angeles has revealed that newscasters who could reduce the anxiety level of audiences and present the news in a context of reassurance had tremendous appeal. The most successful personalities on the air were those who could take the edge off what was unpleasant.

It could be demonstrated that, deliberately or unconsciously, broadcasting organizations do choose personalities to give such an impression of reassurance in order to attract audience. TV executives might be hard put to define precisely what qualities they are looking for, but basically they want men who will sound authoritative while making the audience feel comfortable.

It would be fascinating to know more about what goes on in the minds of regular viewers. It may be that the broad reaches of the American public have become so inured to falsity in wide areas of the advertising and mass entertainment media that they are incapable of discrimination. From the early days of network radio when movie stars with melodic, sexy voices assured fawning announcers that they always used a certain soap, while both read from a script the audience could not see, to the television newsmen of today may seem a giant and improbable step, but what if the newsman, so impeccably dressed, so calculatedly believable, is a man who simply does not know what he is talking about and is reading from a script on a TelePrompTer the audience cannot see? Are these merely "conventions" of mass communications which Americans in their sophistication accept as unimportant? If viewers are so healthily cynical, where do they start and where do they stop believing? Or are they so buffeted by spurious information, by half-truths and comforting slogans, that they believe everything? Does a viewer believe and respect the newscaster and then a few seconds later greet the commercial announcer with skepticism? These questions represent crucial mysteries which have yet to be clarified.

As we have seen, networks and stations tend to fit journalism into the other big world of television. Thus the news comes not as objective observation of the environment but as *part* of the environment. It is what philosophers would call part of the "flow," part of the "given." When the commentator is also a commercial pitchman, the effect is further reinforced. Can the audience take seriously the pronouncements on world affairs of a man who ingratiatingly tries to sell them barbecue forks or dog food a few minutes later? There have been instances when newsmen refused to read commercials in order to protect their credibility as journalists, and the practice is increasingly less common. That they were asked, however, is typical of the misunderstanding of the journalistic function in the broadcasting industry. Because of this danger of a credibility gap, a case could be made for removing commercials altogether from news programming. The selling could be done in time segments before and after, but not during the news. After years of living with the system, the networks and local broadcasters know how incongruous commercials appear. It is standard practice, for example, to fade out to a few seconds of black if a particularly tragic or moving story appears just before a commercial. There are also arrangements to avoid embarrassing sponsors with the irony of, for instance, a commercial rhapsodizing air travel in a newscast with a report on an airline crash. In such situations, the commercials are not run, although there are occasions when the decision is made only after discussion about whether the news value of the story warrants the loss of revenue.

If, as Marshall McLuhan says, people perceive information on television in an intuitive, "mosaic" form, how do they see the news as they drink in the reassuring voice of the commentators and the surrounding commercials? Surely, many must regard it as part of the numbing, relaxing, mesmerizing "stuff" that comes at them out of the glowing box, a fraction of life size, inseparable from the total "television experience."

Ideas are bad business

There is yet another aspect of television journalism which lends it common identity with the other programs: it has too little opinion about the subjects it covers. Broadcasting has made a virtue of neutrality. Many critics believe that it is not merely neutrality but noninvolvement. V. O. Key and others have theorized that what is controversial is bad business for the mass media. A week's exposure to commercial television would suggest that the networks believe that even ideas are bad business unless they have already been sensationalized in other media. Michael Arlen believes that certain gods have been kept out of television, "the gods of Wit and Unprofessionalism, the nasty gods, the gods that get into noisy arguments, the dissenting gods."[2] The short of it is that television does not want to offend anyone. When Pauline Frederick, NBC's United Nations Correspondent, once interviewed General Maxwell Taylor rather more aggressively than usual on the *Today* show, Hugh Downs later felt it necessary to apologize to the audience for the vigor of her questions: a few people had written in to complain. At the beginning of *Meet the Press* each week, the announcer reminds the audience that the questions the panelists ask do not necessarily reflect their own points of view. Only in extreme cases—as in the period of disillusionment about Vietnam in the spring of 1968—do network commentators burst through the blandness.

The television news departments offer what sound like respectable arguments to defend their avoidance of controversial stands. They operate under the restraints of FCC regulations, which require them to present both sides on matters of controversy. When they do examine controversial matters they are fair, but sometimes fair to the point of irresponsibility. William S. Paley, defending Edward R. Murrow's broadcast on Senator Joseph McCarthy in 1954, said that fairness cannot be reduced to a mathematical formula. He went on: "And it must be recognized that there is a difference between men, ideas and institutions: some are good and some are bad, and it is up to us to know the difference—to know what will hold up democracy and what will undermine it—and then not to do the latter."[3] That was powerful stuff in 1954. It would be today. Unfortunately, today only the critics complain about the absurdity of mathematical fairness, not the broadcasters.

It is exceedingly difficult to believe that it is genuinely a fear of government regulation which keeps broadcasting so sterile of opinion. Government regulation by the FCC does not appear to be nearly as effective in bringing broadcasters to heel as is the occasional direct interference of an elected official or the general awareness of being part of a business community with a large stake in the economy.

Taken together, all these influences suggest that the television industry, including its news operation, does not enjoy rocking the boat, politically or commercially. It enjoys the status quo. It identifies with the establishment, nationally or locally.

Television can be pushed around

People in government have not been slow to recognize television's desire to stay out of trouble. They have often assumed that the industry could be made to do what this or that government department wanted, without regard for journalistic independence. The instances which have found their way into public knowledge are, of course, those occasions when broadcasters resisted the pressures.

One was in 1959 when the State Department tried to tell the networks when they could, and when they could not, show the Nixon-Khrushchev Kitchen Debate. The film of the encounter actually belonged to NBC because it was at the pavilion of the network's parent company, RCA, that the two statesmen had their famous argument. The State Department had undertaken on its own to make an agreement with the Russians that the film would not be shown on American television until it had been shown on Soviet television. The networks discussed it among themselves. Robert Sarnoff of NBC was doubtful about using it but was persuaded by CBS to run it.

In 1962, the networks were again disturbed to find that the government was committing them in advance, and without consultation, to carry a program on which President Kennedy and Khrushchev would appear jointly. Officials were reported to have rationalized this interference by pointing to the fact that television is licensed by the government while newspapers are not.

Later, the State Department tried very hard to stop NBC from putting on its exclusive and dramatic film of the digging of a tunnel under the Berlin Wall, through which a large group of refugees escaped. Robert E. Kintner, who was then NBC President, said it was the network's "worst encounter with the government" and that they had been subjected to unremitting pressure for a month.[4] NBC's Berlin office had heard of a tunnel being dug and contracted with the diggers to let them film the escape. The building of the tunnel was filmed in its entirety and in great secrecy and so was the climax when the refugees finally slipped through. Before it was completed, however, a Deputy Assistant Secretary of State came to NBC to say that the tunnel had been discovered by the East Germans and that further work on it would be dangerous. He was wrong. Kintner charges that the higher levels of the State Department were "unbelievably timid and remarkably ignorant of what was really happening in Berlin." In spite of the pressure, NBC did air the film, to tremendous critical acclaim, and the United States Information Agency later distributed it overseas. The incident was not marked by consistent boldness within NBC. There was much soul-searching and at one point the network was even proposing that all the faces of the Germans involved should be blacked out (an incredibly tedious and costly procedure on film). In the end, journalistic freedom asserted itself and NBC brought off one of the television coups of the Cold War.

More important than these occasions on which the industry had the fortitude to resist official pressure is the knowledge that such pressure can be brought to bear so often. It is bound to have an influence on the conduct of television executives, and, as we shall see in a subsequent chapter, television does not always resist. Obviously, the susceptibility to yield is present.

Jack Gould pointed out in 1962: "When you operate under a government license, you are never indifferent to the possibility of reprisal." Ferdinand Lundberg suggests in *The Coming World Transformation* that "the private holders of public broadcasting franchises must give government and government personnel so much respectfully neutral and even sympathetic attention that in effect they become semi-government agencies. . . ."[5] How true that is depends very much on how the television industry, most importantly the national networks, views the possibility of government reprisal against its franchises. The fact of the matter is that revoking a license has been so rare a procedure on any grounds that it is scarcely credible today as a threat. When the networks are pusillanimous, the motive is more likely to be a general fear of government than a specific fear about licenses. And that general fear may have a solid commercial foundation.

One example, which has been the subject of comment in the press and in the FCC, is the relationship between large corporations which have multimillion-dollar defense contracts and the broadcasting stations they also own. In July, 1967, *Variety* noted that six such corporations with broadcasting interests—General Electric, Kaiser, Westinghouse, General Tire and Rubber, Radio Corporation of America and International Telephone and Telegraph—had received substantial increases in defense contracts between 1965 and 1966. The trade paper asked: "Can a major news medium like television do a thorough, honest job when it is owned and controlled by a parent corporation that has a financial involvement with the government?" And it added: ". . . it's not unreasonable to conclude that none of the broadcasting subsidiaries of war contracting corporations acquitted its news obligations in a way upsetting to the contractor, the Defense Department."[6]

This fear was very much in the minds of three FCC Commissioners who dissented from the majority decision of the Commission, which approved the merger of ITT and the ABC Television Network. Commissioners Bartley, Cox and Johnson wrote that any threat to the integrity of ABC News must be a matter of serious concern to the FCC and the American people. The fact that ITT had sensitive business relations abroad and at the highest levels of the U.S. Government meant that reporting on any number of industries and economic developments would touch on ITT interests. The dissenting Commissioners then identified what is probably the chief kind of pressure that network news departments feel, the anticipation of trouble through a subtle, almost unconscious process. "The threat is not so much that documentaries or news stories adversely affecting the interests of ITT will be filmed and then killed, or slanted—although that is also a problem," they wrote. "It is that the questionable story idea, or news coverage, will never even be proposed—whether for reasons of fear, insecurity, cynicism, realism or unconscious avoidance."7 As it turned out, the Justice Department took the merger question to court and, before there was a ruling, ITT withdrew from the agreement.

The whole dispute had been very instructive. It revealed the morality of a large corporation like ITT in the kind of pressure it thought permissible to exercise on the press. Reporters of the *New York Times* and the *Milwaukee Sentinel* declared that ITT had tried directly to influence the stories they were writing on the merger hearings. It also revealed the opinion of several FCC Commissioners that RCA had considerable influence on the public behavior of its broadcasting subsidiary, NBC. The episode reinforces the impression that the broadcasting industry finds itself in a highly sensitive position as regards both its business connections and its relations to government. When this fact is added to the normal commercial orientation of the industry and its connection with the mass advertising business, the extent of the extraordinary pressures on television journalism will be apparent. When it has to program for the widest audience to stay profitable, keep one eye open for displeasure in Washington and occasionally consider the larger interests of parent corporations with a vast stake in government and defense, it is not surprising that TV news is cautious.

Shooting bloody in Vietnam

By the end of 1967, NBC and CBS were each reported to be spending $2 million a year on covering the Vietnam war, and ABC $1 million. Each network maintained a staff of two dozen or more people in Saigon and the film shot in the jungle battles had appeared prominently on the news programs virtually every night for two years. Much was written about "the first television war" and the probable political effects of having a war which so divided the nation brought so vividly into American homes. No one is certain what that effect has been. Morris Janowitz, a University of Chicago sociologist, has said that television coverage had "hardened and polarized public sentiment." He added: "Those people who are skeptical of the war now have a vehemence in their skepticism. Those who are for the war see Americans being killed and they don't want those sacrifices to be in vain."[8] Other observers have echoed that view.

Another point of view suggests itself, however, if the nature of television's coverage is considered. Overwhelmingly, what has been seen on the home screen has been battle action. Camera teams and reporters in Vietnam found that no matter what they filmed, the networks wanted action footage. At CBS, Vietnam hands used the expression "shooting bloody" to describe the filming they had to do to get on the air. It was not that they were ordered to shoot only war scenes, but when they shot a political story or the progress of the pacification program as well as war scenes, it would be the action film which the program producers selected. Night after night for two years, American families have seen episodes more vivid and gripping than those concocted for entertainment shows later in the evening.

They have seen a considerable amount of horror: badly wounded Americans, sacks of dead Americans being loaded for shipment home, sprawled heaps of small, dead Vietnamese bodies. There are those who believe that this portrayal of horror has sickened Americans and turned many against the war, which has seemed increasingly pointless. Yet the horror has been heavily edited, and that may also have had a political impact. By exposing the mass audience to more vivid and horrible battle events than have ever been brought into American homes before, but by cutting out what is most unbearable, it may be that television has built up a tolerance for the frightful, a feeling that war really is bearable. The grisly truth has been shown in the screening rooms of the network news departments. There would be close-up footage, with sound, of a young soldier, whose leg had been shot away a moment before, screaming obscenities at the medics, pleading with them in desperation to stop his agony. As someone who believed from before 1964 that this war was a futile and stupid waste of American energies, I often wondered as I watched this uncut footage at NBC whether we should not be putting on even more of the horror, so as to arouse people more. We did not because, as one man put it, and not facetiously, "We go on the air at suppertime."

He said that that afternoon we screened a story showing American soldiers cutting the ears off dead Vietcong as souvenirs. A U.S. sergeant took out a straight razor and the zoom lens followed him in. The ear came off like a piece of soft cheese, and the sergeant put it away in his pack as the party went crunching off through the forest. The NBC reporter explained in a careful commentary that this barbaric practice was not uncommon. The story was referred to an executive in the News Department, who said not to use it. We were divided on whether we wanted to, in any case. Again, to have shown such an incident would have said a good deal about the brutalizing effect of the war. Six months later, a CBS crew filmed a similar scene, which was seen on the *Walter Cronkite* program.

The political impact of the war coverage could have been far greater if more such scenes had been shown, possibly causing the American people to protest to their government more strongly that it was too much. The effect of TV coverage, in convincing people they are seeing the worst, may have been to inculcate a spirit of pained but loyal tolerance of the war.

Michael Arlen, of *The New Yorker*, believes that the cumulative effect of all these short film reports has been "bound to provide these millions of people with an excessively simple, emotional and military-oriented point of view." Arlen also feels that the physical size of the screen had diminished the horrors of war—"a picture of men three inches tall shooting at other men three inches tall and trivialized, or at least tamed, by the enveloping cozy alarums of the household."[9]

It is also possible that the conditioning of the audience to the staged violence of television serials has diminished the emotional impact of the Vietnam footage. Real violence often seems curiously tame and insignificant compared with violence constructed by film producers. It was remarked at the time that Lee Harvey Oswald's shooting by Jack Ruby, as carried by TV, looked amateurish; the action occurred too quickly, there was no buildup. Cameramen risking their lives to record a sudden battle in Vietnam cannot provide intimate close-ups of both sides: they cannot often record all the elements that make for a satisfying film sequence.

Perhaps all these factors have helped to minimize the impact of the nightly war coverage. It was not until the sudden reverses of the Tet offensive in February, 1968, that a majority of Americans seemed decisively moved by the events of the war. Then television appeared to be moving with public opinion rather than leading or molding it.

Until the Tet offensive raised the rate of American deaths to over five hundred a week, television had not treated the story as a crisis or a national emergency. Throughout 1967, when only two hundred Americans were being killed a week, Vietnam tended to appear on television as just another story. Many critics complained that TV had not put the war into perspective. There were efforts at longer treatments of the political and economic issues, but for the most part not when a majority of the television audience was around. NBC ran a *Vietnam Weekly Review* for over a year at midafternoon on Sundays, but finally took it off in 1967 when no sponsors could be interested. The program was hastily resurrected after the Tet offensive. *ABC Scope* was a weekly series of half-hour programs, also run at odd weekend hours, and discontinued for financial reasons in January, 1968. It had first been scheduled on

Saturday evening in prime time, was then moved to 7 P.M., and finally pushed off by a teen-age rock-and-roll program to Sunday afternoon. By the end of 1967, the United States was engaged in a major war and the nation's most important news medium was not even reviewing the war week by week.

This business-as-usual attitude probably assisted President Johnson in playing the war down. It is interesting to consider what the effect might have been on the Administration if one network had decided that the war needed greatly expanded coverage and deserved at least one hour of prime time on a weekday evening. Assuming that the other networks would have followed suit, the impact might have been very great.

In 1967, a member of the White House staff told me he thought that network policy was working on two levels. There was a policy filtering down from the top and another policy bubbling up from the bottom. He went on: "The latter may not survive long. It sometimes does not get to the surface. When it does it can be very antiestablishment before the word gets down from the top. For example, Morley Safer's piece on the Marines in Vietnam was antiestablishment and no doubt after that it was decided all over to scrutinize Vietnam pieces more carefully."

Safer's piece (on CBS-TV), showing Marines setting fire to the huts in a Vietnamese village with cigarette lighters, infuriated the Pentagon. Defense Department officials tried to pressure CBS into removing Safer, who is a Canadian, from Vietnam. Perhaps it is significant that the one piece of television war reporting which notoriously went against the grain in the Pentagon appeared on a network which had no affiliations with large defense contractors.

The Vietnam war obviously presented the television networks with a dilemma. It is the best and most exciting story going and therefore merits vivid coverage. At the same time it has seriously divided the country. The industry has reacted in a manner that is now habitual: it has covered the action, done a minimum of explaining and taken no moral stand until very late in the day. One wonders how television would have treated the Second World War. Presumably because the nation was almost unanimous in support of the President's policy, television would have acted as a cheerleader for the country. That is closer to the natural inclinations of the industry than frosty detachment. Thin bits of cheerleading can even be heard through the coverage of the Vietnam war.

Have the networks behaved correctly? Whether the White House wanted it said or not, Vietnam had obviously become a national emergency for the United States by 1967. It was having a profound impact on the economy, on the strength of the dollar overseas and on the race problem at home. Hundreds of Americans were being killed each month. It was not a time in which most intelligent people felt neutral. The best-known TV commentators were by no means neutral in their own minds. Yet there was a curious reaction. Those who were inclined to be hawks let their hawkishness come through on the air. Listening to Chet Huntley, for instance, over many months, one would have little doubt that he was in agreement with Administration policy. David Brinkley was, apparently, opposed to the war, but little evidence of that came across in his broadcasts. In June, 1967, Brinkley told *TV Guide:* "We should stop the bombing—there is not much evidence that it has ever been as effective as the Air Force thinks it is, in this or any war—and I think we should take the first settlement that is even remotely decent and get out without insisting on any kind of victory. It was a mistake to get committed there in the first place, but this country is big enough and secure enough to admit it, survive it and go on to something else."[10]

If a man with David Brinkley's following had said precisely that, at that period, on nationwide television, it would have created quite a stir. The question arises whether a man who is a communicator of such stature should not communicate what he believes when the issue is so important. Why could Brinkley say it in print and not on television? *TV Guide* has an enormous circulation. Why is neutrality necessary in one medium and not in another? It is not a question of compromising the credibility of a news commentator. Comment can easily be separated from what is reported as fact, and even when it is not clearly labeled, a good deal of contraband comment slips through anyway.

If a commentator wishes, he can make his attitude known in a multitude of subtle ways by varying his expression or intonation.

More important, however, are the facts the commentator chooses to use and the form of words used to report them. In a situation like the Vietnam story, which appears night after night, it is possible consistently to accentuate the positive elements in the news and to give less emphasis to the negative. Simply by beginning each story with the American initiative that day and the number of Vietcong reported killed, you can create a sense of American achievement and progress. By beginning your story with an account of the *enemy's* initiative, you convey the opposite impression. This is putting it crudely, and I am not imputing to all well-known TV commentators a deliberate attempt to slant the news. Personal attitudes and emotions, however, are a factor in how a story is told.

My complaint is that it took television so long to tell the American people frankly how disastrously the war was going. By the time the industry did, and then almost to a man, in February, 1968, the evidence was so overwhelmingly conclusive that a good proportion of the public had made up its mind anyway.

The Vietnam war is a good case over which to argue the morality of television's refusal to take an editorial position. It is true, as we shall see later, that some stations do present editorials, chiefly on local issues. The networks do not, but it is time they did. What tended to happen, at least over Vietnam, was that stealthy editorializing in support of the Administration slipped through, but criticism did not. There was implied cheerleading in the nightly preoccupation with battles and body counts and often cursory treatment of Congressional debate.

Television does not have to come on with flags waving to appear in agreement with the Administration. It takes that side by default. If the networks argue that they have no business editorializing, when they serve some two hundred diverse affiliates, that is an argument for changing the system.

Television and the Negro—revolution or counterrevolution?

On a hot day in late spring, 1963, a police chief named Bull Connor decided he had had enough of civil rights protesters. There was something alarming in the air of Birmingham, Alabama. Day after day, crowds of young Negroes had come marching and singing down the streets demanding an end to racial discrimination in shops, restaurants and employment. Each day, Connor had carted many of them off to jail, but each following day more kept coming. On May 2, schoolchildren were taken to jail. On May 3, still more marchers appeared. Connor turned police dogs and fire hoses on them, on women and children as well as on the men. That evening, film of the dogs lunging at the Negroes and of the high-pressure hoses tearing at the marchers' bodies was seen on television news all over the country. The Negro Revolution became vividly known to white America.

Because we are still living through that revolution, it is too early yet to assess conclusively what role in its course television has played. For several years after the Birmingham explosion, it was conventional to talk about the beneficial impact of television coverage of nonviolent demonstrations. Television was a primary agent in conveying to fair-minded white Americans for the first time the depths of Negro humiliation and frustration. From the days of the Freedom Riders, through the March on Washington of 1963, to the march from Selma, Alabama, in 1965, television moved with the fresh tide of goodwill that swept the country. Through those years, television presented a sympathetic picture of the Negro struggle. It was sympathy dictated by events. In each of the major episodes of those years, the Negro demonstrators were on the defensive. They were taking the initiative in provoking confrontations but they were under physical attack, by the fire hoses of Birmingham, the stone-throwing mobs in Cambridge, Maryland, the charging police in Selma.

Then, after Selma, the mood in America changed. More militant Negroes tried to supplant the moderates in front of the cameras. The tide of goodwill had been stemmed and white intransigence had set in. By the summer of 1966, President Johnson could not get his open-housing bill through a Congress with a more liberal complexion than is likely to exist again for a long time. Now, by the nature of events, television was presenting Negroes, not on the defensive, but attacking, looting, burning and shooting as they rioted in the big cities. It was not a sympathetic picture and undoubtedly it helped to reinforce the fears and hostility of many white people.

More and more Congressmen and others began to claim that television was a bad influence, that it was stimulating and provoking the violence. Theodore White charged that television, "reaching for a distorted dramatic effect," had ignored decent Negro communities for garbage-strewn slums and the moderate Negro leadership for those who were inflammatory and provocative. He was talking about the summer of 1964, when the "white backlash" became an emotional political issue. By the summer of 1967, when big-city riots had assumed the proportion of small wars, many officials were uneasy. Some claimed outright that the riots in Detroit were fanned and inflamed by local TV coverage. There were similar charges in Cleveland, leading to an inquiry which exonerated television news. The Ohio legislature passed a bill permitting newsmen, including television newsmen, free access to scenes of riots and disturbances. The impact of television and the other news media on the riots of 1967 was studied closely by the Commission on Civil Disorders appointed by President Johnson. The Commission reported in March, 1968, that despite some incidents of sensationalism, television and the other media had made a real effort to be balanced and factual in their riot coverage.[11] The media had made the disorders look more widespread, more destructive and more of a black-white confrontation than was the case, the Report said, but could not be generally accused of helping to intensify the rioting. The Commission's chief criticism was that the media tended to reflect too much the attitudes of the white power structure, that they neglected the causes of ghetto unrest beforehand and then, when disorders broke out, concentrated on efforts of the authorities to suppress the violence.

The Commission produced a warning which has particular relevance to television: "Reporters and editors must be sure that descriptions and pictures of violence, and emotional or inflammatory sequences or articles, even though 'true' in isolation, are really representative and do not convey an impression at odds with the overall reality of events."[12] Although the Commission directed this admonition to all news media, one aspect of television news method justifies some apprehension.

When a reporter and camera team go out to cover any story involving action, they are looking for the best of the action. I have covered demonstrations and riots and street fighting for television in many cities here and overseas. The point for television is always the same: to extract the most extreme scenes. One can argue for hours about the ethics of such behavior, but this policy is not far removed from the wire service practice of pulling the most sensational detail up into the lead. Any incident involving crowds of people—a ticker tape parade for John Glenn or battles between French troops and nationalist demonstrators in Algiers—has lulls and pauses. Much of the time little happens; then there is a little violence, which flares up into bigger violence. Unless, by a mixture of bravery, instinct and sheer luck, a TV crew is to film the peaks of the violence, they will not feel they have covered the story; they will have missed what newspapermen call the "lead." From several hours' shooting, they will send back perhaps 1,000 or more feet of film. The longest television news story will use only five minutes of film (180 feet of 16-millimeter) and part of that five minutes will probably be taken up with someone talking. So the editors will obviously select the scenes of peak violence and the television audience will see the very worst of what happened. In a ghetto riot, they will not see that 75 percent of the Negroes were staying in their homes with the doors locked. In a journalistic sense, this is not distorting the story. From the point of view of public order and the good of society, however, it could be very damaging if such selected coverage hardened the white audience in their resistance to Negro advancement or stimulated Congressmen to make wild calls for heavier police forces as the solution to urban problems. Television conveys such an intensity of emotion in a few scenes, and is so much more powerful a kindler of emotional reactions in the audience, that its responsibility to society, in this case, is greater than that of print journalism.

The President's Commission dismisses any idea of government restrictions on television and press coverage of racial disorders. It does advocate voluntary adherence to guidelines and codes mutually agreed on by local authorities and the press. The chief feature of such codes is a brief moratorium, of thirty minutes or so, during which the media do not rush out with bulletins. Such an arrangement is useful because it not only gives the law time to mobilize, but permits television and radio stations to check their facts before going on the air.

Television, particularly, must carry through the next generation a great part of the burden of educating white America about the Negro problem. The responsibility is greater even than that which television bears to enlighten Americans about the Vietnam war. The needs are the same, however, in both crises: a major effort toward creative, analytical, exploratory journalism, rather than reliance on a ritualized coverage of violence. If the Vietnam war is again worth a half-hour weekly review, so is the racial crisis. On occasion, the television networks, and some local stations, have made commendable efforts to explore the meaning of Negro unrest in special programs and documentaries. The two programs Stuart Schulberg produced in Watts for the NBC *Experiment in Television* series were a good example of the kind of imaginative effort that is needed to bring sympathetic white understanding to bear on the ghetto.

The reasons why there have not been more such programs will be apparent in the next chapter.

4 Documentaries and Special Events

William S. Paley is said to have once told a group of CBS executives: "In this country play it down the middle. Overseas you can be tough."[1]

Nowhere is this attitude more clearly seen than in the extended treatment of important public issues occasionally offered by the network news departments in their documentaries. The history of television documentaries is a history of struggle against fear of controversy. Brief phases of boldness have been followed by relapses into timidity, when commercial and political considerations overrode journalistic instincts. Although there have been some notable recent attempts to break out of the web, we are still in a phase of timidity. The industry talks boldly but acts cravenly.

Critics and frustrated television journalists look back with nostalgia to the middle 1950's, at what they regard as a Golden Age in television, when electronic newsmen were flexing their new muscles apparently with less fear of the consequences than they feel now. Fred Friendly has recounted some of the more exciting episodes of that period, which was dominated by the personality of Edward R. Murrow.

Murrow and Friendly established landmarks in television journalism with some of the broadcasts in the *See It Now* documentary series, particularly those dealing with McCarthyism. But in 1958, CBS took *See It Now* off the air. Accusing the network of retreating into blandness in the face of economic and political pressures, critic Jack Gould commented at the time: "The pretense of public service is maintained by the presentations of interesting yet harmless documentaries on the past. Topics can be so chosen that the illusion of dealing with controversy is preserved, yet the risk of forthright examination of really vital issues is avoided."[2]

In the period of profitable self-indulgence which followed, the television industry was disgraced in the public eye by the quiz scandals. There was an orgy of remorse, nourished by the enthusiasm of President Kennedy and Newton Minow, at the FCC, for better TV, and something like a second Golden Age emerged. In his 1961 "vast wasteland" speech, and in other equally strong statements, Minow attempted to arouse public opinion to bring a kind of pressure to bear on the networks that would be beyond what the FCC and the Congress could muster. In January, 1962, Minow alarmed the industry by calling hearings of the FCC to discuss direct regulation of the networks. They protested violently, but President Kennedy came to Minow's support. In public, he said that Minow was using encouragement, not force. In private, he urged Minow on. He also got unexpected support from Governor Leroy Collins, then head of the National Association of Broadcasters, traditionally a bastion of industry support.

As a joint consequence of the backlash from the quiz scandals, Minow's pressure and the personal attractiveness of the new President to television, there was an increase in public service programming. The A. C. Nielsen Company reported that from October to January, 1959, the networks presented a total of 94 hours of public service broadcasts. In the same period of 1960, the total had risen to 109 hours, in 1961 to 151 hours. Thereafter, it leveled off, with a sizable burst at the time of the Kennedy assassination in 1963.

The networks grew not only more generous with their time but more daring. In November, 1960, NBC produced a documentary on the U-2 debacle which was extraordinarily specific in its criticism of Washington officials, although by that time the people under attack were members of the lame-duck Eisenhower Administration. Gould noted in February, 1961, that, increasingly, network documentaries were "delving into controversial issues and letting the chips fall where they may." Fred W. Friendly says that as Executive Producer of the new series *CBS Reports,* "my job was to create a series of bold documentaries which would help restore the prestige of CBS and, indirectly, the broadcast industry recently tarred by the quiz scandals."[3] One early broadcast in the series took an unusually hard look at the horrors of an air crash in Boston, another examined the hotly controversial topic of the quality of medical care in the United States. Both were subjects that major advertisers on television would have preferred ignored. Edward R. Murrow helped to resurrect the social conscience of television with *Harvest of Shame,* a program on the lives of migrant workers.

This period of comparative excellence reached its peak in 1963, after which the networks appeared to have exhausted their reserves of moral courage. On September 2, 1963, the NBC network turned almost its entire prime-time schedule over to NBC News for one three-hour program on civil rights. It was unusually timely for news documentaries and was justifiably hailed as a turning point in the journalistic evolution of television. The same evening, probably by no coincidence, CBS expanded the *Walter Cronkite* program to thirty minutes and a week later NBC followed suit. On the weekend of November 22 to 25, network television performed an extraordinary service to the nation. In the sentimental aftermath there were commentaries saying that the industry had redeemed itself and that electronic journalism had "arrived."

Since then, it has lapsed into a period of commercialized timidity, which is marked in the documentary field by an avoidance of controversy and significant topics and by an outpouring of popular-culture and history shows. As David Brinkley told an interviewer: "Television is lacking in excitement these days." He went on to say: "In the non-news areas, like documentaries, we lean toward soft, pastel programs—trips through the Louvre, or up the Nile with gun and camera—that seem to me to be somewhat irrelevant to the time we live in."[4]

The commercial pressures are considerable and inevitable. As a general rule, advertisers using television do not want their products associated with ideas that are unpleasant or disturbing. Robert L. Foreman, then Executive Vice-President of the New York advertising firm Batten, Barton, Durstine and Osborn (BBDO), told an FCC hearing in 1959: "A program that displeases any substantial segment of the population is a misuse of the advertising dollar."[5] There is scarcely a subject that has any relevance to contemporary American life which is not going to displease some segment of the television audience if it is handled arrestingly in a documentary. In times when competition between the networks for profits is even greater than competition for prestige, such subjects will be avoided as much as possible.

No one posts a list of forbidden subjects on a bulletin board. On the contrary, the networks are full of talk about being hard-hitting and controversial. However, somehow in the process of sifting and bargaining that determines which ideas are accepted, the bland ideas get through and the controversial ones do not. Or, when strong ideas are accepted, the treatment is so suffocatingly bland that all the sharp edges are filed down. Again, there is a strong odor of public relations. As Newton Minow put it, the networks "want provocative programs that don't provoke anybody" and the advertising agencies "want a strong, hard-hitting, non-controversial show that won't offend anybody—and above all no gloom."[6]

The crudest pressure is the direct approach: refusal to sponsor controversial programs; withdrawal of sponsorship from completed programs which promise to arouse controversy; encouraging the networks to make candy-floss documentaries. Sometimes these pressures leak out and the networks can pick up a little cheap prestige by being seen to resist. The B. F. Goodrich Company withdrew from an ABC documentary, *Nurses—Crisis in Medicine,* in June, 1967. The rubber company was currently being struck by its workers and the program showed nurses picketing for higher pay in San Francisco. Evidently Goodrich felt the association of strike ideas would harm its image. Apparently an association with war is better for image than association with striking nurses, because Goodrich subsequently agreed to sponsor a special on the Middle East war instead. In the same month, the Insurance Company of North America withdrew its sponsorship of an NBC documentary entitled *The Pursuit of Pleasure*. The program, which took a titillating look at contemporary morals, was considered to have a climate "unsuitable for our selling message," the insurance people said.

The squeamishness of a large portion of American industry about having its name associated with any but the coziest glimpses of contemporary life is not usually felt so directly. It does not often come out into the open. The effect operates long before the programs are made. NBC negotiated a remarkable contract with the Gulf Oil Company, which agreed to give blanket sponsorship to news specials and documentaries the network might wish to present as events dictated. It was regarded as an enlightened partnership and removed some of the chronic network anxiety about how to pay for unscheduled specials. By 1968, however, there was uneasiness in some quarters at NBC because Gulf did not want documentaries on the Middle East troubles or on race problems in the U.S. Since those were two of the major stories of 1967, the Gulf deal was inhibiting.

Usually, however, the influence is more subtle still. It is not always a question of direct sponsorship. An hour-long network documentary filmed in color now costs in the vicinity of $150,000 to produce. Sponsors rarely pick up the full cost. Moreover, large advertisers increasingly spread their commercials over many different parts of a network schedule. It is estimated that 75 percent of all national television is paid for by this so-called scatter plan. Network salesmen often sell not an entire documentary to a sponsor, but one or more commercial spots in that program. The scatter plan encourages network programmers to build the highest possible ratings all over the schedule, so there is pressure to select for documentary treatment subjects that will gather large audiences. That means using big-name entertainment stars and avoiding gloom. Such pressures do not help the television journalists.

The climate in which network executives work contains a factor that discourages controversy generally, operating like an undetectable nerve gas in the corporate atmosphere. Burning controversy looks good in press releases and TV reviews. It looks awful in ratings, sales, comments from aggrieved affiliate stations and nasty letters from offended viewers. Constant, warm, bright reassurance is the emotional climate in which American business, including the television business, feels most at home, and television executives instinctively work to maintain that climate.

Subject matter is also influenced when network salesmen and an advertiser make deals that relate the particular sponsor's product to the content of a documentary. The most blatant example of this in recent years was the ABC "documentary" *Blondes Have More Fun,* a title taken from the slogan of the program's sponsor, Clairol. In January, 1968, NBC produced a documentary on the future uses of outer space called *Beyond the Sky.* As Jack Gould pointed out, the program not only leaned heavily on the opinions of commercial companies involved in space technology, but was sponsored by utility companies whose commercials borrowed the program's theme—predictions of the future—to glorify the free enterprise philosophy. Such arrangements, even when the content of the program is innocent and nonpolitical, must lessen the discriminating public's confidence in the authority of the network's newsmen.

Occasionally, the networks are lucky enough to find firms which are highly public-spirited in their approach to the sponsoring of informational programs. The Xerox Corporation is one. It refused to be frightened off when the John Birch Society launched a campaign to kill a series of programs Xerox was sponsoring on the United Nations. The firm financed a nationwide survey which found that a majority of viewers liked and wanted such programs. Not many large companies are as ready to court unpopularity from any source.

In self-defense, the networks occasionally leave a documentary unsponsored to ensure freedom from pressures. Programs on serious subjects are difficult to sell and at most they would recoup a fraction of the cost. By presenting without sponsorship a documentary which is bound to get a low rating, the network also protects its overall rating position. The television and advertising industries place considerable importance on the weekly rating reports, in which one network's share of the audience in prime time is averaged out over the week. Only sponsored programs are included in this average. If a documentary is unsponsored, its low rating will not affect the weekly showing.

The networks claim they are also hindered, in their efforts to be fearless and concerned, by the weight of government regulation, especially the FCC's Fairness Doctrine.

A survey conducted by ABC's research department listed one hundred and sixty-four documentaries produced by the three networks in the years 1963 to 1966. It is significant that in those four years, when two exceedingly important things were happening to the United States, the Vietnam war and the Negro Revolution, there were only nine documentaries on Vietnam and five on the race problem, and of those five, three were about the police. Of the 164 programs studied, only sixteen fell into the category of "U.S. Social Conflicts and Problems." In other words, in their filmed documentaries at least, the networks devoted only 10 percent of their time to the real problems of life in America. In fairness, it should be pointed out that the networks produced many other special programs on public affairs during this period. NBC, for example, presented three evening-long programs, dealing with the Negro problem, crime and foreign policy. Nevertheless, because the documentary is particularly valuable in giving television journalists an opportunity to prepare carefully and to take more time than usual to look at an issue, it is significant and unfortunate that the form was used so little by the networks in these four years.

TV Guide did a breakdown of the ABC survey to discover what qualities made a documentary popular with the audience.[7] It found that documentaries which attracted between 30 and 50 percent of the available audience tended to have certain characteristics: "Hero worship, including the heroic view of America, dominates the picture—the heroes emerging from a great variety of realms: movies, politics, history, sports, exploration and the military." In this category were *The World of James Bond,* which got a 49.8 percent share of the audience, *The Legend of Marilyn Monroe* (45.0 percent), *The World of Jacqueline Kennedy* (35.5 percent), *The Journals of Lewis and Clark* (30.5 percent) and *The Real West* (42.1 percent).

The same romantic-dramatic elements were present in the next group, which got between 19 and 30 percent of the audience. The viewers responded to admired figures of the same type, political, show business, military, artistic, literary. They also watched some documentaries on social problems if the shows featured clear-cut dramatic conflicts such as law vs. criminals and whites vs. blacks, the most successful being those with the most dramatic construction. Some examples were: *The Age of Kennedy* (28.3 percent), *The World of Sophia Loren* (27.5 percent), *Cuba: The Missile Crisis* (27.6 percent), *Letters from Vietnam* (19.0 percent), *Black Power—The White Backlash* (21.7 percent), *The Stately Ghosts of England* (26.4 percent), *The Fischer Quintuplets* (19.5 percent) and *Our Man on the Mississippi* (27.1 percent).

The third group, documentaries which attracted 18 percent of the audience or less, involved different subject matter, of a drier nature, were more sedate in treatment and contained fewer heroic central figures, such as Winthrop Rockefeller or Everett Dirksen. *TV Guide* said that "what the public seems least likely to watch is the 'social problem' documentaries—shows discussing inflation, water and air pollution, disease, poverty, racial oppression and dope addiction." The audience was not resisting specific subject matter but holding out for "drama, meaning and an approach to reality that is idealistic and exciting."

Quite clearly, relatively few documentaries really delve into the acute problems of our time, because, in so doing, they will not attract sufficient audience to make them commercially appealing, or they will make the programming adjacent to them seem less attractive. The pity in all this is that a substantial number of people nevertheless do watch serious documentaries. CBS did an exceedingly interesting and original study of teen-age values in a prosperous suburb of St. Louis, Missouri, called *Sixteen in Webster Groves*. It was imaginatively filmed and utterly absorbing. It got a 14.5 percent share of the audience. A follow-up program, exploring what the people of Webster Groves thought of the first program, attracted 14.1 percent. That is a small rating for prime time but still represents an audience of many millions. Again, an evil of the American system of television is that so many people can still constitute a minority whom it is not economically feasible to satisfy very often. To have made this revealing study attractive to a wider audience, it would have been necessary, apparently, to jazz it up with a Hollywood star as narrator and to introduce dramatic conflicts that might have distorted the story.

Constant conditioning by the entertainment programs produces expectations which informational programming can fulfill only at a cost to truth. Theodore White raises an interesting question in this connection: "How does one conduct a public discussion of issues before the people of America in an age of television, in which, increasingly, the market and art insist that discussion be dramatic—and serious matters are permitted display or discussion only if they can hold the attention of Americans by visual or dramatic tension?"[8]

In 1967, there was much talk in the industry of more forceful and probing documentaries. Julian Goodman of NBC told an interviewer: "I think we have to put on tougher documentaries and we plan to do that during this coming year," although Goodman said he did not see "any wild surge of sponsor demand for the type of deeply searching investigative programs we're going to put on."

When one examines the documentaries on serious subjects that the networks did produce in 1967, the relevance of Paley's dictum to play it "down the middle" at home and tough abroad is clear.

Leaving aside what David Brinkley would call "pastel programs"—like *JFK—The Childhood Years* (CBS), *Gauguin in Tahiti: The Search for Paradise* (CBS), and *American Profile: The National Gallery of Art* (NBC)—the networks were fairly aggressive abroad, in the eyes of responsible newspaper critics. NBC's coup in securing candid home movies of *Khrushchev in Exile* in a country home outside Moscow was praised as a "notable historical document." Both NBC and CBS turned in solid documentaries on the Arab-Israeli war. CBS took a very hard look at *The Germans* in what *Variety* called "a bone-chiller of contemporary history" and NBC gave Canada's problems a searching look in *Canada Faces the Future*.

Coming to documentaries that directly affect people at home, the networks' performance was not always so forthright. Here is a sample of comments from *Variety* and the *New York Times,* two publications which maintain fairly consistent critical standards:

The Pursuit of Pleasure (NBC)
"A quickie ground out largely for instant rating effect . . . never rose above a pedestrian level."—Gould, *New York Times*

After Civil Rights . . . Black Power (NBC)
"A certain impotency . . . the bland voice of NBC News, dulling to distraction . . . a tardy summation of warmed-over events."
—*Variety*

Robert F. Kennedy (CBS)
"Totally deficient in insight, original or other, and contributed but zero."—*Variety*

The Loyal Opposition (NBC)
"Although billed as a critical analysis of the Republican party, there was little analysis and no criticism."—*Variety*

Can We Prevent Tomorrow's Riots? (CBS)
"Exercise in futility and a case of piddling while U.S. cities burn."—*Variety*

Who in '68? (ABC)
"Spent virtually all of the hour replowing old ground."—*Variety*

The Learning Process (NBC)
"Not an especially spirited presentation of a subject already rather extensively covered . . . notably shy of detailed data."—Gould, *New York Times*

Barry Goldwater's Arizona (CBS)
"Here is another glowing example of CBS News lending its considerable skills to a timely, hardhitting, subject in a troubled world . . . an improvement on the theatrical James C. Fitzpatrick travelogue."—*Variety*

There were, on the other hand, a number of much-praised documentaries in 1967: *CBS News Inquiry: The Warren Report,* an innovation because it lasted four hours spread over four evenings; *CBS Reports on Homosexuals; The Huntley-Brinkley Report Special: Just a Year to Go* (NBC); and *Same Mud, Same*

Blood, NBC's look at the role of Negro soldiers in Vietnam. Yet the number of documentaries which looked penetratingly at important matters of concern to Americans and did not flinch in doing so was still pathetically small. The best commentary on the situation is the fairly general agreement that the best documentary shown on American television in 1967 was the French-made film on Vietnam, *The Anderson Platoon,* which CBS had the good sense to buy. At the year's end that film was running at a movie theater in New York City.

One NBC program deserves separate mention because it did represent an unusual effort both to do some original reporting and to tackle a highly controversial subject. At least the subject *appeared* to be controversial—the case of Jim Garrison, the New Orleans District Attorney, who has claimed to have uncovered a Kennedy assassination plot, and has charged that the FBI and CIA are conspiring to cover it up. The nation's newspapers regarded Garrison's investigation as being very casual.

It is an indication of the state of affairs in TV public affairs programming that a network's motives are seldom believed to be pure. There was some suspicion in the industry that NBC pushed the Garrison program on the air in order to take the edge off the four-part *CBS Reports* on the assassination. The CBS investigation had been getting puffy advance billing for weeks and, well in advance, was turning into one of those publicity occasions when TV is fulsomely praised for a major contribution to society. Jack Gould did in fact call it "a thoroughly valuable social service." Words like that are emeralds and diamonds to a television network, but such publicity gems are rare. People in the industry were fascinated that NBC would dive into the murky waters of Louisiana justice and politics, but no one thought to call it "a thoroughly valuable social service." Such was the thickness of mystery and rumor that no one could quite clear his mind of the suspicion that Garrison "may have something after all," and that the "establishment" (variously, the FBI, CIA, White House, Justice Department and assorted Kennedys), working through NBC, was now trying to squelch him.

NBC had on its staff an investigative reporter, Walter Sheridan, who was a former member of Robert Kennedy's staff at the Justice Department and one of those chiefly responsible for the conviction of Teamster Union President James Hoffa. Sheridan did an investigative report on Garrison's conspiracy investigation and found a witness who said Garrison offered him money to make certain key points in his testimony. Garrison appealed to the FCC, claiming that NBC had the calculated objective of destroying his case and had "gone far beyond the pretense of merely gathering and disseminating news." The FCC refused to stop the program. Afterward, Garrison was given time to reply, which he handled effectively, continuing to insist that his case was sound. In the meantime, Sheridan was charged in New Orleans with having bribed a witness. Sheridan and NBC denied the charge and Sheridan avoided appearing in New Orleans court to answer it. Such refreshing excitements are rare.

When controversial subjects *are* tackled, the necessary process of journalism by committee often blunts the sharpness of the coverage. The Carnegie Commission recognized this: "A public affairs program or a news analysis sometimes will deteriorate as it passes through the various stages of production because the producer is seeking desperately for some device to increase its rating. Whatever the intentions, and they are good more often than the critics of television ordinarily concede, they are carried out in an atmosphere which is not conducive to the soundest selection of quality programs and their best performance."[9]

One of the troubles with the production of network documentaries goes back to the economics of news. Too often the reporter is absent. To make a documentary appealing to the audience, the network will put its biggest news name on the program. The biggest names cannot afford to spend a month or six weeks away from their regular appearances in front of the studio cameras and the networks cannot spare them. So a high percentage of network documentaries are made by a producer, with a writer, who is often the same man. When it is finished, the name commentator is handed the completed script and he spends an hour recording it. To lend this exercise a little more authenticity, he may actually travel to a location and stay there just long enough to record a few pieces with his face on camera. An NBC producer has said: "I am sick of this hypocrisy that reporters actually report on documentaries. You know how we have to fake up these specials. That is because they will not make it possible for the reporter to spend any time actually reporting. When I say that they simply look out the window and murmur, 'We know it's a problem!' "[10]

It is a problem because on television the name and face are still more important than high journalistic standards. The fees system encourages parasitism. When a commentator actually does the basic reporting on a documentary, as Frank McGee did in Vietnam for NBC's *Same Mud—Same Blood,* it is considered remarkable.

All these limitations of subject matter and treatment mean that one of the most potent instruments of TV journalism very seldom comes to grips with the vital issues of the day. There is no regularly produced series of documentaries today with a reputation inside the industry or outside for lively, consistently strong journalism. Individual programs, like the CBS documentary *Hunger in America* (May, 1968), which produced a violent public reaction from the Administration, are too-rare exceptions. Agriculture Secretary Orville Freeman demanded equal time to reply. CBS refused and repeated the program, adding to the presentation a review of the substantial efforts made by the Administration and Congress in the program's aftermath to remedy the conditions the documentary had exposed. It is significant that this example of excellent television journalism in fact grew out of an informal suggestion to CBS by a United States Senator, the late Robert F. Kennedy.

The one group of people who may feel that this is a Golden Age of television are the politicians. Buffeted by newspaper and magazine criticism, they know that they have something of a safe haven on television, along with the widest and most effective exposure. Television does not probe at issues with the frequency and pertinacity of the press and is usually very gentle with politicians. Herbert Mitgang said after a few years at CBS that a "take it easy" attitude was implicit; there was an awareness at lower management levels "that you cannot go in there and tear the hide off Senators and Presidential candidates, or Governors, especially those heading toward the Presidency."[11] Mitgang added that "the effect is to remove from TV what could be an important regulating tool, the analytical process of a correspondent himself—he has had one of his tools removed." Television's chief analytical tool is the hour documentary. It very much needs sharpening.

Special coverage: tonnage or selectivity?

The greatest strength of television is that the American people have learned to rely on it in moments of national crisis. When the story was supreme, the industry has been willing to throw off all selfishness and devote itself to the public. At times like the Kennedy assassinations it is difficult to conceive of television doing anything other than it did. Nevertheless, to say that is not to minimize its achievement.

It is probably an exaggeration to claim, as some commentators outside the industry have, that the broadcasting industry saved democracy in this country that November weekend. The nation survived President Lincoln's assassination, which occurred in far more precarious times. Certainly broadcasters did knit America into a tight and probably unprecedentedly intimate community. As *Newsweek* put it: "The greatest escapist medium ever devised made escape impossible." At one time or another that weekend, a total of 175 million Americans were drawn to the TV screen. On the day of the funeral, 93 percent of television homes were tuned in. The coverage was estimated to have cost CBS and NBC $4-million each and the advertising losses were colossal.

It is interesting to ponder why broadcasters almost automatically dropped the commercials. Newspapers did not drop their advertising; why did television and radio? One can speculate that some feeling of guilt may have been operating. Obviously many broadcasters felt that it was inappropriate to intrude advertising messages into a nation's grief. Yet if it was inappropriate, why are commercials considered appropriate in other emotionally charged contexts, such as newscasts and specials showing Americans being killed in Vietnam? The advertisers themselves were not unanimously generous about it. Some, like Pan American, agreed to let the networks consider the missing spots as run. About 50 percent agreed to accept "make goods," to have the same commercials run without charge to them at a later time.

Not all the information that poured over the airways that weekend was uniformly uplifting. Unavoidably on the networks and local stations there was much reporting of unsubstantiated fact as well as repetitive and confusing material.

That said, broadcasting was elevated that weekend to a role of unaccustomed prestige and respect.

It was again in 1968 when the death of President Kennedy was echoed in the assassinations of Robert Kennedy and Martin Luther King. The networks canceled two hundred hours of television and radio programs at a cost of more than $7 million to cover Senator Kennedy's shooting, hospitalization, death and funeral. One New York station, WNBC-TV, kept an all-night electronic vigil by the coffin in St. Patrick's Cathedral. NBC's Edwin Newman told *Newsweek:* "There's something unreal about this. All the wheels go around; we handle it as we did before. Nothing changes—only the names." National expiation by television (and perhaps for television) had become a ritual.

Similarly, in other stories of great national importance, television has come into its own. Heavy live coverage of big events is now taken for granted by the public.

There were moments, in the early days, when it seemed that television would not rise to its opportunities or would crassly exploit them. For example, NBC and CBS revolted many people by inserting commercials into religious parts of the long telecast of Queen Elizabeth's coronation in 1953. Another was the meeting of the United Nations Security Council on October 30, 1956, the day when Britain and France attacked Egypt and vetoed an American resolution. No television or radio network carried the session, and the industry was much criticized for this neglect. Today, coverage of important U.N. debates is almost routine. In June, 1967, the three networks spent an estimated $6 million providing almost continuous coverage of the United Nations deliberations on the Middle East crisis.

The same coverage, however, demonstrated a weakness in the

present methods of live broadcasting on important occasions, which deserves more discussion because of its political implications. There is at present much debate in the television industry on the pros and cons of so-called tonnage coverage. Unfortunately, some of the merits of the argument are lost in the war of prestige. Continuous live coverage too easily puts the network which adopts it on the side of the angels.

It can be argued that live coverage, as at the political conventions, relieves a network of editorial responsibility. It is true that during sessions like the United Nations debates, network commentators do attempt to explain the significance of what is happening. But being dragged on from moment to moment as they are by the need to discuss what is actually happening and who the actors are does not give them time for much analysis. The need, Jack Gould wrote after one Middle East session, "is for some appraisal of such a hectic day by dispassionate foreign affairs specialists, the introduction of an element of perspective and critical judgment to accompany the telling of the running story." Similar criticisms were made after the networks had devoted ninety minutes of prime time on a Sunday evening later that month to live coverage of Premier Kosygin's press conference after his talks with President Johnson at Glassboro. "Ninety minutes of prime time are so valuable that the webs cannot provide much more than perfunctory analysis following their coverage before returning to regular programming," *Variety* said. Gould added: "One segment of astute analysis can be worth many hours of pictures." The strength of live television as journalism can at the same time be its weakness. There is very little journalism in the flow of a live event straight into the eyes and ears of the public. Such exposure is like plugging a reader into twenty-four hours of a novelist's stream of consciousness to save the writer the trouble of selecting what is significant and putting it into words.

At the time of Fred Friendly's battle with CBS over its refusal to cover the Fulbright Vietnam hearings live, the argument of network executive Jack Schneider was that the TV journalist had a duty to present a thoughtful summary. Schneider's motives were suspect at the time, but his argument has some validity and in fact reflects official policy at CBS. In June, 1966, after NBC had devoted fourteen hours and CBS eight to a Gemini space shot, Richard Salant said: "We hope to establish that the American people can rely on CBS News to be there when it counts, and that when CBS News is not there it is because there is no significant and noteworthy news."[12]

This dispute within the industry has political ramifications. *Whether* an event is covered live by television may determine its impact on the country; whether an important event really penetrates the national consciousness or is just another distant incident fleetingly referred to on news bulletins and reported in newspapers unread by millions can influence yet other events.

In the case of happenings like the Fulbright hearings on Vietnam, the political implications of television's decision about live coverage are obvious. We will discuss this more fully in looking at the relations of Congress and the White House to the television industry.

There are those who believe that live coverage is television's most important contribution to journalism. NBC's Julian Goodman says that the medium's journalistic growth "may depend on how well it can employ its unique strength to transform the viewer into a witness of the event."[13] President Johnson's former Press Secretary, George Reedy, now a special adviser at the White House, thinks that the "electronic media should present the public with what is happening right now. The printed media should present the public with what has happened."[14]

My own feeling is that such an approach surrenders too much to the mere technology of television, which is too powerful an instrument to use merely in making viewers eyewitnesses. Untrained witnesses miss significant detail. Journalists are witnesses trained to recognize what is significant in a series of events. Only the retrospective view, when the event is over, can perceive such significance. Television needs much more of that approach.

This debate within the industry about continuous vs. edited coverage has its most obvious political impact at the nominating conventions, which we shall examine next.

In fact, the quality of news presentation vitally influences television's approach to all political campaigning, and our politicians' uses of the medium.

PART II

*"I Give You
the Next..."*

5 Conventions and Election Nights

When the Republican National Convention opened in San Francisco on July 13, 1964, the 1,308 regular delegates who had gathered to nominate a Presidential candidate were outnumbered by the 1,825 accredited representatives of the three television networks. If the equal number of alternate delegates were included, there were 2,158 representatives of other broadcasting organizations to outnumber *them*. In all, 3,983 badges were issued by the Republican Party to authorized representatives of broadcast journalism (editorial and technical) to report on the activities of only 2,616 party delegates and alternates.

Since 1952, the television industry has engulfed the national conventions, not only covering them and interpreting them to the rest of the country, but (with the active cooperation of the parties) reshaping them, molding them into happenings more appropriate to television.

More than 180 tons of television equipment was moved to San Francisco in 1964. Twenty-three mobile units arrived, some having driven thousands of miles from the East Coast. The networks built a power substation near the Cow Palace which could generate over 2 million watts, enough to light a small town. CBS alone rented 556 hotel and motel rooms at an average cost of $19 a day.[1]

Why, every four years, do the networks spend millions of dollars they never recover? What do they get out of it? What do the Republican and Democratic parties get out of it? More important, what good does it do the American voter? And most important, are the nominating conventions still as significant as the networks and the parties say they are? Has television brought the nominating process into the open or driven it underground?

What do the networks gain?

Edwin A. Roberts, Jr., of the *National Observer,* wrote that "attracting a large audience during the conventions and the ensuing campaign can yield important dividends in the next four years. Viewers' preferences since 1960 indicate that the network winning the greatest following during the campaign is the one that will dominate the news field for the following four years."[2] William R. McAndrew, President of NBC News, told *Time* magazine: "It's an intangible, but sales people say that our news image definitely makes sales for the whole network schedule."[3]

The losing network, by general critical agreement in 1960, was CBS. A top member of the CBS editorial team at the conventions four years later said: "CBS went to the San Francisco Convention with the desire to beat NBC, not to cover the Convention in its most thoughtful and original way as the story developed. The goal was to beat NBC to get a bigger audience and critical acclaim."[4]

One particular incident illustrates the competitive pressures working on high network personnel. Early in the 1964 Republican Convention, the CBS News correspondent in Germany, Dan Schorr, sent a filmed report stating that Barry Goldwater had contacts with extreme right-wing groups in West Germany. Several of us were sitting with a number of Goldwater aides down the corridor from the Senator's suite in the Mark Hopkins Hotel when Schorr's report appeared on the television screen. Goldwater's people were furious, taking it as proof that CBS was trying to sabotage the Goldwater nomination. The Senator had borne a grudge against Columbia ever since the Kennedy assassination. He had learned that in the hectic first hours of broadcasting on November 22,

Walter Cronkite had read a piece of wire service copy suggesting that Goldwater was unmoved by the President's death and was going about his normal business. In fact, Goldwater was in the process of taking the body of his mother-in-law to Muncie, Indiana, for burial when he heard the news at Chicago airport. As a man with a warm friendship for Kennedy, he was shaken by the assassination. Eight months later, he had still not forgiven CBS. Now Schorr's report from Germany reopened the wound.

The repercussions created consternation at CBS. All the top-level executives in San Francisco were called into a meeting, which included William S. Paley, Chairman of CBS, Fred Friendly, President of CBS News, and Bill Leonard, head of the election unit. Friendly telephoned Schorr in Germany and told him the story was being denied. Schorr retorted that the story was true. Friendly said: "You're giving me a clubfoot out here. This is hurting CBS News and we can't function." As an executive who observed this commented later: "The question was not whether the story is right and do you believe your reporter but what the politician is saying." There was discussion about whether Schorr should be called back to the United States as a public reprimand, but in the end he was not.

The year 1964 marked the fourth time television had attempted gavel-to-gavel coverage of the conventions. The audience was beginning to show signs of boredom. The networks had 17 percent fewer viewers than they would have attracted by sticking to the regular dreary summer schedule of rerunning old programs. Nevertheless, the competition between them for the election year honors was, if anything, fiercer than ever.

The networks do not only compete to be best at covering the conventions: they are in competition to make news themselves. A young political scientist, Herbert Waltzer of Miami University in Ohio, who studied TV coverage in 1964 at the invitation of CBS, reported: "Each (network) had a press information staff at the conventions that distributed to the newspapers and press wire services announcements of network 'scoops,' transcripts of televised interviews with convention personalities, stories of the adventures and misadventures of its reporters, and anthologies of the perceptive or humorous comments of its correspondents."[5] NBC, for example, released sheets of "Brinklies," collections of David Brinkley's wry asides.

The public relations activities of the networks are as well financed as the efforts to cover the conventions. NBC flew a number of newspaper TV writers to San Francisco in 1964 and put them up in central hotels where it was impossible for many reporters to get rooms.

In the 1950's, CBS enjoyed the reputation of being the leader in electronic journalism. That reputation was captured by NBC in 1956, when it had the inspiration to make Chet Huntley and David Brinkley its convention anchor team. The refreshingly unpompous tone these two, especially Brinkley, brought to the hours of ad-lib commentary won NBC the critical honors and the ratings that year. NBC's preeminence was clinched at the conventions of 1960. Although, by 1964, the critics were beginning to find fresh virtues in CBS, NBC continued to reap the harvest of those golden years. Generally speaking, when the three networks were competing in live reportage of a special event—from space shots to election coverage—NBC's audience would be substantially larger. On election night, 1966, for example, NBC had a 43 percent share of the total audience, while CBS had 39 percent and ABC 18 percent. The allegiance of viewers won during the conventions spilled over to the regular evening news programs featuring the same anchormen. In the long run, the networks are not making such colossal efforts at convention time purely as an exercise in charity or patriotism.

The other major benefit has been just as tangible. The early conventions on television stimulated people to buy television sets. Westinghouse and Philco, both TV manufacturers, were prominent sponsors of the conventions of 1952. In that year, "the industry was moving toward a profitable basis and was eager for various means of increasing its public," a study by the Brookings Institution reported. "The television industry, in its advertising and public statements, widely hailed the conventions as the greatest political show on earth, a special event of magisterial proportions."[6]

The growth of television can be traced by the increases in convention audiences. Filmed excerpts were carried by the embryo industry to up to 100,000 New York and Philadelphia viewers in 1940. The war interrupted progress in 1944, but by 1948 an estimated 10 million people saw parts of the Dewey and Truman conventions. In 1952, with the first nationwide coverage, peak audiences were about 25 million; by 1956, over 40 million. Some 100 million people were said to have seen some part of the 1960 conventions. The Goldwater convention of 1964 drew at one time or another 83 million viewers.

These figures somewhat exaggerate the average American's appetite for a massive diet of convention politics. Independent stations, running routine entertainment programs, have often done very well while the networks were off at the conventions. Viewers drift in and out of the audience as proceedings grow exciting or dreary. In 1956, the average audience for the conventions was 33 million, compared with an average of 54 million for Elvis Presley or Ed Sullivan. In 1952, Nielsen reported that the Republicans attracted 13 million homes at their most gripping moments, but that their following dwindled to 881,000 homes during discussions of the credentials committee in the afternoon. In 1964, as we noted earlier, the ratings were below the summer averages.

Up to 1964, network enthusiasm for the convention battle showed no sign of flagging. In 1960, CBS sent 287 people to cover the Democratic Convention in Los Angeles, where John Kennedy was nominated. Four years later, the same network employed about 600 people in San Francisco. The major difference for 1968 was the introduction of color, which the industry hoped would give the perhaps overfamiliar spectacle fresh appeal. For the first time since 1952, broadcasters were wondering about the cost, while the political parties had begun to take it for granted that the networks needed to cover the conventions, and to make fewer concessions to the broadcasters. When it was all new and thrilling in 1952, the parties sat down with the networks and agreed to hold both conventions in the same city because of the physical and cost burdens to the networks. Television executives, faced with the greatly increased cost of color equipment, tried to persuade the Republican and Democratic national committees to do the same in 1968. The Democrats, however, refused to follow the Republicans to Miami Beach and the networks estimated that having to shift to Chicago would cost them an extra $3 million. In addition, with the Vietnam war causing some economic uncertainty, 1967 had not been a good year for network profits. ABC settled for briefer, more selective convention coverage for 1968. NBC and CBS cut back their convention budgets. The end of gavel-to-gavel coverage would mean that the networks had decided that the conventions had, to an extent, outlived their usefulness to the industry, having helped to build television's penetration of the country, and to make television a more effective medium for mass advertising—after having helped to make stars of its leading commentators, and to give television journalism more justification in the eyes of network time salesmen.

Such a curtailment would be welcomed not only by the few millions who prefer summer reruns, but by a substantial body of critics in the industry and outside.

Almost since it was introduced, people have been saying that gavel-to-gavel coverage was passé. In 1956, describing the second set of conventions to receive blanket coverage, *Broadcasting* magazine said in an editorial: "It is evident that the public doesn't like all it sees and hears. The ratings of both conventions prove this. Important keynote addresses, yes. Balloting on nominations, yes. But the sameness of officially stimulated demonstrations and dull-as-dishwater speeches drives audiences away."[7]

The same year, Charles Thomson suggested that "a combination of edited and live coverage will be most effective for future conventions." He continued: "The opportunities for public service are enormous, as a good edited account could well conserve the public's time, bring the account at times and places when most of the public could watch it, and include the most relevant parts of concurrent events."[8]

Despite the efforts of the parties to streamline the proceedings, much of the political ritual is of little interest to most people. If casual viewers are driven away by activities that are tedious, they may be less likely to return for events that are important. In their efforts to keep the show interesting, the networks have developed the habit of cutting away from droning platform speeches to more lively incidents on the floor or outside the convention hall. In doing so, they have been accused either of not covering the meaningful part of the convention or of manufacturing "events" to stimulate the audience. That charge usually comes from party officials who would prefer not to have the national audience witness spectacles of party disunity. At the 1964 Democratic Convention in Atlantic City, President Johnson himself personally intervened to stop what he thought was excessive and harmful coverage of the Mississippi "Freedom Delegation." He is reported to have telephoned an NBC executive with an order to "get those cameras off that Mississippi delegation and back on the speakers!" As a result, coverage of the efforts of the Freedom Delegation to unseat the regular Mississippi Democrats was, for the moment, dropped. By no stretch of the political imagination was that struggle a manufactured event, however much it spoiled the air of harmony and consensus Mr. Johnson was anxious to demonstrate. If the cameras had remained on the platform, they would have been shirking a journalistic responsibility, as was the case when Presidential pressure forced them off the events occurring on the floor.

A borderline case was NBC's John Chancellor's bodily removal from the floor of the Republican Convention by a sergeant at arms who was trying to clear the aisles. "Clearing the aisles," a traditional and futile exercise at national conventions, is an attempt by frustrated chairmen to restore some order to the seething mass of chatting delegates, camera crews and others milling around the floor in what is usually good-humored chaos. But the effort to remove Chancellor—ostensibly for causing an obstruction—symbolized the obvious hostility of the Goldwater delegates to the press in general. The ludicrous spectacle of a man reporting his own arrest to millions of Americans conveyed a true picture of that hostility. It also came close to making the right of television to be on the floor the chief issue of the day.

If the conventions are a real event in themselves, then television's function is to report that event, not to become part of it. The dividing line was manifestly crossed when ABC hired former President Eisenhower as one of its commentators for the same convention. On one occasion, Eisenhower the political commentator was interviewed by fellow commentators Bill Lawrence and Jim Hagerty as Eisenhower the political partisan. The General lent support to William Scranton's efforts to put a firmer civil rights plank in the Republican platform. In the interview, Eisenhower said he believed the plank could be "helped some" if it called on all Americans to "adopt a moral commitment" against racial discrimination. His intervention was not very effective. The civil rights plank was the weakest the GOP had adopted in years. But in airing the interview, ABC was not reporting the convention, it was part of it.

Gavel-to-gavel coverage is criticized, in part, because of the mass of trivia that is used as a diversion from dull proceedings, the kaleidoscopic switching from, say, a floor interview to a civil rights demonstration to a platform speaker to an anchorman's anecdote to a candidate's hotel corridor to a floor demonstration. The result for the in-and-out viewer is too amorphous and impressionistic to be meaningful. Bruce Felknor, former head of the Fair Campaign Practices Committee, who attended most of the televised conventions, says that a selective approach, which is impossible when the broadcasting is continuously live, would "permit the networks to present an accurate summary of what is going on. If they could do an hour retrospectively, you would have the advantage of the newspaper and many people would look at it. In continuous coverage you avoid the responsibility for editorial judgments you don't have to make."[9]

That is not strictly true, because with multiple eventlets to choose from, the networks are constantly making little editorial judgments.

This is what it looked like in NBC's main control room in the closing moments of the Goldwater convention. Stacked up together, making a solid wall of television screens, were two dozen monitor sets. On one side of this display were three sets, labeled NBC, CBS, ABC, showing what each of the three networks was putting on the air at that moment. Another was marked POOL, representing the feed from the cameras on the convention floor which the three networks used in common.* On the pool screen was a picture of Barry Goldwater delivering his acceptance speech, which startled the country by its refusal to make the customary conciliatory gestures to defeated opponents in the party. On each of the other twenty screens was a different picture as NBC's cameras inside and outside the convention hall stalked the people and happenings for telling shots. From memory, it seems there was a close-up of Goldwater speaking from another angle, a very long shot on another, showing the widest view of the hall, a close-up of Mrs. Goldwater listening, on another monitor a picture of civil rights pickets—Negroes and whites—demonstrating outside.

Facing the huge bank of these flickering, moving images were three tiers. On the lowest, the man choosing which image to select from moment to moment, director Walter Kravetz, was speaking quietly to the technical director: "Take four." Then, pulling another switch on the intercom connecting him with the headphones worn by all the camermen, he would say, "Camera six, pan a little left and give me a close-up of Peggy Goldwater." On the next tier up were Reuven Frank, overall producer of the election coverage, and Shad Northshield, the General Manager of NBC News, each watching the array of screens, and occasionally suggesting to Kravetz that he take a different shot. On the third tier were NBC News executives Bill McAndrew and Julian Goodman, also watching. Behind them, but out of sight, was the President of the NBC network, Robert Kintner, watching ceaselessly, behind thick tinted glasses (worn to rest his bad eyes), the output of all three networks. At his side was a white telephone which he picked up occasionally to pass an instruction to the control room.

The whole room suddenly became more tense. Goldwater was still speaking, but one of the monitors showed a stirring in the rows of chairs.

---

* A "pool" is an arrangement by which all three networks take basic pictures of the conventions from one camera in a single location, instead of three. It reduces costs and space needed. "Pool" pictures are supplemented by exclusive cameras elsewhere.

"Watch the New York delegation."

"Camera five go in tighter." One of the monitors swirled as the cameraman changed his lens to zoom in.

"Get me a reporter. Who's near there?"

"This is [Sander] Vanocur. I'm near New York."

"What's happening there? Someone's moving."

"Give me a minute to get over there."

Goldwater finished his speech. Over the loudspeakers came a deep roar. The wall of monitors flashed with changing images: Barry Goldwater in a glare of spotlights, raising his hand high—a short man with a shock of white hair, pushing his way through the crowd on the floor with others after him—still the civil rights demonstrators outside—a row of empty chairs—a big close-up of a card on one of the empty chairs saying THE STATE OF NEW YORK—reporters pushing through to get at the man who was leaving—sound: "Senator Keating, Senator Keating . . . ?" Another monitor showed the Stars and Stripes caught in a spotlight. The audience was cheering and applauding—pictures of the Goldwater family smiling. Then the sound of "America the Beautiful. . . ."

Northshield and Frank shouted directions to Kravetz: "Get close on Keating—take the civil rights people—what are they singing? What? Let's hear it louder." And as Kenneth Keating, the liberal Republican Senator from New York State, sickened by the intransigence in Goldwater's speech, walked out of a convention that had been captured by the right, the sound of the civil rights demonstrators singing "We Shall Overcome" crept over the sound of "America the Beautiful." The Goldwater crowds applauded frantically, joyously. Big close-ups of their clapping hands and radiant faces were followed by a shot of Keating's white head bobbing in the crowd, a shot of the flag, of Goldwater, of his family, of the demonstrators outside, of the empty New York delegation chairs—all woven into one orchestrated visual impression of a moment of history.

The moment was gripping and highly emotional. Was it art or journalistic judgment or a sense of instant history which called for the quick intercutting of pictures and mixing of sounds? There had been very little talk in the control room. The decisions, orders, suggestions, were transmitted in a few words. The coverage could have been quite different, stressing the loyalty of the Goldwater fans, for example, instead of making heavily ironic comments by deliberately juxtaposing different images. Keating could have been ignored. In fact, it was very hard to tell in the crush of people that it was a walkout. The Senator tried to deny it afterward. The television audience at home need never have known that the demonstrators for Negro equality were singing the deeply moving "Deep in my heart I do believe/That we shall overcome someday/ . . ." while people inside were singing "America, America, God shed his grace on thee,/And crown thy good with brotherhood,/From sea to shining sea."

Editorial judgments *are* made during live coverage, although there are few moments where so many separate elements come with such a rush and demand such quick reactions. Even if the network had not been broadcasting "live," but videotaping for later, edited use, the same process would have been followed. The edited version would have appeared very much as the live one, the sum of tiny editorial decisions from second to second. Edited convention coverage will never be, as some advocates perhaps believe, the difference between a running account of a horse race and a retrospective account of the same race. Broadcasting is not journalism recollected in tranquillity.

Nevertheless, some modification of the system is probable. Richard S. Salant, President of CBS News, says he thinks gavel-to-gavel coverage is "excessive and an abdication of news judgment."[10] He continues:

I would much rather see us just go for live coverage of the truly significant happenings at a convention—and, in addition, provide a daily, prime-time summary and wrap-up. But so far there are two things which stand in the way of this sensible journalistic procedure. The first is just plain guts—which we don't have. We are too afraid that we will be condemned by the television critics for making a money judgment (actually such coverage would be no cheaper) and we are too afraid that our competition will be regarded as the white knights for its tonnage coverage. Second is the problem of the inflexibility of the television network entertainment schedule which makes it extremely difficult to move in and out of that schedule if and when the convention events dictate; after all, it is argued, we can't cut away from the last ten minutes of Perry Mason and leave the poor public dangling with a whodunit.

George Reedy, President Johnson's former Press Secretary, says that a considerable amount of the television coverage is wasted: "Because of technical limitations, about the only contribution that television, as a medium, can make is to present the more dramatic moments and these are rather few and far apart. Therefore the networks are presented with the problem of filling in a great deal of time with conversation that frequently is lame."[11]

The networks have gradually evolved systems of collecting the mass of information available at the convention and channeling it through anchormen who can bring the methods of journalism to bear on the raw material of the event.

The networks use their anchormen to personalize the coverage and reduce the myriad impressions to an understandable pattern. Naturally, a great deal depends on the anchorman's skill. "Covering a convention is a very hard job," according to David Brinkley. "You have to keep about eight tennis balls in the air at one time. You have to listen while you're talking, you have to know everybody, and you have to know everything about the political situation."[12]

To assist them, each of the networks ties the scattered components of the convention together with its own news wire service. At NBC, every correspondent covering a candidate or major political figure (and no one is uncovered) is instructed to phone the least bit of information he picks up to a central news desk. There copytypists take it down, the desk edits it and it appears moments later on teletype outlets at a dozen NBC locations around the convention city. The most important outlet is in the "anchor booth," where Huntley and Brinkley sit overlooking the convention hall. The wire is essential to give them a running flow of incidents, important events, changes of schedule and humorous anecdotes to supplement their own knowledge and what they can observe by watching the floor through binoculars. The system is similar at the other networks.

NBC brings one newsman from an affiliate station in each state to stay with the convention delegates from that state, waking and sleeping. Each of these reporters phones information to the wire. The service's information is so complete that no other news medium in the convention city is kept as well informed, or as up to date. Therefore, hundreds of newspaper reporters can actually cover the convention more efficiently by watching and listening to television. If a political personality leaves his hotel, there will be a private network phone somehwere near the entrance. The reporter covering him will phone the wire and within a minute Huntley will have a piece of copy in his hands enabling him to say, "We see Governor Rockefeller left his hotel half an hour earlier than expected this morning." When Rockefeller returns to his suite, there will be an NBC phone in the service stairway as close to the Governor's rooms as his security men will allow. The reporter will go to it the minute he is back.

The anchormen and all other editorial personnel for the networks are supplied with huge looseleaf notebooks prepared months in advance by election research staffs, with as much information on personalities, political history and previous conventions as they could require. The men in the glass booth high over the convention floor are thus better informed than any single delegate or political figure on the floor about the general flow of events.

Keeping abreast of the information, however, accounts for only a few of Brinkley's eight tennis balls. The anchorman's next function is to keep the public interested. He can drone on authoritatively for hours, delivering prodigious amounts of information, but unless he does it captivatingly, he will bore the audience and they will switch off. Brinkley uses brevity and wit. When Brinkley first appeared in 1956, Jack Gould wrote in the *New York Times* that "Mr. Brinkley's extraordinary accomplishment has been not to talk too much." Huntley's is a low-pressure affability. Neither of the other networks was able to offer an anchorman or combination of them who could make the tedious hours pass so pleasantly. The others, Edward P. Morgan (now with PBL) and Howard K.

Smith at ABC and Walter Cronkite, with Eric Sevareid, at CBS, has each a following of millions and a great store of political information to impart, but in terms of audience chemistry they never quite matched the NBC convention team.

If they have the manner or magnetism to keep an audience of many millions in their grip, the anchormen then have the duty of making what happens coherent, which is probably most difficult of all. With one's attention constantly flicking from the sound of the network program on the little plastic speaker plug in one ear, to the instructions of the producer who can override it, to the sound of whatever is being said on the floor, to conversation with editors delivering copy, to reading that copy, to watching the TV monitors, it requires extraordinary concentration and orderliness of mind even to keep straight all the incoming bits of information. That the commentators do not always provide wise and detached analysis is not surprising. To do that consistently, they would probably have to stay away from the distractions of control rooms and studios.

The networks or their anchormen may have left their critics unsatisfied, but they have convinced millions of people that the national conventions are important. The impression TV has given American voters is, according to Professor Waltzer, responsible for people's willingness "to accept the authority of the national convention, and thereby of the national parties, to determine the field of choice of candidate and the programs in Presidential elections."[13]

What have the parties gained?

A citizen gives his allegiance to the Democratic or Republican Party because he has in his mind an image of that party. The party identity is not the same in the minds of all who consider themselves Republicans or Democrats. Each organization provides a home for many views. In fact, the ability of each party to remain many things for many people is what has kept the United States a two-party country. Sometimes the party identity may seem clear and specific to its adherents, who express their understanding in phrases like "the party of the little man" . . . "the party of big business" . . . "the party that believes in free enterprise" . . . "the party of social reform." Sometimes it may become blurred and vague. The art of running a large and diverse political party is in keeping its image or identity specific enough to attract new members and general enough not to repel old ones.

Most of the furbishing of party identity occurs at election time, in the candidate it chooses to symbolize what it stands for, and the policies it adopts in its platform. The national conventions thus serve the function of imprinting afresh the identity of the party in the minds of the voters. As in all other fields where communicating an image to a large number of people is the task, television is an ideal tool.

Perhaps the greatest benefit to American politics of complete television coverage of the national conventions is the opportunity to penetrate every corner of the nation with a week of identifying material. Both parties have been willing to modify their convention procedures quite drastically to exploit this opportunity. The television industry, for its part, has wanted to produce a spectacle that would attract big audiences and particularly to avoid long, dull periods that would drive viewers away. Usually these motives of the politicians and networks have been in conflict; sometimes they have harmonized.

From the first days of extensive television coverage, there seemed to be a common interest in streamlining the proceedings. The party organizers did not want to bore the television audience any more than did the networks.

Most of the radical changes were made before and just after the first taste of full television coverage in 1952. There was a battle at the Republican Convention to get TV into the platform and credentials committees. TV eventually won the right, but the politicians later arranged matters so that the committee met the week before to hammer out their differences, before live coverage of the convention proper began.

Convention programs were turned around to eliminate most of the business during the daytime, when the television audience is small. Important business which the parties wanted seen—the keynote addresses opening the conventions, nominating speeches, balloting and acceptance speeches—were pushed into prime time.

The halls were decorated with slogans designed to be seen on television, big-name entertainers were hired to attract viewers, stands full of dignitaries behind the speakers' platform were redesigned so that inattentive faces did not show up comically in long-lens close-ups of the speakers.

Large camera platforms were tolerated in the middle of the convention floor to accommodate cameras shooting platform speakers. When delegates on the floor complained that their view was obstructed, they were given TV monitors to keep them happy.

An important reform was urged on the Democrats by Hubert Humphrey after the 1952 experience when obscure delegates held up proceedings with indiscriminate demands that their delegations be polled. Now the opportunities for requiring a poll are limited.

The parties provided the networks with "shooting scripts" and hired TV advisers from the profession to guide them.

Instead of the most senior or most worthy political figures, young and vigorous-looking politicians were given key convention jobs. For instance, in 1964, the Republican Minority Leader in the House of Representatives, Charles Halleck, would by tradition have been made Permanent Chairman. Instead, Senator Thruston Morton—who was thought to project a better image for the party on television—handled the gavel. The Governor of Oregon, Mark Hatfield, a handsome, clean-cut young Republican, was made keynote speaker.

The Republicans fought a battle with television over its right to station reporters and portable cameras (called "creepie-peepies" by NBC) on the floor, but surrendered to the wishes of television.

The "writing press," who traditionally occupied honored places on the floor directly in front of the platform, gradually were pushed to the sides, with their space much diminished. In 1964, they were even relegated to a basement garage by President Johnson, who personally stage-managed the Democrats' convention at Atlantic City.

All these concessions to television, however, did not change the basic character of the conventions, which are still filled with acres of procedural pomposities, about as sparkling as the formalities at a Rotary luncheon.

Take this excerpt from the proceedings of the 1964 GOP Convention schedule:

3:45   Preconvention entertainment.
4:00   Clear the aisles: marching and singing groups participating. Temporary Chairman Hatfield calls Convention to order. Presentation of colors by Oakland Police Department. Pledge of allegiance by Terry McDermott, 1964 Winter Olympics gold-medal winner.

National anthem by Robert Weede.

Invocation by Dr. Morris Goldstein, Rabbi of Congregation Sherith Israel, San Francisco.
4:30   Temporary Chairman calls for report of Credentials Committee. Report of Credentials Committee Chairman. Temporary Chairman appoints committee to escort Permanent Chairman Morton: Miss Edith Napier of Kentucky, Congressman Charles S. Hoeven of Iowa, Mike Stepovich, Candidate for Governor of Alaska, Toshio Anasai of Hawaii, Mrs. Tom Abernethey of Alabama, Mrs. Florence G. Morris of Ohio.
5:00   Temporary Chairman calls for report of Rules Committee, etc. . . .

and so on through endless tiny, pointless ceremonies with participants carefully balanced ethnically and racially, by religion and by region.

By the schedule, one hour and fifteen minutes went by and only one piece of business was accomplished. Does the national television audience really have to see the worthies of the Oakland Police Department present the colors, or listen to a winter sports star lead the Pledge of Allegiance? Does Temporary Chairman Hatfield really need to appoint a committee to escort Permanent Chairman Morton, on national television, just for the sake of giving that morsel of political patronage to a few deserving party members?

If the alterations have never satisfied television's craving for a show that scintillates from gavel to gavel, the political parties have never been quite happy about what television likes to show.

From 1952 onward, there have been fresh attempts at every convention to make the delegates arrive on time—respectably dressed—take their seats and try to stay awake during the sessions. If the delegates insist on behaving like children, as they are prone to do, the party's managers will treat them like children. They have cut down as much as possible on the carnival side of the convention, the floor demonstrations, because without the emotion that comes with actually being in the hall, demonstrations quickly begin to look silly and contrived to people at home. The power of a long and noisy demonstration to stampede a wavering convention behind a particular candidate is almost an anachronism anyway. Today, delegate loyalties are kept under constant review by representatives of the candidates in command centers near the convention hall.

The surveillance system was improved and refined by the Kennedys in 1960 and by the Goldwater team in 1964. F. Clifton White, who had charge of the nomination for Goldwater, knew from moment to moment—by walkie-talkie and telephone reports from his men with each delegation—how the delegate count stood. White is sensitive to the way television pictures floor demonstrations, especially what he calls the "constant snide remarks of the commentators."[14] He believes that demonstrations still have a useful function: "They let off steam in a highly emotional situation. Everyone wants his team to win. Initially demonstrations were an emotional response. In 1952, there were grown men in tears. They had spent twelve years trying to nominate Bob Taft and it was finished. Now there are more staged demonstrations. The commentators always mention that they are paid demonstrators and it is true in some cases. But the public has the attitude that the demonstrations are meaningless and it is not true."

Some demonstrations can be far more harmful to the party's image than the sight of happy supporters whooping it up behind a band. There was a demonstration in 1964 which Clif White and other Goldwater aides tried desperately to stop: the shouting down of Nelson Rockefeller. The Goldwater delegates on the floor had been well disciplined, but when the eastern Republican who had fought Goldwater's nomination from New Hampshire to California rose to speak to the convention, the galleries would not let him. It was a few minutes of great embarrassment to the Republican cause, as Theodore White describes: "As the TV cameras translated [the hecklers'] wrath and fury to the national audience, they pressed on the viewers that indelible impression of savagery which no Goldwater leader or wordsmith could later erase."[15] In written instructions, booing and heckling had been strictly forbidden to Goldwater delegates, but television, understandably, concentrated on what could be seen happening, not on what was supposed to happen.

Attempts are still being made to censor or restrict what television can show to save the parties embarrassment. At Senate hearings on political broadcasting in 1967, Democratic Senator Vance Hartke, of Indiana, said it was up to broadcasters to make the convention look serious: "It's not the responsibility of the people running the convention to keep the delegates awake," he said. "People fall asleep in church too, and televised church services could be made to look ridiculous by focusing on someone dozing. Likewise the antics of people participating may be funny, but the conventions are serious business. The broadcasting industry has a responsibility to show that."

The classic, and perhaps most courageous, response to this attitude came from CBS after an incident at the 1956 Democratic Convention. The network refused to carry two films made by the party and shown during convention evening sessions. One of the films was a propaganda effort called *The Pursuit of Happiness* and was narrated by Senator John F. Kennedy. Paul Butler, the Democratic National Committee Chairman, complained that CBS had broken faith with the party organizers. The network retorted: "The right of CBS to be bored must be defended."

Eight years later, a film tribute to the dead John F. Kennedy was shown at the Democratic Convention in Atlantic City. It was carried by all the networks and left millions of viewers and delegates at the convention in tears. But the tears came when President Johnson thought them appropriate. One of the trickiest pieces of scheduling at Atlantic City was the placement of that film, which was to be introduced by the late President's brother, Robert F. Kennedy. Ever since the assassination, nine months before, a movement had been building to force President Johnson to take

Bobby Kennedy as his running mate in 1964. In the spring, the President had issued a statement saying that Bobby was not on the list of those acceptable to him. Stories of bad blood between them were becoming general. If the Kennedy film was shown to delegates before the nomination of a Vice-Presidential candidate, would it not provoke a wild demonstration for Robert Kennedy with all the nation watching? Mr. Johnson decided it would and rescheduled the showing for *after* Hubert Humphrey's nomination for Vice-President.

Fear of bad television publicity also caused the Republicans to do some last-minute rescheduling in 1964. The organizers had planned to have only twenty-five minutes of the platform read to the convention (a concession to televiewers' patience). After it had been adopted, President Eisenhower was due to speak. But Governor Scranton and others insisted on challenging some planks of the Goldwater platform. To avoid a floor fight on television, General Eisenhower was put on first, and then the entire platform was read. It took 90 minutes. The platform's opponents—including Nelson Rockefeller—were pushed out of prime time and the session closed at 4:30 A.M. in the East.

The parties, understandably, are ambivalent about television. They want the most searching attentions as long as they are flattering; when television pries too deeply they grow worried and want to banish the cameras from sensitive areas. After 1964, former President Eisenhower proposed that a committee be formed to work out convention reforms. One of those who tried to talk some sense to the committee at a meeting in the fall of 1966 was the late Paul Tillett, a political scientist from Rutgers University. "All the critics want to change is the appearance of things," Tillett told them. "And, I'm afraid, if they succeeded in driving the media men from the floor, in gaining absolute control of demonstrations, and in keeping the delegates and spectators sitting like schoolchildren, it would become all too apparent to everyone that nothing of consequence was happening on the rostrum."[16] Tillett said that besides the nominating function, there is only one role that can be performed fully before the public: the function of a mammoth rally to kick off the Presidential campaign. The other functions—

hammering out a statement of party principles and settling disputes between contending state organizations—had to be performed partly in private.

Clif White complains that television cameras and microphones were so thick near Goldwater's headquarters at the Mark Hopkins Hotel in 1964 that the need for new ground rules was clearly indicated. "There is a really serious and fundamental conflict between the politician who feels the need for secrecy and the TV cameras," White says. "As in any negotiating situation there is a need for total candor. In 1968, the candidates will be chosen in meetings in private rooms held with the greatest candor. You can't say that Henry Cabot Lodge is a bad campaigner because he likes to sleep four hours a day, in front of 180 million people!"[17]

One of the misleading impressions television coverage has given is that it has brought the whole convention process into the open for public scrutiny. The efforts television makes, by its hot pursuit of candidates through hotel kitchens and underground garages, may give the false impression that the camera eye is all-seeing. The more assiduous the networks have become (in 1960 one crew broke a hole through a hotel-room wall to get a picture), the more enterprising the politicians have become in evading the creepie-peepies. When, before the convention, NBC and CBS installed camera pickup points and telephones right up to the Goldwater suite in the Mark Hopkins Hotel, Goldwater's aides simply removed them. A force of security police guarded parts of the hotel floor that were "off limits" except by special invitation.

The only reason the smoke-filled room is disappearing is that for health reasons fewer politicians are smoking. The harder television tries to crash the party, the farther away the politicians will gather. Some parts of the machinery for building up steam in these two giant engines every four years are simply not visible. Increasingly, it may be that the real nominating process will not be visible.

Only the TV coverage sustains the myth

John Kenneth Galbraith has written that the main point of the modern political convention is that it can decide nothing. He says:

"Rather it is a ratification of weeks and months of effort designed to sew things up and thus avoid the risk of action by the convention. The delegates and other so-called bosses, in consequence, have about the same power of self-determination as a carload of prime steers at the Kansas City yards. Only the TV coverage sustains the myth."[18] John F. Kennedy's nomination in 1960 and Barry Goldwater's in 1964 are well-known cases in point.

This applies not only to the nominating function but to the preparation of platforms, which, in Paul Tillett's description, "are prefabbed elsewhere and shipped in for erection, display and ratification."

In 1960, Governor Rockefeller forced Richard Nixon to modify the Republican platform at their secret Fifth Avenue meeting, but it was an acknowledgment that Rockefeller had bowed in advance to the inevitability of Nixon's nomination. Theodore H. White has described how the Rockefeller workers and volunteers cheered and demonstrated in Chicago as though they were taking part in a convention. "But the real Convention, the deciding Convention, had already met and all but concluded its work before the gavel pounded and called the public Convention to order."[19]

Paul Tillett gave the Committee on Convention Reform examples of delegates to recent conventions whose actions "were supremely unimportant in the sense that they simply went to the convention cities to carry out decisions made elsewhere."

One was at the 1960 Democratic Convention in Los Angeles. The Illinois delegation's sixty-nine members caucused the day before the convention opened. Their choice of candidate for the Presidential nomination was controlled by Mayor Richard J. Daley, of Chicago. Their only decision-making was to elect Daley and State Chairman James A. Ronan as Chairman and Secretary of the delegation. They confirmed preliminary appointments to convention committees and reelected a National Committeeman and National Committeewoman for Illinois. All that was done in one caucus; never during the entire convention which nominated John F. Kennedy did they caucus again. In the thirty-five states which hold state conventions, key aides of various national contenders for nomination are out months before the national convention, making deals with political leaders right down to the precinct and election-district level, to line up delegates. It is always the party activists who bother to attend all these early sessions. Naturally they make the decisions. If the ordinary, casually motivated voter believes it all happens at the big conventions in July and August, as television's emphasis may lead him to think, he will not be involved in the crucial groundwork.

Television's emphasis on a few major primary elections in states which do not hold state conventions merely helps to reinforce the impression that the road to nomination is clear and open all the way to the national convention.

Of course, in a year like 1968, when more than one contender acquires a large number of preconvention delegate commitments through primaries, or when the early ballot test of strength results in a deadlock, the national convention again becomes the decisive arena. Then, however, as Clif White puts it, "candidates are chosen in meetings in private rooms," as happened when President Truman persuaded key delegations to switch from Kefauver to Stevenson and break the deadlock in 1952.

By its nature, television cannot be where matters are actually being decided in private, except under conditions that would destroy the journalistic function. Cameras of historical record could be admitted to the most secret sessions, but they would inhibit people and would contribute nothing to the coverage of a convention while it is happening. A film crew hired by the Goldwater forces stayed with the Senator and his aides through many private moments of the San Francisco convention. One segment of the film showed the Senator, dressed in blue jeans, watching television in his hotel suite as the delegations were polled to nominate him. When the balloting passed South Carolina and his victory was confirmed, there was a short pause while aides congratulated him. Then the phone rang. Denison Kitchel, his campaign manager, answered, covered the telephone with his hand and said, "Barry, it's Nelson!" There was a moment of shock. In the correct tradition, the man who had futilely done everything he could to prevent Goldwater's nomination was calling to congratulate the winner. For a moment the accumulated feelings of the prenomination campaign welled up against Rockefeller, who had branded Goldwater an "extremist" and worse. Goldwater swore and made a spitting gesture. Then he picked up the phone and in the friendliest tone said, "Hi, Nelson. Do you want to come up?" If such intimate glimpses into the hotel suites and back rooms at convention time were a routine part of live television coverage, the result would be farcical.

Party leaders could help television reporters to get the real story, Tillett told the Committee on Reform, "but it would require *leveling* and despite the confidence of leaders, there's many a slip twixt cup and lip." He went on: "Public interest does not have an intrinsic right not to be bored; but it has an effective sanction, it can do something else. Public interest does require that the important work of the convention be exposed. Television and other media can contribute to this, but not if their agents are kept away from the point of resolution."

As long as they are kept away from the point of resolution, the result will be to some extent spurious.

There would seem to be an argument, then, for the television industry to draw back, so to speak, from the conventions. By trying to tell and show less of the story, it might with less stress and more contemplation tell more. At present, the immense burden of the competition for network prestige, on TV reporters and producers, puts too great a premium on speed and picture. To have succeeded by whatever devious means in snatching a live picture of a candidate sneaking through a hotel kitchen becomes the network "coup" of the moment. The network reporter works under such anxiety to be first with the merest tidbit of information and must devote so much ingenuity to wangling cameras and microphones into this caucus or that hotel room, that he has little time to get the real story. The truth is most often revealed, as any journalist knows, by a series of quiet and often leisurely talks, in confidence, with several important people, which he then weaves into a story. Important figures are most willing to tell a reporter something quite significant if they are alone and the politician knows his indiscretions will be protected. In delicate moments of a convention, when every public word is a tactical maneuver, no sensible politician is going to be candid before a microphone carrying his words to millions of people.

If news departments could convince the television networks that the story is more important than considerations of mass-audience prestige, everyone would be better served.

Election night: second fiddle to the computers

The other predictable television spectacle which Americans find most absorbing in years of major elections is the coverage on election night.

In one generation, TV has transformed the anxious, all-night ritual into an incredible display of electronic virtuosity. It has dazzled, and not always pleased, the voters with its ability to tell them who won, before some voters have even finished going to the polls. The public is still mystified and a little annoyed that there is no longer any "horse race." There never was, of course, except in very close elections. Old-fashioned reporting techniques merely created that pleasurable illusion.

Television journalists, on the other hand, show some anxiety about being themselves gobbled up by the computers. Increasingly, the work of the commentators and political pundits is being preempted by machinery. The election coverage is in danger of becoming dehumanized in its fascination with the new technology.

On several recent election nights, it has been not only the networks competing with each other, but the computers. Network competition, which is ferocious all through election year, rises to a climactic pitch on election night. Every nerve is taut in the anxiety to outdo the other networks in the last round of the battle whose consequences will be felt commercially for four years thereafter. There is also a desire to sell computers. The reputations of RCA (NBC), IBM (CBS) and Burroughs (ABC) are on the line as much as is the prestige of the networks themselves. There is extreme pressure from both industries to get the results fast and right. Sometimes, in the feverish atmosphere, they have been less right than fast.

The role of the computers has not stopped with vote counting and projection of winners. It has now moved into the business of explaining to the voters what the election was all about. The journalists, who thought this was their job, are disturbed to discover the mechanical tail wagging the editorial dog. It is not a question of jealousy as much as a concern for meaning. At both NBC and CBS, there was antagonism in 1966 between the experts, who wanted the computers to tell the story, and the commentators, who felt the computers did not know what the story was. Network executives were backing the machines. The computers had been crammed with demographic information and fitted with devices enabling them to display that information in graphs and maps on the television screen. Technically, it was remarkable to be able to ask the computer whether middle-income Poles voted for Charles Percy or Paul Douglas in Chicago and an instant later have the answer in a picture. The complaint of commentators like Sevareid and Brinkley was that too much information was left out. The computers could not yet cope with politicians' personality, style of campaigning, relevant remarks—all the ingredients that make political journalism interesting and human. Statistical comparisons sorted mathematically cannot generate the intuitive insights of a well-stocked human mind. The torrent of raw information the computers and election experts could produce needed to be filtered through a journalistic screen. Like so much else in the television industry, it is a struggle between what is exciting and flashy and what is helpful to the public. One can expect the election night struggle to go on.

If the TV newsmen are uneasy about the mechanical takeover, so are the voters and politicians, although their fears are different.

At 7:22 P.M. Pacific Daylight Time on the day of the California Republican Presidential Primary in June, 1964, CBS declared Barry Goldwater the winner over Nelson Rockefeller. In southern California the polls had been closed for twenty-two minutes but in San Francisco and to the north, there was still thirty-eight minutes of voting time left.

In the general election, CBS declared President Johnson a firm winner at 9:04 Eastern Daylight Time, when polls were still open in many western states. Politicians of both parties jumped on the networks, charging that irresponsible predictions might have influenced the outcome. Just before the election, the Republican National Chairman, Dean Burch, had formally asked the three networks to withhold "early and unwarranted interpretations of the first returns" and to make no projections until polls on the West Coast had closed. When the networks ignored his request, the impression spread among politicians and others that the networks were tampering with basic democratic institutions.

Pierre Salinger, for one, charges that the 1964 election coverages raised "a grave threat to the democratic process" and claimed that 300,000 Californians had not bothered to go to the polls once they heard the outcome of the Presidential election. Salinger thought "it could have been the deciding factor in many close races for state and federal offices across the country."[20]

In fact, there is no objective evidence that the early projection of results had any effect in 1964. A number of studies were undertaken to try to find out how, if at all, the voters in western states were influenced by hearing the projection from network computers in New York. In one, 344 people were interviewed at polling places in Berkeley, California,[21] between 4:00 P.M. and 8:00 P.M. Most of them (67.1 percent) had heard a broadcast prediction of the outcome before they voted; not all interpreted the broadcasts in the same way. Only 4.4 percent thought Johnson had actually won. The largest percentage thought he was leading heavily and 1.3 percent even thought Goldwater was leading. They were asked whether hearing a computer prediction of a sure Johnson victory had made a difference in their desire to vote. An overwhelming percentage (84.4) said it made no difference, 10.6 percent said it made them more interested and 5.0 percent said it made them less interested.

Two New York University sociologists, Kurt and Gladys Lang, in a study financed by CBS, examined 364 voters in the East Bay area, near Oakland, California, and found "no evidence that the broadcasting of election returns caused any significant number of persons to abstain from voting altogether, or to abstain from voting in the Presidential and Senate races."[22] The Langs found that, like politicians, voters had a widespread belief in a bandwagon effect but they could not find one person in their sample who could document the effect "by references or anecdotes concerning either themselves or anyone they actually knew." When they were asked what elements in election broadcasts voters found most helpful in deciding how the Presidential race was going, only 16 percent said the computer predictions. The actual vote count was thought most helpful (33 percent) and the electoral-vote tally almost equally so (32 percent).

At least for the time being, these and other studies apparently satisfied the anxieties of Congress. The Senate Communications Subcommittee took up the question in 1967, and concluded that there was no immediate emergency and that "no legislation restricting the broadcasting of election returns and predictions is warranted." However, the Chairman, Democrat John O. Pastore of Rhode Island, did suggest that the networks label projections more carefully as such, since *declaring* winners might have an effect in swinging elections.

All the same, there remains some residual doubt about what the effect might be in a very close race for Congressman or Senator if even very few voters were dissuaded from voting because they heard the big race was over. In 1964, the networks took pains to urge citizens in the western states to vote, even though the LBJ victory was evident long before the polls had closed.

One suggestion, put forward by CBS's Frank Stanton and others, is that new election laws be passed so that polls would remain open for the same twenty-four-hour period in all states. Both NBC and ABC said they thought a uniform poll closing time was the best way of avoiding any danger from early vote predictions, but Senator Pastore said that he had polled all the Governors and that most of them were opposed.

What still appears to mystify a great many people is how the networks can declare a winner "before the votes are in." It is really quite simple. If the networks make mistakes, as they do occasionally, it is because the system is always capable of refinement and because the pressure to be first with a projection can override caution.

The networks do precisely what seasoned politicians have always done: they look at the early results in a few key areas and see by how much the vote differs from the way those areas voted in the past. They then apply that variation to the state as a whole or to the nation as a whole and predict the outcome. The difference is that the networks do it much more extensively and scientifically than do the politicians. Each network election unit hires experts on election behavior long before the election campaign has even begun. Each team has its own system, but they are all basically the same. The experts study the electoral map of the United States to find the smallest election units that are typical, in as many ways as possible. Precincts, or election districts, are examined by all the usual demographic criteria: income range, professions, ethnic backgrounds, race, religion. Their pattern of voting in the past is also carefully scrutinized. Finally, out of the nation's 172,500 precincts, each network selects a group it thinks most typical so that, taken together, they form an accurate profile of the nation. In 1964, NBC used 6,000 "barometric" precincts; CBS had some 2,000 "model election districts," and ABC relied on only 1,020 "key" precincts. One factor each of the precincts chosen has in common is that the vote is usually counted there very early. The networks then hire one person just for the evening to handle each of the sample precincts and a special private phone line is provided. In the New Hampshire primary in 1964, NBC made a $5,000 contribution to the League of Women Voters and got 206 ladies from the organization to staff the precincts. CBS used state and local government officials, paying them $20 apiece, while ABC got college students for $15 a head. These special employees have only one job. The moment the vote is counted in their precinct, they phone it in to network election headquarters on the private telephone provided. At election headquarters, teams of women sit at long tables answering these calls. Runners carry the results on slips of paper to the men operating the computers and each precinct is fed in. Instantaneously, the computer compares the vote in each precinct with what was expected. When enough of the key precincts have reported, the trends are averaged out by the computer and a prediction can safely be made. By that time, viewers may still see almost no vote total because the general vote tally has not yet caught up with the swift counting and reporting from the key precincts.

The system goes wrong if the initial research and choice of sample precincts were done carelessly or if a particular race is so close that a clear trend is not discernible.

There have been some notorious mistakes. In the off-year elections of 1954, CBS, using a UNIVAC computer, wrongly predicted a sweeping Democratic landslide. In 1960, both CBS and ABC predicted a Nixon victory and had to correct themselves, while NBC took its time and made the correct prediction. In 1966, NBC had Lester Maddox elected Governor in Georgia, and shown on television in a victory interview, only to find that the result was too close and that there had to be another election. CBS incorrectly elected Democrat George P. Mahoney Governor of Maryland, but later had to switch to Spiros Agnew, Republican, while ABC had the misfortune to call eight races wrong.

When the sample precincts are well chosen, the system can be uncannily accurate. CBS employed pollster Louis Harris for its Vote Profile Analysis system. In the 1964 California primary, he used only forty-two of California's 32,000 precincts. The prediction, twenty-two minutes after the first polls closed, came within 1 percent of the final result. In the 1968 California primary CBS did less well. It went off the air with the inaccurate prediction that Kennedy would beat McCarthy with more than 50 percent of the vote. The actual result was much closer, and the other two networks played it safe.

Besides the excitement of projections, the television viewer has also benefited from the immensely faster total vote count inspired by television. For a few years, the networks hired thousands of their own reporters to phone in results and then counted them more quickly in the computers, instead of the hand adding machines used by the wire services. Finally, in 1964, the three networks reached a sensible agreement with AP and UPI to share the vote-reporting task. In the Presidential election that year the new National Election Service employed 130,000 reporters, nearly one for every precinct in the country.

It is regrettable that the extraordinary performance of television on election nights cannot be spread out a little during the election campaign. Many authorities feel that television's magnificent performance on election night is partly wasted. Too much information is unloaded in one evening. By that time it is too late to educate the voter about the issues and personalities of that election. A lot more could be done, using the same techniques and the same computers, during the campaign.

Another way to exploit the resources mounted for the election results would be to make two nights of it instead of one. The night after the election could be devoted to an explanation of what happened. For that matter, there is no reason why the networks should not turn on the big machines for the entire evening the night *before* an election to explain all the issues and give millions of disinterested voters a last-minute cram course.

The skills and equipment the networks bring together on election nights are impressive, as they are for the national conventions. Yet if each convention is worth five days of heavy coverage, the election itself should deserve more than one evening.

Just as television is refining and sharpening its techniques in covering politics, politicians are constantly discovering how to use the medium for their purposes. The conventions are an important part of any campaign, but they are still the termination of one campaign phase—in the cases of some candidates, lasting months and years—and the start of another. Through the campaign the candidates move, and for a large portion of the public that progress to triumph or defeat on election night is charted on the television screen. Seldom does a candidate seem the same at the end as he did at the beginning. His image takes form, and television itself has much to do with the transformation.

6 The Televisible Candidate

In spite of the warnings of some critics about the enormous selling power of television, most American politicians first approached the medium in a manner that seems ingenuous today. They were so impressed by its ability to carry their faces and voices simultaneously to millions of people, that for the most part they gave it only their faces and voices to carry. As politicians in the 1920's and 1930's had used radio, they used television as an extension of their platform presence.

They quickly found, however, that they were not speaking to audiences like those who left their homes for the town halls and high school auditoriums at election time. This was an audience accustomed to Bob Hope and Milton Berle, to Ed Sullivan and to swiftly moving news reports which themselves were usually shaped by the strategies of the entertainment business. The politicians found that televisionland is a world impatient with gravity and scornful of platform rhetoric. Some, like Richard Nixon, adapted well. Others, like Adlai Stevenson, pursued a style too dry and intellectual. It became clear that few of them had natural gifts that could compete for attention in an industry where the greatest failure was to be boring.

Through expensive and painful experience they discovered that television was a medium that projected images and impressions better than facts and reasoned argument. And when they discovered that, Madison Avenue took over.

Broadcast politics really began when Calvin Coolidge chose to stay in Washington through much of the 1924 campaign and make his speeches by radio.[1] Coolidge outspent the Democratic candidate, John W. Davis, three to one ($120,000 to $40,000) for time on private stations—and outpolled him on election day by two to one.

Campaigning was so much more expensive by 1928, when there were 8 million radios reaching 40 million people, that Democratic candidate Governor Alfred E. Smith had to tell his audiences: "Save your applause to the end of the speech. It doesn't cost anything then."

Even the way Smith mispronounced the instrument—"raddio" —became one of the issues of the campaign. Yet so well did the medium discourage overblown oratory, that the *New York Times* called radio "the greatest debunking influence that has come into American life since the Declaration of Independence."

The three Presidential candidates of 1932 together spent an estimated $5 million on broadcasting, which helped Franklin D. Roosevelt to the first of four election victories.

In 1936, advertising agencies and political spot announcements appeared for the first time as part of a heavy campaign effort by the Republicans to dislodge Roosevelt. By 1940, commercial techniques were being employed so heavily on radio that the parties were charged with surrendering to Madison Avenue.

In the campaign of 1948, television made its first significant appearance and radio made its last big political stand. The major innovation that year was a broadcast debate between two Republican contenders in the Oregon primary, Thomas E. Dewey and Harold E. Stassen. Who won the debate was not clear, but Dewey narrowly won the primary.

Dewey, who worked hard to train his voice and manner, used some television in 1948 but used it much more extensively in the New York gubernatorial election of 1950. That year Senator Robert Taft won a substantial victory in Ohio with a campaign managed by an advertising agency. Possibly because of their business and advertising contacts, Republicans appeared more willing to exploit the new techniques. The Republican National Committee helped Congressional candidates to use television during the 1950 campaign. The Democrats, with a smaller budget, were more conservative. In 1952, they reserved extensive amounts of television time for speeches and panel programs, while the Republicans spent an estimated $1.5 million in a heavy closing-weeks campaign of spot announcements aimed especially at the nonvoter. In overall strategy, the Republicans relied on national familiarity with General Eisenhower's face and personality. His whistle-stopping was supplemented by regional television campaigns, while the Democrats, needing to build Stevenson into a national figure, spent their money on national programs.

Nevertheless, television remained what Frank Stanton of CBS calls "a source of uneasy or wistful concern" to many politicians. Thomas Dewey discovered he had to combat an impression of aloofness which his TV appearances conveyed. President Eisenhower felt uneasy before the camera and resisted the use of visual aids and gimmicks. Adlai Stevenson tried to overcome criticism that he seemed cold and intellectual on the screen by assuming a folksiness which did not suit him.

One candidate who was not uneasy or wistful was Richard Milhous Nixon.

In 1952, Nixon was a successful young Senator of thirty-nine, with good vote-getting ability and a moderately conservative voting record in the Senate. He was a lawyer and former Navy Lieutenant Commander, who had been elected to Congress in 1946. Nixon came to national attention in 1949 through his vigor, as a member of the House Un-American Activities Committee, in pursuing the investigation of Alger Hiss, the high State Department official eventually convicted of perjury in connection with alleged espionage in the 1930's. An astute politician, who projected an image of energetic anti-Communism suitable to the times, Nixon was chosen to be the running mate of the famous, but somewhat apolitical, General Eisenhower.

With the campaign well launched, a crisis broke on September 19. Nixon was accused in the press of having accepted $18,235 put together by seventy-six wealthy Californians as a "slush fund" for his "financial comfort." In the next few days, even Republican newspapers criticized him for accepting the money. The Democrats demanded that he retire from the race and were supported in this by Republican papers. All General Eisenhower would say was that he was keeping an open mind on the matter. Nixon, feeling that the party was deserting him without cause, grew despondent, but then decided—with advice from Governor Dewey—to go on national television to explain. Nixon said later that they put the broadcast off from Sunday until Tuesday night to give him time to prepare and to build up an audience. "We wanted to create suspense," he said.

He arrived at the Los Angeles studio twenty minutes before the broadcast, on September 23. With no script or TelePrompTer, and only five pages of notes, he went on to give a thirty-minute talk which dramatically transformed the situation.

More than 9 million homes, almost half of the total television audience, were tuned in.

"My fellow Americans: I have come before you tonight as a candidate for the Vice-Presidency and as a man whose honesty and integrity have been questioned."[2]

He disposed quickly of the "slush fund" charge: not one cent of the money had gone for his personal use. In case some listeners might think that he had "feathered his nest" while in public life, he devoted most of the half hour to a folksy recital of the domestic finances of Pat and Dick Nixon, an accounting unique in American politics: they were heavily mortgaged; they were in debt; Pat didn't even have a mink coat. "But she does have a respectable Republican cloth coat and I always tell her that she'd look good in anything."

The climax, which gave the speech its name for posterity, was still to come. He had to admit, Nixon said, they had received a political gift.

"A man down in Texas heard Pat on the radio mention the fact that our two youngsters would like to have a dog. And, believe it or not, the day before we left on this campaign trip, we got a message from Union Station in Baltimore saying they had a package for us. We went down to get it. You know what it was? It was a little cocker spaniel dog in the crate that he sent all the way from Texas. Black and white spotted. And our little girl—Trisha, the six-year-old—named it Checkers. And, you know, the kids love the dog and I just want to say this right now, that regardless of what they say about it, we're gonna keep it."

Then came a promise to campaign up and down America "until we drive the crooks and the Communists" out of Washington, a plug for Ike, and he was off.

Nixon had not only succeeded in making his family sound exactly like the average middle-class American family of the fifties, but, as one commentator noticed, "the common man was a Republican, for a change."

Although the speech created bad feeling for Nixon as well as good (many thought it vulgar and tasteless), it made him regarded as the country's most skillful television politician. Later, he used much the same technique for another successful appearance to tell the story of his involvement with Whittaker Chambers, a key witness in the Hiss conviction.

The Democrats' response to the Nixon sensation was a TV "fireside chat" with Adlai Stevenson, which was in stark contrast to the theatricality of the Nixon appearance.

Nixon's technique was much discussed at the time. It was noticed that he preferred to talk to only one camera, to eliminate the distraction of switching from one camera to another for a variety of angles. Some of those close to Nixon believe that these successes on television went to his head. A close associate in a later campaign said Nixon made the gross miscalculation of thinking that his efforts had been crucial to Eisenhower's election in 1952. In fact, there was a serious effort to drop him from the ticket in 1956.

Television, however, may have had less of an effect on the outcome of the 1952 election than the candidates' preoccupation with the medium would suggest. A study by Miami University of Ohio concluded that television was less of a factor in projecting the Eisenhower personality than were newspapers. Although people who watched television *thought* they were making the largest gains of information, the researchers found television inferior to newspapers as an instrument for communicating the issues. Stevenson gained more from television because he began the campaign less well known than Eisenhower. Another factor was television's ability to circumvent an unfriendly press.

Fair TV and the unfair press

Often cited as one of television's most important contributions to campaigning in the United States has been its injection of an element of fairness. American newspapers have been overwhelmingly Republican in ownership, and although some enlightened owners might permit Democratic candidates a fair hearing in their news columns, the number of papers endorsing Republicans was always greater.

It is interesting to speculate how much broadcasting may have contributed to the Democratic hold on the White House since 1932. It has been estimated that 90 percent of the nation's newspapers were opposed to FDR. By 1936, press hostility was so virulent that James A. Farley, the Democratic Party Chairman, later wrote that FDR's reelection that year would have been impossible without radio. His broadcast election speeches, of course, were reinforced between campaigns by the "fireside chats." These intimate, highly personal broadcasts in which the President could take his case, unedited, directly to the people made such an impact that those who lived through the New Deal often think they occurred very regularly. Like President Kennedy's televised news conferences a generation later, the "fireside chats" outshone the more orthodox means of Presidential communication. In fact, during twelve years in office, FDR gave only thirty such broadcasts, and in the years before the Second World War gave, on the average, only two a year.[3] They were massively outnumbered by the President's efforts to woo American newspapers. He held a total of 990 press conferences, averaging more than eighty a year.[4]

The same issue was still alive in 1964 but the open battle between the conservative and liberal Republicans produced a complication in press loyalties. Faced with the desertion of even staunchly Republican newspapers, Barry Goldwater leaned on television. He told me once: "I would say that 75 percent of the press of this country are against me. The columnists with one or two exceptions are against me. The news commentators on television are definitely, so I had to go on television. I found so much distortion of what I had been doing that I had to resort to the televised press conference, in some cases cutting down on regular press conferences. So I went to television merely because I could not depend upon objective reporting 100 percent."

Televised press conferences did not always help, because in public, Goldwater's mind tended to wander creatively into paths he had not explored privately beforehand. Highly controversial new elements were often thus dropped casually into the campaign. But he believed that the press was the enemy: "I would pick up a paper, for example, the morning after having made a speech. The headline would be a complete distortion of what I said yet the story, the body, would be all right. So if I'm going to be faced with this fact of life, then I have to use what I call the greatest lie detector ever developed—television."

The growing tendency of television stations to broadcast editorials and particularly to endorse candidates may cause politicians to think less rhapsodically of the medium as a means to bypass the press. Many Congressmen are opposed to television's finding an editorial voice, even though stations are required by law and government regulation to give both sides of controversial issues. One of the troubles of American television in the informational field is that politicians want to use it only on their own terms and have made sure that at election time at least it is largely kept that way.

The ad agencies move in

By the time Eisenhower and Stevenson were running again in 1956, the parties had made a big effort to jazz up their TV campaigning. For the President's sixtieth birthday, for example, in October, at the height of the campaign, they put on a nationwide television show with a heavy emphasis on show business. Appearing with the President were stars like Helen Hayes, Irene Dunne and James Stewart.

One of the main issues in that campaign was the President's

health. Late in 1955, Eisenhower had suffered a heart attack. To counter mounting doubts about his ability to continue in office and to run for reelection, he addressed the nation on television in February, 1956. The President said that he would not campaign "in the customary pattern" but would rely heavily on the "means of mass communications" to inform the American people of the issues. The country could see that he looked well and there was much comment about how useful television was in such a situation. Still, the whole question was reopened in June when Eisenhower had to undergo an emergency operation for ileitis. He had not finished convalescing when the campaign began. If he had campaigned solely through television, it would have fed the rumors about his fitness to continue as Chief Executive. Adlai Stevenson drew attention to the issue by waging a vigorous campaign. In the event, the President was forced to make several campaign trips to be seen to be well enough to do so. Television coverage of his campaigning, of course, helped to spread that message. Aided possibly by the Suez and Hungarian crises, which erupted just at the end of the campaign, Eisenhower defeated Stevenson by a wider margin than in 1952.

The President had steadily improved his own technique on television. Although he still said that it made him feel like an actor, commentators felt that his appearances were becoming increasingly effective.

The parties began to feel the greater campaign costs imposed by increased use of television, but the medium itself came to their rescue. An interesting innovation in 1956 was a fund-raising dinner, called a "Salute to Eisenhower," which was held simultaneously in fifty-two cities linked by closed circuit television. The interconnection cost the GOP a quarter of a million dollars but 70,000 Republicans paid $100 each for their dinners and the party netted $5 million.

For financial or other reasons, political exploitation of television was still somewhat restrained in the Presidential campaigns of the 1950's. All the techniques were in use—the straight political talk, the staged conversations, filmed programs, telethons and the short commercial. However, the medium had not yet come to dominate the campaign. Something in the characters of the two men nominated for the Presidency in that decade may have been a restraining influence. It is more likely that the men who could visualize the wedding of television with the mass advertising techniques were still not influential enough with the parties. The advertising agencies were very important in campaign planning but not paramount; pollsters were not yet elevated to become strategists and policymakers. Politics had not yet been taken out of the hands of the lawyers. What that development needed was a new breed of campaign manager, part public relations man, part advertising executive, part pollster, part film-maker, part computer programmer.

The new manager began to emerge in the planning for the 1960 Presidential election. A man who gave politics a lot of thought after 1956 was Carroll Newton, a senior executive in one of the country's biggest advertising agencies, Batten, Barton, Durstine and Osborn. Newton had worked for the agency on both Eisenhower campaigns but felt that television could be used more creatively. In 1956, he had begun to discover the power of shorter political programs that viewers did not have time to turn off. Newton wanted to carry that further, to eliminate the candidate's "earnest" talks to the camera, and, instead, to use film to build his image. Newton wanted to "market" a candidate. To the advertising industry, that is a perfectly respectable exercise based on thorough research, careful testing of attitudes and a blend of highly developed arts and sciences in a campaign.

The perfect candidate for such a campaign would be the Republicans' vital young Vice-President, the "wonder boy" of political television, who was certain to be the Presidential nominee. Nixon was thinking along the same lines. Even before the 1956 campaign, he knew that buying air time was only the beginning of a modern television campaign. In September, 1955, he had told a group of broadcasting executives in New York that "candidates should be prepared to spend as much money on building up a program, through advertisements and organization work, as they do on air time." So when Carroll Newton took his creative thinking to Nixon well before the 1960 campaign, there was a meeting of minds.

Another of the new breed was becoming seriously interested in politics at the same time. In 1958, the market research firm of Louis Harris had been hired by John F. Kennedy to take polls and analyze public opinion in Massachusetts before Kennedy's campaign for the Senate. In October, 1959, as Kennedy began to plan his assault on the Presidency, Harris was called into the most intimate councils. In the twelve months that followed, Harris took and analyzed more samples of American public opinion than had ever been attempted in a political campaign. According to Theodore White: "Upon his description of the profile of the country's thinking and prejudices as he found them, were to turn many of John F. Kennedy's major decisions."[5]

At least in the early planning, both the Nixon and Kennedy campaigns of 1960 were based on fresh thinking about how the techniques of manipulating America's mass consumer market could be applied to politics. The Kennedy campaign explored much new ground; Nixon's could have, if his own hesitations had not undermined the efforts of his creative team. But in those campaigns the union of television, polls and advertising was firmly cemented. For all who dared, or could afford, to use it, a new image-making machinery was available to the politicians of the 1960's.

An end to older-looking men?

It was a warm day in late June, 1964, in Senator Barry Goldwater's office on Capitol Hill. The convention in San Francisco which was to put the formal stamp on Goldwater's nomination for President was still several weeks away but that day in his office on Capitol Hill, he was relaxed. Leaning back in a leather chair, surrounded by mementos of his carefree days as junior Senator, jet flier, student of the Southwest Indians and photographer, Goldwater talked knowledgeably about the problems facing a modern candidate.

As often happened that spring and summer, his conversation kept turning to the politics of his own state, as though some part of his political instinct had predicted the debacle with Lyndon Johnson and was already sorting the problems of returning to the Senate. When he got around to the effects of television, the example he turned to was Arizona's senior Senator, Carl Hayden, then eighty-six, who would be up for reelection in 1968. "Some of our best Senators are older men," Goldwater said. "My colleague, for example, Carl Hayden. I consider him to be one of the most outstanding Chairmen of the Appropriations Committee we've ever had. But he'd have a hard time running against a young-looking person. I don't like this but it's a fact of life." He added that the off-year elections two years earlier "probably marked the end of older-looking men being elected to national office."

Carl Hayden has been in Congress longer than the state of Arizona has been in the Union. He is deeply respected. Yet he has begun to look old and frail. As one of Goldwater's Arizona strategists put it: "We had to keep him out of the state during election campaigns because he looked so decrepit." They never put him on television. Hayden's own version of the story was, laconically: "I got tied up and couldn't get away."

At just about the same time in 1964, advisers of the handsome young Illinois Republican Charles Percy may well have been regarding veteran Senator Paul Douglas and thinking that he would have a hard time running against a younger-looking person. In the fall of 1966, Senator Douglas was challenged by Percy—the very prototype of the candidate made for television—and the older, much respected man was defeated. In 1968, Carl Hayden announced he would not seek reelection, thus removing himself from any trial by age with Barry Goldwater.

A few days after Barry Goldwater formally declared his candidacy for the Presidential nomination, on January 3, 1964, Democratic Senator Clair Engle of California announced that he was seeking reelection. At the time, Engle could scarcely walk, one arm was paralyzed and he was almost unable to speak. The previous August he had undergone brain surgery but had not recovered. His condition was kept secret from the California voters. The declaration in January was made to them in a carefully edited film lasting only forty-two seconds. All that Californians saw on television was a middle-aged man saying with some hesitancy: "The medical men have given me the green light and I am running."

In some doubt, the Democratic party leadership in California sent a group to Washington to find out Engle's real condition. They were shocked when they saw him, and Governor Pat Brown finally demanded that Engle's wife provide medical proof that her husband could run. Some doctors obliged by saying they felt "certain that the Senator will be fully able to take on the active phases of his election campaign." The Democratic State Central Committee refused to accept the report, but only after another operation was Engle persuaded to withdraw from the primary. He died in July. It was too late to remove his name from the ballot and, although he was dead and not a candidate, he received more than 100,000 votes.[6]

Engle's case raises the possibility that a politician physically or mentally unfit for office might be passed off as fit on television. It is conceivable that by propping a sick man up, making him up to look healthy, filming many takes and editing together a reasonable-sounding phrase from here and there, the deception might work. It is difficult to exaggerate the power of a medium such as television to make *appearance* seem to be *reality*.

From the earliest days of televised politics, it has been a rule of thumb among professional party workers, campaign managers and politicians themselves that the man who makes the best appearance on television stands a better chance of being a candidate in the first place and that the candidate who makes the better appearance has more chance of being elected. Obviously there are many other factors—incumbency, ability to raise money, familiarity of a name—but a face and personality that televise well are increasingly important qualifications.

In 1955, when television was still comparatively new to politics, the Republican National Chairman, Leonard Hall, told the National Federation of Republican Women: "We must choose able and personable candidates who can 'sell themselves' because TV has changed the course of campaigns."

When the Democratic party bosses in New York State were looking for someone to turn Nelson Rockefeller out of the Governor's office in 1962, they finally settled, under pressure from New York Mayor Robert Wagner, on United States Attorney Robert M. Morgenthau. An able but mild-mannered man, Morgenthau was not a popular choice and his nomination was railroaded through the state convention, full TV coverage notwithstanding. But one of the stages in making Morgenthau acceptable to the political bosses who would decide whether he should run was a quietly arranged television audition. The leaders watched him on the monitors and decided that his appearance was acceptable.

According to Bob Price, campaign director for John V. Lindsay, the very telegenic Mayor of New York: "You don't have to look as good as Lindsay, but if you look bad, it's a minus. An ugly, able man is less likely to be nominated today than fifty years ago."[7]

It would be wrong to overemphasize the importance of a handsome face in the politics of the television age. Yet when that requirement is so firmly implanted in the thinking of the people who choose candidates, whether they are cigar-chewing pals in the back room, delegates to a convention or voters in a primary election, it cannot be ignored. Television has encouraged the selection of candidates who conform to the values of a commercial entertainment medium. A physically pleasant appearance is one of those values, as Richard Nixon discovered. It is not enough to have regular features and to be free of deformities. Nixon's features are regular and strong. In person, they give him, as Theodore White noticed, "a clean masculine quality." On the television screen, however, with his features scanned electronically, converted briefly into a flow of electrical charges, and then reassembled by another scanner in the receiving set, Nixon's appearance was transmogrified. In *The Making of the President, 1960,* White describes watching "the deep eye wells and the heavy brows cast shadow on the face and it glowered on the screen darkly; when he became rhetorically indignant, the television showed ferocity; . . . when he smiled and his fine white teeth showed, it was the smile made meaningless by the grin of all the commercial announcers who appear with similar white teeth showing."[8]

In 1966, I accompanied Nixon for a week while he campaigned for Republican senatorial and congressional candidates in the

South. Toward the end of the tour, in Miami, there was a revealing experience. Nixon had an appointment to be interviewed at CBS station WTVJ-TV. In a control room overlooking the interview studio, there were several black-and-white monitor sets in addition to the colored monitors. The interviewer chatted with Nixon as lights were adjusted and the makeup checked. We could watch Nixon both in color and in black and white, and the difference was startling. When the technical director punched up the camera taking a close-up, there was the Nixon of 1960, much like the Theodore White description, although not now under any strain. On the color monitors, a few feet away, was another Nixon, much nearer the man in the flesh, whom we could also see through the control room window. Nixon in TV color was altogether a more personable individual. Technically speaking, color affords the camera a greater range of contrasts between light and dark than does black and white, particularly in shadowed areas of a picture. Nixon's eyes were quite visible in color and his whole countenance had a more cheerful cast. It is intriguing to speculate that this man might have been kept out of the White House in 1960 by a tiny lag in technology.

In the 1950's, youth and confidence and skill before the camera made Nixon the political television star of the decade. In 1960, he suffered by comparison with John Kennedy, who looked and sounded better than any of his contemporaries on TV. By 1968, Nixon the TV performer had made a successful comeback.

It's how you say it

Television has conditioned a generation of people to expect certain standards of articulation in the stars they treat as household names. They are not always the standards that political scientists would like politicians to adopt. Campaign director Joseph Napolitan says: "It's not what you say, it's how you say it. The general impression that is left is a lot more important than the individual words and phrases. For example, the Kennedy-Nixon debate."[9]

Others in the new breed of campaign directors agree. F. Clifton White, who masterminded Goldwater's nomination, believes:

"When either party has options in the selection of a Presidential candidate, one of the major conditions they are going to make is the capability of that candidate to campaign through the TV medium. He has to be able to get the mush out of his mouth."[10]

Critic Gilbert Seldes, who wondered what expectancies the years of entertainment programming had created in the audience for the Kennedy-Nixon debates, came to these conclusions: "It has taught the audience to recognize certain moves and attitudes as being desirable or unworthy. The tempo of television has, for instance, put a premium on speed and this is reflected in the superinduced admiration for the quickness rather than the quality of wit and has somehow equated the process of contemplation—the painstaking working out of a judgment, the careful consideration of what has been said before replying—with slow-wittedness, with the stooge for the popular comedian's brightness."[11]

The ideal candidate for television campaigning may not be a man with any original insights to offer his country, he may not be capable of grasping the immensities of the office he aspires to. What he must be is articulate and expressive in ways acceptable and effective on television. He needs to be able to stress the appearance of competence rather than the fact of it. He needs an ability to appear assured and confident, because that is the impression he will leave with viewers long after his words and picture have faded out.

Napolitan thinks that Robert Kennedy had this ability. While Kennedy was still alive Napolitan said: "It doesn't matter what he says, as much as appearing to know what he is talking about. He can make a really impressive appearance even if he is saying nothing. There is nothing wrong with a candidate who says: 'I don't know, I'll find out. I'd rather not comment right now,' or 'We're working on it.' You have to look confident," Napolitan says, "and act confident. That is what leaves the aura." One professional political worker, Harry O'Donnell, a New York Democrat, says: "There is an aura around Kennedy that makes what he says seem more profound than it is."[12]

It was not Robert Kennedy whom the older style politicians worried about for this ability to project an image of assurance and competence. Beside Ronald Reagan, Robert Kennedy looked like an amateur. A veteran New York politician, Frank O'Connor, believes that "With men like Reagan, there is a horrible danger that a person who is glib and articulate and an actor can create an impression that may not be backed up by the facts."[13]

Politicians and journalists are still arguing about whether Ronald Reagan, the cowboy star of the *Late Late Show*, was the first nonentity television has elected to high political office. Such speculation would never have started if Reagan had emerged from the ranks of business, law or journalism to become Governor of the nation's most populous state. He is a bright and personable man who might have done well in many professions if he had not become a movie actor. As an actor, however, he found that while America may heap riches and fame on movie stars, it does not rate their intellectual capacities high. Reagan has been mocked by almost every political commentator in the nation. To them, it was effrontery that an actor, a hired pitchman for a business corporation, should leap into a governorship and even aim his sights at the White House without having been elected to any lower political office. Reagan's leap was, in fact, a classic demonstration of how many of the techniques of mass persuasion can be applied to politics.

*Remember it was an actor who shot
Abraham Lincoln*

Ronald Reagan entered the year 1966 with an image that needed doctoring if he was going to capture the California governorship. He had acquired a vehemently right-wing image from his conservative-oriented speeches before and during the 1964 Goldwater campaign. The first thing his public relations firm, Spencer-Roberts, had to do to groom him for the Governor's race was to soften that image. It was the nicest of ironies that the same firm, when retained by Nelson Rockefeller during the 1964 Republican primary in California, had done its best to label Reagan as an archconservative. Highly skilled in the techniques of getting information to the right quarters in the press, they had branded

Reagan, like Goldwater, an enemy of the progressive income tax, civil rights and the TVA, and, for good measure, a John Birch sympathizer. Two years later, with client Rockefeller back East and client Reagan at the door, Spencer-Roberts found it in their hearts (for a campaign fee estimated at $150,000) to undo that little misunderstanding and to sell Reagan as a decent, responsible and moderate man.

The machine now circulated 50,000 copies of Reagan's as-told-to autobiography, *Where's the Rest of Me?*, named for a line Reagan spoke in a movie called *Kings Row,* in which he awoke in the hospital to find his legs amputated.

California's volatile politics nourished the growth of the new-style campaign management firms long before other states. Spencer-Roberts is one of the newest but most successful. Stuart Spencer and William Roberts were both volunteer officials in the Los Angeles County Young Republicans (Spencer was a recreation director, Roberts a TV salesman) when they joined forces to create a public relations firm in 1960. The first campaign they managed they won, sending the conservative Republican John Rousselot to the U.S. Congress. When Rousselot became prominent in the John Birch Society, they dropped him. In 1962, Spencer-Roberts assisted Senator Thomas Kuchel in being re-elected and, in 1964, picked up the Rockefeller account.

Two years later, Bill Roberts, declaring that "the right-wing issue is now old hat," proceeded to make the firm's new client, Reagan, appear a moderate, to extract the maximum support from California Republicans. Reagan stopped uttering remarks like "there can be no moral justification of the progressive tax," which had made him a favored political speaker for the General Electric Company. He was encouraged instead to perfect a standard political speech that would be innocuously appropriate for all occasions. The *New York Times* described the typical Reagan speech as "a skillful script combining moral platitudes, pseudo indignation, homely examples and harmless jokes." With a lifetime of memorization and professional delivery to draw on, Reagan became an extremely polished platform and television speaker, handsome and bronzed by the sun, with a particular knack of conveying sincerity.

The content was still basically conservative but bland. The strategy was campaigning by style and personality, not by programs or convictions. Columnist Joseph Alsop said during the campaign that Reagan resembled "a carefully designed, elaborately *customerized,* supermarket package, complete with the glossiest wrappings and the slickest sort of eye appeal." It was like selling soap, but soap that had been made to a formula based on elaborate surveys to discover which perfumes would offend the fewest consumers. This approach showed a profound understanding of the political realities in California.

The population of the state was growing and changing so fast that political allegiances had not had time to jell. Political writer Joseph Kraft reported that from one decade to the next, half the electorate were new voters. Many were strangers to politics, indifferent to past records and with feeble party identifications. It was a state that gave minimum political credit to old loyalties and the maximum advantage to the periodic "new face." Political decisions thus turned on the ability to appeal to a constantly new electorate. Victory could depend on how many new voters candidates were able to lure to their party's registers in an election year, and not on how successfully existing voters were wooed.

The situation was ready-made for Reagan in 1966. Pat Brown, the amiable Democratic Governor who had done much in eight years to stimulate California's fantastic growth, had been around too long. He traveled the entire state and spent a great deal of money telling Californians that he had been a good Governor, as in fact he had, but the polls revealed indifference. Some people admitted they did not think very highly of Reagan but simply wanted a change. A nuclear engineer was quoted as saying: "I don't think Reagan would be very good as Governor. But I'm going to vote for him. I'm tired of that Brown."

California Democrats, furthermore, were not united behind Brown. Assembly Speaker Jesse Unruh, the second most powerful Democrat in California, stayed out of the race, fearing to be associated with what many saw as Brown's predictable defeat. Los Angeles Mayor Sam Yorty, who won nearly a million votes when he opposed Brown in the Democratic primary, refused to endorse him. And some New Leftists, accusing Brown of having moved to the right of his power base, talked nihilistically of voting for Reagan.

By wearing only the vaguest conservative colors, Reagan became the beneficiary of the discontent that was simmering beneath California's prosperity, overhigh taxes and high prices, government expenditure and welfare payments, iconoclastic youth at the State University and, particularly, Negro riots.

The strategy that Spencer and Roberts mapped out for Reagan on the basis of their polls was therefore principally to be nice and to wait for nice things to happen to him. In addition to filing down his right-wing horns, they also had to make him credible as a candidate, to show that a movie actor who considered *Bedtime for Bonzo* one of his better films could be taken seriously in politics. Reagan's movie roles and his years of television exposure as host on *Death Valley Days* had given him a clear identity. "The problem we had in the campaign," Bill Roberts said later, "was to transfer this identification to a serious individual who was interested in government—which he did very effectively."[14]

What is fascinatingly relevant to our examination is that television was the instrument in both processes: by showing his films and appearances as an announcer, television, even more than the films, made Reagan a household name and face, with a lightweight, actor's image; television then made him a political figure to be taken seriously.

Judicious injections of substance by Spencer-Roberts gave a serious tone to the image of sincere concern that Reagan was cultivating. Many newsmen who reported on the campaign were impressed by the sheer professionalism of the blending. Listening to Reagan speak, it was extremely difficult to decide how much depth of knowledge and understanding there was beneath the surface of this handsome and apparently intelligent man. At press conferences, it was a different matter.

Reagan seemed less sure of himself when detached from his script or led by questions beyond pat answers drawn from campaign rhetoric. During a press conference at Chico, California, on October 6, Reagan gave contradictory views on open-housing laws. When reporters pointed out an inconsistency, he said he was tired and broke off the conference. After that, no more press conferences were scheduled.

With familiar material in a set speech or on television, he was formidable. While his old movies continued to run on the late shows, Californians could see him throughout the campaign, on fifteen-minute programs once each week, five minutes every day and on commercials.

There were prolonged negotiations with the Brown camp over the form for a television debate. Insisting that he would not engage in "a declamation contest with an actor," Brown wanted the Nixon-Kennedy format with a panel of newsmen. Reagan wanted a straight debate. In the end, Brown allowed himself to be maneuvered into a compromise that probably did Reagan as much good as formal debating would have done.

Brown agreed to appear in three quasi debates with Reagan in which they were questioned separately, one after the other, on scheduled television panel programs. The first encounter, on NBC's *Meet the Press,* brought an exchange of charges of extremism. Reagan said Brown's administration was controlled by "militant left-wing radicals." Brown, in turn, said that Reagan's "extremist" views had made him an "enemy of the people." After the program, President Johnson telephoned to congratulate Brown, but the effect had probably been to make Reagan seem more credible as a candidate. The next joint appearance occurred a few days after an outbreak of rioting in San Francisco. Brown had acted forcefully to put down the disturbance, but Reagan charged on television that the disorders indicated a "lack of leadership in Sacramento." There was a third appearance the next day, on ABC's *Issues and Answers,* and immediately the polls showed a sharp decline for Brown. Whether this was attributable to the riots themselves or to Reagan's exploitation of them on television was not clear.

At this point, Brown became worried. His campaign was handled by the firm of Baus and Ross, which had been managing political candidates since 1948. Their strategy was to have Brown stand by his record and demolish Reagan's candidacy with ridicule. The theme chosen was right-wing extremism. Brown's television speeches and commercials played upon the most conservative remarks Democratic researchers could find in Reagan's early speeches. "Reagan is both for and against Social Security—on the same day," the Governor would say. "Extremists see their opportunity to put their blueprint on the largest state . . . the California we know would be starkly different if he should prevail." They recalled that Reagan had once said, "When you've seen one tree, you've seen them all," and used it to show that the Republican was cool about expensive conservation measures by the state. They hammered away at Reagan for not denouncing the John Birch Society.

It did not work. There was a slight narrowing of Reagan's lead in September but then Brown fell back in October.

With Baus and Ross, Brown suddenly decided to alter the strategy. If Californians refused to believe that Reagan was the wicked agent of the far right, they might be made skeptical about an actor trying to be Governor. It was a desperation measure, far too late in the day to start building a new issue. Nevertheless, Baus and Ross drew up a crash program to saturate California with the idea that an actor was not qualified to govern them. Charles Guggenheim, one of the nation's foremost political film-makers, was flown out. He produced a series of television commercials whose pitch reflected the desperate situation. Well-known movie actors were filmed saying things like, "I'm a cowboy and I play western roles but I couldn't play the role of Governor." One of the spots even said, "Remember, it was an actor who shot Abraham Lincoln."

Drawing on his success in the recent Pennsylvania primary with a brilliant film made for gubernatorial candidate Milton Shapp, *The Man Against the Machine,* Guggenheim made a similar half-hour film for Pat Brown called *Man vs. Actor.*

Guggenheim said later that Brown might have done better—that is, lost by less—if these commercials had not been shown. "Brown was a loser and looked like one," he said. The desperation commercials merely helped to drive home the message.

The television blitz with Brown's new theme began in the last two weeks of the campaign. A total of 4,500 radio spots were scheduled and 400 one-minute television commercials, roughly forty apiece each week on major TV stations. In addition to screening *Man vs. Actor,* Brown delivered a five-minute talk on television each evening and took part in an hour-long telethon. At the same time, Reagan's managers switched from fifteen-minute shows to five-minute, one-minute and twenty-second commercials. A strategy from the very beginning to attack Reagan where he was most vulnerable—his lack of experience—might have made a difference. Adopted only at the end of the campaign, it did not. The miscalculation was widely criticized at the time by newspapers sympathetic to Brown.

It seems doubtful in retrospect, however, that the "actor" issue would have been as convincing to the electorate as it seemed to Brown and to many liberal newspapermen. There were two forces working the other way—the nature of politics in California, and the wider effect of television on political life generally. The weak organization of both parties at the grass roots level in California had driven candidates to television earlier and more completely than in some other big states. Like the movies, television was largely a California industry. Politicians felt at home with it and the voters expected a heavy overlay of show business with their politics. Campaigning national politicians surrounded themselves with the biggest and most glamorous Hollywood names they could find. For many Californians, especially after George Murphy's election to the Senate, it was not unusual or preposterous to see a well-known actor on television talking politics.

It can be argued that for the whole nation, television has made the actor-politician inevitable. Television is indispensable to politicians, and the television audience is conditioned to like glamour and style. Therefore, politicians become glamorous and stylish. During the Reagan campaign, the *New York Times* analyzed this in an editorial: "With its neatly segmented half-hour programs, its well-crafted dramas with their simplified issues, clearly discernible heroes and villains, and fully resolved denouements, and its *sincere,* well-rehearsed announcers and masters of ceremonies, television has created a new reality, or at least a new way of looking at reality, for millions of viewers."[15]

Brown's decision to mount an all-out attack on Reagan as an

actor suggests that he and his advisers did not understand how deeply this influence had gone. The Governor complained at one point in the campaign: "I'm not running against Ronald Reagan. I'm running against Spencer-Roberts. That's the candidate." But he was also running against the influence of television.

Kennedy versus Reagan

A few months after Reagan began grappling with the real problems of governing California, the national television audience was given an intriguing foretaste of what the future may hold. Having had barely five months in which to familiarize himself with the complexities of state government, Reagan was drawn into an international forum to discuss the Vietnam war. He and Senator Robert Kennedy were persuaded by CBS Television to take part in a *Town Meeting of the World*. In a studio in London there gathered a group of foreign students angry about American policy. By means of a communications satellite, they hurled difficult and hostile questions across the Atlantic at Kennedy in New York and Reagan in California.

That evening it did not seem fanciful to regard what followed as the opening television debate of a future campaign for President. Reagan, whose bellicose generalities about the war had seemed irrelevant and laughable during his campaign for Governor, had prepared carefully for this appearance. It emerged later that he had asked for a detailed briefing on Vietnam and his staff had prepared a twelve-page memo. After Reagan studied it, they subjected him to a long question-and-answer session the day before the program. That was the technique John F. Kennedy had used in preparing for the debates with Nixon in 1960 and later for his televised press conferences.

No one was more familiar with the procedure than was Robert Kennedy, but his staff later said he made no special preparation for the appearance with Reagan. Admittedly, Kennedy had less need. As a close adviser to his brother he had confronted the problems of the war while in the Cabinet, and later as a Senator had wrestled with his conscience about how to exploit his differences with President Johnson over this issue. Even so, his familiarity with the subject did not come across that evening to the 15 million Americans watching *Town Meeting of the World*.

Reagan fielded the questions with such a wealth of information and good humor that even liberals in the East thought he came off "better than Bobby." Kennedy projected a diffident, hesitating manner. His ambiguities of expression left a sense of vagueness or uncertainty. He seemed to be trying to convince the students in London that he had no philosophical differences from them, that he was on their side. Reagan, while smiling pleasantly across the world at the questioners, was obviously talking straight to the American public. His syntax was pure and his speech fluent; Kennedy's was cluttered and confusing. If Reagan and Kennedy had been debating formally that evening, Reagan would have been called the winner.

Behind Reagan's TV manner is what *Newsweek* called "his unmatched ability to convince people that the honest face they see on their TV screens is an accurate reflection of the inner man." His rise, the magazine added, "sometimes seems an eerie fulfillment of those prophecies of the early 1950's that TV would revolutionize American politics, producing comfortably charismatic candidates cast very much in the Reagan mold."

If you like William Penn, you'll love Milton Shapp

Possibly the *least* charismatic candidate to run for any major office in recent years has been Milton Shapp, Democratic candidate for Governor of Pennsylvania in 1966. His startling campaign demonstrated the image-making possibilities of a thorough exploitation of television advertising.

Shapp's campaign manager was Joseph Napolitan, who has been described by *Life* as a "master strategist" and by the *Washington Post* as "one of the shrewdest professional political managers in the business."

Napolitan, an energetic man in his mid-thirties, is of Italian descent, stocky and voluble. He comes from Springfield, Massachusetts, and was a newspaperman until he and Lawrence O'Brien (for a time, President Johnson's Postmaster General) became partners in a public relations business. When O'Brien moved off to serve John Kennedy and Lyndon Johnson, Napolitan struck out on his own as a political pollster, aiding Kennedy in 1960 and Johnson in 1964. He now heads his own political counseling and research firm and is a consultant to the Democratic National Committee. (Upon Robert Kennedy's declaration for the Presidency, O'Brien resigned from the Cabinet to aid him.)

Napolitan says: "If you had unlimited funds you *could* elect a nonentity to office. But this implies if you don't do it this way, someone who is other than a nonentity will get elected."

"We had problems with Shapp," he said. "People who were negative on him pictured him as an arrogant little Jew. The Republicans were trying to foster that image and we had to do something to counter it."

Milton Jerrold Shapp (born Shapiro) was the first Jew to run for statewide office in Pennsylvania. He was an aggressive, dryly humorous man who was able to transmute a $500 investment in TV aerials just after the war into the $12 million Jerrold electronics business twenty years later. Then he sold the business and, at fifty-four, decided to try his golden touch at politics.

He had been divorced and remarried. He had a physical appearance Napolitan thought "not impressive—small, stoop-shouldered." He was not a powerful speaker and he had no base of power. And he was almost totally unknown. A private poll in April, 1965, revealed that only 3.3 percent of Pennsylvanians knew who Milton Shapp was. If these were not disadvantages enough, Shapp encountered active hostility from the state Democratic organization. And there was his religion. He was Jewish in a state with only 5 percent Jewish population. His one claim to fame was the assertion that he had been instrumental in persuading President Kennedy to adopt the idea of the Peace Corps. When the Republicans accused him of inventing this cozy niche in history, Shapp produced certification from Vice-President Humphrey. Late in the campaign, he even got Robert Kennedy to do a TV commercial recalling Shapp's role. Napolitan says the rebuttal never received as much attention as the charge by Republican Senator Hugh Scott that the claim was a fabrication.

Such misfortunes were in the future when Joe Napolitan and Shapp settled down late in 1965 to calculate how they could shove this unknown businessman past the defenses of the Pennsylvania Democrats and into the nomination for Governor.

The primary election which he had to contest was on May 17. Napolitan gambled and kept his mass media campaign under wraps until only fifteen days before the election. When it was released, it covered Pennsylvania in the thickest blizzard of publicity ever recorded in a political campaign.

In the months preceding the primary, while Shapp campaigned routinely, Napolitan and the image-makers were preparing. They researched issues and voter responses with such fine detail that they even ascertained which billboard colors were most likely for psychological reasons to catch the eye. They decided on orange and red. They invented slogans worthy of a canned soup campaign; the most famous was "If you like William Penn, you'll love Milton Shapp." Most important, they hired Charles Guggenheim, the best film-maker Napolitan could find, to make the basic campaign film. Guggenheim employed a technique he had attempted with Robert Kennedy in New York in 1964—following Shapp on the campaign trail. The thirty-minute "documentary," called *The Man Against the Machine,* was regarded by Napolitan and others as the best half-hour political film ever produced.

"I don't believe in putting on poor TV," Napolitan says. "The competition on TV for a viewer's time is so heavy that people who are not competitive are losing out. The only way to compete is to put on quality material."

He thinks two other things are essential. One is not to try to tell the film-maker how to do his job: "It would be better if more campaign managers and candidates would get out of the way and not tell the film-maker what to do. Just let him do it."

The other essential is to be willing to spend money in making and promoting your film. "If you do a half-hour film you should promote it heavily. We spent as much time promoting ours as we did buying the time," Napolitan said. He thinks most politicians are not willing to spend enough money on production. "People must go to experts," he says. "If they have $100,000 most people want to spend only $5,000 on production. But it is better to spend $50,000 on production."

His emphasis on the half-hour campaign film contradicts the trend since the 1950's to shorter political programs. Napolitan also uses one-minute and thirty-second commercials in great quantity, but he avoids the five-minute piece because he says the structure of television schedules does not permit politicians to buy good time slots. What is different in his half-hour films is that he uses them as other campaign directors use one-minute spots. Once it is made, the film is shown and reshown as often as the time segments can be bought.

On May 2, Napolitan unleashed the carefully prepared media campaign to force the name and image of Milton Shapp into the consciousness of millions of Pennsylvanian Democrats who had never heard of him and to persuade them to vote for him only two weeks later. To any experienced campaign manager of the old school, the very effort would sound ridiculous.

Only newspaper ads were run the first day of the blitz media campaign. The next day came radio spots. Television commercials began running on May 6, and on the ninth, with only eight days of the primary campaign left, the half-hour film was introduced. It was run thirty-five times in those eight days, including ten showings on the night before the primary. Thirty-five showings of a half-hour film—seventeen and a half hours—in just over a week is a staggering amount of television time by conventional standards. The primary cost Shapp $1.5 million of his personal fortune—but he knocked out the machine-backed Democratic candidate by 50,000 votes.

The party regulars, who had regarded Shapp as a joke or an "egotistical buffoon," as *Time* put it, caved in. The state's former Governor and Democratic king-maker, David Lawrence, told a party dinner: "Crow should have been the main dish. I must admit I am eating mine."

Napolitan had been taking regular soundings with name-identification polls. In January of the election year, Shapp's name was familiar to 5.2 percent of Pennsylvanians. In July, a few weeks after the primary blitz, the figure had leaped to 65.5 percent. The whirlwind of advertisements and spots and the saturation showing of *The Man Against the Machine* had made Shapp even better known than the man he now had to face in the general election, Raymond P. Shafer. Shafer had served two terms as a State Senator and been William Scranton's Lieutenant Governor for four years, but was known, the polls said, by only 59.1 percent of the voters.

The Scranton administration had been popular enough and Shafer, as the chosen heir, had counted on an easy campaign until Shapp won the Democratic primary. Although Shafer's campaign manager, Robert Kunzig, was soon charging that the Democrats were marketing Shapp "like corn flakes," the Republicans quickly adopted the same methods. "By using TV effectively in the primary," Napolitan says, "we forced the Republicans to use it and to spend money on it."

Shafer had obvious assets as a candidate, in addition to the legacy and backing of Scranton. He was six feet two inches tall, athletic and sandy-haired, a Protestant minister's son whose very conventional family life was stressed in the campaign. According to Napolitan's analysis, other Shafer attributes that mattered were an ability to memorize speeches and read them well, possession of the full support of his party, coverage by a friendly Republican press, and previous campaign experience which enabled him to answer questions without getting into trouble. He avoided mistakes and, like Shapp, was amply financed.

Ten days after Shapp's primary victory, the candidates began the now ritual dance of the TV debates. Shafer challenged Shapp to debate. Shapp immediately accepted (the right behavior for an underdog). Seven weeks went by and they heard nothing further from Shafer. Then Shapp reopened the discussion. Napolitan, with the various Kennedys' experiences in mind, demanded a panel of newsmen while Shafer wanted none. Eventually one debate took place, on October 14, with newsmen as questioners, but it was not shown on a statewide hookup. Napolitan thought Shafer did better in the memorized opening and closing statements, while Shapp handled the questions better. The encounter was regarded as a standoff.

Having closely observed Shapp's techniques in the primary, the Republicans picked up the best film-maker *they* could find, David Wolper, who had produced highly regarded television specials, including *The Making of the President*. With Wolper, the Republicans prepared four different half-hour programs, three of which were put on film.

Since Shafer was campaigning largely on the Scranton record and did not offer any radically new programs, he concentrated on denigrating Shapp, whom he accused of "arrogance and lack of insight" and of espousing programs that would send Pennsylvania "crashing downward to a state of chaos and tax her to the wall."

Shapp had original and unconventional solutions for everything. The one which brought most ridicule from Shafer was a proposal to offer free tuition for all higher education and finance it with a huge bond issue. "Shifty—dangerous—desperate—cunning—crafty—grandiose—obsessed—crack-brained," were some of the adjectives Shafer applied to Shapp, while the Democrat attempted to pin the Goldwater label on Shafer.

Napolitan and Shapp ridiculed the Republicans with the funniest and most expensive campaign joke of that year. Shafer had been campaigning on the slogan "Something wonderful is happening in Pennsylvania." One evening, hundreds of Republicans attending a Shafer dinner found a glossy, twenty-six-page pamphlet with the same title at each of their dinner places. They assumed it was a piece of Shafer campaign literature. When they opened "Something Wonderful Is Happening in Pennsylvania," they found page after page of frightening photographs of slums and dumps, unemployed miners, shoeless children and polluted streams. On the last page was the grinning face of Milton Shapp.

This time, the polls were not responding to Napolitan's treatment. Although Shapp continued to emerge as better-known than Shafer (70.9–66.8 percent in September and 78.2–74.4 percent in October), he was not better liked. In mid-September, one pollster, E. John Bucci, hired by the Republicans, found Shafer leading

Shapp by 53–47 percent, while Public Opinion Surveys, Inc., the firm that conducted the name-identification polls, reported Shafer leading by 47–34 percent, with 19 percent undecided.

Analyzing the polls, Napolitan decided that Shapp was slipping because the Republicans and his own actions were spreading an image of arrogance. Shapp had publicly boasted, for example, "I know more about Pennsylvania than any other one man in the state." The media campaign, particularly on television, was therefore redirected to improve Shapp's image, especially to give him some charm. Parts of some commercials, Napolitan recalls, were shot as many as twenty times to extract just the right expression and feeling from the candidate.

The change had a curious effect and exemplified the kind of image manipulation that those who are anxious about the implications of the new campaign techniques like to point to. One man who knew Milton Shapp personally and who felt this anxiety as he followed the campaign was FCC Commissioner Robert E. Lee. Lee knew Shapp as a smart, cold businessman who was honest and conscientious. "Milton Shapp would have made a good Governor," Lee said, "but some of the things they put together for him were projecting a personality and charm he didn't have."[16] Lee feared that the same techniques might be used to elect just anybody. To the contrary, there may have been something of a backlash reaction to the charm commercials. Napolitan says that in trying to "soften his image" through the television campaign, "something of a credibility gap was produced."

Another half-hour film about Shapp was made for the general election. Possessing a dreamy, poetic quality, it showed Shapp walking in the rain, visiting poor people, eating breakfast at home, strolling affectionately with his daughter, talking to students. Whenever possible, Guggenheim designed his shots so as to have Shapp framed in soft, leafy trees, or moving against the sun. Snatches of warm, concerned conversation by the candidate were interspersed with soft guitar music. Viewed outside the context of the election campaign, the film is a small masterpiece of persuasion, with a strong emotional quality that is hard to resist even when the viewer knows he is looking at a propaganda film. There was not a suspicion in the entire thirty minutes that Shapp was arrogant or aggressive or brittle in personality. He came across as a gentle, easily moved intellectual.

The film was held back until eight days before the polling and then was shown some seventy times in that period. In addition, the film from the primary campaign, cut down to half its length, was broadcast thirty times.

Both sides had trouble buying all the television time they wanted. The Republicans sent out orders to their agents to buy every available twenty- and sixty-second prime-time spot in Philadelphia and Pittsburgh for the final four days of the campaign. All they could get were three twenty-second spots in Pittsburgh; none were available on the main stations in Philadelphia.

Each side spent close to half a million dollars on television air time and production.

On the night before the election, Shafer forces mounted a new style of television program which Napolitan thought very effective. It opened in a TV studio, where paid professional actors pretending to be newsmen brought in election-eve reports from different parts of the state. Announcers in the various stations contacted made the reports. Napolitan later said he was surprised that the stations had permitted their employees to take part.

Shapp lost the election by a substantial margin. Nevertheless, Napolitan claimed that his candidate was the only Democrat running for major office in 1966 who improved on his party's performance compared with the previous off-year election.

Napolitan believes that "it is impossible to change a candidate, although it is possible to change his image somewhat." He admits trying to change Shapp's image but he disputes the Republican charge that they were trying to sell Shapp like a product. "Shapp is the very antithesis of the know-nothing candidate who is maneuvered into office by shrewd unscrupulous handlers," Napolitan says. "He knew the issues, was aware of the problems, offered positive programs."

Nevertheless, Napolitan prided his campaign organization on its ability to select and develop the issues Shapp presented according to the findings in the polls. He said during the campaign that if a view the candidate was supporting was shown to be unpopular, it was "deemphasized." What was found to be positive was stressed. That is how campaigns for soap and other consumer products are conducted, on the basis of market research. When Napolitan says Shapp was not sold like soap, he means Shapp was not a nonentity, which is true. But good soap and bad soap are both sold the same way, and Napolitan's handling of the Pennsylvania campaign was full of lessons for managers with candidates to sell, whether brilliant or empty-headed, if they have the money.

Emily Post, or the casual voter

It is an article of faith held by many in politics that television inevitably unmasks the phony.

Frank O'Connor, Democratic City Council President in New York, says, for example: "I feel that if a man is on TV long enough, no matter how phony he is, sooner or later they're going to catch up with him."[17]

While it is true that television quickly punctures rhetoric and makes a broad platform manner look ridiculous, recent developments in television campaigning make it necessary to reexamine the idea that the television camera searches out falseness.

Defending the influence of television on politics, CBS President Frank Stanton wrote in 1964: "There is no such thing as a 'telegenic' personality. It can only give a personality that exists a wider audience. . . . Far from creating synthetic personalities, television can only unmask them."[18]

On the contrary, I believe that television can, in a real sense, "create" a personality by filtering out some facets of a man's own personality and letting through certain others, as happened to Nixon in 1960. The television audience is conditioned to expect certain traits as attractive by its prolonged exposure to the star-oriented entertainment system.

Charles A. Siepmann, head of New York University's Department of Communications in Education, believes that television puts a high premium on facets of a politician's personality "that are impertinent to the choice of party precisely as they divert our interest from the matter of his discourse to the man. Note, also, that the diversion of our interest is not merely to personality but to the distinctive and adventitious attributes of *TV personality*."[19]

Obviously television can do more than merely enlarge the audience. It can inhibit an otherwise confident man—Lyndon Johnson for example. It can exaggerate traits, put a premium on appearance, favor the man who is glib and seemingly sincere—again a result of audience-conditioning by a generation of formula entertainment which stresses the slick rejoinder, the ready phrase, professional assurance, the right word on the lips.

Can television "only unmask" synthetic personalities? President Johnson, for example, often exhibits on television something as close as one could come to a "synthetic personality." It is not his own, as people who talk with him are relieved to discover, but his TV persona screams at some people oppressed by his speech style and unctuous manner. He may thus offend people but is he "unmasked"? Is Reagan unmasked when he uses his benign, avuncular manner to sell his political ideas? The truth is that a skillful performer can more or less choose which personality he will exhibit on television. The more it draws on his own, real personality, the easier the exercise will be. Only the unskillful subject is the victim of his own unattractive manner. Some performers "make it" on television because their own personality, as transmuted through TV, is what the mass of the people want at a certain time. Others present a more studied persona, constructed by them and calculated to appeal. There is no reason why politicians of special ability in this field cannot build images as well as actors do.

This assumes that a politician, like an actor, is deliberately playing a part on television. Ronald Reagan is said to believe that it is very difficult to hide the "real person" from the television camera. According to his "communications director," Lyn Nofziger, Reagan says: "One thing that the television camera can pick up quicker than anything is insincerity, phoniness."[20]

In the type of modern campaign we are discussing, however, it is not left to the candidate to survive alone on television. He is not required to expose his naked personality. Each of his appearances is a strictly controlled event. In the case of commercials, it will be a rehearsed and calculated image of the candidate.

Joseph Napolitan cites a case in which effective control produced an instant image of a candidate which voters did not recognize after the election. The candidate was Endicott Peabody, gubernatorial candidate in Massachusetts in 1962.

"Peabody was a big, handsome guy," Napolitan says. "Immediately after the election he started holding press conferences and people said he seemed entirely different than in the campaign. The trouble was he was getting tough questions and giving bumbling answers. Not the clean, crisp image of the prepared spots [made by Vision Associates of New York]. Because maybe you waited eighteen times in filming the spots to get just the right thing. His TV image dropped afterward like a lead balloon. They had elected him on one basis and he seemed entirely different."

Peabody, who scraped into office by 5,000 votes on the coattails of Edward Kennedy, was defeated in the Democratic primary two years later. Questions of image were probably reinforced by the annoyance Peabody caused many old-line Democratic workers and appointees by proposing government reforms which would have blocked traditional channels of patronage.

Clif White says: "I still believe that the gol'darned camera shows the man's real personality. You can't dress him up and make him up and still not have his real personality show through. You can get away with a couple of shows and hide a man's basic personality but not continuously."[21]

Yet is it a question of hiding a man's basic personality? It is a question of finding men as candidates who have agreeable personalities on which the image-makers can build. Dwight D. Eisenhower was such a man. Although he started with the tremendous advantage of being a household name for ability and integrity in service to his country, what made him a successful political commodity year after year was his personality. The political superstructure was erected on top of that, and during his last years in the White House, commentators (while not questioning Eisenhower's integrity) found almost as many unpleasant things to say about his executive ability as they have said about Reagan's. If they can possibly avoid it, party officials do not choose a candidate with an obviously nasty personality that needs to be hidden by TV makeup and careful staging. The question that arises as television becomes indispensable to political campaigners is how much agreeable personality is coming to outweigh other assets.

It is dangerous to attribute to the inanimate television camera a human or even a supernatural ability to read and reveal character. The circumstance of being on television, as all of us know who have worked before the camera for a long time, can put even professionals under unusual stress. Frank McGee of NBC, who is perhaps the most skilled of all television commentators at keeping cool under the extraordinary pressures of the trade, has to contain and suppress a great amount of nervous tension. Ability to cope with stress may be an indication of strength of character, but inability to suppress it completely on camera is not a sign of character weakness. Eric Sevareid of CBS gives evidence every night of a nervous reaction to the medium; but that does not make his observations less astute. As Charles Thomson has written in the Brookings Institution study of *Television and Presidential Politics:* "Possibly a more reasonable approach would be to state that television *can* unmask a charlatan, if those responsible for the use of camera and microphone want to do so. But given control over the television situation—makeup, lighting, camera angles, speechwriting, teleprompting and the like—there is no reason in the world that the basic appearance of a candidate cannot be acceptable. It may not be a crashing success, but there are specialists in the field of public relations and deportment who could get a man past either Emily Post or the casual voter."[22]

In *Kennedy Campaigning,* Murray B. Levin worries about the possibility "that men skilled in the arts of communication and persuasion can successfully merchandise a vacuous or hollow shell, or a dim-witted fool, or, what is really more to the point, a very average fellow, by creating for him a public image that bears little or no resemblance to his private reality, but is so astutely constructed and sold, that it is accepted as the real thing."[23]

Make him a star by calling him a star

Does television spontaneously create candidates? Whenever that question is raised, the late Senator Estes Kefauver of Tennessee is the first example offered. Kefauver was just another United States Senator to the public until the Senate appointed a special committee in 1951 to investigate crime in interstate commerce. Kefauver was made chairman and through extensive television coverage of the hearings became a national figure almost overnight. He was raised, as Bernard Rubin put it, "from being an interesting 'comer' from Tennessee to a pinnacle of national popularity and international interest."[24]

This impetus pushed Kefauver to make an immediate frontal assault on the Presidency in 1952 and he won enough primaries to come close to the Democratic nomination.

Obviously, not every chairman of a Senate committee is catapulted into the Presidential arena by televised hearings. Senator Joseph McCarthy was badly hurt by the most explosive hearing ever televised. Extensive television coverage of Washington and of prominent politicians around the country is doubtless a major factor in giving likely candidates public recognition much faster than they could attain it elsewhere. It is perhaps tempting to rely too much on this power, as William Scranton may have done in thinking he had any chance at all of wresting the Republican Presidential nomination from Barry Goldwater. Television cannot, as Rubin points out, give people "instant memories of a man."

It may be that the use of free television is most significant when it is timed to coincide with another sequence of events. In the early spring of 1962, when President Kennedy's youngest brother, Edward, let it be known he wanted to be a Senator, there was vigorous opposition in the Democratic Party both in Massachusetts and nationally. The youngest Kennedy seemed too green; he was scarcely past the minimum age for a U.S. Senator (thirty years) and with President Kennedy's relations with Congress touchy enough anyway, it looked too much like nepotism. The President himself did not want Teddy to run but changed his mind when the advance polls showed that he would win easily. On March 11, 1962, Edward Kennedy appeared on NBC's *Meet the Press,* a launching platform for many campaigns, and said he wanted to be the Democratic candidate for the U.S. Senate from Massachusetts. Four days later, he went to Massachusetts and formally announced his candidacy. It may be that his appearance on *Meet the Press* helped to give his desire to run some legitimacy and to provide him with the appearance of being a candidate. To the simple mind it might appear that a man who is important enough to appear on *Meet the Press* must be of the caliber to run for the Senate. From that time, as Professor Levin has recorded, Kennedy's image-makers took over: "The political campaign makes him a star by calling him a star—on radio, on television, in documentary films, in billboards, in press releases, in ghost-written speeches, in brochures, in handouts, in one-sheets."[25]

It is probably true that television has merely speeded up a process that was long established. Well before television's advent, there were recognized occasions when likely prospects were given a moment of glory—like seconding a nomination at a national convention—to push them forward. The press always seized upon these and quieter opportunities, such as an unusually provocative speech on the Senate floor or able questioning of a witness in hearings, or the battles of a certain governor with a hostile legislature. Columnists in search of something fresh would pull names out of obscurity and politicians with influence would float trial balloons. All this still happens now, but it happens much faster.

These, then, are the qualities that the television era demands of political candidates: personality above all else—a personality not too specific and not the least abrasive, a personality which is pleasantly neutral enough to be built upon; a pleasing appearance with no features which may light unflatteringly on television; assurance—a way of comporting yourself that suggests, with modesty, that you know more about anything than anyone else and could handle any crisis; articulateness—an ability to put anything you say, even if it is "I don't know what we're talking about," in such a commanding and authoritative way that your grasp and leadership qualities will flow through into every living room. In other words, you should be an actor.

7 Debates

One evening at the end of the 1960 campaign, after watching a replay of one of his television debates with Richard Nixon, John F. Kennedy remarked to Pierre Salinger: "We wouldn't have had a prayer without that gadget."[1]

For a short period after 1960, the televised debate was a feature of campaigns all over the country. The fashion appeared to exhaust itself after the midterm elections of 1962. What was hailed as "an event of monumental significance in the history of our Constitution" at the Presidential level became merely another campaign device to be embraced or ignored as tactics demanded. Now politicians have accepted the popular view that the television debate is something freshly honorable, signifying decency and clean campaigning. Avoiding a debate is therefore a matter to be handled with careful attention to public relations and as a crucial part of campaign strategy.

When, in 1964, Robert Kennedy was trying to unseat Kenneth Keating, the Republican Senator from New York, Kennedy's advisers did not want him to risk a debate with the older, much respected Senator. One aide, Gerald Gardner, has said that "the Kennedy forces were not hungering for debate if it could be honorably avoided."[2] It could not be "honorably avoided," but Kennedy and Keating each staged an elaborate charade, trying to make the other appear the reluctant debater.

Such games have become a ritual when a candidate feels a debate would put him at a disadvantage. The experienced man fears to allow his untested opponent seem his equal. The incumbent does not wish to lend an opponent the prestige of his office by sharing a platform with him. The famous politician may be anxious not to help the other man become better known. The young challenger may worry about looking callow beside a distinguished officeholder; the older man may in turn fear he will be thought decrepit beside the younger. An incumbent may be trying to keep some issues dormant as he seeks reelection. Any candidate may be uncertain about how his television personality will contrast with his opponent's when they are together.

One of the startling discoveries of 1960 was that since the founding of the Republic, no Presidential candidates had ever been joined in a campaign debate. Americans who had something like a folk memory of Lincoln and Douglas breathing health into nineteenth-century democracy had to be reminded that it was in a contest for the U.S. Senate that they debated in 1858.

Another fact was that few Americans of differing persuasions listen to each other at election time. Loyal Republicans would pull on their galoshes to wade though the Vermont snow to hear Republicans, but wouldn't flip the radio dial to hear a Democrat. Democrats were deaf to talk from the other side. Many newspapers contributed to this one-sided approach.

Many thoughtful people found serious weaknesses in the 1960 debates, but no one denied that the encounters encouraged Americans to listen to the other side. Sam Lubell, an acute student of public opinion, noted a further benefit. The debates made "both the candidates and the election result more acceptable to the electorate." The Democrats saw that if Richard Nixon won, it would not be a catastrophe; Republicans could not help noticing that John F. Kennedy was an intelligent, reasonable human being.

Many other claims were made for the debates, especially by the television industry, which felt it had acquired, by association, much prestige. Most of these claims—that the debates greatly heightened voter interest, increased the turnout and clarified the issues—are contested. What the industry could legitimately claim was that adapting the tradition of political debate to the mass medium did encourage voters to emerge a little from their partisan shells.

There had been various experiments with broadcast political debates before 1960. Dewey and Stassen met on radio in the 1948 Oregon primary. Two Democrats, Kefauver and Stevenson, appeared together on national television with a moderator in May, 1956, and commentators praised the quiet seriousness of their conversation. Robert F. Wagner and Jacob Javits, who were contesting a U.S. Senate seat, debated in New York. John Kennedy and Hubert Humphrey took part in a televised debate during the West Virginia primary in May, 1960, and the program was picked up by a number of other stations around the country.

Nevertheless, it was the fact that Richard Nixon suddenly changed his mind in the summer of 1960 and ignored the advice he had been given that made the broadcast debate an important part of modern political history.

The Great Debates

Nixon never explained at the time what prompted the decision. Carroll Newton, the BBDO advertising agency executive in charge of media planning for the campaign, says that the Vice-President told his staff during a planning session: "Absolutely, I will never just stand up in front of a camera and talk and I will never debate or discuss debates."[3] That was the understanding of his top strategists as Nixon went into the Republican Convention in Chicago. The day after Nixon's nomination, on July 27, Robert W. Sarnoff of NBC sent telegrams to Nixon and Kennedy proposing a series of debates. Kennedy discussed the matter at a luncheon meeting with his campaign staff in Hyannisport and then quickly accepted. His advisers said they felt it was important to be first and thus appear to "challenge" Nixon, who they felt would procrastinate. Nixon did not immediately respond in person. A statement accepting the proposal in principle was issued to the press by his press secretary, Herb Klein. The other members of his campaign staff, including Republican National Chairman Len Hall, learned of Nixon's acceptance through newspaper reports. Four days after the network invitation, Nixon himself confirmed that he had accepted, with a telegram stipulating a "full and free exchange of views without prepared text or notes and without interruption."

Carroll Newton believes that Herb Klein talked Nixon into accepting. Among those who had urged Nixon not to debate Kennedy was President Eisenhower, who says in his memoirs that his objection was practical: "Nixon was widely known; Kennedy was not: dramatic debates would therefore help Kennedy."

In his own book, *Six Crises,* published two years after the debates, Nixon said he had been doubtful about the wisdom of building up an audience for Kennedy, but could not refuse for fear that Kennedy would say he was afraid to stand on the Eisenhower record.

On August 24, in a postconvention session, the House of Representatives approved Senate Joint Resolution 207, suspending the Equal Time provisions for the Presidential election, and networks began planning the debates with representatives of the candidates.

The complicated negotiations, described in *The Great Debates,* edited by Sidney Kraus, quickly revealed that the candidates were more show-business-minded than were the television executives. The networks wanted the traditional format, the so-called Oregon Debate, in which the candidates would make opening statements and then question each other directly. Both candidates rejected this in favor of a panel of journalists to question them. Their representatives said that a straight debate would not hold an audience and that campaign issues were not sufficiently clear-cut to stimulate good debate. The latter observation was an extraordinary piece of behind-the-scenes candor. Kennedy's plenipotentiaries went further, saying they were not as interested in the format as they were in getting him on the same television program with the Vice-President. On the other hand, Herbert A. Seltz and Richard D. Yoakam reported, "They realized Kennedy's skill with the question and answer setup and were really happier with it than a straight debate format."[4] Douglass Cater, who covered the debates for *The Reporter,* said that Nixon's people feared they would be too polite if they interrogated the other side. A Kennedy aide said, "since nobody likes the prosecuting attorney type on television, it was better to turn this thankless task over to others."[5]

At Senate hearings the following year, Republican Senator Hugh Scott, of Pennsylvania, made a point of insisting that he had good information that the networks had imposed the panel format. Frank Stanton, the CBS President, denied it at the time and the evidence in the Kraus studies published by the University of Indiana would appear to support him.

It is interesting that the politicians were so aware, before the debates, of how important considerations of image might be. A political candidate concerned about not appearing to be the nasty prosecutor shows an awareness of the difference of television as a campaign medium and a willingness to let that difference influence behavior. A politician willing to modify the traditional structure of a formal debate because he fears he may be branded with too aggressive an image is a politician concerned not primarily with the weight of his arguments but with projecting a favorable image. Later, it was widely agreed that the first debate, at least, turned on questions of image. From the available evidence, Kennedy seems to have been more aware beforehand than Nixon was that the general impression he made on the viewers could carry more weight than what he said.

I had an unusual perspective on the first of the 1960 debates. NBC had sent me to Berlin to film some advance material on the attitude of West Berliners to the American election. One evening in October, the United States Information Service arranged a screening of the first Nixon-Kennedy debate in the ballroom of the Berlin Hilton. The room was filled not only with Americans but with intensely curious Berliners. At that time, feeling was strongly pro-Republican among the West Germans. They knew Nixon's reputation for tough anti-Communism and were confident that with him in the White House there would be no softening of the Western position in Berlin. Kennedy was an unknown quantity, reputed to be a liberal, and that worried the Germans. When the lights went on after the debate film had run, most of the Berliners were very glum and went away convinced that their man, Nixon, had put on a poorer showing than Kennedy.

What perhaps emerges most persistently from all the studies of the debates (and few political occasions have been so minutely scrutinized) is that the appearance and behavior of the candidates, the way in which their personalities were transmitted, overshadowed what they said. Those factors, and the argument over Nixon's tactical wisdom in agreeing to debate, appear to carry the most important lessons for politicians and the public about the true significance of televised debates. The conclusion is reinforced by a study of other TV debates in later campaigns.

All the contributors to the Kraus study stressed the importance of image and the relative unimportance of content:

Douglass Cater said that the Kennedy-Nixon dialogue "was largely a paste-up job, containing bits and snippets from campaign rhetoric already used many times. As the series wore on, the protagonists were like two weary wrestlers who kept trying to get the same holds. What became clear was how limited the vocabulary of the debates really was and how vague were the candidates' ideas about what to do."[6]

Samuel Lubell was concerned that the debates put pressure on the candidates "to project some contrived 'image' across the screen into the national living room."[7]

Kurt and Gladys Lang, who did a study of voter reactions in New York City, found that voting intentions changed much less than did the candidates' images for the voters. Kennedy changed from "an eager, affable, young and ambitious political aspirant into one that epitomized the competent, dynamic and quick-thinking candidate"; Nixon, who had been seen as an experienced politician with reputed great skill in debate, emerged as a disappointing, nervous, complicated personality.[8]

Theodore White believed that the greatest opportunity ever for a discussion to clarify the issues in a Presidential campaign was missed. He attributed this to the tyranny of timing in broadcasting, "which cannot bear to suffer a pause of more than five seconds." Nixon and Kennedy were thus reduced "to snapping their two-and-a-half-minute answers back and forth" and could not stop to think.[9]

Thirteen different surveys were undertaken to determine reactions to the debates. They revealed that more people thought that Kennedy won the first debate, that the second was very close, that Nixon won the third, with the fourth also close.

A study by the Mass Communications Research Center of the

University of Wisconsin concluded that "Kennedy did not necessarily win the debates, but Nixon lost them."[10]

Certainly the first debate, for whatever reasons, gave the Kennedy campaign a substantial boost. Ten southern Governors who had not been overly enthusiastic about his candidacy immediately sent Kennedy a telegram of warm congratulations. A worker in the Kennedy-Johnson campaign headquarters in New York said that before the first debate there had been trouble finding enough mature volunteers; afterward, there were more than enough applications.

Through August and September, Kennedy had been running slightly behind Nixon in the Gallup Poll, with one exception on September 14, when he was ahead (48–47 percent). In the poll published on October 12, after the first two debates, Kennedy had a substantial lead (49–46 percent), and although the gap narrowed toward election day, Nixon never regained the lead.

There has been no attempt, however, by students of the debates to suggest that Kennedy "won" because of any demonstrable forensic superiority. Some people who only heard the debates on radio thought that the two candidates had scored about evenly. Even among his close associates, the focus was on the way Kennedy had closed the maturity gap by appearing, in Pierre Salinger's words, "a mature, knowledged attractive man."

There was an outcry by disappointed Republicans the day after the first debate. The *Chicago Daily News* headlined its story "Was Nixon Sabotaged by TV Makeup Artists?" but modified the account when the Nixon camp revealed that it was their own man, not a CBS saboteur, who had applied the makeup. The lighting was blamed, until it was discovered that the candidates' advisers had been fully consulted. In fact, they had at the last minute asked that technicians put more light into Nixon's eyes to eliminate shadows. Republicans said the background was the wrong shade, that Nixon had been badly advised and wore a suit which did not contrast sufficiently with the background. They accused CBS of selecting cutaway, or reaction, shots of Nixon that caught him unawares, wiping the perspiration from his face and nervously tapping his foot.

The other two networks went even further than CBS in the

subsequent three debates to protect themselves from such criticism, redesigning the sets and lighting to be more flattering to both debaters. By the second debate, Nixon's health was restored and there was marked improvement in his appearance.

Besides the opinions of voters about the content of the debates and which candidate they considered had won, some studies tried to determine what effect the debates had had, if any, on the actual voting. None of them found any positive evidence that the debates alone had either caused an important switch in voting intention or significantly increased the voter turnout. Lubell's interviews across the country made him think that "religious prejudice was much more powerful in getting out the vote." The Opinion Research Corporation found that viewers of the debates, if anything, changed less in the strength of the commitment to their party than nonviewers, who only heard or read about the debates. Charles A. Siepmann concluded: "It is by no means certain that, as some people assert, [the debates] contributed to the making of more intelligent decisions by the voters. Nor has it been established that the debates were responsible for the record turnout of voters at the polls."[11]

We are left with the paradox that most commentators think the debates harmed Nixon, but with no objective evidence that they swung the election to Kennedy. Perhaps, if the result had not been so close, the effects might have shown up more conclusively in the surveys. It is remarkable that more adult Americans watched the first debate—the average estimate is 70 million—than actually voted. Nixon and Kennedy received a total of 68 million votes and the difference between them was only 112,702. It seems inconceivable that a political event with so many participants did not make some contribution to the result. Both Kennedy and Nixon thought that the debates had decided the election.

Another area worthy of more research is what effect reports by other media and word of mouth about the debates had on people's attitudes. Some voters heard the first debate on the radio and thought it a draw, but within hours they were hearing from many commentators that it was a clear-cut victory for Kennedy. The Opinion Research Corporation study already mentioned suggests that such secondhand accounts may have had more influence on voters' decisions than firsthand viewing.

There is yet another feature of such encounters, which was remarked on in 1960: the advantage to the loser of being exposed to viewers of the winner's party. It was argued by Frank Stanton of CBS that Nixon as well as Kennedy had something to gain by the nature of the audience. Those who watched the 1960 debates were found to be roughly one-half Democrats, one-third Republicans and the rest independent. Since Nixon, the better-known candidate, came from a party with roughly one-third fewer members and thus had to look to both the Democrats and the independents for support to win, he stood to gain from the exposure. As Stanton further points out, the sheer size of the audience (CBS put the total viewers at 120 million for the four debates) was of help to both candidates equally, as was its willingness to stay with the programs and not tune out. The typical television family was said to have kept its set tuned to the debates for fifty-four minutes of the hour. Nine of ten television families tuned into some part of the debates; more than half watched at least three and one out of four watched them all. The four debates attracted television audiences that were on average 20 percent larger than the entertainment programs they replaced.

By any standards the Great Debates of 1960 were a remarkable experiment. In further attempts at the Presidential level, it needs to be decided whether the weaknesses they exhibited sprang from the nature of the television medium or could be avoided by modifying the format. The chief criticism of the Nixon-Kennedy encounters was that they stressed personality and image at the expense of reasoned argument. Undeniably, that arose partly from the psychological difference between the impact of television and radio, on the one hand, and newspapers, on the other. The novelty of the occasion and the fact that there were only four encounters may have also contributed to this effect by not giving the viewers time to adjust to the personalities. If such debates between candidates became a tradition of Presidential campaigns, it is arguable that voters might gradually pay more attention to what is being said. Similarly, if there were more debates during a campaign, one a week for example, or if they lasted two hours instead of one, fascination with personality might wear off to a degree.

The interposition of a panel of questioners was also much criticized in 1960. If they had been made to use the traditional form of debate and argue to one specified point, speaking directly to one another, there would have been less chance of their sliding off into superficialities.

If televised debates were to become a tradition of Presidential campaigns, they would be harder to dodge. As a rule of thumb, however, incumbents are probably going to avoid debates whenever they can. Besides, no one—political scientists, journalists or television executives—can really tell any candidate how he should campaign. That is his and his campaign manager's prerogative.

Still, a line of evolution which would result in greater use of TV debates in Presidential elections can be visualized. There may be in the future so much concern about the encroachment of commercials into campaigns that steps will be taken to limit their use. Then politicians and broadcasters will be faced with the need to produce some kind of television broadcast that will continue to hold an audience. Solid half hours of talk by candidates do not; debates do. Writing about the 1960 debates, Frank Stanton said: "Straight exposition in any form is always the most difficult way to engage and hold the attention of anyone. Conflict, on the other hand, of ideas in action, is intriguing and engrossing to great numbers of people. Drama has always got more attention than essays."[12] An understanding of that truth is of course the foundation of the highly successful formulas of network television. But it may be many years before Presidential candidates accept that their own interests coincide with those of the public and the television industry in the debate formula.

As long as they toy with the television debate, shadow-boxing with the public and the networks, lesser politicians will do the same.

Another Kennedy debate

In his book *Kennedy Campaigning,* Murray Levin has given a fascinating account of how, in 1962, Edward M. Kennedy borrowed his older brother's techniques for two television debates in Massachusetts. The youngest Kennedy was challenging Edward McCormack, nephew of the Speaker of the U.S. House of Representatives, John McCormack, in the Democratic primary for Senator. Kennedy was without experience, whereas McCormack was a seasoned state politician who had twice been elected Attorney General of Massachusetts.

Campaigning energetically and leaning the weight of his illustrious name on the state convention, Kennedy had edged McCormack out of the nomination he expected in the spring. Reviving an older political feud between the two Massachusetts families, McCormack challenged Kennedy in the fall primary. The most important incident in that campaign was a televised debate on August 27 in South Boston.

McCormack had challenged Kennedy to eight debates. Kennedy stalled for sixteen days, and then took four days to negotiate. He emerged with an agreement to two debates, having insisted on a format with a panel of newsmen, and on being free to choose the site for the first debate. The choice, the South Boston High School, Levin says, cleverly served to draw attention to what McCormack preferred to live down, the image of the corrupt old South Boston Irish politician.

For weeks before the debate, McCormack and his advisers wondered whether they should attack Teddy. Kennedy was known to have a fierce temper and it was argued that if McCormack could provoke him to anger on the television screen, Teddy would be lost.

McCormack decided to attack. Teddy came well prepared and gave answers heavily seasoned with place names and topical items in the news to give an appearance of familiarity with current events. McCormack opened by charging Teddy with running on his name, not on any qualifications, and said Kennedy's campaign was insulting to the state.

In his summing up, Kennedy was emotional. During his last few sentences—about the tradition of free speech in Massachusetts—his voice broke and he appeared to be weeping.

Then McCormack delivered the body blow. Turning to Kennedy, he said, "If his name was Edward Moore, with his qualifications, with your qualifications, Teddy, if it was Edward Moore, your candidacy would be a joke, but nobody's laughing because his name is not Edward Moore. It's Edward Moore Kennedy. . . ."

According to Levin, Kennedy sat unbelieving, "stunned, rigid and ashen."

But the result surprised them both. It quickly became clear from newspaper, political and public reaction that Kennedy had won. He had inspired a remarkable wave of sympathy for his courtesy in the face of McCormack's attack. Women, especially, sympathized with Teddy, who looked, observers said, like a little lost boy whom all the women wanted to cuddle. McCormack, on the other hand, spoke out of the side of his mouth, sneeringly. They also noticed that McCormack's head looked strangely little on his shoulders, while Teddy's was handsome and well-proportioned.

On such considerations are TV debates won or lost. Teddy won the primary.

Then he was challenged to a television debate by his Republican opponent for the Senate, George Lodge. Kennedy repeatedly refused to take up the challenge. Lodge attempted to embarrass him by holding debates with the Independent third candidate, H. Stuart Hughes, always with a vacant chair to symbolize Kennedy's absence. It did not help Lodge. The voters of Massachusetts did not hold it against Teddy that he had refused to debate; they sent him to Washington with 57 percent of the vote.

The gentle art of avoiding debates

The television debate has grown into such an important yet unpredictable factor that one of the skills a modern campaign manager must develop is the technique of keeping his candidate out of debates that might be damaging, without losing face. The interest of the public in hearing a reasoned discussion of the issues is seldom a consideration.

This is how Joe Napolitan has revealed he would approach the question: "If I had a candidate who was a clear favorite, I'd try to keep him off TV debates. But I would never openly refuse to debate. If challenged to a debate, you say, 'yes, sure. How about my campaign manager meeting yours at 4 P.M. on Thursday?' Then at five to four on Thursday, you call and say, 'We've had a real crisis here, can we make it on Saturday?' And on Saturday you put it off till next Wednesday . . . and so on."

Few politicians can match the Kennedy family in such skills. What John demonstrated in 1960 and Teddy exploited in 1962, Robert Kennedy adapted to a somewhat different situation in New York in 1964.

His opponent was Kenneth Keating, the silver-haired Senator respected in the liberal wing of the Republican party. Keating had irritated the Kennedys prior to the Cuban missile crisis, by repeatedly charging that the Russians had given Castro offensive missiles. Despite Administration denials, the charges became an issue in the 1962 off-year elections. As it happened, Keating turned out to be right, although evidence displayed by the U.S. Government at the height of the crisis suggested the Senator had been right before the fact.

Two years later, Keating found his Senate seat challenged by the man who had been President Kennedy's right-hand aide throughout the missile crisis. The Kennedy clan suspected Keating of having exploited rumors from Cuban refugees about missile installations for political ends. But Robert Kennedy's advisers in 1964 recognized that Keating's public reputation was solid. As mentioned earlier, they did not want Kennedy to debate him if it could be "honorably avoided." One important Kennedy aide told a reporter: "We're not going to let him appear with that wise old man."

However, the polls turned against Kennedy and a debate seemed to be the only way to reverse the trend. Not sure whether Keating would want to face a confrontation, Kennedy decided to make the challenge. He proposed that he and Keating buy the time, each paying half, to get around the Equal Time regulation, because there was also a Conservative candidate in the race.

The maneuvering began. Keating suggested that there be a panel of young people or no panel with only the two candidates speaking. Kennedy's reaction was, "Does he call that a debate?"

CBS then offered an hour of prime evening time and both sides accepted. By the afternoon of the program, however, the candidates still had not agreed on the format. Keating still paid for the first half hour. Gerald Gardner, in *Robert Kennedy in New York,* says that when Kennedy tried to buy the other half hour, he was refused. He telegraphed William Paley, the CBS Board Chairman, in California and secured the half hour. By this time, Keating had announced that he was going to debate an empty chair.

There was a frantic scene at Kennedy headquarters. Bobby said: "I can't let him debate an empty chair."

With a retinue of reporters, Kennedy turned up and demanded to be admitted to the studio where Keating was preparing to go on. A CBS official refused to let him enter. When Keating left after his broadcast, he was besieged by reporters but refused to talk. Aides hurriedly pushed prop furniture in the reporters' paths, while the candidate escaped. Kennedy went on with his own half hour, with radio personality Barry Gray, and afterward portrayed the incident as a victory. When Keating bought more time on NBC for $10,000 and invited Kennedy to appear, Bobby refused. Most of the New York newspapers regarded this competition in trickery as a draw. It was the conclusion of some experienced reporters that Robert Kennedy never had any intention of debating Keating and that the incident of being locked out of the studio was merely a device.

The bumper year for television debates was 1962, the first general election after Nixon-Kennedy. There were hundreds of debates all over the country. George Romney debated John Swainson four times in the gubernatorial election in Michigan and won. Unchastened by his experiences with Kennedy, Richard Nixon confronted California's Governor Pat Brown on television. They exchanged personal charges and neither was considered a winner, although Brown remained Governor.

The art of avoiding debates was already advanced. In Pennsylvania, William Scranton was running against Richardson Dilworth for the governorship. Dilworth kept challenging Scranton to a debate, and when he was refused, arranged to go on television alone with an empty chair. Scranton turned up at the last minute with a bucket of whitewash and walked into the studio accusing Dilworth of trying to smear him. Scranton won the election easily.

It is apparent that politicians are as alert to the hazards of TV debating as they are to the advantages. Many politicians have been frightened off. Others wait indecisively on the sidelines, like nervous gamblers eyeing the roulette wheel, wondering if this is their moment to take a chance. Their nervousness may be killing the genre.

In 1964, the most remarkable absence was that of a Presidential debate. After his election, John F. Kennedy had announced that he would take part in TV debates if he were the Democratic candidate in 1964. The prospect of an incumbent President in such a direct partisan confrontation alarmed some people. A panel formed by the American Political Science Association decided: "It may be contrary to the national interest for the President to engage in debates." Nevertheless, the panel said that the 1960 debates had added "a useful dimension to American public life" and recommended a series of seven debates between Labor Day and the election.

In *Political Television,* Bernard Rubin suggests several grounds for anxiety about debates involving an incumbent President: he could not be drawn into argument involving his thoughts on delicate matters of national security; he could not easily attack the policies of allied countries; success as a partisan spokesman might lessen his effectiveness as the nation's leader; and in a crisis that coincided with the debates, the President's arguments would carry undue weight.

These are possible pitfalls for a President campaigning in any form, however, and it is not inevitable that the risks would increase because of the pressures in a debate situation.

President Kennedy demonstrated in his press conferences that delicate issues and sharp questions could be safely handled on live television. It is not clear why the debate form would uniquely restrict a President's freedom to comment on the policies of allied countries. Any policies he did not like would already have brought some response from his Administration, which he could defend. If something new burst on the scene, the President would respond with some public explanation. In the case of a crisis, a President's arguments inevitably weigh more heavily in public opinion than the arguments of other politicians. Again, why should TV debates make a difference? Debates with an incumbent President would perhaps make him a more obviously partisan spokesman than recent Presidents have liked to appear at election time. Still, the dignity of the office is not likely to be casually jettisoned. It is too valuable a commodity at election time.

It may be a long time before these questions are put to the test. They might have been in 1964 if President Kennedy had lived. The machinery was already in motion to suspend the Equal Time rule once again. President Kennedy had appointed a Commission on Campaign Costs—with Herbert E. Alexander as Executive Director—which recommended the Equal Time suspension for 1964. Although there was considerable support in Congress, Alexander said that "it appeared to be high Democratic policy to avoid suspension."

The failure of an otherwise amenable Democratic Congress to pass legislation making debates possible was generally taken to mean that President Johnson did not want to take part in debates. Senator Goldwater challenged the President and offered to pay for the broadcast time. To forestall the national-interest argument, he even offered to have the debates filmed in advance to guard against inadvertent security leaks. But President Johnson did not accept.

Politically, Johnson was probably wise. Accepting Senator Goldwater as a debating opponent would have narrowed the credibility gap between the two men. It would have shrunk the psychological distance that separated them in the minds of many voters. To voters in the middle ground of American politics, inviting Senator Goldwater into the same TV studio with President Johnson would have been to haul him back from the outer reaches of that extremist wasteland to which the Democrats had consigned him. Conservative Republicans, taking the measure of the two men side by side on the TV screen, might have been willing to raise Lyndon Johnson a few notches out of the socialist hell they were convinced he inhabited and was planning for them. But the intention of any healthy politician is the reverse; it is to put an infinity of wisdom and humanity between himself and his opponent.

Furthermore, Lyndon Johnson did not want mere victory. The earliest polls told him he had that. He wanted a landslide. It is probable that by doing Barry Goldwater the honor of debating with him, Johnson would have lessened the margin of triumph. In that case, his mandate for the vigorous social reforms he initiated after the election would have been less convincing, and possibly the Democratic majorities in Congress would have been smaller. On every *political* ground, his decision not to debate appears right.

When the interests of the voter are considered, however, the arguments are different. A useful dialogue between the two candidates was possible. One feature of the President's campaign was the extreme mistiness of the future he was promising. The Great Society was a personal vision of which he vouchsafed the public only tantalizing glimpses. No one pinned Mr. Johnson down on specific programs. By focusing public attention on the supposed radicalism of the Republican candidate, the President was able to imply a program rather than to delineate one. The voters might have appreciated an effort to make him spell it out. Vietnam was also treated vaguely, the problem being reduced to the proposition: President Johnson seeks no wider war—Senator Goldwater does. It was not long after the election that Republicans were jokingly saying: "They told me if I voted for Goldwater we would be bombing Hanoi. So I did and we are!" It is difficult to see how the national interest would have been harmed by having the two men discuss the issue, in person, for an hour.

There is a third consideration: the effectiveness of each of the two men on television.

In one sense, Goldwater had gifts more suitable to the medium than Johnson. The Senator was a man refreshingly unstuffy in his approach to politics. Naturally leaning toward informality in moments that put others stiffly on their dignity, he often exhibited an absence of pomposity that made him seem open and undevious. His clean-cut, handsome features reinforced this impression of candor, which showed particularly when he was speaking extemporaneously and not following a text.

Mr. Johnson's television demeanor, on the other hand, has always suggested a man more calculating, a man making an effort to ingratiate himself with the millions. He has often seemed like an insincere preacher at a routine funeral, twisting his features to look grieved. By all accounts he was inhibited by the example of Kennedy's graceful mastery of television.

Yet everyone who has ever talked at length with Lyndon Johnson in person knows that he is the most persuasive and forceful individual in politics. Arthur Schlesinger, Jr., for one, telling of being exposed to the Johnson "treatment," says that he "staggered away in a condition of exhaustion," feeling he had been "under hypnosis."[13]

In common with many reporters who traveled with the Johnson campaign in 1964, I found myself overwhelmed by the first encounters with the burst-dam quality of his personality. Freed of the unctuous manner he adopts when speaking directly to the television camera, the President was a man who projected genuine charm and concern. It is difficult to believe that these qualities would not have emerged in a television debate.

Mr. Johnson made no effort to get Congress to permit Presidential debates in 1964 but his withdrawal from the campaign stimulated new efforts in 1968. Richard Nixon and Vice-President Humphrey, the two leading Presidential hopefuls, both said they favored such action by Congress. Nixon rejected requests by his Republican rival, Governor Nelson Rockefeller, for a preconvention debate, but shortly before the GOP convention he did announce that, again contrary to his aides' advice, he would be willing to debate the Democratic nominee. When he made this statement, however, the measure that would have made a Presidential debate possible was still bogged down in committee.

In the struggle for the Democratic nomination, Senator Robert Kennedy dodged a debate with Senator Eugene McCarthy until McCarthy defeated him in the Oregon primary. It was a measure of Kennedy's desperation that he consented to a joint appearance on ABC in California on June 1. Most commentators gave the "debate" to Kennedy because he appeared more aggressive, although McCarthy benefited from the exposure. Kennedy's victory in the California primary three days later was less substantial than many observers thought he would have needed (had he lived) to give him the momentum to win the nomination.

By ingeniously calling the Kennedy-McCarthy confrontation a "special edition" of *Issues and Answers,* ABC did not have to give equal time to other candidates. Regularly scheduled news and news interview programs are exempt.

In 1961, Frank Stanton, urging repeal of the Equal Time rule to make TV debates a permanent feature of American campaigns, said he could not believe that any responsible politicians would seek to resume outlawing them. "It would certainly be incredible cynicism," he said, "for any public official to conclude that the people were entitled to see and hear candidates in face-to-face discussions only when it served the political interests of a candidate."[14]

It was incredible—and it was true.

8 Campaigning by Commercial

On the screen, two GI's crouch near the ground, talking about the war. They think it is futile and can see no goal worth fighting for. Suddenly, shooting breaks out again and one of the men is hit. The other GI sees his buddy die, and then, in his frustration, deliberately exposes himself to the enemy and is killed. An announcer's voice urges, "Vote Republican."

It is not 1968, but 1952—the Korean War. This melodramatic commercial was one of the first ever made to sell a political candidate on television.

Sixteen years later, what was once a startling innovation is the rule. In that time, politicians have virtually abandoned television as a campaign platform, preferring to concentrate their money and ingenuity on its power to make a selling pitch. By the 1968 Presidential election, with a tormented country desperately needing rational debate, political argument on the airwaves has largely been reduced to one-minute commercials. The crude radio commercials broadcast on behalf of President Johnson in New Hampshire, accusing Senator Eugene McCarthy of helping the Communists in Vietnam by advocating "fuzzy thinking and surrender," indicated to what depths even the White House had been brought by the availability of mass advertising.

In the same period, the new managers have not been blind to the opportunities afforded by free television. Before we examine the latest techniques for exploiting paid television, let us see how politicians secure valuable exposure at no cost at all.

Ever since politicians first began to use the broadcasting media to reach voters, some have claimed that the industry should not be making them pay for air time, but should give it. It was argued that the airwaves broadcasters used belonged to the public; radio and television exploited the airwaves profitably, under a franchise; and a condition of that franchise, laid down in the Federal Communications Act of 1934, was that broadcasters should operate "in the public interest." What could be more truly in the public interest than to provide an opportunity to hear the issues confronting the nation discussed by candidates at election time? The broadcasters did not agree, on the grounds that the government had saddled them with a regulation that tied their hands at election time. Under Section 315 of the 1934 Act, broadcasters must give equal time to all candidates for a particular political office. If there are two candidates for a Senate seat, for example, and a television station gives one of them a half hour of free time to make his pitch, an equal amount of time must be offered to his opponent. If there should be five candidates for that seat and one is given a half hour, each of the other four must be given the same time. The regulation appears most onerous and ridiculous to broadcasters in Presidential campaigns. In addition to the two, and sometimes three, serious contenders, there are inevitably a host of lesser candidates, sometimes as many as fifteen, representing fringe groups like the American Beat Party, the Church of God Party and the Vegetarian Party. If the Republican and Democratic presidential candidates were given an hour of network time each, by law each of the others would have to be treated equally. The television industry has campaigned vigorously to have the regulation removed, so far without success.

The Equal Time provision does not apply to appearances for which the candidates pay, except that if a television station sells time to one candidate it must be willing to sell it to the others. The broadcasters quickly found it in their hearts to sell virtually as much time as candidates could afford to buy, with the result that candidates with big campaign funds swamp the airwaves and the poorer ones disappear.

There have been three kinds of response to this situation. One has been to continue the pressure to repeal the Equal Time provision.

Another has been to try to overcome the inequalities of exposure imposed by the enormous cost of television by finding some way to finance campaigns with public funds. President Johnson proposed such a system in 1967, but Congress did not act on it.

A third response, which has attracted less attention than the others, is the increasingly skillful exploitation by candidates of the free time that is available.

In 1959, the FCC removed regular news and news-interview programs from the Equal Time restriction. The only condition remaining is that broadcasters are still required to be "fair" in their treatment of candidates. For instance, in 1964, if President Johnson spent a day campaigning in New York and a five-minute report appeared that evening on *Walter Cronkite,* the Republican candidate was not entitled to mathematically equal time on the same program. CBS was required, under the Fairness Doctrine, to ensure that, on balance, during the campaign, the Republican views were presented as thoroughly in news programs as Johnson's. The Fairness Doctrine makes broadcasters even unhappier than the Equal Time provision, for reasons we shall see later.

Now, with hours of television news and panel programs open to them every week, the new campaign managers have made it part of their art to get their candidates on those programs. Their skill is considerable, although television often makes it very easy for them.

By appearing on a television news program, the candidate is guaranteed an audience that has some interest in public affairs and is predisposed to consider them at that time of day. He is not competing with entertainment programs and runs no risk of antagonizing the audience by preempting its regular fare. The audience, as we have seen, is an almost perfect demographic cross section of the electorate. For this audience largely dependent upon television for its information about current events, news programs form the windows to their minds: if a candidate is to reach them, those windows are the openings where there may be least resistance.

Perhaps the most important benefit is the intuition of authority in the audience. Vitally important things are happening in the cities, the country and the world, they are told, and it is on news programs that they learn about those happenings. A man whose activities are part of the news is credible, his doings have the authority of a news event. He is a bona fide news happening, not a commercial. And he is, if we believe the surveys quoted earlier, a more believable event on television than he is in a newspaper or magazine report.

The major disadvantage to a candidate is that he cannot control all the aspects of an appearance on a news program. He cannot edit the film and write the commentary. But if he is alert to the possibilities, he can control a great deal.

His campaign manager must first have a real understanding of the value of the "pseudo event." To make television and the other news media cover his activities, he must invent happenings which are likely to interest them. They are not real events because they are manufactured simply to attract the media, especially television. In the old days of campaigning, a candidate tried to meet and speak to as many people as he could. Today, if he understands his business, he still goes about meeting people and speaking, but he does not do it with those voters principally in mind. His attention is directed to the hundreds of times greater number of voters who will see him that evening on the television news.

If the events of his campaign are too repetitive, the coverage will dwindle, so there must be constant variety. The speeches he delivers must make different points and the type of setting should vary. But, principally, he should be placed in circumstances where something news-like will happen. If the first sentence that comes to the mind of a reporter summing up the day is: "Republican senatorial candidate Charles Percy today continued his campaigning through southern Illinois . . ." Percy has not succeeded. If the day can be constructed so as to provide a lead sentence like: "Senatorial candidate Charles Percy today held a vigorous curbside debate with angry Negro demonstrators in Chicago," the incident has the appearance of an event. While it has always been an elementary rule not to run a dull campaign, television's hunger for visual incident has made that precept imperative.

Television hunger has also made it easier. As we have seen, in recent years the network evening news reports have expanded from fifteen minutes to thirty, and there is pressure to make them an hour long. The local news programs which precede the network shows have been lengthened to one hour by many stations. They can be very profitable for the stations but they consume what is for television a staggering amount of material. With so insatiable an appetite to feed, a candidate who runs a creative campaign has an excellent situation to exploit.

This is less true for Presidential campaigns—which will attract constant TV coverage in any case—than for congressional, gubernatorial or municipal races, where the coverage on local stations might be sporadic.

Election coverage for television is an arduous business in which technical and logistical problems are so important, just to get a piece of properly exposed film on the air, that the editorial considerations often come last. The campaign manager who enters most sympathetically into the problems of television journalism will be rewarded by the coverage his candidate gets. Television covers an election by sending reporters and film crews to record the doings of the candidates. There is always an early deadline to meet. They must return with the film to their own station (or, if a network crew, to an affiliate station), where the film can be processed and edited and the commentary added. That may mean breaking off from the campaign as much as five hours before air time. The alert campaign manager, therefore, will try not only to devise an event interesting enough to bring the TV people out, but schedule it before the early afternoon, when they must leave.

If a TV crew wants to travel with the candidate's plane, the manager should do his utmost to permit it and to let them film whatever they want. Holding things up a moment to let a film crew be first off an aircraft or a bus in order to get a shot they want; providing an extra car in a motorcade for TV equipment; or getting the candidate to exchange a few words with a TV reporter who has to leave to make a program deadline is a small price to pay for the exposure that results.

Some politicians have gone so far as to do some of the broadcasters' work. In Michigan, in 1966, Governor Romney's campaign apparatus regularly produced tapes of his remarks, already edited for use, which were made available to radio stations. The Romney people estimated that they received half a million dollars in free radio coverage with that device. If broadcasting pieces preselected by a political candidate seems an abdication of journalistic responsibility, such a lapse is certainly not going to worry the candidate.

Bob Price, campaign manager and later Deputy Mayor for John Lindsay, thinks it is easy to use the television stations in New York. "You have to make the stations give you free time," he says. "If you are imaginative you can get them to use thirty seconds on any news program. In New York City, it's duck soup. You just have to think of the personality of the individual TV newsman and think in terms of what he is likely to use."[1]

Although Governor Nelson Rockefeller spent over $5 million to be reelected in 1966, his staff were very alert to the opportunities news programs provided. Leslie Slote, the Governor's press secretary, says it is easier to get the cameras out during a campaign than in day-to-day affairs. "It needs inventiveness," he says. "The challenge is when they get there to make it good."[2]

He referred to the efforts of Rockefeller's chief opponent in 1966, Democrat Frank O'Connor. For a variety of reasons—late nomination, too little money and too many advisers—the O'Connor campaign had an amateurish air. Frequently, reporters would turn up at a place designated on the campaign schedule to find that no advance man had been there to produce a crowd. O'Connor would be seen pacing on an empty street corner or talking to people who were hostile. One night in late fall, the campaign motorcade with O'Connor, his aides and the press was streaming along a road outside New York City. The lead car made a confident turn off the highway, all the other cars followed and the press found themselves sitting with the candidate in a deserted drive-in movie theater—which had been closed for the winter.

It was not the same in Rockefeller's campaign, where the effect of every campaign stop was calculated. Slote went on: "It's not difficult getting the cameras out. It's showing up the Governor in a setting of enthusiasm and response. One of the keys is young people. We had lots of rallies at schools and universities. Most people are working during the days but there are always people at the schools. He goes to a school and there are six hundred kids. The Governor shakes hands and the TV cameras are cranking away. It is an enthusiastic, warm occasion. The locals will see it that night on the local station. In the middle of that sort of day we would stick a Kiwanis luncheon in as a way of getting the media."

All three Kennedys showed great ability to attract the attention of the media to their activities, both between campaigns and during. It did not happen accidentally. When Senator Robert Kennedy appeared in a full front-page photograph in the New York *Daily News,* leaning in the door of a squalid Puerto Rican tenement in Spanish Harlem, it was not a coincidence that the photographer was there. Nor was he pulled there by a high-pressure public relations man calling to say, "Hey, we've got a great picture for you today." It was all managed more subtly, but it *was* managed.

It is much easier for an incumbent than a challenger. In the opinion of his critics, President Johnson's sudden flight to Honolulu for a conference on Vietnam during the 1966 Senate hearings on the war was the pseudo event of the year. The press cannot ignore a President, so the newspapers and television shows were full of the Honolulu conference. However much the White House denied it at the time, the conference was very suddenly arranged and did divert public attention from the hearings, which were heavy with criticism of the Administration.

The need for visual incident to give variety and action to a television news program can have political effects that worry serious journalists in the medium. The practice is less true in the news departments of the major networks, which are peopled by trained journalists, than in the news operations of local stations around the country. There are more than six hundred of these and many of them still do not have extensive news resources, either in facilities or in personnel. Whenever a political candidate turns up, there is competitive anxiety to put him on the local news. In the rush and excitement of getting to the politician and recording an interview, the last thing that may be considered is the content of the interview. The interviewer may be so preoccupied by other factors that his questions are sycophantic, or so uninformed as to let the politician simply walk away with the occasion. Such interviewing results in little more than a public relations exercise for the politician. Television viewers, seeing the interview on a news program in the context of other, real events, may give it the benefit of the same trust they bring to that station's other news items. Nor are such lapses unknown at the network news level. For economic reasons, however, the local station may be particularly vulnerable. To send out a cameraman and have him expose a roll of sound film (four hundred feet, or ten minutes, is the standard length) is an investment which stations operating on small news budgets cannot afford to sacrifice. Even if the politician's speech, news conference or private interview results in nothing significant or newsworthy, it is difficult not to run it once the film has been exposed and processed. For that reason, politicians both during campaigns and in normal times get uncritical television exposure that is of great benefit to them.

News programs provide particularly valuable exposure because they are scheduled most often on the fringes of prime time, just before 7:30 P.M., when the large audience for the evening's entertainment programming is beginning to build up, or just after 11:00 P.M., before the big audience goes to bed. Other opportunities for free television exposure, the regular panel or interview programs, usually occur on the weekends, when the audience is smaller, but their effect is still important.

Almost every television station runs at least one half-hour public affairs program a week as a comparatively inexpensive way of demonstrating public service. The most influential of such programs are these on the three networks on Sunday afternoons: *Meet the Press* (NBC), *Face the Nation* (CBS) and *Issues and Answers* (ABC). Appearance on such programs is by invitation, and to a relatively unknown figure an invitation from a network can be an important event (for example, the appearance of Edward Kennedy in 1962 on *Meet the Press*). Prominent politicians are invited often. At election time, these programs become "events" and can have an influence on the momentum of a campaign. Robert Kennedy agreed to appear on *Meet the Press* during his 1964 New York senatorial campaign only after careful thought and preparation. He followed closely the standards set by the late President in schooling himself for such an appearance. The day before the program, Kennedy spent several hours on the lawn of Gracie Mansion, the official residence of New York's then Democratic Mayor, Robert Wagner, with a group of advisers. Arthur Schlesinger, Jr., flew in from Washington to join the others in throwing at the candidate every hostile and tricky question they could think of.

Programs of this nature have an important built-in advantage for politicians in that the panels of questioners tend to protect them as much as they expose them. Competition among members of the panel each to shine with his own favorite questions may prevent any searching pursuit of a subject. *Meet the Press,* in particular, often conveys the impression that it is being much tougher with its interviewees than is the case. Any skilled politician knows how to exploit this appearance of being under attack and gain audience sympathy. In March, 1968, two days after his announcement that he was entering the Presidential race, Robert Kennedy again appeared on *Meet the Press.* His motives at the time were being severely questioned. By repeatedly diverting the discussion away from the harm he might do to Eugene McCarthy and by advertising his wider concern for the fate of the country, Kennedy probably helped to make his candidacy more acceptable.

These interview programs may not be good exposure for a candidate who is too exhausted from campaigning to bring a fresh mind to the studio. One of the incidents most harmful to Senator Goldwater occurred in May, 1964, shortly before the California primary, where victory was thought to be crucial to his nomination. Appearing on *Issues and Answers,* he seemed to suggest that atomic weapons could be used to defoliate the jungle trails used by the Communists in Vietnam. At least, that was the way the Associated Press interpreted Goldwater in a bulletin flashed to every radio, television and newspaper office around the country a few minutes after his appearance. That was the last thing Goldwater should have been saying, from a point of view of campaign tactics. His opponent in California, Governor Rockefeller, had kept Goldwater on the defensive on "the bomb" issue all year. A major effort of Goldwater's California campaign was to escape from that issue while reassuring people that he did not have an itchy trigger finger for nuclear weapons. As soon as they heard of the Associated Press version, Goldwater's press people quickly produced the full text, but the operative sentences were ambiguous enough to keep reporters seeking clarification for the next two weeks.

"There have been several suggestions made," Goldwater had told Howard K. Smith on the program. "I don't think that we would use any of them. But defoliation of the forests by low-yield atomic weapons might well be done."

However valuable such nationwide exposure may be, it is quite possible to turn it to disadvantage if the candidate does not and his managers do not approach it with care and preparation.

In 1960, forty-four editions of these three network interview programs were devoted to politics, thirteen of them in the final two weeks. In 1964, there were twenty-eight during the campaign. At thirty minutes a program, that adds up to a great deal of free television time for the candidates, or supporters, who can use them well.

In addition, the networks mount a number of political news specials and documentaries in election years, in which politicians in prominent races are covered. Like regular news programs, they have the advantage of giving the politician wide exposure in a context not manufactured by his own publicity apparatus. For the most part, a candidate is treated gently on such programs because television does not usually consider itself as free as newspapers to put politicians under too searching or unfavorable a spotlight. Even when television has decided, because of the personality of the reporter or producer, to attempt a deeper analysis of a man, time limitations work against it. Campaign specials tend to be compendia, surveys of a group of candidates, with five or seven minutes devoted to each race in a series. Often that is simply not enough time to be thorough.

Herbert Mitgang, a journalist who returned to the *New York Times* in 1967 after several years with CBS News, has said: "I can't think of one profile either of a general nature or of a national political figure that really stripped away the sham and allowed the correspondent to be as outspoken as Reston and Wicker [two *Times* columnists] are in the press."[3] Mitgang further said that at

CBS "the attitude on political documentaries was always not to jab the guy—it was never to go as far as any of the writers like Kraft or Lippmann would go."

In an effort to acquire even more sympathetic free exposure, national political figures have frequently accepted invitations to appear on completely nonpolitical programs. Richard Nixon was interviewed on *Open End* by David Susskind for nearly four continuous hours in May, 1960. Susskind asked the friendliest of questions to stimulate his subject to reveal himself. For a seasoned politician willing to relax, it is an opportunity to present himself in the most favorable light. Some entertainment programs, such as NBC's *Tonight,* with Johnny Carson, the *Merv Griffin Show* and others, use big political names to give prestige to their operations and for that reason go out of their way not to embarrass the illustrious guest. If veterans like Hubert Humphrey *are* embarrassed by being so cloyingly interviewed on these occasions, they have the good sense not to show it. Such shows do not fall within the category of programs exempt from the Equal Time ruling, however, so politicians are invited only before they have actually declared themselves candidates for office. Still, their supporters can continue to appear right up to election day. In 1952, the Eisenhower-Nixon forces estimated that appearances on such programs as *Junior Press Conference of the Air* and the *Kate Smith Show* by speakers favorable to their candidates were worth a million dollars in television time.

Such attention from the media, especially television, does not happen accidentally. A politician determined to exploit it can do so by cultivating the right people and by making news. Robert Kennedy was able to hook all the national media simply by shooting rapids in a rubber dinghy or climbing a mountain. If you are a lesser luminary, the effort is greater but the technique is the same. It consists in being active, making provocative suggestions, challenging the White House, going on foreign trips, investigating and criticizing. Whatever it is you do, you must unashamedly cause it to be publicized beforehand (to create suspense), while you are doing it (to report the event that all the suspense led up to), and afterward (to feed curiosity about the event everyone is discussing).

In New York, any candidate could get several television crews out at the crack of dawn because it was traditional to open campaigns with an early morning exchange of pleasantries at the now removed Fulton Fish Market. President Johnson, who is very adept at stimulating the mass media, merely has to embark on marathon walking press conferences. Senator Everett Dirksen tweaks his gray curls into a pompadour and growls mellifluously, but never begins the performance until every network camera is in position. Other senators ask interminable questions of hearings witnesses who have already answered them in their opening statements. Lady Bird Johnson formally inaugurates a dam that has survived, uninaugurated, for a generation.

The only politician I ever saw balk at an opportunity to gladden the national heart by an appearance on the television screens was President Kennedy. Shortly before the President was killed, representatives of the nation's turkey raisers had turned up in the White House Rose Garden for the traditional presentation of the Thanksgiving turkey at the White House. The President was so acutely embarrassed by the tawdry commercialism of the occasion that he delivered only the minimum courtesies and refused to be photographed with the turkey.

It is a matter of style and sophistication whether you willingly make small talk with turkey growers or don't. But an ability to attract publicity, always a prerequisite for political success, is the key to much free exposure on television.

News is what the market will bear.

In theory at least, the medium still retains editorial control over politicians appearing without charge in its news programs. But a much greater part of political campaigning on television today consists of advertising, with which the industry only rarely interferes. The greatest medium for democratic political communication is increasingly dominated by the huckster.

The morality of the new politics

If a television commercial makes you like the image of one brand of toothpaste enough to buy a tube, it is no great matter if you find you don't like the stuff after all. You can quickly revert to the brand you like. If a television commercial makes you like the image of a politician, it may be six years before you can change him and he is next to impossible to throw away.

For one brand of toothpaste, commercials showed an attractive and concerned young mother going to the local library for information on a dentifrice her kiddies should brush with. By one of those miracles that abound in TV land, the librarian happened to have the very information right at her elbow and Mrs. America departed much relieved. The purpose of the commercial, of course, was not to provoke the rest of us to go to the library to do research on toothpaste, but rather to save us the trouble. All the information, direction and reassurance we needed had been distilled into that sixty-second film drama.

That is precisely what happens in political commercials, which are intended to influence us vividly and emotionally in as short a time as possible. They imply that the ingredients of a political decision can be encapsulated like the ingredients of any trivial commercial decision. They reduce the complexities of public life to a formula cunningly devised to cure everything.

They are so indefensible by any criterion of public service that politicians do not even pretend otherwise.

It probably would not matter if political commercials had continued to occupy only a small part of the political campaign time on television. But in terms of money, air time and creative energy, the political commercial is now forcing other forms of political television off the air. In some recent campaigns it has virtually taken over all television time bought for the candidates.

The recognition that political candidates can be mass marketed like consumer products has led politicians to the proposition that persuasiveness equals truth. A product is good because it is well sold. A man will make a good governor because his campaign is clever. We are conditioned to expect large doses of half-truth and deceit in business advertising. We also expect a good deal of exaggeration and deceit from politicians. But if their attempts to persuade us are increasingly going to be fitted into a commercial formula that almost *requires* deceit and half-truth, our political life can only degenerate.

The mass marketing ideas that politicians have adopted bring with them another danger. Advertisers about to market a product try to find out two basic things—what the public wants and what the public can be induced to accept. Applied to politics and elevated to the highest levels of campaign strategy, such an approach turns the political function on its head. Whatever they may pretend, candidates will no longer offer themselves as leaders but as followers. Since what they follow will be the common denominator of what their polls tell them the public wants, the result is a perversion of the political role. Of course, some politicians have always used this approach, but before this decade they never had at their command powerful devices such as the television-advertising industry has given them.

So far there has been little organized complaint about what is happening. It is true that the occasional losing politician complains about the distortions and half-truths of his opponent's commercials. What worries most politicians is what the new developments are costing. President Johnson and other elected officials have devised interesting proposals to meet the cost with public money, but they are not asking how the money is to be spent. Since the techniques under discussion have been widely used in their own campaigns, that is not surprising. Nor is the television industry leading any crusade against this manner of using the medium. Broadcasters are quite happy with the trend. Short spots keep the politicians happy, do not annoy audiences by interrupting their entertainment, and make money.

Nevertheless, some isolated voices of protest have been raised. Here are some from various professions:

This development can only have the worst possible effect in degrading the level and character of our political discourse. If it continues, the result will be the vulgarization of issues, the exaltation of the immediately ingratiating personality and, in general, an orgy of electronic demagoguery. You cannot merchandise candidates like soap and hope to preserve a rational democracy.
—Arthur Schlesinger, Jr., historian[4]

There doesn't seem to be a safe approach to taking a position on the use of television commercials during campaigns, so why equivocate?

As a voter, I resent them. As a citizen, they alarm me, and as the president and founder of an advertising agency, I do not believe advertising agencies should accept such assignments.

—Carl Ally[5]

The dominant goal of political broadcasts paid for by a political party is obviously the promotion of a candidate, not the enlightenment of the voter. This promotion takes its very worst form in the thirty-second or one-minute commercial where political issues are so oversimplified or ignored that the voter is given no information or, worse, misleading information.

—Elmer Lower, President, ABC News, and
Samuel L. Becker, political scientist[6]

It would require a carefully organized and well-financed study, probably lasting a number of years, to determine precisely what effect political commercials are having. Until such a study is undertaken, it is very hard to argue that the effect is a good one. Most people who stop to think about it conclude that the effect is bad.

Another possibility sometimes raised to explain the complacency about this shaping of our political life is that commercials do not have much effect and are therefore not a cause for alarm. This argument is based on the idea that voters are more sensible than advertisers assume and that they absorb all commercials through a critical filter. The argument is demonstrably untrue in consumer marketing. Large corporations do not spend hundreds of millions of dollars a year with advertising agencies and the television networks without some proof of results. Could politicians be throwing away the bulk of their campaign funds on an illusion? They and their advertising experts believe that political commercials are worth the huge cost of surveying and research, production and air time that they now represent.

Richard Nixon, one of the first to realize the full potentialities of television for politicians, was at first not entirely comfortable exploiting the opportunities. According to Carroll Newton, Nixon did not want his 1960 campaign to be associated with a large Madison Avenue firm. Accordingly, he asked the management of

BBDO to permit Newton to set up a separate organization. They called it Campaign Associates and located it, at Nixon's insistence, on nearby Vanderbilt Avenue to get away from the Madison Avenue image.

Because he looked upon the press as an enemy, Nixon desired to use television to reach the people. Newton and Nixon's personal TV adviser, Ted Rogers, worked out the details of a television campaign that would introduce two new concepts: getting the candidate away from the old style of talking directly into the camera, and making more use of films constructed so as to show an appealing image. One film was to be called "Khrushchev as I Know Him" and would portray the Vice-President traveling abroad in defense of democracy and clashing with Khrushchev in the famous Kitchen Debate. The other new concept was to shape the TV campaign into a crescendo of impact just at the end, to exploit a fresh interpretation of American election behavior coupled with the marketing techniques of mass advertising. Carroll Newton's explanation[7] of this theory is worth reproducing at some length because it is the basis of all the thoroughgoing TV-admass campaigns of the present.

Most products, Newton said, are marketed in a few very simple steps. They are developed and tested in homes in so-called blind tests. Then the research people find out what the people liked about the product and the advertising agency develops its strategy from that. Newton added: "I see nothing wrong in following this kind of a process with a political candidate. You go around and interview people, discuss the candidate, find out what they like and what they don't and develop emphasis (i.e., emphasize certain issues) based on this kind of research."

Surveys showed there was one group of people, one-third of the electorate at the most, who were vitally interested and who followed the campaign in newspapers and magazines as well as on television. Then there were varying degrees of interest down to almost complete indifference. "We find that it is the people who are quite indifferent who get almost all their news and impressions of the campaign from television because it comes on and because it requires a positive action to get away from it. People who will not take the positive action to read a story will sit and listen to something if it is not too long. We used a lot of five-minute segments in 1956. You are not directing a mass media campaign at the informed voter," Newton said.

Research into election behavior showed that 60 to 65 percent of the electorate had roots deep in one party or the other and made up their minds as soon as they learned who the candidate was unless there was some strong personal prejudice against him. Then there was another 10 to 15 percent who gradually made up their minds in the course of the campaign. There was a final group of people who did not make up their minds until the last few days. They considered themselves open-minded until the last.

That analysis was responsible for the strategy attempted in Nixon's campaign. Newton went on: "We set out the financial requirement and started with the night before election day and worked backwards to less and less activity, with a burst when the campaign gets underway. A really mass saturation campaign would have everybody fed to the teeth and have the opposite result it is designed to have. You can give people too much. There is initial interest and then the curve of interest drops. But it is important for the candidate to make sure that he has at least equal exposure in the public mind."

Following this strategy, Newton said, Campaign Associates spent between $3.5 and $4 million (out of total estimated Republican expenditure on the Presidential campaign of $11.3 million).*

One unexpected element was a decision only four days before the election to put Nixon on the air for an extended telethon the afternoon before the election. It strained the fund-raising abilities of the GOP to produce the money (estimated from $2 to $6-million) which it cost to go on the ABC network for four solid hours, answering questions phoned in. Theodore White called it "the most expensive and probably the most effective burst of television electioneering since the medium invaded American cul-

---

* Official reports of campaign expenditures are always the result of imaginative bookkeeping after the fact. While Newton admits spending up to $4 million through Campaign Associates, the official GOP figure for what the agency spent was $2,269,578.

ture."[8] The telethon climaxed a Republican television blitz in the last week of the campaign featuring a fifteen-minute program with Nixon at 7:00 P.M. every night, in addition to spot commercials. In effect, the impact of this campaign was somewhat old-fashioned. Much of the time went to appearances by the candidates or their supporters speaking, and not to pieces using the image-building skills of the film-maker. In conception, though, the campaign use of television was quite up-to-date.

What sabotaged it, from the strategists' point of view, was Nixon's hesitancy in giving wholehearted approval to their plans and his decision to debate with Kennedy. As we have seen, he had promised he would not debate, and the image he projected in the debates undid their efforts to sell a different image. Newton says: "Many more people vote on an emotional basis than through a process of cerebration. The appearance and character that a man projects in front of that dirty hole is quite crucial. You head for disaster if you try to project something different from your own character. Ike projected his and people warmed to it. Stevenson did and they did not warm. Nixon projected his and a friend said he looked like an earnest undertaker."

As we have seen, left to himself in front of a TV camera, a politician can *only* project his own character unless he is a skilled actor. But modern techniques can doctor that character and present those facets likely to be most ingratiating, if the candidate will leave the work to the experts.

Nixon's unwillingness to leave the campaign to celluloid image-making is typical of the ambivalence of sophisticated politicians toward the new devices. They hesitate to put their fate completely in the hands of opinion manipulators. On the one hand, many fear the opprobrium of being "marketed"; on the other, they increasingly respect the evidence that marketing can work. Their feeling about opinion polls, which are an essential part of this process, used to be the same. For years politicians had a healthy skepticism about pollsters, especially after Harry Truman's experience in 1948, which was the classic example of how wrong polls could be. But polling techniques have been much refined in the twenty years since Truman upset them. Moreover, politicians have discovered that what is most important to campaign strategy is not what the pollsters say about who is ahead or behind, but what the voters feel about the issues. In a well-run campaign, the issues-and-attitude surveys are now essential to organizing overall strategy at the beginning and to guiding tactical decisions as the campaign progresses.

Let us look at one detail of John F. Kennedy's beautifully run campaign to see how closely a pollster worked in harness with the candidate in day-to-day tactics.

West Virginia's Democratic primary was pivotal in Kennedy's efforts to secure the Democratic nomination. In West Virginia, he decided to tackle the issue of his Catholic religion openly, and there he knocked Hubert Humphrey out of the running. Theodore White records that Kennedy had used Louis Harris as early as 1958 to take a survey for him in largely Protestant West Virginia. It was the first sounding outside his home state of Massachusetts of what sentiment might be for his candidacy two years later. In December, 1959, Harris took another sample and discovered that Kennedy was a 70-to-30 favorite over Humphrey. But by late spring, the issue of religion, brought to national prominence by the attention Kennedy received for his Wisconsin victory over Humphrey, left the outcome in doubt.

According to White, most of the Kennedy staff thought that the issue was too explosive to raise in public, but Louis Harris believed on the basis of his latest soundings that it had to be met openly and wiped out of the voters' consciousness as an issue. Kennedy in the end agreed with Harris.

The vehicle chosen for this delicate and possibly fatal exercise was a Sunday-night paid telecast in which the candidate was questioned about his religion by Franklin D. Roosevelt, Jr. The program lasted half an hour and is described by White as "the finest TV broadcast I have ever heard any political candidate make." Kennedy assured West Virginians that he was as dedicated to the Constitutional separation of church and state as any Protestant.

This device was backed up with a campaign film (described as a "documentary") that was a model of image construction. Carefully selected footage evoked the war hero, the thoughtful author of a Pulitzer Prize-winning book, the family man, and ended with

Kennedy's own statement about the separation of church and state. The film was broadcast repeatedly on West Virginia TV stations. Harris took surveys on a day-to-day basis and found sentiment swinging to Kennedy even in the most die-hard areas of the state. This effort became a prototype in campaign procedure, and was followed closely by Kennedy's brothers and other politicians in later campaigns. It required three things: accurate polling by a pollster who was trusted and followed by the strategists; a willingness to use TV production and air time extensively for films designed to spread a particular image of the candidate; and especially the money to pay for it, which Kennedy certainly did not lack. Official records, which may not tell the whole story, show that he outspent Humphrey four to one ($100,000 to $23,000) in West Virginia.

Humphrey's campaign, by contrast, became a much-quoted example of how the new techniques can crush a candidate who cannot put together the right ingredients. In Humphrey's case it was not only money that was lacking, but professional advice on how to use television. In a last desperate fling to turn the tide, Humphrey bought time for an evening telethon. Telethons, which had been used as far back as 1950, required stage management, to filter out embarrassing questions and keep the program moving. Humphrey had no professional staff to make the program work. He went unassisted before the television audience of West Virginia with only two telephones and no intermediaries. The unscreened questions were predictably embarrassing and prevented him from making telling points. The effect was comic but sad.

Which of the many elements of John Kennedy's assault on West Virginia was decisive in his victory is impossible to say. Harris' findings in the last day before the election suggest that it was the double-pronged television campaign that turned opinion Kennedy's way. This effort was supported, it should be remembered, by an impressive array of Kennedy friends and relations working the state for him, by an organization that penetrated to every courthouse, and by the candidate's own personal campaigning.

Since, in the course of this description of televised image-making and its effect on democratic politics, there is much to report that is disturbing, we should note that Kennedy used the techniques to convey impressions that had a substantial basis of truth. He was a genuine war hero and there was nothing deceitful in using a film to remind people of that. Whether from devotion to the Constitution or political expediency, Kennedy did firmly believe that he was an American first and a Roman Catholic second. He *had* written a Pulitzer Prize-winning book, *Profiles in Courage,* and proved his authorship when others claimed it was ghostwritten. The image presented in the skillfully edited "documentary" films was not constructed out of nothing, but was the truth, suitably dramatized and embellished to give it impact.

What disturbs many people about the new techniques of marketing a candidate is that nonachievements can be projected almost as effectively as real ones and an impression of experience and qualification can be constructed that has little basis in fact. To many observers that was the case when John Kennedy's campaign techniques were borrowed, as we have seen, by Edward Kennedy two years later.

Experience was not the issue, however, when Robert Kennedy left the Johnson administration to run for the Senate in New York in 1964. He needed to divert attention from charges that he was carpetbagging, and to dispel the impression that he was ruthless. The way in which the image of ruthlessness was attacked is instructive.

Everywhere he was scheduled to appear, Kennedy deliberately encouraged crowds of children to form around him. He had a naturally warm and easy manner with them. He was filmed, by his own hired camera crews, and by television news teams, as being relaxed and joking. These scenes and others of him answering questions from voters while on the stump were made into commercials by the firm of Papert Koenig Lois. In the view of some of his staff, the qualities of grace and spontaneity they saw in Kennedy in the streets did not always come across in the commercials. Charles Guggenheim made a half-hour campaign film from an appearance by Kennedy at Columbia University. Again rapport with youth was stressed. The film showed a crowded gathering in a gymnasium with Kennedy good-humoredly answering students' questions.

Again, the image-making was the result of extensive polling and analysis to discover which issues were hurting him. It was his showing in the polls that finally convinced Kennedy that he had to bring the debate issue to a head, in the manner already described. It was a complex election, with New York's very large, liberal Jewish vote torn between its traditional attachment to the Democrats and its regard for Keating. In the end, it was thought that the Johnson landslide nationally was of some help to Kennedy, who won by more than 700,000 votes.

At the same time, on the West Coast, Pierre Salinger was employing the Kennedy techniques in his campaign against Alan Cranston in the California Democratic senatorial primary. Salinger's strengths were an ebullient, outgoing personality and a national reputation for his close association with President Kennedy. His weakness was his relative innocence in California politics and possibly too lighthearted an image.

Since he had no organization of his own and in fact had to combat the regular Democratic organization, which backed Cranston, Salinger put more than half of his campaign funds into a campaign of television commercials. One of them, intending to project the image of a man of action, showed a helicopter landing, and Salinger dashing from it. Others worked hard to exploit his association with Kennedy. These commercials saturated the airwaves, giving the voters an image of Salinger as vivacious and energetic in contrast to the drier, more intellectual and older impression which Cranston projected. While the technique worked against Cranston, it could not carry Salinger to victory over screen actor George Murphy.

It was the Presidential election, however, which made 1964 a memorable year in the evolution of commercial techniques for political television.

Early in 1960, plans were drawn up in the Democratic National Committee to spend $400,000 on a campaign of television commercials and cartoons to "cut down" Richard Nixon. None of the potential Democratic nominees would accept the plan, and it was dropped.

The Democratic opportunity to experiment with the medium to

destroy an opponent instead of building up their own candidate came in the Goldwater-Johnson election. The campaign became, at this level, a battle of giant advertising agencies—Doyle Dane Bernbach for President Johnson and the Democrats, the Interpublic Group for Goldwater and the Republicans. There had been a major escalation of the TV battle since 1960. In that year, Kennedy and Nixon forces produced and broadcast 9,000 political commercials during the general election period on television, with 29,000 on radio. In the same period in 1964, there were 29,300 television commercials and 63,000 on radio. Sixty percent of the money spent in the general election period went for spot announcements of a minute or less and only 40 percent was spent on program time.[9]

Neither Johnson nor Goldwater was prepared to submit himself completely to the image-makers. The real ingenuity of 1964 was reserved for offensive warfare.

Early in the year, Richard Kleindienst, one of Goldwater's closest aides, said: "These advertising people just love to get their hands on a guy like this. They treat him like a block of wood, cutting him into the shape they want. Barry just won't put up with that. If it means losing the nomination because he won't adopt the image they want, then he'll lose."[10]

This antagonism between the "Arizona Mafia," including Goldwater himself, and the different public relations and campaign management firms associated with him at various stages persisted throughout the election year. The campaign was constantly making fresh starts, when a new group would convince key aides that the candidate had to stop giving impromptu press conferences, to rely more on taped spots, to gear his speeches more closely to what the polls showed the issues were. Goldwater did grow more amenable to control by the experts after the nomination, but although there were money and experts and techniques in abundance, the campaign was never a fully coordinated event. Those people, like Clif White, who would have been able to draw all the needs together and match them with appropriate techniques were not permitted to be close enough to the central planning to be of use. There was no "masterminding" of the Goldwater campaign.

There was in the Democratic camp, but the mastermind was the President himself. Voracious for polling results (which he often got on the cheap by asking other Democratic candidates to send him duplicates of their soundings), Johnson weighed the issues and waded through the United States of America like a Gulliver trying to grasp the strings of every tiny ship. While he was thus out drawing huge crowds to augment his vast television exposure as the White House incumbent, key aides were plotting gleefully with Doyle Dane Bernbach how to undo Senator Goldwater. What they concocted was some of the most poisonous television advertising ever shown in this country. Two commercials, in particular, were so powerful ("reprehensible," the Republicans said) that each was shown only once.

At 10 P.M. on Monday, September 7, millions of Americans were watching NBC's *Monday Night at the Movies*. There was a break for station identification; then on came a film of a pretty little girl pulling the petals off a daisy and counting them slowly. As she counted, a man's voice came in over hers, also counting: ". . . ten, nine, eight, seven . . ." As he finished, the scene dissolved into the explosion of a nuclear bomb and an announcer's voice urged listeners to support Johnson and the Democratic ticket.

Thousands of people phoned television stations and political headquarters to complain, and they were not all Republicans. The commercial was regarded as a viciously clever attempt to keep alive doubts that had been an issue all year, of Goldwater's trustworthiness with the nation's nuclear arsenal. Goldwater was ultimately responsible for this insecurity. He had suggested in New Hampshire that the Supreme Commander of NATO should be given the power to order the use of nuclear weapons. He had raised the possibility that nuclear weapons could be used to defoliate the Vietnam jungles, although he firmly denied that he was proposing such a course. The doubts his statements inspired were thoroughly exploited by his opponents in the Republican Party and by the Democrats to paint the Senator as a trigger-happy cowboy or a Dr. Strangelove (some posters called him "Strangewater") ready to "shoot from the hip." In fact, when his statements were explained and analyzed, Goldwater was seen as merely expressing the conventional military view that nuclear weapons were just another form of armament and should not be shrouded in emotion and fear. In the Pentagon this was a respectable point of view. To civilian America, emerging from a generation of Cold War anxiety, it was terrifying.

As the protests poured in to Republican (and Democratic) headquarters, the Republican leaders roused themselves to complain. Yet before they did so formally, the Democrats had detonated another commercial that added to the fallout.

On Saturday evening, September 12, the peak prime-time audience just before 11 P.M. saw another little girl, licking an ice cream cone. A warm, tender, protective woman's voice was saying that people used to explode nuclear bombs in the air and that radioactive fallout made children die. But then, the voice went on, there was a treaty banning all the tests in the air, although a man who wanted to be President voted against it. "His name is Barry Goldwater. So if he's elected, they might start testing all over again." Her voice was lost in the frantic clicking of a Geiger counter, as an announcer said: "Vote for President Johnson, November third. The stakes are too high for you to stay at home."

On Monday, September 14, the Republican National Chairman, Dean Burch, wrote to the Fair Campaign Practices Committee, saying he was asking the three television networks to take the spots off the air, "as a matter of common decency." Burch said the daisy spot "represents a new low in American politics and violates the American sense of fair play and good taste." Senator Thruston Morton of Kentucky, who had been Permanent Chairman of the Republican Convention, had the text of the ice cream commercial entered in the *Congressional Record* to record his protest. Robert Kintner, then President of NBC, said the network had carried the two commercials unchanged although many of the affiliate stations were concerned about the content. The Fair Campaign Practices Committee passed all the complaints on to the Democrats and reported later that "the controversial messages were not shown again, even though the Democrats never formally withdrew them."

In the meantime, the Democrats went on showing a number of

other commercials, each in its way as damaging to Goldwater, but not stimulating the same protests.

In one, the screen showed a telephone that rang and rang. A hand reached toward the receiver and then stopped. A solemn voice asked, "Who do *you* want answering the phone when Khrushchev calls?" One showed a pair of hands carefully tearing up a Social Security card, to remind voters that Goldwater was supposedly going to do away with Social Security. The Senator had gone so far as to suggest that Social Security could be made voluntary, although he had never proposed, in 1964 at least, that it be abolished. A particularly pointed commercial showed a number of Rockefeller for President posters lying on a floor, with feet trampling on them. This was directed at those Republicans angered by the treatment Rockefeller and other Republican liberals had received at the San Francisco convention.

There was another, more lighthearted, which pictured a large map of the United States. A saw could be seen cutting off the eastern states, which then floated away. That was to remind people of a remark Goldwater had made in a genially reckless moment in 1961, that "sometimes I think this country would be better off if we could just saw off the Eastern Seaboard and let it float out to sea."

The Republicans had their own surprise film package, but leaked reports of what it contained aroused such a storm that it never got on the air.

It was not a short commercial but a long film entitled *Choice*. It was produced in response to an analysis of the situation that said Goldwater needed to counterattack. The film, produced under cover of an organization describing itself as "Mothers for a Moral America," painted a lurid picture of the Republic under Lyndon Johnson—Negroes rioting in the streets, rampant moral decay typified by girls in topless bathing suits and a man, suggestive of the President, driving a Lincoln Continental and throwing beer cans out the window. (There had been press reports from the LBJ Ranch that the President had driven his Lincoln very fast one day and that someone in it was drinking beer.)

Kintner later said that NBC was prepared to carry the film but had demanded a "few brief deletions of visual material, including the topless bathing suit, a strip tease scene and a magazine cover with the title, 'Jazz Me, Baby!' "[11] Kintner said that he was sufficiently concerned about the "appallingly tasteless production" to draw the attention of Goldwater and the National Committee to the film, which he felt they had not seen. When asked about it, Goldwater told reporters he understood it was "nothing but a racist film" which could incite people to violence, and that he had ordered it not to be shown.

While undeniably clever, there is no doubt that this film and the Daisy and Ice Cream commercials put on by the Democrats all crossed the boundaries of responsibility. They were scurrilous. Each was an attempt to provoke in voters an intense emotional reaction of fear, or disgust, or anger. While milder in tone, some of the other commercials produced by the Democrats were also grossly oversimplified distortions of Goldwater positions. There was at the time an air of levity surrounding the whole question. The commercials were all praised and joked about. Even those who deplored them on ethical grounds would say things like: "Boy, that was a great commercial!"

It is interesting to speculate how much the Daisy and Ice Cream spots benefited from media reinforcement. Each was shown only once, so that only a fraction of the voters were exposed, but they became, by word of mouth and in the press, a major topic of conversation for the whole nation. Even in the process of attacking them, people like Dean Burch and Thruston Morton contributed to spreading the word. They were described again and again, and each time the central message was reinforced. It is possible that even in the most unreceptive minds, the secondary kind of transmission implanted a germ of confidence in the man and the team that could use the mass medium so effectively and ruthlessly.

It is frightening to imagine a national campaign in which there would be a general free-for-all with such commercials. As it was, in 1964, despite the huge volume of short spots, 40 percent of the television time paid for by the parties nationally was used for longer pieces. While they may not have been the finest examples of voter enlightenment, the longer program format usually imposed some restraint. Issues were discussed at length and were not reduced to the emotional sloganeering of the short commercials. Yet the trend was already away from these longer pieces because they failed to attract the huge audiences of the 1950's. President Johnson delightedly revealed privately to some reporters the TV ratings for a program Goldwater did with former President Eisenhower. In an attempt to kill the bomb issue, the Senator videotaped an earnest conversation with Eisenhower at his Gettysburg farm. As such programs go, it was relatively unstilted as the two Republicans draped themselves over fences and sat on Ike's front porch to chat. Although he was personally unhappy about Goldwater's candidacy, Eisenhower was prevailed upon to tell the nation that Barry was not reckless, but a fine, responsible American.

The Nielsen ratings, which Johnson disclosed to newsmen, showed that Ike and Barry had a rating of 8.6, compared to 27.4 for *Petticoat Junction* and 25.0 for *Peyton Place,* which ran at the same time.

By the time the nation had pulled itself together for another general election for Governors, Senators and Congressmen in 1966, the short political commercial had taken an even firmer hold on American political life.

A product like Alka-Seltzer

By the spring of 1966, New York State had apparently had more than enough of Rockefeller. Three things had decimated his political support; his divorce and remarriage; his two unsuccessful attempts to use the state as a springboard into the White House; and his broken promises not to raise taxes. The last of the three was the "gut issue" in 1966. Four years earlier, Rockefeller had promised the people of New York no tax increases for four years. But his programs required heavy state aid, and to finance them he secured enactment of the state's first sales tax, of 2 percent. Coupled with municipal taxes, it meant that people living in New York City, for example, had to pay a total sales tax of 5 percent. It came to be known as the "5 percent for the Governor." Rockefeller later said that campaign promise was "the big blooper I made in politics. I had to swallow my words and I felt very badly about it."

So did the voters. By early 1966, the polls showed that the number of people who gave the Governor a favorable rating had shrunk to 25 percent of the electorate. He was advised not to attempt a third term. However, at fifty-seven, Rockefeller retained the energy and ambition of a much younger man. To give up the governorship would have meant abandoning all national aspirations, and few people believed he had done so. He also loved campaigning. "It's like jumping into a chilly swimming pool," Rockefeller once said. "It's a shock at first but as soon as you get used to it, it's the most exhilarating thing in the world."

Running his campaign machine was William J. Pfeiffer, a man of wide political experience who had begun working on the 1966 campaign immediately after Rockefeller's Presidential hopes had died in 1964.

Pfeiffer says they considered many advertising agencies before finally deciding on Jack Tinker Associates. "They impressed us with their handling of Alka-Seltzer. Who would try to popularize Alka-Seltzer?"[12] Tinker had, and when the Rockefeller organization checked, they found that Alka-Seltzer sales had substantially improved. So the task of refurbishing the tarnished image of the Governor was handed to that agency, which had also persuaded Braniff Airlines to paint each jet in its fleet a different violent color.

"We looked at the Governor almost as though he were a product like Alka-Seltzer," the firm's Managing Partner, Myron McDonald,[13] told me. "As a personality he was well known. There was no hay to be made in publicizing his political life or personal. Some thought he should explain why he got divorced, etc. We said no. So the strategy was to run not the Governor but the Governor's record. Our strategy was to start early enough with serenely innocent commercials; to look at the record and allow a gentle rain of persuasion to fall rather than to make a big splash at the last minute."

It is interesting to note that Tinker's approach was the reverse of Napolitan's in Pennsylvania, where everything was gambled on the final big splash to win for Milton Shapp.

Tinker believed it was easier to form a new opinion than to change an existing one. McDonald said: "It is true of products when opinions are objective but in the emotional arena of politics it is specially true. We did not try to change the image of Rockefeller the man, but to form a new opinion of his politics with commercials that were so unpolitical that people thought they were probably sincere."

The campaign was broken down into three phases. The first was to remake the public's impression of the Governor's record. "We had to sell the record," Pfeiffer said, "associate it with the Governor. And it had to be done so subtly it crept up on you before you knew what the hell had happened to you."

The points to be emphasized were decided not by the advertising agency alone, but in conjunction with Rockefeller's chief issues man, Dr. William J. Ronan, former Dean of the Graduate School of Public Administration and Social Services at New York University and now head of the Metropolitan Transportation Authority.

Tinker assigned two complete production units to the task. They isolated five subjects, based on Ronan's research, and made thirty-two initial commercials on health, education, crime, road building and politics.

The spots began running on July 5 according to a schedule designed to saturate twenty-two of New York's sixty-two counties where 87 percent of the state's registered voters lived. If a selling campaign is to reach every member of the television audience at least once in a week, the term used is "100 rating points." In the initial phase the Rockefeller commercials were given 150 rating points, or 50 percent more exposure than was theoretically needed to reach the entire audience. That meant running a total of thirty-seven commercials a week on six New York City stations. In five upstate communities with stations serving the remainder of the twenty-two heavily populated counties (Albany, Binghamton, Buffalo, Rochester and Syracuse), eighteen commercials were run every week in phase one. Before the Republican Party met in convention to approve Rockefeller's renomination, the commercials had been shown more than seven hundred times.

They made heavy use of polls. According to Pfeiffer: "Polls cost very little and if used constantly are fantastically accurate. We polled to the last day. We tried to find out what people were concerned about rather than the standing of the candidates."

The polls showed that Rockefeller was most vulnerable on the 2 percent sales tax. "We decided to hit the issue head on," Pfeiffer said. "When you can't run away from something like that, you try to turn it around and make it work for you."

By showing the voters what had been done with the money raised by unpopular taxes, Rockefeller hoped to show that most of the revenue went back to the taxpayers. The TV commercials implied this, but the detailed explanation was left to the Governor himself in his appearances around the state.

The commercials were all memorable examples of the art.

Water pollution: On the screen a puppet in the form of a fish appears and is approached by a hand wearing a hat labeled PRESS, and carrying a microphone. The fish is very bored by the interview which follows.

REPORTER: You, sir.
FISH: Uh huh?
REPORTER: How do you feel about Governor Rockefeller's Pure Waters program?
FISH: His pure what?
REPORTER: Pure waters.
FISH: Oh, oh yeah.
REPORTER: This program, sir, is wiping out water pollution in New York within six years.
FISH: Well, it was pretty smelly down here.

Roads: The viewer is looking at a road as if from the front of a moving car. All he hears is the sound of the car engine as he sees the broken center white line winding by. A voice says conversationally: "If you took all the roads Governor Rockefeller has built, and all the roads he's widened and straightened and smoothed out; if you took all those roads and laid them end to end, they'd stretch all the way to Hawaii." The road ends and the car moves onto sand. There is the sound of surf and Hawaiian music. The car reverses and drives back onto the road, as the voice says: "All the way to Hawaii and all the way back."

Clean air: A man is seated looking at the camera, with his mouth and the fingers of both hands stuffed with cigarettes. A voice says: "You're looking at one day's supply of good old New York City air. Just breathe for twenty-four hours and you get what you'd get from two packs of cigarettes every day. The Governor of New York doesn't want you inhaling that kind of air. Governor Rockefeller has called for air pollution devices on all cars and trucks by 1968 models—and that will help." A hand reaches in and removes all the cigarettes from one hand of the man on the screen. The voice goes on: "He has signed a new law that gives tax incentives to factories that restrict pollution [the hand removes the cigarettes from the other hand]—and that will help. Line for line his air pollution bill is the strongest in the United States [all the cigarettes from the man's mouth are removed]—and that will help. [The man smiles.] Four more years for the Governor, and New York could break the air pollution habit for good. Four years of somebody else [the man frowns and coughs] and who knows?"

Superimposed over the picture at the end is the message: "Governor Rockefeller for Governor. A paid political announcement by Friends of the Rockefeller Team."

Education: Half a dozen kids of various races are playing pick-up basketball in a lower-class neighborhood. Five of them are fast and smooth, but there is one short, fat kid who is so inept he is never given the ball. The camera singles him out, the music fades under and the announcer says: "Hey, kid. Want to go to college? Maybe you could catch the eye of some coach, get yourself a scholarship. No, you don't have to be nine feet tall to get a scholarship, or a blooming genius either. Why, if you can get *into* college, you can get the money to help you *go* to college. From New York State. Two hundred thousand new state scholarships are sitting there waiting, every year, even for you, shorty . . . tubby . . . butterfingers. The man who did it, the man responsible for those new scholarships, is Governor Rockefeller. Who was no Bob Cousy himself."

Crime in the streets: A police car cruises down a silent, dark street with its lights flashing. Then you hear the sound of someone walking alone. A voice says: "If you walk home at night, or if there's a teen-ager in your family, you should be worried. Governor Rockefeller's worried. As much as half the crime in New York is caused by addicts. That's why the Governor has sponsored a tough new law that can get addicts off the street for up to three years."

The voice in all these spots was that of Edward Binns, a voice millions of Americans hear on television every day talking about various products. It is a neighborly, reassuring voice.

The commercials were designed to cover aspects of the record that Tinker felt would not be given free coverage in the news. McDonald said: "We tried to cover things that were noncontroversial. We were just trying to be persuasive."

Old-line people in the Republican Party were skeptical. Many of them felt Rockefeller was too weak in the polls to be running for reelection. His campaign organization gathered a group of county chairmen one day and showed them twenty-three of the Tinker commercials. Afterward, they came up and said, "You know, Rockefeller's a pretty good man!"

McDonald spelled out further his ideas on how to be persuasive. "We find in selling products all the time the first thing is to find out what the people know. You must really find out what they know, and then you can find out what they can be made to believe, not what you want them to believe. You must form a common denominator of belief and ignorance. . . . You operate on two levels, visceral and intellectual, and visceral may be more important than the intellectual. We were directing more to the visceral."

The TV image-building was intended to be supplemented by news coverage of the Governor during his energetic campaigning. In each place, whether he was asked about it or not, Rockefeller would launch into an explanation of how sales tax revenue went back to the local communities as state aid to education and so on. His researchers had provided him with fact sheets containing figures appropriate to each community. He could thus say, in Elmira, that without the sales tax, local property taxes would have been much higher to pay for improvements in education. Television news crews, as well as the local newspapers, picked these up.

In the second and third phases of the campaign, the spirit grew more ruthless. The second phase was designed to draw attention to a lack of stature on the part of the Governor's opponents (it was a four-way race) and the third phase, to zero in on the Democratic candidate, Frank O'Connor.

As soon as O'Connor had been nominated, after a fight at the Democratic Convention in August, the rate at which the Rockefeller commercials were aired was doubled. Fifty to sixty commercials were shown in New York City every week from the beginning of September to the end of the campaign.

The same gentle commercials continued to run, but were interspersed gradually with attacks on O'Connor, in new commercials which unloaded their messages in ten or twenty seconds.

James M. Perry of the *National Observer* said that at this point the commercials became clear distortions, and he gave two examples.[14]

One script said: "Frank O'Connor, the man who led the fight against the New York Thruway, is running for Governor. Get in your car. Drive down to the polls and vote." In fact, what Frank O'Connor, then a state legislator, *had* opposed was the Republican-backed toll road. O'Connor and the Democrats in Albany wanted a free road.

Another commercial near the end of the campaign said: "Frank O'Connor from New York City is running for Governor. He says the New York subways should be free. Guess who he thinks should pay for them." That commercial was run only in upstate New York, not in the city. O'Connor had never made any such proposal but was, in Perry's words, "musing about long-term goals."

The most *emotional* issue of the campaign, all the news people thought, was crime, especially in New York City. That was because the election coincided with an effort by New York Mayor John Lindsay to bring the city's large police department under the supervision of a Review Board dominated by civilians. The idea was to give fairer hearings to Negro and Puerto Rican charges that the heavily-white force discriminated against minority groups. The Policemen's Benevolent Association fought hard against the proposal, managing to get the issue placed on the ballot for a referendum. They ran a saturation campaign of lurid TV commercials and newspaper ads suggesting that the Civilian Review Board would emasculate the police force. For example, in one advertisement they showed a pretty girl walking down a dark street at night. The copy suggested that the Board would prevent police from protecting her from "the addict, the criminal, the hoodlum." The police campaign against the Board took several nasty turns, with cases arising of pro-Board demonstrators being arrested or intimidated. It was even charged that "Communism and Communists are somewhere mixed up in this fight." But the basic appeal of the campaign was blatantly racist.

The issue surveys being quietly taken by Rockefeller and others showed, however, that crime was an issue very far down the list of priorities for most of the voters of the state. Rockefeller's own polls and the identity of the pollster were kept secret. But a survey similar to his taken by Oliver Quayle and Company for the National Broadcasting Company showed that taxes, not crime, were what bothered most voters. In September, Quayle found that 26 percent of all voters thought taxes were too high and that Rockefeller should not have raised them. Fewer than 1 percent thought he had not done enough to reduce crime. That was obviously viewed as primarily a city responsibility.

Knowing this, the Rockefeller campaign nevertheless zeroed in on the crime issue, hoping perhaps to pick up votes in New York City and to smear Democrat O'Connor, who was City Council President in Lindsay's administration. O'Connor, with backing from Democratic Senator Robert Kennedy, supported the Civilian Review Board. Rockefeller stayed away from the issue.

The Governor touched a special chord among certain groups of city voters with his program for control of narcotics. This was a drastic proposal, to get addicts off the streets by making it legal to force them to be treated. O'Connor attacked the program as unworkable and disturbing to liberals concerned with civil liberties.

In the last stages of the campaign, Tinker produced quick commercials on videotape. One showed an empty table on which a hand laid down one by one the implements used by a drug addict —the powder, spoon, a hypodermic—and then in the same row, a gun, a knife and brass knuckles. Then, as a voice explained the Rockefeller program to reduce crime by getting addicts off the streets, the hand picked up all the implements until the table was again bare.

Finally, after being carefully withheld, the Governor himself appeared in short commercials, saying: "If you want to keep crime rates high, O'Connor is your man."

The polls showed a dramatic response. In September, only 36 percent of the voters viewed Rockefeller favorably, but by October it was 50 percent, a progress Quayle described as "nothing short of a miraculous comeback."

Rockefeller was helped immeasurably by the picture of confusion and ineptitude in the Democratic camp. The O'Connor candidacy, decided at a convention in which Senator Kennedy, the state's leading Democrat, did not get his way, left the party split. Franklin D. Roosevelt, Jr., was defeated for the nomination and decided to run as the Liberal Party candidate. This siphoned off much Democratic support in New York City and caused traditional sources of money to dry up. Moreover, the campaign organization O'Connor put together was an unwieldy troika, with representatives of Robert Kennedy, the regular state Democrats and O'Connor's own cronies from Queens often pulling different ways. Although Kennedy's highly experienced brother-in-law Stephen Smith became overall coordinator, his people were dismayed by what they regarded as the amateurishness of the O'Connor people. They, on the other hand, considered that the Kennedy people were just paying lip service to O'Connor and suspected that Kennedy had motives for not wanting a Democratic Governor as a rival for power in the state. O'Connor's chief press aide, Harry O'Donnell, said later: "In the end Kennedy campaigned but he was just going through the motions."[15]

The dismayed Kennedy advisers, meanwhile, were saying to the O'Connor people: "You fellows are so gentlemanly about this campaign. Why don't you get nasty? Make charges!" Getting nasty was not O'Connor's style. During the campaign he told me: "I don't go in for all the gimmicks, all this artificial business. I don't think people like it. Maybe I'm too sensitive for a guy in this business. But I just think there are better ways to campaign."

Mutual suspicion continued throughout the campaign and

weakened its effectiveness. The New York City Democrats, who did cut an old-fashioned figure, were no match for the Rockefeller organization.

They were also desperately short of money. Late in the campaign, when Governor Rockefeller *admitted* spending $4.3 million, the most the O'Connor forces could boast was $278,000. Naturally, they spent a lot of time charging that Rockefeller was buying the election, but that did not help. When the Democrats did attempt some TV commercials, these were too late and too sparsely shown to be of use.

The press, including television, always tends to be more sympathetic to politicians who act professionally and know their business. Stories abounded of O'Connor misfortunes. In one, his advertising managers took the candidate to a dirty street in Harlem to film some commercials intended to reveal Rockefeller's neglect of the ghetto. He sat on the steps of a crumbling tenement and said his piece. But the film had to be thrown away, because a screening showed clearly visible just over O'Connor's shoulder a filthy word chalked on the house. O'Donnell said: "Our TV stuff just blew up from poor production."

Looking back on the campaign, O'Connor praised the professionalism of Rockefeller's television material. But he said that his own personal reaction had been that the Tinker commercials would not have an impact, that "people would see through them."[16]

"I had always used TV and we planned as much as funds would permit," O'Connor said, "but I never thought that the American public would buy a campaign sold like soap or corn flakes." He was not so philosophical about it during the heat of the campaign, and accused Rockefeller of conducting a "massive brainwashing" of the electorate by "bombarding it with television advertising."

Roosevelt complained "that there is something fundamentally wrong with a system that places candidates who cannot pour millions into television at a fundamental disadvantage."

There was some question about how faithfully the Rockefeller commercial campaign mirrored the truth. O'Donnell for the Democrats said bluntly that it was an "absolute fabrication" of Rockefeller's achievements. It was not that—Rockefeller *had* doubled aid to local schools, trebled university enrollment, built or rehabilitated 10,600 miles of highways (enough to go to Hawaii and back), pushed through the nation's most generous state Medicaid bill, raised the minimum wage and tackled water pollution. However, there was something in the Democratic charge that much of this had been done suspiciously close to the election, when Rockefeller turned his energies from national campaigning to state matters.

Ethical questions aside, the Rockefeller campaign was an impressive display of techniques. Whereas Milton Shapp's primary campaign in Pennsylvania showed the extraordinary potency of a last-minute blitz for a candidate who is unknown, Rockefeller's demonstrated the power of a long, low-key saturation of opinion. No doubt, the respective virtues of the "terminal blitz" and the "gentle rain" approaches will agonize campaign planners for a long time. A comparison of these two campaigns suggests that when there is something unfavorable in the established image of a candidate (Shapp's arrogance, Rockefeller's tax promise), the slow treatment dispels it more efficiently, like irradiations of a cancer. Rockefeller's experience may also show that when it is a question of modifying an existing image, as opposed to creating an image for an unknown, the short commercial may pay more dividends in voter penetration than the long film.

The People Machine

It can go much, much further. Television continues to open doors to the more imaginative people in campaign management. Some of those doors lead into a future that may be exhilarating to politicians in its prospect of efficiency and alarming to others for its possibilities of control and manipulation.

In 1960, the Democrats made use of a computer system they called, frighteningly, the People Machine. In an experimental project financed by the Democratic Advisory Council, social scientists put data on public opinion from sixty-six nationwide surveys into a computer and tried to show what effect different campaign strategies would have. The experiment was interesting but was not carried far enough to be of practical use.

There are a number of people interested in reviving the idea.

Carroll Newton would like to see a well-financed center established at one of the universities. Every conceivable detail from public opinion surveys, demographic profiles and election analyses would be stored there in a large computer bank. It would then be available for the political parties to draw on as needed.

Joe Napolitan began negotiations with the International Business Machines company in 1967 to exploit a similar idea. IBM was already working on a "consumer profile" of the nation, breaking down in the greatest possible detail what kind of people Americans are in their buying habits and tastes. Napolitan thought it would be easy to feed in political data on top of the consumer information. He was able to offer a simple form of computer campaigning to clients for the 1968 election.

Napolitan thinks that once the basic information was stored in the computer, it could constantly be updated with the latest polls so that the computer would always know what the American people felt about any issue. It would also be able to tell a politician what specific groups of people thought and how influential their opinions would be. What do Democrats in Portland, Maine, think about costly federal programs for rehabilitating Negro ghettos in the big cities? What do automobile dealers think about federal car safety regulations? Are car dealers more often Democrats or Republicans? Are Iowa farmers bothered more by the price of corn and hogs this year or by threatening developments overseas? A candidate need merely ask the machine to find out instantly.

Such a profile would serve several purposes. It would do much to eliminate the old style of politics-by-intuition, which grows ever more risky in a nation as diverse and complicated as the United States. It would make possible instant access to more pertinent information from the past and present than any highly skilled team of political researchers could physically manage. And the system could make rapid and complex comparisons of voting statistics, preferences, ethnic behavior and class attitudes with whatever new element was relevant. Thus, both long-range strategy for a campaign and hour-by-hour tactical decisions could be based on more complete and more accurate and recent information than is possible at present.

Napolitan thinks, for instance, that the system would be invaluable for deciding how to schedule a Presidential candidate. He believes that Richard Nixon might have been saved by such a system in 1960. Nixon had pledged that he would visit all fifty states. He doggedly kept that promise and spent thirty-six hours at the very end of the campaign on a trip to Alaska. He was behind in the polls and every hour of campaigning was vital, but not in Alaska, which did not have enough electoral or popular votes to make any decisive difference. Two states with large electoral votes (Illinois, 27, and New Jersey, 16) were balanced on a knife edge of indecision and could have swung the election to Nixon. Illinois went to Kennedy by 8,858 votes, or two-tenths of 1 percent; Kennedy won New Jersey by 12,091 votes, or seven-tenths of 1 percent. These razor-edge margins gave him all the electoral votes of those states, a total of 43. Kennedy won a total of 303 electoral votes to Nixon's 217. If the 43 from Illinois and New Jersey had gone to Nixon, the electoral vote would have been tied. With a version of the People Machine, humming with the very latest intelligence from all corners of the country, Nixon might well have decided that those vital thirty-six hours were better spent campaigning in downstate Illinois and in New Jersey than in a quixotic chase to Alaska for three electoral votes.

The Machine could be programmed with voting behavior in every county in the nation. There are some counties with a vote of 200,000 that have never had a variation to one party or the other of more than 5 percent. There may be neighboring counties with a vote of 200,000 but with a record of real variations of 30 percent. According to past performance, the first county would have only 10,000 voters susceptible to campaign influences. In the second, 60,000 might be. If time or money were short, it is obvious which county should receive the candidate's attention, literature and television pitch.

The Kennedy team showed in 1960 that the old politicians who run their bailiwicks "by feel" often simply do not know the realities. One keen politician might ascertain by talking to a handful of people in his area what the feeling was. Another would do his thinking wishfully, one of the commonest weaknesses in political life. The Kennedy people came in with a new, pragmatic attitude and demanded to know the facts.

In the future, a computer would far more easily decide which political personality clamoring for the prestige of a candidate's attention should get it. A good deal of a candidate's time is still spent on useless trips to places that cannot make a difference, because the organization does not know how to refuse some local politicians. The People Machine could send out refusals on IBM cards and would not be available for aggrieved telephone calls.

Napolitan envisages a further use for such a machine, the allocation of media dollars. He says that no one has analyzed a campaign scientifically enough to determine how much should be spent in each medium. It is all done by rule of thumb. There are particular groups of people or areas that might be served better, and more cheaply, by a direct mailing or a telephone campaign than by television. The Machine could eliminate the guesswork.

Such concepts did not spring up before the era of heavy campaigning with television, partly because computers and some mass advertising techniques have evolved concurrently with television, but also because television has introduced something basically different. In many kinds of political races, a candidate is now able to reach virtually every member of the electorate. It is no longer true that he reaches only those willing to listen to him speak at election meetings or on television. He is no longer confined to influencing those interested enough to read about him in the newspapers or magazines. Television has given him the eyes and ears of the voter who does not care very much. Expressed as melodramatically as that, it sounds like a marvelous leap forward in the democratic process. However, the way politicians are using television is not so splendid.

Let us pull together several sets of facts that have already been discussed.

First, the composition of the television audience. We have seen that the average audience for the news programs of the television networks is very close to a cross section of Americans in education, income, profession, sex and place of residence. We saw also that in terms of the magazines they read, a very large proportion of the network news audience did not exhibit an avid desire for information about current events. They told opinion samplers, and their own viewing and reading habits confirmed, that they depended on television for most of their information.

After the evening news programs, the television audience gets bigger and remains very large throughout the prime-time entertainment schedule. If, however, the networks occasionally interrupt the entertainment for an informational program, the audience invariably shrinks. For example, in the week of October 22–29, 1967, the regularly scheduled *CBS News Hour* in prime time (10–11 P.M.) on Tuesday had only a 10 percent share of the audience in New York for a program called *Vietnam: Where We Stand,* while ABC collected 28.2 percent for a television remake of the Broadway musical *Kismet* and NBC pulled in 43.5 percent with the Beatles' film *A Hard Day's Night.*[17] On Friday evening, NBC's fortnightly informational program (10–11 P.M.) got an 11.4 percent share for a documentary called *Justice for All,* while ABC had 17.0 percent and CBS 50.9 percent with entertainment programs. It is therefore a safe assumption that only a minority of the television audience is deeply interested in public affairs questions. And the nature of the news audience shows that among those viewers who *are* interested in public affairs, many do not actively seek information beyond that offered by television. To put it another way, it appears that, by and large, the regular American television audience is not greatly exercised by the day-to-day details of what is happening in the world, and is not strongly motivated to seek detailed information. A majority of television viewers prefer not to watch much of what television does offer in informational programming.

During political campaigns, Carroll Newton found that there was one group of people, one-third of the electorate at the most, who were vitally interested and followed the campaign on all media. The people who were quite indifferent were those who got almost all their information about the campaign from television because it required a positive action to get away from it. Those were the people the mass media campaign was aimed at, Newton said, not the informed voter. This group corresponded to the 25 or

30 percent of the electorate with weak political motivation, who made up their minds very late in the campaign.

Newton's opinion is supported by Richard Scammon of the Election Research Center, who says: "Those who care most make up their minds early. . . . The Lower Middle Class make up their minds late and therefore are most subject to influence by television."[18] According to Herbert Gans, the lower middle class *is* the mass TV audience.

Now add to these observations another fact known to the advertising industry and to social scientists: the less people care about something, the more easily they believe what they are told about it. In his study of the impact of television advertising, Herbert Krugman found that "in cases of involvement with mass media content, perceptual defense is very briefly postponed, while in cases of non-involvement, perceptual defense may be absent."[19] In other words, people do not put up critical defenses for subjects that they do not care about.

This is the heart of the matter. Politicians, with their advertising advisers, have discovered that the television audience is there and will not bother to turn off political spots. It is a group with weak political motivation and is not generally well informed.[20] It does not care much about politics and for that reason will believe what it is told. The audience contains that group which makes its voting decisions very late. For all these reasons, it is this group to which the campaigns of persuasion are directed.

At the top of the television audience, other researchers have found a group of "high media users," people vitally interested in political developments between and during campaigns, who read newspapers and magazines and watch television. At the other end, according to Angus Campbell, is the other group, which is "very incurious about politics; its demand for information is exceedingly modest."

This group, perhaps as large as a quarter or a third of the electorate, is the captive of the political commercials. It is easy for well-educated and well-informed people to scoff at these commercials, to be amused by them and to base their own judgments on other information. College-educated people may be opinion leaders but they still comprise only a quarter of the adult population. Even though their percentage turnout is often higher, they influence elections less in numbers than people with high school and grade school education. Since it has been demonstrated that all classes of American voters can be induced to change their party allegiance from election to election,[21] it matters a great deal what influences the submerged and disinterested third of the electorate. And when it can be argued that for reasons of their cultural conditioning by commercial television they raise no critical defenses to information which does not excite them, it is a serious matter indeed.

It is difficult to see how the present trend toward short commercials will be halted. In 1960, when the parties put on evening programs longer than five minutes, the Republicans got an average 19 percent share of the audience and the Democrats 20 percent. In 1964, the Republican share of the nighttime audience for such programs had fallen to 13 percent and the Democratic to 15 percent. The fall-off for daytime programs was even sharper. The audiences for five-minute programs, slotted into the last segment of regular entertainment shows, remained about the same.[22]

So far this approach has been confined to elections for offices with a fairly wide constituency: the Presidency, senatorial seats, governorships and mayoralties of big cities. Adoption of the television-admass approach has been impracticable for many congressional and lesser candidates. It costs too much to be used effectively and there are technical limitations. Few congressional districts are neatly served by one television station. In many cities, if a candidate buys time on a station, his messages slop over into many other congressional districts. It is wasteful for him and not attractive to the TV station, which risks the boredom of its audience in the districts not concerned with that candidate.

New Hampshire is such an area, but the 1968 Presidential primary showed that even limited television may be effective.

George Romney, who ran an expensive and modern campaign complete with computerized voter lists, used almost no television. John Deardorff, a partner in Campaign Consultants, the Boston firm which ran the campaign, said they spent only $20,000 out of $200,000 on TV. The programs were one half hour of a speech on Vietnam, a half-hour interview by TV personality Mark Evans, and a one-hour telethon limited to the city of Manchester. Almost as much money went into radio spots. It was an old-fashioned approach.

There are only two television stations in New Hampshire, and the other two active candidates in the primary, Richard Nixon and Eugene McCarthy, bought television spots on Station WBZ-TV in Boston. These spots cost up to $1,300 for twenty seconds, and $1,700 for sixty seconds. The Romney managers thought such expenditure a waste because they were paying for 8 million viewers in Greater Boston and reaching only 200,000 voters in fringe reception areas in New Hampshire. It is interesting that the two candidates who did buy extensive television time, McCarthy and Nixon, both did well, whereas Romney's campaign fizzled out. Nixon's commercials were slick and dramatic, showing him as a world traveler, meeting important statesmen, stressing that wherever he went "people listen and things happen." McCarthy's spots, in keeping with his unhistrionic campaign, showed excerpts of remarks by the Senator about Vietnam. Both Nixon and McCarthy flooded the airwaves with radio commercials. So did those running the high-pressure write-in campaign for President Johnson. In the last week, the Johnson people, who used no television, were running a total of 450 radio commercials a day on thirty New Hampshire stations. One of the spots said: "The Communists in Vietnam are watching the New Hampshire primary. Don't vote for fuzzy thinking and surrender. Support the men who are fighting in Vietnam. Support your Commander in Chief. Write in the name of President Johnson on March 12." McCarthy played a tape recording of this commercial at a press conference and accused the Johnson forces of smearing him with the methods of the other Senator McCarthy.

In the ensuing primaries, candidates demonstrated greater dependence than ever on short commercials. They were reported to have spent $20 million, four times the cost of the preconvention campaigns of 1964. The television competition reached its peak in California, where Kennedy and McCarthy each spent between $500,000 and $1 million in a blitz of spot commercials.

Immediately after Kennedy's death, Governor Rockefeller turned to television in a desperate attempt to stop Nixon's nomination.

His agency, Jack Tinker, produced a series of commercials shown nationally in prime time and coordinated with full-page ads in newspapers across the country. The vastly expensive drive was designed, the agency said, not to reach the people, but "to get the polls moving in Rockefeller's favor."

Especially among academics, there is still considerable doubt about the real ability of television to influence voting behavior. That is partly because they, quite properly, demand more objective proof of the medium's efficiency than any research has so far revealed. But they have not yet grappled fully with the problems of commercials.

People in television, advertising and politics, operating in the thick of events, have not had time for doubts. Broadcasters and advertising men have a vested interest in demonstrating the power of their methods. Politicians, who are creatures of fashion, have found their claims irresistible. The new politics have captured most of the men who feel impelled to guide the larger destinies of the states and the nation. No one has yet proved that the methods are not effective, and candidates are paying heavily for their faith.

Until some far-reaching research is undertaken, it is impossible to prove that campaigning by TV commercial is doing injury to American political life. All the authorities *assume* that it is and one can scarcely find an argument to gainsay them. One can say that American politics have survived dirty practices and many excesses in the past. It can be demonstrated that there has been no sudden invasion of public office by rascals and charlatans. And, as we have noted, some complacent people take refuge in the argument: "Oh, well, nobody really pays attention to all those commercials anyway."

At least, in earlier times, the passive, disinterested voter was master of his own mind. Voting by instinct, by emotion, by prejudice, by bribery as he may have done; ignorant of the issues, unfamiliar with the candidates, putty in the hands of political bosses, perhaps; each voter still had the power, if he wished, to resist, and to make a decision in a private corner of his own thinking. Will that still be possible if the minds of ordinary persons can be bored into and filled with subliminal influences? The dangers are well worth contemplating.

9 The Cost

In the Presidential election of 1912, when Woodrow Wilson was first elected, nearly 15 million votes were cast. In 1928, when Herbert Hoover defeated Al Smith, the vote totaled more than 36 million. The costs of campaigning had also increased steeply but it has been calculated that on average each Presidential vote cast between those years represented an expenditure of 19–20 cents.[1]

In 1956, when President Eisenhower won his second term, costs had again increased and the total votes cast had risen to 62 million. Each vote still cost the parties 19 cents.

Then came a sudden increase. By 1960, the 68 million votes cast for Kennedy and Nixon cost the Republicans and Democrats 32 cents each. In 1964, 70.6 million Americans voted and each vote cost 41 cents.

Television is a principal factor in this escalation. It is not simply the money spent on buying television time but the fact that television has created an entirely new syndrome of campaign costs. Because of television, larger sums of money are now spent on advertising firms, opinion surveys, film and videotape production, and—recently—computers. Higher costs of telephones, printing, mailing, salaries, jet transportation, office rental, and incidentals like renting typewriters and feeding staff, have all contributed to campaign-cost inflation. But television is the great squanderer both in itself and by encouraging a more extravagant mode of campaigning.

A year before his election, John F. Kennedy wrote: "If all

candidates and parties are to have equal access to this essential and decisive campaign medium, without becoming deeply obligated to the big financial contributors from the worlds of business, labor or other major lobbies, then the time has come when a solution must be found to this problem of TV costs."[2]

Eight years later, no solution has been found, although many have been proposed. What Kennedy feared has come to pass: all candidates and parties do not have equal access to television. The fact that, in 1966, Rockefeller could spend roughly twenty times what O'Connor did in New York is an example.

Nor have the politicians avoided becoming obligated to the major lobbies. Vice-President Hubert Humphrey wrote in 1964: "The costs of radio and television, particularly of television, are getting so extraordinary . . . that some study should be made of limiting the amount of television that may be used by political parties and candidates either in terms of time or terms of amount."[3] Despite the Vice-President's concern, no one has attempted to limit the amount of television politicians can use.

It is now widely believed that the new scale of campaign costs has seriously narrowed the field of talented men who might become political candidates. Politics is increasingly a game for the very rich. Congressman James C. Wright, a Texas Democrat, wrote in 1967 that it was nearly impossible in most states for men of modest means to seek high elective office, unless they were "willing wards of the wealthy." Wright added: "The price of campaigning has risen so high that it actually imperils the integrity of our political institutions. Big contributors more and more hold the keys to the gates of public services. This is choking off the wellsprings of fresh, new thought, and severely limiting the field of choice available to the public."[4]

The foremost authority on campaign expenditure, Herbert E. Alexander, Director of the Citizens' Research Foundation of Princeton, N.J., has estimated that the overall costs of political campaigning in Presidential election years has risen in a geometrical progression since 1952. Including Presidential, senatorial, congressional, state and local campaigns, plus the nominating processes, $150 million was spent in 1952. In 1956, it was $155 million; in 1960, $175 million, and in 1964, $200 million.[5] If the rate of increase remained the same, the totals would be $228 million (1968) and $268 million (1972).

All this money has to come from personal wealth or donations; records show that usually most of it is not raised by small contributors. It comes in large amounts, often $500 or more, and it is naïve to think that such impressive donations do not carry influence with them. From the industrialist invited to dine at the White House as a member of the President's Club (for contributors of $1,000 or more) to the construction company director who has the ear of a big-city mayor, contributors expect and get something for their money.

The cost of political broadcasting

Since 1960, at the direction of Congress, the Federal Communications Commission has been compiling records of money spent on political broadcasting. There are detailed reports available for each election year since, with expenditures on the Presidential elections reported separately. Before 1960, the figures available are not precise.

In 1952, according to *Sponsor* magazine,[6] a total of $6 million was spent on political broadcasting, both radio and television, with the Republicans spending $3.5 million and the Democrats $2.5 million. Of the Republican expenditures, $2.1 million was spent on network broadcasting; $1.5 million of the Democrats' funds went to the networks. Thus, the amount spent on broadcasting for the Eisenhower and Stevenson campaigns was probably at least $3.6 million, plus some local or regional broadcasting on behalf of the Presidential candidates.

By 1956, broadcast expenditures had risen to $9.8 million for the general election period when Eisenhower and Nixon were campaigning for reelection.

With fuller documentation by the FCC, a more detailed picture is available for the Kennedy-Nixon election. Broadcast expenditures went up by 45 percent to $14 million.[7] The Republicans spent a total of $11.3 million on the Nixon campaign. Of that, 23 percent ($2,269,578) was reported paid to Campaign Associates, the agency created specially to handle the election for Nixon. The bulk of that amount was spent on television. Kennedy's campaign (from September 1 to November 8) cost the Democrats $10,587,000, and 40 percent of that went to their advertising agency, Guild, Bascom and Bonfigli.

These figures do not include amounts spent through other firms. The Democrats, for example, paid Jack Denove Productions, Inc., $377,500 for campaign films and tapes.

The temporary suspension of the Equal Time regulation for the 1960 Presidential election brought the candidates more free time from the networks than in previous elections. Nevertheless, charges for network broadcast time and facilities, for the Presidential campaigns, were only 7.5 percent less than in 1956. So, according to Herbert E. Alexander, although there was a small reduction in broadcast expenditure at the national level, because of the free time available, total expenditures for political broadcasting, at all levels combined, increased by about 50 percent from 1956 to 1960.

Four years later, broadcasting expenditures had risen 73 percent.

The Republicans spent $14,416,324 on Barry Goldwater's losing Presidential campaign, while President Johnson's election cost the Democrats $8,757,000.[8] The GOP admitted spending $5.6 million on broadcasting time and production. The Democrats, who did not publish detailed accounts, estimated $4 million for advertising agency spending, mostly for broadcasts.

Total broadcasting costs for the general election period were $24.6 million. If the cost of political broadcasting in the nominating period is included, the total expenditure on radio and television for the 1964 election year was $34.6 million, which, Alexander says, accounts for 18 percent of all political spending and thus probably makes broadcasting "the largest single political cost."

The extent to which television has crept into statewide and congressional campaigns is shown by comparing broadcast expenditures in off-year elections with the non-Presidential charges in 1964.

The FCC reported that candidates for various offices in the off-year election of 1962 spent $20,000,000 on broadcasting. In 1964, candidates for similar offices paid, as we have just seen, $22,000,000. In 1966 (the year of the Reagan, Rockefeller and Shapp races we have examined), broadcast charges had risen to $32,000,000.[9]

Two-thirds of that went into campaigns for U.S. Senator, U.S. Representative or Governor.

We have also noted that the great bulk of the money in 1962 and even more in 1966 went into commercials of one minute or less. In 1966, candidates and their supporters spent six times as much for spot announcements as they did for program time.

The Democrats, who faced more numerous strong challenges in primary campaigns, reversed the 1964 pattern and heavily outspent the GOP, $18,500,000 to $12,200,000.

How money is allocated to different media

To get a clearer picture of how broadcasting actually dominates campaign spending, let us look in detail at some campaign expenditures.

After the Goldwater defeat, the Republican National Committee released an unusually specific account of where the $14,416,324 spent on Goldwater had gone. This was the breakdown:[10]

TV and radio	$ 5,608,635
Salaries	1,586,672
Postage and express	955,827
Travel	909,632
Chartered planes and trains	807,997
Printing and reproduction	555,252
Newspaper and magazine ads	529,868
Telephones	398,113
Data processing	155,349
Total	$14,416,324

Broadcasting (39 percent of the total) clearly overwhelmed all other campaign activities in the Goldwater campaign. The figure for TV and radio includes expenditure of $1,066,484 on the production of films and videotape. In a similar breakdown provided by William Scranton after his abortive attempt to wrest the Republican nomination from Goldwater, TV still dominates the picture but, at 29 percent, is proportionately less of the whole.[11]

TV and radio	$245,000
Candidate travel	110,000
Convention	200,000*
Printing	58,000
Polls	12,000
Fund raising	10,500
Hotels	27,000
Miscellaneous	162,425
Remaining bills	2,100
Total	$827,025

Including some TV.

Scranton had an urgent need to make himself widely known in a short time to lure convention delegates away from Goldwater. Within the confines of a much smaller budget, his strategists, as did Goldwater's, devoted roughly one-third of their resources to television. Of course, it is a rare campaign in which media needs can be accurately plotted and money allocated completely in advance. Initial plans are often tempered by how the money is coming in. Different emphasis may be required to meet day-to-day crises that arise; an adverse poll may force a sudden increase in the use of television. An operation thrown together as hastily as Scranton's may have to survive on a hand-to-mouth basis. Nevertheless, in 1964, it happened that television (and radio) absorbed campaign funds in approximately the same proportion in a number of campaigns.

Joseph Napolitan is very doubtful whether newspaper advertising or many of the other traditional forms of publicity are worth the money in the electronic age. He thinks that the "gimmick" materials are useless. Things like combs, book matches, rain bonnets, nail files and balloons, he says, are expensive and probably never turn a vote.

William Pfeiffer, Rockefeller's manager, says that 25 percent of the money in any campaign is "leaked right out the window." In 1966, he told the *New York Times:* "The trouble is that you're never sure which 25 percent. Somewhere around this city there are

2 million Rockefeller buttons. Where are they? You can stand all day on the busiest street corner in this city and not see one of them. On the other hand, if you didn't have them, you'd hear from every county chairman in the state that you weren't doing anything. Someday, somebody's going to have the guts to throw the buttons out."[12]

Buttons were a small part of the gigantic budget for Rockefeller's reelection. The record of his expenses over three elections offers an interesting example of how campaign costs have soared for those politicians who feel they have to make heavy use of television.

In 1958, when he first ran for Governor, Nelson Rockefeller spent $1.8 million, and Governor W. Averell Harriman, whom he defeated, spent $1.1 million. The next time around, his opponent, Robert M. Morgenthau, was less formidable, but Rockefeller spent $2.4 million in 1962 while Morgenthau spent less than $500,000. In 1966, as we have seen, Rockefeller was in serious trouble and spent accordingly. There is no completely reliable figure on what his campaign cost. The official figure filed with the State of New York was $4.8 million. William Pfeiffer told me they spent $5.1 million. James Perry of the *National Observer,* who studied the financing closely, estimated something over $6 million, while the Democrats charged that Rockefeller poured over $10 million into the election. A Democratic spy who studied operations at Republican headquarters during the campaign told the press that the Rockefeller forces were spending $410,000 a week, with $312,000 of that going on television commercials. At that rate, they would have been devoting 76 percent of the budget to television. Such a figure is roughly what Rockefeller's advertising agency, Jack Tinker, said later was spent on TV. Myron McDonald, of the agency, told me that 70 percent of the media budget went to television, 15 percent to radio, 10 percent to newspapers and 5 percent to outdoor advertising. He said he would have preferred to spend 95 percent on television.

McDonald said his media budget was about $4.4 million. Eighty-five percent of that (70 percent TV, 15 percent radio) would be $3,740,000. Yet the Federal Communications Commission Report for broadcast expenditure in the 1966 primary and general elections lists only $1,683,525 for the Republican Party in New York State.[13] This suggests that the TV stations responding to the FCC questionnaires on political broadcasting are not telling the whole story. McDonald told me that the production budget for Rockefeller's commercials, including both filmed and videotaped spots, was $250,000. If that is added to the FCC figure on Republican broadcast expenditures, it still leaves $1,806,475 which the agency says was spent but which broadcasters did not account for to the FCC. If it turned out that such discrepancies were common in the FCC reports, political broadcasting could represent an even larger campaign expenditure than it does now. Merely adding the missing $1.8 million from the Rockefeller campaign to the FCC figure of $32 million would raise the total of broadcast expenditures by politicians in 1966 to $33.8 million.

As it is, the totals are quite high enough to alarm many politicians. For most candidates seeking national office, there is no escape.

Why is it so expensive to use television for campaigning? A glance at the rates broadcasters normally charge commercial advertisers and politicians will show where the money goes.

What television time actually costs

In the earliest days of television, broadcasters made time available to politicians as a public service. Then, in 1952, NBC and ABC offered to sell time to legally qualified candidates, and the practice began in the Presidential election that year.

The rates for television time are set by the number of viewers likely to be reached. As a particular TV station attracts more viewers to a particular time segment, the time rates will be raised, and then lowered if the audience falls off.

A Presidential candidate contemplating a full hour of network television time in the evening, when the audience is largest, will have to pay something in the vicinity of $100,000 just for the time. On top of that will be a charge sometimes almost as great for preempting the show normally seen at that time. If he has planned an extensive program of film and videotape, by the time he has paid for all production costs, the total bill might be $250,000. The cost of spots is even higher. If one-minute commercials in a Presidential campaign are to be seen by the maximum audience, they will have to appear in intervals of the most popular programs. In 1964, for example, one-minute spots on NBC's *Mr. Novak* cost $37,000 each, and those on *Dr. Kildare,* which had a higher audience rating, $55,000.

Candidates for Governor or U.S. Senator in one of the big states pay only a fraction of such costs for one minute of time on local stations in the major metropolitan centers. But the sums mount up quickly. In New York City, one of the most desirable spots for politicians is ten seconds on the flagship station of the NBC network, WNBC-TV, immediately before and immediately after the *Huntley-Brinkley Report.* The rate during the 1966 election was $600 for ten seconds. In New York, twenty seconds at prime time would cost in the vicinity of $3,000; in Philadelphia, $2,500; in Los Angeles, $1,200.

The rates are constantly being adjusted, usually upward. William Pfeiffer said the Rockefeller team found television costs had gone up 17 percent in the four years since the 1962 election.

Hiring the best people to produce first-rate commercial spots is also expensive. A one-minute filmed commercial made in New York can cost from $5,000 to $100,000, depending on how much filming and editing is involved. The Rockefeller commercials discussed earlier cost about $15,000–$16,000 each to make.

Color television has also raised many costs in the industry.

Raising the money

There is little doubt that this system favors rich candidates. A glance at the relative expenditures of the three Kennedy brothers and their opponents in three elections which the Kennedys won suggests that great private wealth is no disadvantage.

In 1960, John F. Kennedy outspent Hubert Humphrey $100,000 to $23,000 in West Virginia. In 1962, Edward Kennedy officially admitted spending $481,442 to defeat Edward McCormack, who spent only $78,765, although unofficial estimates put their actual expenditures at $1,200,000 to $200,000. Two years later, Robert Kennedy spent $1,300,000 in his New York Senate battle with Kenneth Keating, whose expenses were $750,000.

At the national level, there have been serious attempts to broaden the base of political financing to escape from the pressures and the opprobrium connected with large individual donors. The Republicans, curiously, have recently been more successful than the Democrats. In 1960, large donations made up the bulk of both parties' Presidential campaign funds. The Democrats received 59 percent of all their contributions in gifts of $500 or more, and the Republicans 58 percent. In 1964, with President Johnson's appeal for businessmen, 69 percent of the Democrats' funds came in donations of $500 or more. But the Republicans, because of Barry Goldwater's grass-roots appeal among certain types of Republicans, raised far more money from all contributors, and gifts of $500 upward made up only 28 percent of GOP funds. This phenomenon was partly explained by the success of Republicans' fund-raising appeals on nationwide television.

The fund-raising innovation which caused most discussion and considerable unhappiness was the President's Club. It was established in 1961 by President Kennedy along the lines of previous clubs in both parties for large donors. Membership was granted to any Democrat who gave more than $1,000. Under President Johnson, the Club became what Herbert Alexander has called "a personal financial-political organization dedicated to the support of his election." The members got special attentions from the President for their largess. If the President attended a party fund-raising dinner, an exclusive cocktail party would be held for President's Club members. The President would slip in and try to talk personally with each member. They were the party's guests and expensively entertained at the Democratic National Convention in 1964 and were invited to attend the Inaugural Dinner. White House officials met groups of members in various cities for special briefings on public policy.

The President's Club has angered Democrats working at the state level because it has skimmed off too much of the readily available money. During the 1966 gubernatorial race in New York, when Frank O'Connor, the Democratic candidate, could not raise even $1 million, they blamed the President's Club. His chief aide, Harry O'Donnell, said the President's Club had taken $800,-000 out of New York State in 1966 and all that came back was $1,000 to each of eight congressional candidates whom the President favored. The Kennedy forces in New York were equally incensed by the political control this gave President Johnson all over the country.

With the strains inherent in such a competitive system, it is not certain that the President's Club can continue to be a successful device. That is possibly one of the many factors that prompted President Johnson and others in 1967 to try to find a way out. The much tighter race for the Presidency in 1968 was even more competitive, resulting in more expensive use of the mass media.

Should the taxpayers pay campaign costs?

After his election in 1960, President Kennedy expressed the hope that before another Presidential campaign came along, a system could be worked out by which the Federal Government would pay the major costs of campaigning for both parties.

In 1967, President Johnson submitted such a proposal to Congress. He suggested that every four years, Congress should appropriate money to subsidize the costs of radio and television, other advertising, campaign literature and travel in Presidential campaigns. Other expenses would be paid, as now, by private contributions. The two major parties would get equal shares. Minor parties could have their expenses paid only if they polled 5 percent of the vote.

A number of Senators later made proposals which resembled the President's but were different in emphasis. Senator James B. Pearson (Kansas Republican) introduced a bill aimed at encouraging small political donations by providing a 50 percent tax credit for gifts up to $10 to candidates for federal office and to state and national party committees. His bill also provided for a tax deduction on contributions up to a maximum total of $500 per year. Introducing this bill in a Senate speech, Pearson noted that the Federal Corrupt Practices Act limits a candidate for U.S. Senator to $25,000 in campaign expenses and a candidate for U.S. Representative to $5,000. "These figures are patently ridiculous and are easily circumvented by establishing a number of ostensibly independent committees to support the candidate's cause," he said.

Senators Robert Kennedy and Joseph Clark also suggested income tax allowances for campaign contributions instead of direct Treasury subsidies. Kennedy said the President's proposal would result in a "centralization of political power" and a "national domination of local politics." Kennedy suggested that one-half of contributions up to $20 for individuals and up to $40 for married couples should be tax exempt.

There seems to be another weakness in these proposals, given the growing reliance on political commercials in television campaigning. President Johnson's proposal for direct government subsidies especially would have the effect of passing large quantities of public money from the Treasury to the broadcasting industry. As most of it would be spent on short commercials and not on full programs, little straightforward information would pass to the voters in the process. An FCC official very familiar with the problems of political broadcasting said: "If Congress passed some scheme to give public money to candidates, it will merely go into spots with no appreciable increase in public information."[14]

Obviously the system is beginning to get out of hand and politicians recognize it. But they are tied with the broadcasting industry in a stumbling, three-legged race. The broadcasters insist that, freed of irksome and unwieldy regulations, they could play a more generous and responsible part in the election process. They would give more free time to all important candidates if they were not forced by law to treat nuisance candidates and serious contenders with equal importance. The politicians suspect, perhaps with some reason, that freed of a legal requirement, not all broadcasters would operate in as public-spirited a fashion as they now claim. But not all the responsibility is on their side. Politicians, as we have noticed, want to control their appearances, and it is not for the broadcasting industry to tell candidates how they should campaign.

The problems can be seen clearly only by looking more closely at the question of government involvement with and regulation of broadcasting.

PART III

"Speaking to You from Washington . . ."

10 The Congressional Image

Imagine the situation of a street peddler who sells old-fashioned patent medicines. He needs a license to stay in business, and the city official who issues them is dubious about most of the peddler's wares. Yet it just happens that one product, a magic elixir, is the only thing that will cure the official's rheumatism and keep him in health. So the two coexist in a tense mutual interdependence, the peddler getting his license, the official his magic elixir.

The relations between the broadcasting industry and Congress are similar. Their interdependence—a two-way umbilical cord, as Bernard Rubin calls it—is behind many of the political effects of television. It is also responsible for the impotence of the FCC in any efforts to squeeze more worthwhile programming out of the broadcasting industry. Elizabeth Drew says in a critical study of the FCC in *The Atlantic:* "The more politically powerful is the industry to be regulated, the more likely are Congressmen to frown on regulation. A broadcaster's friendship can mean life or death for a member of Congress; his stations may treat the Congressman's every utterance as newsworthy, or give aid and comfort to the enemy."[1] When he was Chairman of the FCC, Newton Minow said: "A Congressman is under terrific pressure from his local broadcaster. Chances are that the broadcaster *gives* him some time on the air for a program to report to his constituents. The broadcaster may or may not support his campaign for reelection, and the broadcaster may own the local newspaper as well—and if this is the case, there is probably no other constituent in his district who means more to the Congressman, and that may even include his wife!"[2] Minow concluded: "Under the circumstances, the Congressman is generally bound to heed the broadcaster's urging—and the message is transmitted loud and clear to the FCC through Congress." Robert E. Lee, a long-standing FCC Commissioner, says members of Congress have "long since learned that they are going to have to use the media to get elected and for that matter they are more sympathetic to broadcasters than to any other group. The broadcasters have a great responsibility not to abuse it."[3] Nicholas Johnson, the newest FCC Commissioner, states: "The broadcasting industry dominates Congress. By these standards, the AFL-CIO, the AMA, the Chambers of Commerce and General Motors are turned into pygmies by comparison with the broadcasting industry. The ownership of TV stations by Congressmen is overemphasized and is less important than the fact that every Congressman is totally beholden to the man who owns the TV station in his community."[4]

On the broadcasters' side, the main interest is in securing Congress as an ally to prevent the imposition of further regulations on broadcasting and in trying to remove the present ones. Throughout this first generation of television, there have frequently been demands that Congress, or the President, or the FCC *really* control the broadcasting industry. There have been occasional efforts within Congress to force the networks to shift the emphasis in their programming away from tawdry commercial fare and closer to the concept of public service, but such efforts have always been blocked. Lester Markel of the *New York Times* has attributed such resistance to "the influence of the TV lobby in Congress." Markel believes that "because of direct financial interest in TV stations or because of pressure from newspaper publishers who also own television stations, or, most of all, because television appearances are vital for politicians, the TV industry gets favored treatment."[5]

When the Kennedy Administration and Newton Minow tried to reorganize the FCC to make it more effective as an overseer of broadcasting, Jack Gould reported that "stations at the grass-roots level turned the heat on their Congressmen, many of whom were elected with the help of TV, to defeat the Kennedy Administration's plan."

The principal worry that broadcasters affect is that they stand in danger of losing their license to operate, but, as we shall see in the next chapter, this fear is baseless.

Newton Minow believes that the industry has followed a sequence of events inevitable in any regulated business. It began by welcoming government guidance and assistance, but as it prospered and won an increasingly powerful voice in Congress, it began to dictate the terms under which it would accept government regulation. Minow has said: "Having won a *privilege,* often at government expense and with government accommodation, they now demand freedom from interference with their *rights.*"[6]

The broadcasters feel, or say they feel, themselves under a constant threat from Congress. The most serious threat is that some future action by Congress will limit the profitability of television. At the news department level in the networks, the threat is seen as a limitation on journalistic independence. Richard Salant of CBS News says: "The threat is always there, and sometimes is explicit —that if the Congressman or Senator doesn't like our news treatment of an issue in which he has an interest, then he will push for legislation to license the networks, or limit their profits—or some other regulatory scheme entirely irrelevant to anything but punishment for the exercise of news judgment."[7]

When we examine the history of recent futile attempts to regulate broadcasting, it should be clear that the industry fears a lot more than it needs to. It can also be argued that the threats broadcasters fear are merely a sublimation of their own guilt. In any case, they now go to extraordinary lengths to cultivate their relations with Congress. Each network keeps lobbyists in Washington. Their work is supplemented by the National Association of Broadcasters, the industry's trade organization, which can be relied upon to mount effective opposition to any suggestion harmful to the industry. On occasion, individual stations go out of their way to be nice to Congressmen. For example, in June, 1967, WNBC-TV, NBC's New York station, gave a dinner party in Washington for Congressmen from the New York, New Jersey and

Connecticut area. After the dinner, the Congressmen were given RCA tape recorders and their wives transistor radios. Only a few of the Congressmen did not think it proper to accept the tape recorders, and left them behind.

This, then, is the context in which politicians on Capitol Hill approach television to compete for access with the occupant of the White House, whose relations with television, as we shall see, are simpler and more direct.

Two kinds of exposure are of particular interest to Senators and Representatives. They need "bread and butter" exposure back home, on television stations in their constituencies, to keep their image well tended there. And, to impress their constituents and further their own higher ambitions, Congressmen need national exposure in Washington.

Local exposure is more important for U.S. Representatives than Senators because, with elections falling every two years, they are in an almost constant state of campaigning. In a number of ways the structure of the television industry and its needs at the local level have made it relatively simple for the Congressman to get on the air back home.

As we have seen, the fundamental fact of television's need for news meshes with the politician's need for exposure. Politics is news, and even stations with small concern for a thorough coverage of the news are anxious to broadcast stories involving political names familiar to their viewers. This appetite serves the Congressman well if he can find the means to get his image sent to stations in his constituency on film or videotape. When he is visiting the constituency, of course, he can appear live if he can persuade local broadcasters that he has something important to say. Still, his most valuable exposure is in reports sent back regularly from Washington. It has been estimated that 70 percent of U.S. Senators and 60 percent of Representatives regularly utilize free time offered by their stations back home. Free time can take the form of appearances on news programs or a scheduled segment of time offered by the station to the politician as a public service. If a politician sends back regular reports, say every week, he may be used in either of these formats, depending on the sophistication of the market his station serves, its own news sense and the content of the politician's report. Free time for extended reports, fifteen or thirty minutes, is not often given in prime time. The traditional time for a station to get rid of its public service obligations is Sunday morning or afternoon, television's so-called Sunday ghetto. If his message lands there, the audience the politician reaches may be quite small but still very useful. If he can contrive to say something which quickens the interest of a TV station's news department, he may reach a much larger news program audience.

In either case, the problem for a Congressman is to find the money and facilities to put such reports together. If he has the money, he can organize his own small production unit using commercial facilities in Washington. Senator Robert Kennedy, for example, hired a TV producer, Jack Lynn, in August, 1967, to produce a monthly half-hour program for him on videotape to be distributed to TV stations throughout New York State. That is an expensive, though no doubt effective, way of keeping a politician's image in repair among his constituents. Most Senators and Representatives cannot afford such a luxurious approach. For them, the Congress makes available subsidized facilities at very low cost, which are now widely used as politicians in Washington grow more aware of the power of television.

Since these reports from Congressmen are seen by millions of Americans on their local stations, the system by which they are produced is interesting to look at in some detail. The Republican Party has been particularly assiduous in trying to promote cheap television exposure for its Senators and Representatives. The disadvantages the party suffers in having been so long in the minority role has been an added incentive in trying to capture exposure in competition with the officeholding Democrats.

The Republicans run a permanent Congressional Campaign Committee with offices in the Congressional Hotel on Capitol Hill. It operates on a budget of approximately $1.5 million a year and has three main functions. It coaches and helps Congressmen to use television better and encourages their staffs to become more television oriented; it promotes exposure of Republican spokesmen in news programs; and it helps Congress produce filmed and taped spots in the TV studios provided by Congress in the House of Representatives.

Much of the Committee's budget goes into a yearly public relations account of $2,000 for each member. His use of the House TV studios is charged against that account but the costs are so heavily subsidized and so low by commercial standards that the $2,000 will go a long way. For example, to produce one print of a five-minute film will cost about $12. It might easily cost several hundred dollars, if the Congressman had to go outside and pay union rates. If the member wishes, he can supplement the $2,000 with his own money.

The Committee leaves all the business of contact with the local TV station to the Congressman involved. The growing use of this system and TV in general has stimulated new interest, especially among the younger Congressmen. The Committee estimates that about 75 percent of the Republican Congressmen use the facilities.

There is a new tendency for Congressmen to have as their administrative assistants or other members of their staffs men who have been in the broadcasting business. Others retain professional public relations firms which handle several Congressmen. Lee Edwards, former press secretary to the Republican National Committee, runs such a firm. He can keep the costs for each Congressman low by producing more or less identical material which can be used by all members whose districts are not penetrated by broadcasts of other members.

Some particularly obliging television stations will tell Congressmen from districts served by the station: "You are acting as our reporter on Washington activities, so we will pay for the film and telephone charges." The advantages to the Congressman are obviously considerable; how the public, depending on such stations for its news from Washington, is served is another question. In another very favorable arrangement, the Congressman has film shot in Washington, then ships it to a local station, which processes it and sends copies on to other stations.

The Republican Campaign Committee is always on the lookout for longer films which can be acquired cheaply and then doctored to provide attractive exposure for a Congressman if his station back home will run it. For example, the Committee found a film lasting half an hour that dealt with the churches of Washington as representing the center for the nation's religions. Robert Gaston, who directs radio and television operations for the Committee, said: "We were able to obtain it at print cost. We sell it to a Congressman, who puts on a head and tail [i.e., adds an opening and closing of his own]."[8]

Another technique was to acquire films made by the Department of Agriculture or the Department of Health, Education and Welfare, publicizing their accomplishments. Congressmen used to be able to get these films free. Each would film his own opening and closing and renarrate the film, which would then be sent to his local station.

The Campaign Committee utilizes every conceivable opportunity to get Republican Congressmen on television. On Memorial Day, 1967, for example, they produced a one-minute film urging people to drive safely. There was a space left in the middle where the Congressman could come in with his own message.

All this activity, of course, is a subtle form of campaigning. Television has made the chore easier for Congressmen whose districts are a long way from Washington. It also makes things very easy for the stations which receive such ready-made packages at no cost to them. They can demonstrate to the FCC at license renewal time (if the FCC bothers to ask) that they have run a certain amount of public service broadcasting, and also can maintain good relations with at least one Congressman. A legislator would be an ungrateful man indeed if he ignored the station's generosity when legislation affecting the broadcast industry comes his way.

Congressional access to TV news programs

In October, 1966, the Republican Congressional Campaign Committee charged that Democrats were getting a "lopsided" share of time on the television networks. The Committee had commissioned a study by "an independent radio-TV monitoring firm," which checked public affairs and news programs for two weeks in June and August of 1966. The survey produced these findings:

DIVISION OF NETWORK TIME BETWEEN REPUBLICANS AND DEMOCRATS

	Time allotted to Democrats, in minutes	Time allotted to Republicans, in minutes
Week of June 12–18, 1966		
NBC	87.00	23.20
CBS	84.15	38.30
ABC	100.20	6.45
Week of August 14–20, 1966		
NBC	168.24	13.56
CBS	192.50	34.50
ABC	115.00	6.00

These figures certainly show a wide discrepancy. They coincided with a period in which President Johnson was occupying a large amount of network time. Normally, the networks try to maintain some balance in exposure for Congressmen and the ratio would probably not be so extreme. There are natural advantages, however, for the party in power on Capitol Hill. While each Senator and Representative enjoys the advantage of being an "incumbent" in his own constituency, if he is in the minority party he may find it hard to attract attention on the national level. The most obvious source of exposure is in news-making committees. But the chairmen of these committees, who attract the limelight most easily, are drawn from the majority party. Hundreds of worthy Representatives and scores of Senators in both parties almost never appear on network news programs because they do not, in the estimation of the network news departments, make news.

To offset the publicity advantage the Democrats have enjoyed from their long domination of both houses, the Republicans have for many years staged a weekly press conference for the GOP leaders of the Senate and House. By directing as much partisan fire as possible into this occasion, which is a Washington "event," they try to draw the attention of the press and the television networks. The "Ev and Charlie Show"—more recently the "Ev and Gerry Show"—as it is called,* is covered routinely by television

---

* First named for Senator Everett M. Dirksen and Representative Charles Halleck, Republican Minority Leaders, and renamed when Representative Gerald Ford replaced Halleck as House Minority Leader.

news. Almost invariably, some snippet from the press conference appears on the network news programs. That is due in large part to the personality of the Senate Minority Leader, Everett Dirksen, whom television journalists, especially David Brinkley, find irresistible. Dirksen the aging thespian can be quite amusing, but his success causes other Republicans to worry. At the Republican Congressional Campaign Committee, for instance, they complain that "the funny bits get on TV, the serious bits get in the papers." It is true that while Dirksen's antics often provide hilarious "closers" for the *Huntley-Brinkley Report,* they do not always enhance the image of a concerned and vital opposition.

Apart from an elite group of Senators, like Edward Kennedy and his late brother, Robert, Charles Percy or Eugene McCarthy, who attract attention for their supposed Presidential ambitions or other special reasons, Senators and Representatives have a hard time making an impact on national television unless they have an important committee assignment. Important, in this context, means a committee likely to be holding hearings which television will cover extensively.

Televised hearings

Live television coverage of Senate hearings has contributed perhaps as much to public life as the televised conventions. They provide the Congress with its only occasions to equal the audience and the weight of Presidential access to television. But today, each time the question arises, the same haphazard criteria of profit and prestige decide whether this powerful tool is to be available. The most famous televised hearings of all, the Army-McCarthy investigation in 1954, *are* famous because of a commercial accident.

The hearings, which tied up millions of American households that spring, received the extensive coverage they did only because the ABC television network was in an uncompetitive commercial situation. Robert Kintner was then President of ABC and was campaigning to build the network's audience and attractiveness to sponsors. When the hearings began, on April 22, ABC, NBC and the Dumont network all carried them live. CBS, which had the heaviest and most profitable daytime schedule, presented a filmed summary at 11:30 P.M. After the opening excitement, the hearings attracted only a small audience and, in a few days, NBC dropped them. But ABC and the smaller Dumont network hung on. Kintner said it was costing ABC $10,000 a day. Jack Gould commented: "Were all chains currently sold out in the daytime, there might be no live coverage of the Army-McCarthy hearings." Kintner would have thought twice about carrying them if ABC had been on an equal footing with NBC and CBS. As the sessions ground on into May and began to pick up an audience, the two biggest networks came in again for the climax. Gould said the coverage exposed what was then (and still is today) "a fundamental journalistic weakness on television. It is not that television cannot technically cover the hearings as long as they last: it can. The problem is to what extent economics will allow it to do so."[9]

Of course, what happened is more important than what nearly did not happen. Network competition for prestige as well as for audience has frequently produced episodes of historic television, as the McCarthy hearings undoubtedly were. The prolonged exposure of the Wisconsin Senator, who had been feared and admired almost equally, did much to reduce the man and the emotions his activities inspired to reasonable proportions. The hearings caused a rapid evaporation of his mystique. Still, it is intriguing that such a powerful instrument can be wielded or neglected at the whim of a few network officials, whose first concern must be the profitability of their business enterprise.

Television coverage of certain happenings has been more than an educational or informational force. It has also had a significant impact on events. The Army-McCarthy hearings were one example. The Senate hearings on Vietnam in 1966 and 1968 were another.

The United States has never been committed in a major war whose justification was so widely questioned by ordinary citizens. The fact that it is a war that was never openly declared and for which Congress has given only the vaguest authority has encouraged public skepticism about the Administration's behavior. In a stable democracy, such doubts take a long time to seep through the layers of respect and confidence the citizenry automatically grants its elected leaders in times of crisis. The 1966 Fulbright hearings apparently speeded up the penetration of doubt into the public consciousness. For one thing, according to Arthur Schlesinger, Jr., they had the clear effect "of legitimizing dissent," and that marked a turning point in public attitudes to the war.

By his actions, President Johnson made it very clear that Fulbright's parade of eminent witnesses critical of the war had alarmed the Administration. The President, snatching at the opportunity to attend a conference in Honolulu, was widely believed to be attempting to distract public attention from the hearings. If they had received even wider coverage than they did, it is conceivable that the Administration might have felt under even greater pressure to justify its Vietnam policy. They did not receive the maximum attention because CBS, which provides programs for some two hundred affiliated stations, chose not to carry the hearings live. Whether the reason was commercial choice, as Fred Friendly charges, or political pressure, as some suspect, it exposed a frailty in our television system. If the reason was anxiety about profits, something is wrong with the structure of a medium which trumpets its journalistic power but skimps on one of the biggest stories of the decade. If the reason was political pressure, it is equally unfortunate that television journalism is open to such gross manipulation.

The National Broadcasting Company naturally congratulated itself for having been on the side of the angels. The new NBC President, Julian Goodman, who had risen through the ranks of TV journalism, expressed his philosophy on such questions to an interviewer in March, 1967: "I think basically a network should lead the public without getting so far out in front that it loses the main part of its audience. To a great extent, I think we do lead in this way. I think, for instance, the public didn't write in and say it wanted us to cover 72½ hours of the Senate hearings last year on the Vietnam policy. But I think the fact that we put it on interested a lot of people who otherwise would never have been interested."[10]

A few months later, Fulbright's Senate Foreign Relations Committee held another series of hearings on Vietnam, again featuring leading critics of Administration policy. The situation in the summer of 1967 was more acute than during the previous hearings in the winter of 1966. Many more troops had been sent to Vietnam, the American death toll was rising fast, and attacks on North Vietnam were being stepped up. None of the networks bothered to carry these hearings. An NBC spokesman told *Variety* that "the network was only interested in carrying actual policy makers."

A few weeks earlier, all the networks had gone to enormous expense to cover the Arab-Israeli war and had been widely commended for their unselfish devotion to hours of expensive United Nations debates. American opinion on that war was virtually unanimous in favor of Israel. The networks might plead that they had exhausted their budgets for unforeseen news coverage and could not afford to cover the Vietnam hearings live. A cynic might ask whether a desire to avoid the political jungles of the Vietnam controversy was not a factor. Television has its moments of daring and independence; but they are brief moments and not habit forming.

In March, 1968, Fulbright persuaded Secretary of State Dean Rusk to testify publicly for the first time in two years. A much larger section of the public had suddenly grown skeptical about the justification for the war, particularly following the startling reverses of the Vietcong's Tet offensive. NBC alone carried the two days of hearings live, the other networks contenting themselves with taped summaries. The reasoned and sometimes impassioned criticisms of the Administration policy by many of the committee members must have impressed Americans who watched any extended portion of the hearings. Large segments were carried by satellite to television viewers in Europe, but not to regular viewers of CBS and ABC in the United States.

Despite the capricious nature of the coverage, Senators who are lucky enough to get an assignment to one of the prominent committees, like Foreign Relations, are assured much wider television exposure than those who end up on Agriculture and Forestry or the District of Columbia Committee. Even hearings which are not covered live receive considerable attention from television news. Extensive portions are filmed or videotaped and segments used in the evening news programs. A calculating young Senator, with an eye to bigger things in the future, would have some interest in lobbying for assignment to a committee, not for its traditional prestige but for its television opportunities.

A member of the House of Representatives, sadly, has no such opportunities. The House bars television from its committee proceedings. Television fought that battle long ago with Democratic House Speaker Sam Rayburn and lost. Rayburn is dead but his ban, first imposed in February, 1952, lives on. It was lifted when the Republicans briefly took control of the House in the Eighty-third Congress (1953-54), but was reinstated by Rayburn when the Democrats came back into power. The networks have tried various dodges to get around the ban—shooting the closed committee room door while listening to proceedings on a radio line, and getting key witnesses to read their formal statements to the cameras before entering the hearings. The most common device is for television crews to camp outside the committee room all day and try to grab interviews as the principal figures come and go. It is not a satisfactory substitute for coverage of the hearing itself.

Congressmen and interview programs

Far more regular and reliable opportunities for Congressmen to air their views to the vast television electorate are provided by the network interview programs. In fact, from time to time there have been complaints that the Sunday network panel shows are dominated by members of Congress to the exclusion of people from other walks of life.

We have already discussed the way programs like *Meet the Press, Face the Nation* and *Issues and Answers* are used during political campaigns, to give prominent politicians a platform and sometimes to stage quasi debates between candidates appearing back to back. Where these programs discourage the average politician in Washington is that they are not accessible to the relatively unknown Representative or Senator. Their guests tend to be people very much in the news at a particular moment or someone already prominent. It was calculated in 1967 that Vice-President Humphrey, since becoming a Senator, had been on these three programs a total of forty-four times. The producers do their best to attract big names to the studios because that is what pulls in audience. Furthermore, Congressmen have to compete with visiting statesmen from other countries, members of the President's Cabinet or top figures in the armed services. Network sensitivities creep into these programs as well. Senator Warren Magnuson, the Washington Democrat, appeared on the CBS show *Face the Nation*. It was assumed by people in the CBS News Department that he had been invited not because he was newsworthy, but because he was Chairman of the Commerce Committee, which oversees the broadcasting industry. CBS management had for years been trying to impress Magnuson's Committee and its Communications Subcommittee with the need to pass various amendments to the Communications Act. CBS staffers thought the *Face the Nation* invitation was designed to flatter the influential Senator.

Networks can be squeamish about putting on people who are *too* newsworthy. Robert Vaughn, the star of the NBC spy series *The Man from U.N.C.L.E.*, said that he was invited to appear on *Meet the Press* in September, 1967, but that the invitation was later withdrawn. Vaughn was a leader in the Dissident Democrats, a movement trying to turn in a petition with 2 million signatures at the 1968 Democratic Convention opposing the renomination of Lyndon Johnson because of his war policies. *Variety* reported that Vaughn was definitely scheduled to appear with Dr. Benjamin Spock, another antiwar campaigner. "Apparently the show was squelched by NBC brass," *Variety* reported, because of network "uneasiness about spreading the peace-in-Viet views of its star." When Spock did appear, at least one critic thought Lawrence E. Spivak's panel treated him with unusual rudeness, while apologists for Administration policy in Vietnam were handled with much deference.[11]

A Congressional elite also commands much of the attention on NBS's *Today* show, a leading television platform for members of Congress. This program does go further than others, however, in seeking out proponents and opponents of legislation currently in the news. The political interviews, which are a feature of its 8:30 to 9:00 A.M. segment, are closely watched by many people in

Washington, including the President. The program has the advantage of appearing at a time when even the busiest Congressman or Cabinet official has a free space in his schedule. The guests also know that the segments are long enough—usually about ten minutes—to allow more than a cursory explanation of a subject and that they will not be treated too aggressively. At one time, especially when Martin Agronsky was the permanent interviewer in this spot, the *Today* show interviews had the reputation of being very probing. More recently they have tended to be what *Newsweek* called "gentle and chatty rather than hard and digging."[12]

Viewed as a whole, the opportunities for Senators and Representatives to appear on network television are many for the several dozen who are prominent, and few for the remainder. Apart from the more dramatic Senate hearings, which receive live nationwide coverage, the Congress cannot be said to equal the impact of the White House on the television audience. Press conferences by Senate and House leaders are rarely carried live by the networks and prominent members of Congress are not given the chance to make special reports to the nation, as the President is. From a journalistic point of view, there is no reason why they should not be given such a chance occasionally. Television journalism has not set itself up so far to cover Capitol Hill as extensively as the newspapers and wire services do. Interpretive or analytical stories about Congressional opinion do not get the prominent play on television that they do in print. While the hearings that form the groundwork may be covered in part, the Congressional initiatives they produce do not compete in urgency of coverage with proposals emanating from the White House.

If both houses of Congress would reconsider their prohibition on television coverage of actual sessions, they would probably fare much better in the balance of exposure. But they are by nature conservative in their outlook. While individual Congressmen may be well aware of the impact of television on their own campaigning and legislative activities, it seems to have escaped the consciousness of Congress as a whole that the habits of the electorate are changing. If tens of millions of Americans do not pay much attention to newspapers but get their news from television, detailed print coverage of Congressional speeches and debates will pass them by. All they will see are the tiny segments of film shown on network news programs, *if* a Congressman has been willing to come to a television camera to repeat what he said on the floor. Many Congressmen do, but that practice has a staged and artificial air about it. The argument of the television industry that it could cover sessions in the Senate and House chambers fairly and unobtrusively seems convincing. Ground rules would have to be established. Congress would certainly have the power, if it chose for once to be tough with its friends in broadcasting, to stipulate that broadcasters would have to devote a minimum amount of time to such coverage. It could, for example, be edited into a daily half-hour summary of events on Capitol Hill, and run at some time convenient to broadcasters. If a body as tradition-bound as the British House of Lords can experiment with TV coverage of its sittings, it should not be too daring a step for the American Congress.

11 Government Regulation

Television is regulated and it is not regulated. The body nominally responsible, the Federal Communications Commission, is a pathetic organization. Few have anything good to say about it, except to offer excuses. It is small and underprivileged by Washington standards, with a staff of 1,500 and a budget of $20 million a year, less than half the budget of the Bureau of Commercial Fisheries. It works in dreary offices behind the old Post Office Building, and its seven Commissioners (appointed by the President at $27,500 a year for seven years) do not even have a limousine to ride in. Even before the advent of such startling technological advances as communications satellites revolutionized the communications field, the Commission was too bogged down in the minutiae of administration to think creatively about broadcasting and, whenever it tried, Congress slapped it down.

In addition to granting and renewing broadcast licenses, the FCC has to rule on the frequencies of police and taxi radios all over the United States, watch the profits of AT&T, keep an eye on ham operators and an ear to shrimp fishermen who use dirty language on their radios at sea. It also deals with a growing volume of complaints from the public about broadcasting—5,358 of them in May, 1967, alone.

One government study group after another has scrutinized the FCC and come away appalled. A task force headed by Herbert Hoover said in 1949 that the Commission had "failed both to define its primary objective intelligently and to make policy determinations required for efficient and expeditious administration." James M. Landis, former Dean of the Harvard Law School, made a report on the regulatory agencies for John F. Kennedy's new Administration. Landis said the Commission "has drifted, vacillated and stalled in almost every major area." He found that the television networks exerted too much influence. Judge Henry J. Friendly of the U.S. Court of Appeals said in 1962 that the FCC was intolerably inconsistent in its manner of awarding licenses. "The Commission must develop enough courage to penetrate the fog it has helped to create," Friendly said. "What is essential is that the Commission do something so that a policy will emerge." Morale within the Commission is so bad that it is openly criticized by the Commissioners themselves.

The gravest charge against the Commission is its cozy relationship with the industry it is supposed to regulate. Retiring Commissioners traditionally take lucrative jobs in broadcasting. The FCC is more timid about proposing standards for radio and television than even the National Association of Broadcasters, and that is saying a good deal. The FCC has hidden behind a statutory prohibition on censorship of broadcasting to refrain from any interference with program content. Although applicants for new or renewed licenses are required to promise a reasonable proportion of public affairs programming, the licenses are issued whether they keep the promises or not. Licenses are sometimes issued even when the applicants do not bother to make such promises. According to Nicholas Johnson, the youngest of the Commissioners, the FCC has never imposed any regulation which interfered with a broadcaster's ability to make the maximum profit. It issues stern, moralistic guidelines (e.g., "Broadcasting stations are licensed to serve the public and not for the purpose of furthering the private or selfish interests of individuals or groups of individuals"—FCC Report, 1946) and does not enforce them.

Commissioner Johnson says the FCC goes through "the motions of appearing to review programming against a public interest standard, when in fact doing nothing of the sort." It has adopted, Johnson says, "a comfortable, hear-no-evil, see-no-evil slouch in front of the radio and television sets of America."[1]

Louis Cowan, former President of CBS Television, says: "The way it is run in this country the license business is a franchise forever."[2]

How the Commission behaves has depended on the personality and dedication of its Chairmen. Several in recent years have made an effort to improve broadcasting. The record is not one of total surrender to the industry; but with occasional exceptions, it has been a story of unhealthy accommodation. As others have pointed out, if the FCC had done its job, there would be no desire for public television.

The Commission also, in Robert Kintner's words, "necessarily adapts itself to the political tone in Washington." Kintner recalls that in the Roosevelt days, applicants for broadcast licenses who owned newspapers were frowned on, and the Kennedy years were a time of reformist zeal around the FCC. Recently, with a President whose personal fortune rests on television, the Commission has again turned a more compliant eye on the industry. According to Arthur Schlesinger, Jr., Kennedy had urged Newton Minow, whom he appointed FCC Chairman, to press ahead with reform. "You keep this up," he told Minow after the "vast wasteland" speech; "this is one of the really important things." When President Johnson came into office, the FCC Chairman was E. William Henry, another reformer in the Minow tradition. Johnson was reported to have told him: "Bill, I want you to lay off that 'vast wasteland' stuff."[3] Shortly after that, Henry left the FCC and Johnson appointed Rosel Hyde, a man considered by broadcasters as a firm friend and with a preference for as little regulation as possible.

The present philosophy of the majority on the Commission is typified by the views of Commissioner Robert E. Lee: "I think the stations do a good job in public service programming. It is easy to say they should do more but the first obligation of a station is to make money, because if it does not, it won't be on the air."[4] Lee also says: "I would accept a station telling us it is going to do very little public service programming in a place where it could show there is plenty already. That would be broadcasting in the public interest."

In the Eisenhower years, the FCC had a Chairman, John

Doerfer, who tried conscientiously to use what power he had to make broadcasting better. According to Kintner, he once called all the heads of the three networks to Washington and instructed them to arrange among themselves for each network to give a different hour of prime time each week to public-affairs programs. When the networks protested that the antitrust laws would not permit such collusion, Doerfer pulled out a letter from the Justice Department explicitly giving them permission to do so. "NBC already had a one-hour public-affairs program in the evening schedule," Kintner says. "We probably would have had one in the next season, too, but Doerfer's meeting made it a certainty."[5]

That is a fascinating sidelight because, by all accounts, the FCC does not have any specific power to regulate the television networks, only individual stations, which are the licensees.

Minow's tenure resulted in a major achievement which is only beginning to have an effect. He succeeded in pushing through Congress a law requiring that all television sets built after April 30, 1964, be equipped to receive UHF (Ultra High Frequency) broadcasts. As more sets so equipped are sold and UHF stations built, broadcasting is being released from its confinement to the few VHF (Very High Frequency) channels available. That means greatly increased competition in the future and ultimately the prospect of more programming—as there is now in radio—for minority tastes.

Successes like that are rare. It is likely that if the broadcasting industry had recognized that UHF might ultimately be a real threat to the profitable status quo, it would have brought pressure on Congress to resist it. Such pressure can be very effective, as was shown early in 1968.

One (very faint) hope for an escape from lowest-common-denominator programming has been the idea of Pay Television (PTV). A number of experiments were made in order to discover whether it was economically feasible to provide special quality programs for people willing to pay for them in their own homes, but the experiments were inconclusive. Commercial television and the film industry were against PTV. Jack Gould said that "both became almost hysterical at the mere thought of toll video siphoning off any of their income or talent, and their persuasive powers found many attentive ears in Congress, where members do not want to disturb the chief outlets for their campaigning." The House Committee on Interstate and Foreign Commerce (the broadcasting committee) directed the still undecided FCC to take no action on PTV for a year.

When the Commission thought there should be some agreed limit on the number of commercials that could be broadcast in an hour, outraged broadcasters rushed to Congress, which obliged by passing a bill forbidding the Commission to issue such a regulation. The extraordinary thing was that all the Commission wished to do was to give official backing to the code already adopted by the National Association of Broadcasters. Responsible broadcasters who restricted themselves to the NAB recommendation of eighteen commercial minutes an hour would thus have had some protection from their greedier fellows.

Frustrated by Congress, the FCC retreats into its dusty offices and takes comfort in the dry gymnastics of bureaucracy. In February, 1967, it refused a license to Station KOSO, which wanted to locate itself on top of Mount Oso, near Patterson, California. The request was innocent enough: the station wanted to use the name of the mountain as its call letters. The Commission's reason was that regulations say stations are meant to serve a community and a mountaintop is not a community.

On other occasions, the Commission will give important regulations the greatest latitude of interpretation. In March, 1967, the FCC granted a wholesale renewal of licenses for thirty radio stations in Florida which proposed to program less than 5 percent news and public affairs. Several of them had even proposed less than 1 percent news and public affairs.

President Johnson appointed a task force in August, 1967, to look into the whole question of communications policy. Major decisions still have to be taken which will determine the shape of communications in this country for another generation. Perhaps the most important is how a system of domestic communications satellites will be run.

A Cabinet-level Department of Communications might well

result. Considering that communications are as important and as complex as transportation, for which a new department has been created, such a move would be logical. Furthermore, a Secretary of Communications, sitting in the President's Cabinet, with a well-financed and well-staffed department behind him, would carry a lot more weight with the broadcast group in Congress.

Congress jealously controls anything in broadcasting that might affect politics but has no stomach to control anything else. The broadcasting industry continually nags at Congress to remove the only two really important controls on broadcasting—Equal Time and the Fairness Doctrine—which are meant as political safeguards. Congressmen friendly to the broadcasting industry make periodic attempts to change these rules, just as a few vehement critics of television in Congress occasionally try to push through some measure of reform. Much safety for politicians resides in these regulations, however, and majorities are not easily found in either house to tamper with them.

The Fairness Doctrine

Impelled by complex motives, broadcasters rage at the Fairness Doctrine as "censorship" and as an "unconstitutional" threat to freedom of the press.

Robert Sarnoff of NBC says that it means "drawing a government curtain between the public and the free press." He told NBC's television affiliates in 1965: "This is a power over the press that is expressly denied to government by the Constitution. Its very existence is a threat to the proper exercise of the journalistic function the public has come to expect of broadcasting."

Apart from the fact that the television industry itself has some threats to the journalistic function of broadcasting to answer for, better authorities on the Constitution than television executives reject the complaint. In June, 1967, a Federal Appeals Court in Washington upheld the constitutionality of the Fairness Doctrine, in its first court test. The Court said the Doctrine does not abridge the right of free speech guaranteed in the First Amendment: ". . . the Doctrine, rather than limiting the petitioner's right of free speech, recognizes and enforces the free speech right of the victim of any personal attack. . . ."

The Fairness Doctrine, as such, is about as old as network television. It was an administrative creation, first adopted by the FCC in 1949 and later made law in a 1959 amendment to Section 315 of the Federal Communications Act of 1934. Drawing on the "standard of fairness" imposed on broadcasters by the original act, the Doctrine requires broadcast licensees "to afford reasonable opportunity for the discussion of conflicting views on issues of public importance." What prompted the Commission to set this down was a reexamination of the whole question of the right of broadcasters to editorialize. We shall return to that question presently.

Over the years since 1949, as various complaints and issues have been brought to the Commission for adjudication, broadcasters believe the Doctrine has continued to grow new tentacles to enmesh them. In the Commission's view, successive reinterpretations of the Doctrine have been merely a logical outgrowth of the principle enshrined by Congress in 1934.

Restating the Doctrine in 1964, the FCC insisted that it was not attempting "to substitute its judgment for that of the licensee . . . but rather to determine whether the licensee can be said to have acted reasonably and in good faith."

There are two aspects of the Doctrine which have important political applications and both are matters of hot contention between the industry and the Commission.

All sides of controversy

The Commission stated in 1949, and has often restated, that there is a "necessity for licensees to devote a reasonable percentage of their broadcast time to the presentation of news and programs devoted to the consideration and discussion of public issues of interest in the community served by the particular station." Moreover, the Commission said, "it is evident that broadcast licensees have an affirmative duty generally to encourage and implement the broadcast of all sides of controversial public issues over their facilities, over and beyond their obligation to make available on demand opportunities for the expression of opposing views."[6]

To a layman with an open mind, that would appear to mean that broadcasters are being encouraged to give air time to matters of controversy and to present all sides of the issue. The broadcasting industry has tended to take a negative view, however, and to regard the instruction as an infringement of their desire to speak out boldly. Fairly typical is this analysis given to an NAB conference in Los Angeles in 1964 by Reg G. Howell, President of station KREX, Grand Junction, Colorado: "We have the anomalous situation of having received encouragement from the FCC to meet our obligations to the public we serve by exercising our responsibility to editorialize, but on the other hand, the Commission's own doctrine on fairness in matters of controversy is being used to discourage broadcasters from exercising anything but innocuous palliatives in lieu of forthright expressions of opinion."[7]

To many observers it is clear that this is an interpretation the broadcast industry wishes to place on the question, and not the FCC. One of the most thoughtful commentaries on the matter is that of Jerome A. Barron, Associate Professor of Law at George Washington Law School. Writing in the *Harvard Law Review* in 1967, Barron argued that a defect of the regulation is that "the obligation to provide access for ideas of 'public importance' arises only after the licensee had taken a position on an issue." It amounts to an escape route. "By avoiding controversy the licensee can evade the fairness rule—there is no duty to report the other side of silence."[8]

To people familiar with the tendency of even the most responsible sections of the industry—the national networks—to dodge the discussion of controversial issues when they can and to treat them with stifling blandness when they cannot, Barron's diagnosis is very perceptive. He said further: ". . . industry opposition to legally imposed responsibilities does not represent a flight from censorship but rather a flight from points of view. Points of view suggest disagreement and angry customers are not good customers."[9]

That is the nub of the matter. Those broadcast journalists who sincerely believe their journalistic freedom is being tampered with by FCC regulations should consider whether their bosses, the television businessmen, genuinely want to use their opportunities to delve into controversial issues.

Newton Minow accurately exposed this hypocrisy in a speech in 1961 when he said: "The trouble, in my opinion, is that far too many licensees do not regard themselves as trustees for the public. The [broadcast] frequency is regarded as theirs, not the public's; and the license is seen to be not one to operate in the public interest but rather to get the greatest financial return possible out of their investment. When the Commission, in discharging its public interest responsibilities, challenges such operations, the first almost reflex reaction is the cry of censorship."[10] The motive, in Professor Barron's phrase, "is not to maximize discussion but to maximize profits."

That is the primary motive of all commercial broadcasters, from the biggest network to the smallest local station. As we have seen in an earlier chapter, the industry uses public affairs broadcasting largely as a prestige commodity to placate its critics, out of fear that excessive criticism might stimulate some new regulation which would lessen profits. Thus, when NBC announced that it was adding a third evening of movies to its weekly schedule for 1968–69, there was a very hostile critical reaction. To offset it, the network permitted the News Department to announce that it would inaugurate a monthly two-hour series of investigative reports in 1969, in place of one of the new movie nights.

A study of FCC rulings and interpretations suggests that broadcasters could go a lot further in testing the limits of the Fairness Doctrine than they now care to. As Commissioner Frederick W. Ford said in 1963: "No broadcast license has ever been revoked or denied renewal because of questions under the 'fairness doctrine.'" Ford went on to say that none of the "national tragedies" predicted if the Doctrine were not abrogated had occurred because they "stem from a furious chain of reasoning based on a series of false premises."[11] It is understandable if small local stations do not all employ skilled lawyers to provide broadcasters with running interpretations of FCC policy. A survey by the NAB in 1966 revealed that broadcast management's understanding of the government regulations affecting editorializing was confused and "far from thorough." The national networks, however, do maintain impressive legal staffs to advise on such questions. The network lawyers have a very clear idea of how far broadcast journalists can go, but one gets the impression that they prefer to use the Fairness Doctrine as a shield rather than as a weapon.

An example which involved me personally illustrates the complexities and fears which cause the networks to content themselves with much smaller bites of controversy than they could safely chew if they dared.

Late in 1966, I began working with Fred Freed, one of NBC's more spirited producers of documentaries, on an hour program about gun laws, to be called *Whose Right to Bear Arms?* Freed had researched the subject very thoroughly and we were both convinced that the evidence pointed overwhelmingly to the need for federal legislation to restrict the sale of firearms. It was calculated that 17,000 people would die in the United States by gunfire in 1967. No other civilized people have such easy access to firearms as do Americans and no other civilized country has such a high homicide rate. The issue seemed beyond argument. Those states which had passed stringent gun control laws had a substantially lower incidence of murders involving firearms than states which did not have such laws. Every conceivable eminent and qualified authority in the nation—successive Presidents, the FBI, police chiefs, judges and criminal psychologists—wanted tighter laws. President Johnson had said that "to pass stricter firearms control laws at every level of government is an act of simple prudence and a measure of a civilized society." Countless bills had been introduced in the federal and state legislatures in recent years but almost none had passed. In Washington, they had not even come out of committee.

The reason was a powerful and well-financed lobby led by the National Rifle Association, which had mounted successful campaigns to kill gun control legislation. Its chief weapon was the Second Amendment to the U.S. Constitution, which says: "A well regulated militia being necessary to the security of a free state, the right of the people to keep and bear arms, shall not be infringed."

Government Regulation | 269

By playing on the fears of millions of Americans who use guns legitimately for hunting or target shooting that their sport was in danger and their constitutional rights threatened, the NRA had successfully blocked all efforts to prevent guns from falling into the hands of criminals, narcotics addicts, the insane and minors.

Our purpose, as we saw it, was not to go over arguments which had already been well aired, but, after demonstrating the need for new laws, to expose the motives of those opposing them. We were not precisely breaking new ground on television. CBS had handled the subject in a relatively forthright documentary three years earlier. We were bolstered in our conviction by a poll, commissioned by NBC from the Gallup Organization, which showed that 61 percent of Americans wanted stricter laws concerning rifles and shotguns, that 75 percent wanted a ban on mail order sales, and that 73 percent favored a law requiring registration of rifles and shotguns. The percentages were even higher for hand guns.

As the word got around that we were doing such a program, there were interesting reactions. Freed received a letter from Democratic Congressman John D. Dingell, of Michigan, a member of the House Committee on Interstate and Foreign Commerce, which oversees broadcasting. The letter could only be described as an attempt to intimidate us. Dingell said that, as an active sportsman, he took a considerable interest in commentaries involving firearms, and threatened that, if our program actively pressed for a particular legislative position and did not give full expression to the views of opponents of anti-gun legislation as the Fairness Doctrine required, he might find it necessary to bring the matter forcefully to the attention of the FCC and the Chairman of the Commerce Committee. Dingell's interpretation of the Fairness Doctrine—a common one among broadcasters—was wrong, as we shall see.

Shortly afterward, the advertiser who had intended to sponsor the program withdrew, but the documentary was completed and shown to NBC network and News Department executives at the customary pre-air screening.

The final one-third of the film was devoted to a searching interview, conducted by Walter Sheridan and myself, with the Executive Director of the NRA, Franklin Orth. It was designed to bring out very clearly the inconsistencies—in fact, the hypocrisy—of the NRA position, which pretended to support measures to limit misuse of firearms but in fact worked diligently against them. The interview succeeded in doing that. Orth dodged and prevaricated, but the truth did emerge.

The program was to end with a brief summary to camera by me, which would say that responsible opinion throughout the United States agreed there should be a law restricting firearms purchase, but that repeated attempts to introduce such a bill had been frustrated by the weakness of Congress in allowing itself to be pressured by an interested minority. My concluding statement was to be that it was up to Congress to throw off these pressures and pass a bill.

Shortly after the screening the word came down that the program would have to be reedited. The instructions came from the NBC lawyers and were ostensibly based on the need to observe the Fairness Doctrine. It was also mentioned that NBC representatives expected to have to testify in forthcoming congressional hearings on broadcasting and did not wish to be under any cloud of disapproval when they did so. The instructions were resisted by the NBC News Department, whose President, the late William R. McAndrew, thought the program was strong and should be aired as it was. However, the wishes of the network prevailed and the film was reedited. The effect was to soften considerably the impact of the argument and to weaken the case against the NRA. In particular, the lawyers considered that we had been too tough on Franklin Orth. Passages embarrassing to him were cut out and passages were inserted which either put him in a better light or permitted him to filibuster. In one sequence in the interview, I referred to the curious fact that Orth had testified before Congress *in support* of an arms control bill just after President Kennedy's assassination but that the NRA had then sent its 700,000 members a newsletter which conveyed the impression that Orth had *opposed* the bill. When I asked Orth what the NRA had told its membership about his testimony, he said at first he could not remember. Then, during a pause in the filming, the letter was produced from the NRA files and Orth read the entire letter with the cameras running. In the first editing, we selected the paragraph of the letter which made it clear that the NRA was deceiving its membership. In the reediting ordered by the network, the entire letter was put in. Again, the effect was to obscure the editorial point by softening the focus on the relevant part. Selection of material is a common device in responsible journalism and full texts of documents are very seldom used. Putting a full text into a television program, where every second is valuable, is not sound journalistic practice, but evasion.

In addition to other changes which softened the impact of the Orth interview, an exceedingly tame ending was concocted. After hearing Orth say: ". . . as reasonable Americans, we have to find ways and means of solving the problems that there are," the new ending said this: "Reasonable Americans, in Mr. Orth's words, agree a problem does exist. Too many guns do get into the hands of the wrong people. Too many guns are misused. Too many people are killed with guns. Reasonable Americans agree that something must be done, that effective laws are required now. But because reasonable men disagree over the form of these laws, we may get no laws at all."

Since the final moments of any television documentary are often those which stick most in the minds of viewers, people who saw *Whose Right to Bear Arms?* were not left with any urgent message. They were given the impression that the whole subject was a matter for argument between groups of equally "reasonable" men, which was absurd.

Variety, quite correctly, called it a "cream puff" ending.

There was no need for such cowardice, at least as far as the FCC was concerned. The Commission has repeatedly stated that in demanding "fairness," it is not requiring mathematical balance *within a particular program.*

In 1964, the FCC's restatement of the Fairness Doctrine said clearly that, in giving all sides of controversial public issues, there is "no necessity for presentation on the same program . . . the licensee's overall performance is considered in determining whether fairness has been achieved on a specific issue."[12]

One was left with the conviction that NBC had other reasons for wishing to avoid too forceful a presentation of this issue.

A year later, in a country stunned by the assassinations of Martin

Luther King and Robert Kennedy, and crying out for firearms control, it was difficult not to reflect on the faint heart of television. It is so often a powerful force for moralizing after the event. *After* the Tet offensive television was alarmed by the Vietnam war; *after* two outstanding Americans were shot down in 1968 television was aroused about guns. Television is a cheerleader for the team that has already won. In my opinion, that is not responsible journalism.

One cannot see that revoking that part of the Fairness Doctrine would be good for anybody but the broadcasters. Those stations run by irresponsible people would then be free to be as unfair as they like. Responsible licensees would be relieved of the "affirmative duty" to broadcast controversial material. They might carry the retreat into blandness even further.

There is a precedent for broadcasters who wish to advance the frontiers for concerned television documentaries. In 1962, *CBS Reports* presented *Biography of a Bookie Joint,* a well-documented film on gambling in Boston, and NBC broadcast *The Battle of Newburgh,* a study of a controversial relief program in a small town on the Hudson River in New York State. Both programs aroused anger in those communities and there were protests to the FCC. The Commission examined the complaints and upheld the networks, saying the documentaries were responsible and conscientious reports of controversial issues.

The reason why the networks do not jump into such disputed waters more often is not a lack of desire among the people who make the programs or many of the executives. It is just that they are ruled by too many other considerations than the thrill of forceful journalism.

In case of an attack

More disturbing to the broadcasting industry is the part of the Fairness Doctrine dealing with attacks on individuals or groups. This is a more recent interpretation of the fairness requirement and arose through complaints to the FCC about the conduct of many radio stations, especially in the South and West, which regularly broadcast right-wing propaganda, sometimes involving personal attacks. The way the FCC has resolved these complaints can make procedures more difficult for responsible broadcasters and in fact has given NBC and CBS reason for taking the entire Fairness Doctrine to the Supreme Court.

In 1964, the FCC laid down that when a broadcast contains an attack on an individual or group, "the Fairness Doctrine requires that a copy of the specific editorial or editorials shall be communicated to the person attacked either prior to or at the time of the broadcast of such editorials so that a reasonable opportunity is afforded that person to reply."[13]

In August, 1967, the Commission formally exempted bona fide news events from the personal-attack provisions because of the obvious difficulties in rushed news reporting of notifying attacked persons of what is coming.

The ruling has particular significance for politicians, as an exemplary case cited by the FCC reveals. The day before the off-year elections in 1966, station KTLA-TV, Los Angeles, broadcast an editorial endorsing Ronald Reagan for Governor. The editorial was interpreted by the California Democratic State Central Committee as an attack on Governor Edmund Brown and they complained that the station did not notify Brown or allow him air time to reply. The FCC dismissed the complaint but ordered the station rigorously to enforce the Fairness Doctrine in the future. The station signed a memorandum promising to give the Democratic Committee time to reply to any editorial contrary to the Democratic position, to give it copies of all editorials, to let it see the texts of newscasts and screen any films relating to politics. The station was also forbidden to broadcast editorials after the Wednesday preceding an election day.

In another case, which raised different issues, the Commission appeared to go out of its way not to apply the Doctrine in a manner onerous to the broadcaster. It arose from a complaint by the Anti-Defamation League of B'nai B'rith against California station KTYM, charging that it had broadcast editorials by an outside speaker of well-known conservative views, containing anti-Semitic material and attempting to identify the Jews with the international Communist conspiracy. The station management argued that free speech considerations precluded any prior censorship by them. They had offered B'nai B'rith time to reply, which had been refused on the ground that the same audience would not be reached and that the material was not in the public interest. B'nai B'rith wanted the FCC not to renew the station's license. A majority of the Commission ruled that the Fairness Doctrine applied, but because the station had presented evidence of an offer of time to reply, the station had fulfilled its obligation and its license should be renewed. The Commissioners noted that they personally deplored the content of the broadcasts and considered them not in the public interest, but that the wider public interest was served best in letting all views be aired. Commissioner Kenneth A. Cox dissented strongly, arguing that the FCC was bound by law to see that licensees did operate in the public interest and that First Amendment rights did not extend automatically to cover "calculated falsehood" used as a political tool. The case was reconsidered in January, 1967, with Cox again dissenting, and finally resolved by a majority of Commissioners in favor of the station.

Again, the complaints of broadcasters suggest that the FCC is preventing them from airing forthright opinions on urgent topics. Joseph L. Brechner, President and General Manager of WFTV, Orlando, Florida, has argued in the *Journal of Broadcasting* that the Commission makes no provision for "justified criticism, such a criticism of a subversive person or group, criminals or crime syndicates, the deranged and demented, the sham and the deceitful." He believes that the broadcaster "should be relieved of the task of seeking out such individuals or groups who might be considered to have been criticized or attacked."[14]

Brechner's catalogue of people whom he would like to be free to attack commends him for a crusading and fearless spirit unusual in broadcasting, but does it ring true? If his station found it absolutely necessary to broadcast an editorial attacking the "deranged and demented" (although one would hope they had the humanity not to), surely he is not prevented by the Fairness Doctrine. It may be inconvenient to have to discover the whereabouts of the people you are attacking so as to inform them. It may on occasion be impossible, since "criminals or crime syndicates" are not in the habit of putting their addresses in the telephone directory. Nothing in FCC rulings on the subject, however, suggests that if the crime syndicates, untypically, complained to the FCC, a station would be in any trouble if it could show it had tried to notify them. Such complaints often have an air of spurious concern about them. It is well known that broadcasters, on the whole, prefer to attack bad mothers, teen-age delinquency, poor roads and users of LSD.

Brechner says further that "the sweep and speed of broadcasting's news and editorial discussion programs may be and are seriously affected if a broadcaster must submit to nit-picking interpretation of his wisdom, intelligence, judgement and editorial fairness."[15] Were there any certainty that all broadcast licensees possessed wisdom, judgment, intelligence and a spirit of fairness, the argument against nit-picking would be overwhelming. However, for people who worry about it, the FCC reports on these questions are interesting reading. Especially in the question-and-answer style used to clarify instances, they appear models of good sense with a judicial detachment remarkable in an agency so understaffed and so harried.

The 1949 FCC statement on the matter includes this well-reasoned passage: ". . . the standard of reasonableness and the reasonable approximation of a statutory norm is not an arbitrary standard incapable of administrative or judicial determination, but on the contrary one of the basic standards of conduct in numerous fields of Anglo-American law. Like all other flexible standards of conduct, it is subject to abuse and arbitrary interpretation and application by the duly authorized reviewing authorities. But the possibility that a legitimate standard of legal conduct might be abused or arbitrarily applied by a capricious governmental authority is not and cannot be a reason for abandoning the standard itself."[16]

In their public opposition to these regulations, broadcasters often neglect the fact that if they feel there is arbitrary interpretation and application, they have recourse to the courts.

Broadcast editorials

There are many authorities who feel that broadcast journalism will not have matured until stations—and particularly the networks, who set the pace in electronic journalism—regularly take an editorial position. Leroy Collins, former Governor of Florida, said when he was Chairman of the NAB: "If radio and television broadcasters are to achieve full stature, stations must begin editorializing on a widespread basis." Minow, as FCC Chairman, urged broadcasters to editorialize: "We recognize that a station with a strong voice can be a prime target for pressure groups and that the pressure groups may try to put the squeeze on through the FCC. I suggest that the absence of such a pressure-group squeeze may indicate that your editorials are milk-toast. Complaints prove that you are communicating, not toe-dancing with issues."[17] Jack Gould reported in 1963 that some station owners wanted to editorialize as a way of overcoming their inferiority complex in journalism. They were convinced that equality with newspapers could not be achieved, Gould wrote, "until they are a directing force in a community rather than merely a glamorous mirror." The *Journal of Broadcasting,* an academic voice for the industry, says in an editorial: ". . . there is little doubt or argument that if broadcasters wish to participate in this society as full-fledged members, then they must fulfill their duties as extensions of the eyes and ears of members of their community. They must concern themselves with reality, and transmit that concern. In a free society, truth is arrived at in a marketplace of ideas and ideologies. The presentation of opinion necessarily accompanies the gathering and presentation of factual material."[18] The Roper survey of public attitudes to broadcast journalism, quoted earlier, found that a majority of people want broadcasters to editorialize; a bare majority of 53 percent in 1964, increasing to 62 percent in 1967.

Broadcast editorializing first became an issue in 1941, when a Boston radio station was attacked for endorsing political candidates. The case was referred to the FCC and, in the famous Mayflower decision, the Commission ordered stations to refrain from editorializing. "In brief, the broadcaster cannot be an advocate," the Commission said. Reaction to this decision built up and in 1947 the FCC began reconsidering. Finally, in 1949, it reversed the policy and encouraged editorializing. Wary broadcasters were slow to pass through the cage door once it had been opened. A few, however, were remarkably bold. A New York radio station, WMCA, established a landmark in broadcast journalism. It began editorializing in 1954 and in 1960 became the first station to endorse a candidate for President. It then tackled the legislative-apportionment question in the state, and forced the issue into court by filing suit. That led to the U.S. Supreme Court decision of June 15, 1964, establishing the one-man, one-vote concept which is drastically altering the political face of America. Another landmark was a series of editorials broadcast by station WDSU, New Orleans, for a period of two years, urging respect for the desegregation laws during that city's integration crisis. The station was widely praised for providing editorial leadership in the community. There has been a gradual increase in the number of stations broadcasting editorials, from 25 percent in 1958 to 56 percent, according to an NAB survey, in 1966. That the practice is not more general is blamed by the industry on the "confusion and uncertainty" they feel about their position under the Fairness Doctrine. Are they confused and uncertain about the Fairness Doctrine or is it again a case of wishing to avoid antagonizing any section of the public, the advertisers, or the Congress?

The editors of the *Journal of Broadcasting,* which is sympathetic to the industry, do not regard the Fairness Doctrine as a hindrance. They urge stations to stop flogging dead horses and to tackle the problems which matter: "Editorials favoring Christmas and opposing drunk driving are not true exercises of the broadcaster's freedom to make use of his special advantages as a thinking, acting, broadcasting citizen. Without use any freedom may atrophy. Rather than worry about the existence of a 'fairness doctrine,' broadcasters should accept it as a challenge opening the way to the creation of new program forms that can change broadcasting's status, even among its most virulent critics, from *potentially* to *actually* the most important communication force in our society."[19]

The national networks are the pacesetters in caution about editorials. NBC does not permit any editorializing by its Owned and Operated stations or on the network. In a statement to Congress in 1963, NBC said that before deciding to begin editorializing, the network "wished further to analyze the methods and techniques through which effective and meaningful editorials might be developed; to appraise the experience in editorializing of other elements in the broadcast industry which engage in that practice; to assess the restrictions and conditions now placed on broadcast editorializing. . . ." Presumably NBC is still analyzing, appraising and assessing, because it is not (openly) editorializing. CBS permits its O & O's to editorialize, for a time limiting them to local issues, but from June, 1967, allowing them to expand their concern to the national and world scene. ABC O & O's are permitted to editorialize but only on local issues, and are not permitted to endorse candidates. Neither CBS nor ABC broadcasts editorials on the network.

The problems of the networks are infinitely greater than those of a single station wishing to editorialize. The management of one station can gauge the sentiment of its community and tailor its editorials to that sentiment. Unless they were so innocuous as to be meaningless, network editorials would be bound to smoke out angry dissent somewhere in the country. Would that matter so much? It probably would not if the dissenters had to complain directly to the network headquarters in New York. It is more likely that some complaints would go to the local affiliates, who would presumably complain to the network if things became too difficult. Relations between the networks and their affiliates are delicate enough as it is. The affiliates chronically feel that they are being milked for their audience by New York, while there is much sorrow on Sixth Avenue that the affiliates constantly demand a larger slice of the pie. Affiliates embarrass the networks by refusing to carry public affairs programs designed to improve the network's public image. It is, while conducted with the nice diplomacy of a strained marriage, a greed-hate relationship. Network editorials would complicate it.

All the same, it is difficult to see how the networks can shirk the responsibility much longer if they wish to be taken seriously as grown-up journalists. They are eminently well equipped to editorialize. They have cornered a large part of the journalistic talent in broadcasting. Each network has two or three personalities with as much knowledge of current affairs as leading newspaper columnists and with a vast, loyal following in the nation. And the fact is that they *do* editorialize now, in an under-the-counter manner, especially on radio, where they don't get into trouble. Much of what passes as "interpretation" is editorializing in masquerade. It would be far healthier if the networks came into the open and unleashed their Sevareids and Brinkleys and Smiths. Charles Thomson, in his study of political television for the Brookings Institution, argues that the general principle of public policy governing communications in our society calls for a communicator to make his interests known so the recipient can assess his credibility for himself. "Moreover," Thomson says, "it is difficult for the public to imagine that owners and news staffs do not have their preferences. In the face of this, is it possible for broadcasters to preserve full faith and credit in the absence of such a statement of political preference?"[20]

Thomson believes that network editorializing would not affect politics in a manner very different from the impact of weekly news magazines: "One possible gain to come from the taking of a mature editorial point of view by the networks would be an increase in the relative emphasis on the news and public service functions of the medium, over its current emphasis on entertainment and advertising."[21]

Variety, noting that when network newsmen have something tendentious to say they do it in print, says that the networks frown on subjective reporting. "But some observers read this as merely a handy cop-out from the performance of truly responsible journalism," the paper adds. "If it did nothing else a mix of personal (depth) journalism on the air might help disabuse skeptics that the networks are too connected to government to depart from the script."[22]

Behind much of the hesitation about forthright broadcast editorials is the awkward question of whether to endorse political candidates. Far fewer stations have the courage to do this than the overall figures on broadcast editorials would suggest. The NAB survey revealed that no more than one out of ten stations (10 percent radio, 9 percent television) say they have endorsed a candidate even once. Before 1963, it was 4 percent; 6 percent in the 1964 Presidential year; 4 percent in 1966. In that year, 2 percent of the stations editorialized on behalf of local office seekers, 3 percent on candidates for state positions and 2 percent on candidates for the U.S. House or Senate. The FCC reported that only 21 television stations and 110 radio stations broadcast editorials for or against political candidates in 1966. More stations editorialized in the general election than in the primaries. All of the 21 TV stations reported broadcasting "reply" statements, whereas only 61 of the radio stations said they did.

It is surprising, perhaps, that more stations do not feel freer to endorse local or statewide candidates than national personalities. Politicians generally have not welcomed the practice but it is only the Congress which has any legal power of reprisal. Congressional anguish about broadcast endorsements has resulted in hearings on the matter and there have been unsuccessful attempts to ban such editorials. Considering its generally obsequious stance before politicians, the industry's reluctance to be bold in this very sensitive field is understandable. It is part of a total attitude.

Apart from the fear of offending politicians, the reluctance to editorialize boldly also stems from a fear of advertisers. The NAB says it found that "only about 30 percent of editorializing stations have ever had the experience of an advertiser threatening to actually take action as the result of an editorial they have broadcast."[23] It is strange that the Association says "only 30 percent," since that seems a high enough figure to scare off many broadcasters who read the report. Sixteen percent of the stations reported cancellation of advertising or threats to do so. In 8 percent of the cases, the advertiser tried to change the station's editorial position, and 4 percent of the stations said the advertiser had increased his spending in competing media. These figures, disturbing enough, are probably not the whole story. There is a syndrome, as we have noticed, that inhibits broadcasters. It is the anticipation either of offending a particular advertiser or of disturbing the general climate of commercial peace by alienating a section of the audience. How many stations simply do not broadcast editorials because their instincts tell them it would not be good business is not discussed by the NAB.

The Fairness Doctrine, then, appears to be only one obstacle to broadcast editorializing and, in the opinion of responsible authorities (e.g., the *Journal of Broadcasting*), it need not be one. It is significant that the NAB survey found that stations which do editorialize now are less likely to cite the Fairness Doctrine as a difficulty than do those stations which editorialized and have stopped.

Viewed positively, the Doctrine can be regarded as a stimulus to a bolder editorial policy and a protection against outside pressures. Revoking it, as many broadcasters advocate, would be unlikely to result in more forthright expressions of editorial opinion.

Section 315: Equal Time

The broadcasting regulation most intimately connected to a politician's well-being is Section 315 of the 1934 Communications Act. As amended, the pertinent part of that Section says: "No station licensee is required to permit the use of its facilities by any legally qualified candidate for public office, but if any licensee shall permit any such candidate to use its facilities, it shall afford equal opportunities to all such other candidates for that office to use such facilities: *Provided,* That such licensee shall have no power of censorship over the material broadcast by any such candidate."[24]

This requirement is merely an extension of the principle of fairness which Congress decided in 1934 should govern broadcasting in the United States. However, it has caused the industry more anguish and produced more charges of unfairness than all other broadcast regulations. It is also the regulation which the general public knows most about. As it stands at present, Section 315 is partly responsible for the frightening costs of modern political campaigning, and it stands in the way of the most important innovation in Presidential campaigns, the television debate between Presidential candidates. The attempts by the broadcasting industry, led by the networks, to abolish 315 are vigorous and unceasing. Should it be abolished? Does it provide essential protection for politicians or is it being used by incumbent politicians, especially in the White House, as a shelter from the risk of exposure?

Let us examine the merits of the industry's case. Frank Stanton, CBS President and the most vociferous network opponent of 315, has testified repeatedly to congressional committees for its abolition. In 1963, he told the House Commerce Committee: "A statutory device was contrived to impose upon broadcasters a civic responsibility. The device backfired. Far from assuring the execution of that responsibility, it created over the years a chronic situation which has had exactly the opposite effect; it deprived broadcasters, by the unworkable, mathematically implausible and substantively self-defeating equal time requirement, of an opportunity to carry out their responsibility. By forcing them, in defiance of all dictates of relevance and significance, to give equal time to the most trivial and irresponsible candidates of the most bizarre parties, it forced them also to deny time to the busy and distinguished men and women seriously aspiring to serve their nation, their states and their communities."[25]

What Stanton does is to take an argument which applies chiefly to Presidential races (where there is a traditional proliferation of nuisance candidates) and spread it over state and local races.

He sounded the same theme in testimony to the Senate the year before: "It makes no sense to lump together indiscriminately such phenomena as the American Beat Party, the Church of God Party, and the Vegetarian Party, with the Bull Moose Party of 1912, or the Progressive Party of 1924, or the States Rights Party of 1948—all of which represented serious, responsible dissents, which were widely supported at the polls."[26]

There is no doubt, when arguing about Presidential races, that the presence of seventeen-odd candidates requiring equal time is a grave disincentive to responsible coverage of a political campaign. Not only could the networks not afford to give them all time, but that would misrepresent their stature in any case. It is when broadcasting's performance is examined in local and state campaigns when there are no nuisance candidates that Stanton's argument falls down. He implies, and the assumption has always been made, that freed of the need to give equal time to fringe candidates, broadcasters would happily make time available to the serious contenders. Jack Gould wrote in 1967 that "there is no denying that far more hours would be allocated to politics if stations weren't obliged to treat fringe candidates with the same regard as the two men who have a real chance to enter the White House." However, when there are only two candidates running in Senate or House races, broadcasters have not been dramatically more generous. Herbert E. Alexander has reported that in 1962 and 1964, television broadcasters did not provide "significantly more sustaining time when only two candidates are running than when more than two are contesting an election." He adds: "In the past the broadcasting industry has put the burden of proof on the defenders of 315. By way of rejoinder, I believe the burden of proof rests with the broadcasters to show that free time is being given generously where there are only two candidates."[27]

The broadcasters reply to that argument by asking why they should have to give free time to candidates. Richard Salant of CBS has written: "Nobody has yet suggested that a newspaper or a magazine, in return for the second-class mailing privilege, offer the candidate free advertising space; nobody has suggested that the airlines transport candidates free—although they are licensed to use segments of the nation's limited airspace just as television stations are licensed to use a portion of the electromagnetic spectrum."[28]

Nevertheless, broadcasters do promise free time at least for Presidential candidates if 315 is amended or suspended. NBC's President, Julian Goodman, offered to give two prime-time half hours without charge to each of the two major political parties for appearances by their Presidential and Vice-Presidential candidates in 1968, but said the offer would only be feasible if NBC were relieved of the "penalty" of having to offer comparable time to minor candidates. Goodman said that television could do more in dealing with the political process, that television's unique value "should not be confined to candidates' appearances in news and interview programs produced by the broadcasters, or in paid political programs."[29]

There is another problem. Even if broadcasters were willing to give large amounts of free time, in exchange for a release from 315, large amounts of free time are rapidly going out of fashion. As we have seen, what politicians increasingly want are spot commercials. Free half hours on Sunday afternoons, or even occasionally in prime time, are no substitute for the power in short commercials. So repealing 315 would not alone cause a significant reduction in campaign spending at all levels.

Another problem is the fate of minority parties. Abolition of 315 would have to be coupled with some statutory definition of a "major party." There have been a number of attempts to do so. President Johnson's proposal to finance national campaigns with public funds included a requirement that parties win 5 percent of the popular vote to qualify. That was criticized as too high a wall for small parties to climb.

Lowering campaign spending, however, is not the popular argument for eliminating the Equal Time provision. It is the possibility of more Presidential TV debates, and here the burden of proof rests as much with the politicians as with the broadcasters.

As we have seen, the Nixon-Kennedy debates of 1960 were possible because Congress temporarily suspended the provisions of 315 for that race. The suspension followed considerable modification of 315 the year before, exempting appearances by candidates on a variety of news programs. What prompted that, and built up pressure for suspension of 315 in 1960, was an FCC ruling so widely ridiculed that there was speculation that it was a deliberate attempt by the Commissioners to bring the issue to a head. During the Republican primary for Mayor in Chicago, Lar Daly offered himself for election dressed in an Uncle Sam suit and calling himself the "America First" candidate. In a news program on CBS, the incumbent Mayor was shown carrying out some official ceremonial duties and Daly demanded equal time. The FCC ruled in his favor, interpreting Section 315 as literally as possible. Later, at the NAB convention, the FCC Chairman, John Doerfer, argued for repeal of 315. The suspension went through Congress in a joint resolution on August 24, 1960, leaving barely a month to arrange the first debate between Nixon and Kennedy.

After 1960, the networks argued that the success of the debates (in their eyes) justified permanent repeal of 315. Congress, however, did not agree. The Senate Commerce Committee examined the experience of 1960 and concluded that it "did not give us a comprehensive picture of what would happen if the exemption were made permanent." Any inclination to make another experiment in 1964 was squelched by President Johnson's apparent reluctance to debate Senator Goldwater. Herbert Alexander reported that "it appeared to be high Democratic policy to avoid suspension, probably for two reasons: to avoid last-minute pressure on President Johnson to debate Senator Goldwater; and to deny Republicans sustaining time and for them (and Democrats as well) to pay for whatever broadcast time was desired."[30] By constantly linking suspension of 315 with Presidential TV debates, the networks appear to be attempting to indicate to Presidential candidates how they should campaign. Charles Siepmann cautions against hasty action to abolish a law whose intention is sound, however unworkable at present: "Such debates are by no means indispensable, they involve certain risks to the operation of the democratic process on a rational basis, but they have the advantages that, on balance, warrant our support of them. But we should not tolerate their use as the big stick with which to beat down 315 in its entirety."[31]

As the 1968 election approached, with the prospect of a much closer race for the Presidency, pressure began to build up for another suspension. Democrats and Republicans introduced bills to amend the Section but no one really expected passage without high Administration approval. At the FCC and in the industry, there was an assumption that further Presidential debates would have to wait until both candidates, as in 1960, would be non-incumbents. President Johnson's withdrawal in March suddenly made this possible. By convention time, however, the Democrats, expecting the nomination of Hubert Humphrey, seemed reluctant to push a suspension measure through Congress.

Insofar as 315 is linked to the problem of campaign costs, some amendment would doubtless help in the Presidential race. Nixon and Kennedy received far more free time from the networks in

1960, with 315 suspended, than Johnson and Goldwater did in 1964, when it was not. In 1956, both parties got a total of 29 hours 38 minutes of free time on the networks. In 1960, the total was 39 hours 22 minutes. In 1964, it was 4 hours 28 minutes. The two candidates themselves got a total of only 1 hour 18 minutes of free network time in 1964. In terms of news coverage of the campaign, there was not much difference between the two years. The networks devoted 18 hours to political specials, documentaries, analyses and roundups in 1960 and 18¼ hours in 1964.

It does not follow that revision of the Equal Time law would save money for congressional and other candidates. There are people, some within the broadcast industry, who believe stations should be made to increase the amount of free time they give. Peter Straus, of WMCA, New York, says there should be legislation "because the moral argument won't work."[32] Straus says: "We do give some time. We would give more if we had some assurance that our competitor wasn't beating our brains out at the same time." Not many broadcasters would agree with Straus when he says that "315 is the greatest excuse in the world for not giving any time to anything." Nicholas Johnson of the FCC believes "the FCC would be wholly warranted in requiring stations to give more free time." Unless amendment of 315 were coupled with some form of pressure on stations to make more time available to candidates without charge, campaign costs below the Presidential level would not be seriously affected.

To be realistic, Congress and the FCC would also have to consider the use of spot commercials in campaigns. Commercials are the real cause of soaring costs. Some authorities, like Bruce Felknor, formerly of the Fair Campaign Practices Committee, would like to see political spots simply banned. One FCC official familiar with the question of broadcast charges to politicians believes it is well within the power of the Commission to impose such a ban. Political realities suggest that Congressmen would not tolerate it. It might be, however, that a proper test of congressional opinion about political commercials would reveal more concern than the rush to use them suggests. That concern understandably focuses more on inequities of expenditure than on ethical questions. Politicians who have just discovered them are naturally excited about using the latest manipulative techniques, but as the cost mounts, and disqualifies poor candidates from the start, there may be second thoughts. It should be humiliating to a man who is, or aspires to be, a statesman to cheapen his side of the campaign dialogue in this manner. A politically feasible way to limit the use of spots, perhaps to pieces of five minutes or longer, would be welcome.

Repealing 315 recommends itself as a solution to the current problems, then, only if it is conditional on: (*a*) an extension of the Fairness Doctrine or some other means of guaranteeing fair, and immediate, exposure to more than one candidate; (*b*) a definition of "major party" to guarantee at least some exposure to responsible small parties; (*c*) a requirement that stations provide some free time; (*d*) some limitation, either by length or expenditure, on the use of short commercials.

Given the difficulty of reaching agreement on any of these conditions in Congress, and the reluctance of more than one prominent incumbent to debate on television, the outlook for such a reform is not very hopeful. Section 315 is undoubtedly a nuisance and a hindrance to better exposure of political ideas on television. What nags in the background, however, is the suspicion that without it or some other protection, broadcasting could easily revert to the one-sided treatment of politics that used to be traditional in newspapers.

Whether it angers broadcasters or not; whether it requires extra effort; whether it puts a mild limitation on their profits, the principle of Fairness should be very precious to them. As Jack Gould has said: "The greatest asset of broadcasting is the general public belief that for the most part the medium does try to be fair. . . ."

Does television need more freedom?

Robert Sarnoff complained in 1965 of an official attitude "that refuses to recognize that broadcasting, as today's foremost instrument of journalism, is entitled to the same journalistic freedom as other media of information."

In one sense he is right. There are many officials who do believe that broadcasting should remain regulated. In 1961, Newton Minow put it this way: "An analogy of broadcasting and newspapers becomes nonsense. The government does not, cannot and will not ever license newspapers. There is no physical limit to their number; anyone who has the means is free to publish a newspaper. But the government must license radio stations because in radio there is far too little room." Of course, the same has been even truer of television, but the analogy with newspapers is not the same order of nonsense today that it was in 1961. By 1975, it may be possible for virtually anyone with the means to operate a television station. Developments in UHF, which Minow himself inspired, and in cable television have created the prospect of one city enjoying (if that is the word) dozens of television channels. While it is true that the capital cost and operating expenses of broadcasting are great, it is no longer cheap to found or buy a newspaper that anyone is going to read. The decline in newspaper competition, coinciding with the growth in television competition, means that one premise of Minow's argument—which is a traditional one—is changing. There seems to be no prospect of changing the need to license television channels, to avoid the technical anarchy of radio in the 1920's, which in fact caused broadcasters to demand government regulation for protection.

How, then, is the country to resolve the paradox that in most American cities there is already more competition among TV stations than among newspapers, while newspapers are constitutionally protected from regulation and televison is not? By revoking the Fairness Doctrine? By letting TV go its own way, totally free of restrictions except for the libel laws?

At the center of this argument is the question of whether the regulations imposed by the government on television are incompatible with freedom of the press. There is no doubt that in a technical and traditional sense they are incompatible. Freedom of the press means the freedom to be as scurrilous, as irresponsible, as prejudiced as human meanness can devise with no official reprisal except legal protection from slander. The case of B'nai B'rith vs. station KTYM would suggest that regulation of broadcasting did interfere with that freedom to the extent of having to offer, at least, to tell the other side. As far as the freedom to editorialize is concerned, the agency administering the regulations has appeared keener to stimulate it than the broadcasters.

Where broadcasters feel their freedom is limited is that, in theory at least, they are *answerable* to government for their performance. It is important to distinguish between two different concerns: the resentment at interference with the freedom to maximize profits through moral pressure to broadcast public affairs material, and the concern of television newsmen for their journalistic freedom. Only the latter is relevant to any argument about government regulations and freedom of the press, yet the broadcasting industry constantly confuses the two. "The press," as far as broadcasting is concerned, is the output of the news departments of the stations and networks and some related programming. Television entertainment programming, which government officials may occasionally deplore and wish to control, is not concerned with freedom of the press.

The anxiety of serious television journalists is well expressed by William B. Monroe, Jr., Washington Bureau Chief of NBC News: "An increasing number of people are getting their news from a medium which is intrinsically nervous about government."[33]

Why is broadcasting intrinsically nervous about government? It fears the White House. It looks at the President through the eyes of the businessmen (who have the ultimate say in what the TV journalists do) and it sees immense power which—if crossed—might harm the industry in some indefinable way, like a recommendation that the networks be regulated, or that an hour of valuable prime time be sacrificed each evening to unprofitable public affairs programming. So the industry likes to keep on the good side of the President. Where does the limitation on freedom of the press spring from there? Surely from the economic relationship between TV journalism and the TV industry. It is as though each of the big steel companies ran a newspaper and the health of that newspaper depended upon the price of steel, which in turn depended upon the steel company's relations with the President.

The industry fears the Congress. It believes that someday its friends there might betray it and side with the TV reformers to pass legislation that would limit profits. At the same time, the broadcasters have the ultimate deterrent in their hands. They may not be able to refuse access to the President on questions of national importance, but television could be very tough with Congressmen if it wished to be.

Does television fear the FCC? No, but it is diplomatic enough to affect that it does. Smaller stations may tremble a little, coming up for the first license renewal, until they discover how routine that is.

One imagines the minds of top network executives resembling the junction box in a telephone system. Thick bundles of brightly colored tiny wires go in and each pair represents a professional concern. They are reasonable, highly intelligent and dynamic people or they would not have gotten where they are and survived the competition. Many of their little wires lead to concerns one would applaud, like patriotism and a square deal for the Negro. Others lead to concerns which are necessary to survival in the industry, and this is where they appear very confused to an outsider opening the junction box for the first time. It is hard to separate the colors, to distinguish which wires lead to worries about why the White House is calling and which to anxiety about the rating of a new half-hour comedy series which follows a news special. The commercial wires are so inextricably intertwined with the public service wires that they often seem inseparable. That is why people who know the industry well are never free of the suspicion that the chronic complaining about government regulation is not coming down the public service wire but the commercial wire.

Let us go back to Sarnoff's complaint that officials do not think broadcasting is entitled to the same journalistic freedom as other media of information. That is true in a second sense. Many officials, elected or appointed, regard television as a utility existing for their benefit. In the case of the White House, it is hard to deny their view on very important occasions. But on others, it is simply the duty of the industry collectively to resist that attitude. If all broadcast journalists, as a profession, treated public officials with the detachment that the best of them do, and if the broadcasting business would permit its journalists to do so, the attitude Sarnoff complains of would die.

Television has to stand up and prove itself the responsible medium of journalism it claims it is. The network news departments have gone a long way toward proving this, but are still held back by some of the frailties we have attempted to identify. If television wants more freedom (genuine journalistic freedom and not merely commercial freedom), it needs only to exploit the opportunities that lie before it. Kicking the Fairness Doctrine will not strengthen TV news coverage. Fairness is about the only quality in broadcast journalism that makes it editorially superior to print. Indeed, it has been argued by Professor Barron that, far from removing the Fairness Doctrine from broadcasting, it should be broadened into a legal right of access to all media for novel and unpopular ideas he believes are now denied a forum in the mass media.

Broadcasting has not proved that present regulations are an infringement of its journalistic freedom: what it has to prove is that its own behavior is not, either, as a closer look at broadcasting's relations with the White House should demonstrate.

12 Presidential Access to Television

When John F. Kennedy was President, the public opinion analyst Samuel Lubell said that cultivation of the Presidential image had become such a continuous process that it was "virtually impossible to tell the man from the actor in the White House."[1] Many other commentators have expressed anxiety about the special powers television has given to the Presidency. James Reston believes that television is one of the developments that are increasing the power of the White House at the expense of Congress and the press. In *The Artillery of the Press,* Reston notes that the President is able, through TV, not only to keep in constant touch with the people but to identify himself with the noblest ideals while Congress squabbles over mundane details of legislation.[2] Bernard Rubin has pointed out that television attention to the spectacle of the President in action "eclipses any widespread interest in picking apart his words."[3]

To condense these three observations, television has put the President himself in control of what image he will project to the country and enabled him to project it farther and more favorably than was ever possible before, with less competition from Capitol Hill and less interference from the press.

Watching President Kennedy and then President Johnson use television these last few years, it often seemed to me that we were experiencing something very near to government by television.

Urgent White House prescriptions for the country's every ill were rushed onto the airwaves by sympathetic TV newsmen or the President himself. They then virtually disappeared in Congress until they emerged ready for the Presidential blessing at a signing ceremony. When the President was thwarted by the steel industry, the unions, the Congress, the Russians or Fidel Castro, he came right into our living rooms to tell us how he was going to stand up to them. Television has had such an ability to personalize issues that it has sometimes seemed to be making the President personify all the processes of the Federal Government, but emphasizing only the positive, White Knight aspects of his role. It has not always worked, but we have seen enough to notice that the machinery is there. As Reston says: "Someday, we may very well have a President with the looks, the voice, and the charisma to unbalance the system even more than it is unbalanced now."[4]

This imbalance is a state of affairs that some people in the television industry believe could be corrected. Richard S. Salant says that television has tended to give the Executive a stronger voice because "the other two branches of government have turned their backs on sensible use of television."[5] It is true that conservative powers in Congress and the courts have kept some doors barred to television. In the case of Congress, the fear seems to be that regular coverage would catch too many members absent or sleeping. In this vacuum, the White House has followed the rules of any contemporary *coup d'état* and captured television first. It did not involve real fighting because from the beginning the television industry had been coaxing the Chief Executive to exploit the medium. Now the industry is having difficulty reasserting its independence. Of immediate concern is whether the industry is trying hard enough.

It is not merely a question of giving more television exposure to the other two branches of government. The multiplicity of voices on Capitol Hill is never going to allow Congress to speak with the same clarity as can one voice in the White House. Congress, moreover, cannot present to the nation the kind of personal drama television can give the life of an active President. The dramatic initiatives of government are his to command. He can snatch public attention away from Congress as President Johnson did by calling the Honolulu conference in 1966. He can do it by merely getting into his car and rushing about Washington.

LBJ used this tactic in March, 1967, to thwart Senator Robert Kennedy. In order to keep the support of the liberals and young people in the Democratic Party, Kennedy had been clinging for a year to a narrow ledge of disagreement with the President on Vietnam. To reassure those who thought he might have climbed back into agreement with Johnson, Kennedy decided to make a Senate speech. As is often the case, his aides spent two weeks leaking the fact that a Major Speech was forthcoming. Since the press was full of speculation about its contents, the White House could scarcely ignore it. On the big day, President Johnson launched an early counteroffensive. At 11 A.M., he called in newsmen and announced that he had received a letter from the Russians agreeing to talk about antimissile systems. It is not known when the letter arrived, but the timing of the release was good tactics. President Johnson then drove to Howard University and rededicated his Administration to continuing the battle for black equality. From there he hastened to the Office of Education Building and rededicated his Administration to giving every child as much education as it could absorb. Before Kennedy had arrived on Capitol Hill, the President had thus contrived to make three pieces of news with appeal for young liberals. The Kennedy speech, which included an appeal to end the bombing in Vietnam, did receive wide publicity, but it was publicity diluted by the attention commanded by the President. At the end of the day, the White House fired a parting shot by revealing that the President's daughter Luci, about whom there had been interminable coy speculation, was in truth expecting a baby.

Cynical Washingtonians may smile at such blatant tactics, but it is the image that reaches the country at large which is important. This was such an extreme case that the press and television treated it as a game. Since Kennedy's motives seemed at the time as calculated as the President's, that is the treatment the episode deserved. But the President is not always grappling with politicians as powerful as Robert Kennedy was. Usually, if he chooses, he can sit on top of the news at will and television is of invaluable assistance.

Another example is President Johnson's astounding television speech on March 31, 1968. Making it just before the Wisconsin primary, he revealed to the nation his new initiatives toward opening peace negotiations. That alone could have affected the voting. His surprise announcement of withdrawal from the election campaign was like a thunderbolt. He had used television to maximum effect.

A good deal depends on the personality of a particular President, his attitude toward television and his relationship with the networks. There has been a gradual warming toward the medium on the part of the four Presidents who have served since the introduction of television, from Truman's frosty indifference to Johnson's passionate embrace. Simultaneously, there has been a steadily applied effort by the television industry, through improvements in lighting and teleprompting devices, to help Presidents appear more at ease. With a little practice, a President can now become as accomplished and smooth as a professional performer.

Evolution of the televised press conference

Harry Truman was the first President of the television era, but he would not permit television or even newsreel cameras at his press conferences. He preferred to keep these sessions in the Roosevelt pattern, in which the President was usually not quoted directly but could be if certain remarks were placed "on the record."

The important innovation, when Eisenhower finally admitted cameras, was not just that a wider audience could see the President answering questions but that the public heard his actual words. One of the most obvious differences between live broadcast and print journalism is that the microphone at least cannot absorb "background" or "off the record" information. It cannot keep confidences or preserve a secret identity. The President cannot, during a televised press conference, hide behind the traditional "high official" or "White House spokesman" subterfuge. Not only will his syntax be mercilessly scrutinized, as Eisenhower's was, but every statement will be his complete responsibility. If it is factually wrong or antagonizes some people, the President himself must suffer the consequences.

While it is easy to argue that this is a good thing, that the President should be publicly answerable for his stewardship, one can also argue that the totally open press conference is no check on the President. Reston says there is a theory "that the modern Presidential press conference is a restraining influence on the Chief Executive," and concludes: ". . . there is a shred of truth in this, but not much more."[6] The more press conferences have been thrown open to the public gaze, the harder each President has worked to *stage manage* them so that he will appear to best advantage. It is fascinating and valuable for the public to see the Chief Executive in action. Whether more useful information about Administration policy emerges in such sessions than in quieter meetings with reporters in which the President cannot be quoted is open to question.

Shortly after President Eisenhower's inauguration in 1953, his Press Secretary, James Hagerty, suggested that press conferences should be televised. However, the first televised Presidential press conference did not take place until January 19, 1955. The ground rules were that the sound film or videotape could not be aired until the President's remarks had been checked by Hagerty. The White House reserved the right to edit them before broadcast. Even with this limitation, the event was hailed as "an example of democracy at work" by Jack Gould, who said it "represented a significant victory for TV as a journalistic medium." Eisenhower was thought to have made an effective appearance. By this time, the President had employed Robert Montgomery as a television consultant, and the actor had become the first show business personality with an office in the White House. Under his influence Ike's television performances were noticeably more relaxed and natural. Montgomery also introduced some lighting changes which gave the President a warmer appearance.

According to Pierre Salinger, John F. Kennedy initially had misgivings about televised press conferences, which later became a hallmark of his Administration. The President was worried about the danger of overexposure, he did not think print reporters would like televised news conferences and he wondered whether the television networks would make air time available if there was no certainty of a major news break. "The strongest and most persistent argument against live TV press conferences was that a single slip of the lip by an American President could push an already jittery world a little closer to disaster," Salinger said.[7] Regular White House correspondents did object to the innovation. Edward T. Folliard of the *Washington Post* told Kennedy's Press Secretary: "You're turning the Presidential press conferences into a sideshow."

The first Kennedy press conference broadcast live was held on January 25, 1961, in the evening in order to attract the biggest audience. It was widely praised. The *New York Times* called it "an altogether successful innovation for both government and television." It captured 33.8 percent of the available television audience. This respectable "rating" was bettered on February 15, when the press conference was broadcast an hour later (7 P.M. Eastern Time) and 40 percent of TV homes tuned in. In between, there had been two televised afternoon press conferences with lower ratings, and the audience continued to decline. On March 1 and March 8, the programs drew only 18.8 percent and 13.9 percent respectively. Nevertheless, the American Research Bureau (Arbitron) reported that whenever Kennedy went on the air, the number of sets in use rose by 10 percent.

Kennedy soon ran into criticism over the press conferences. In April, 1961, after there had been seven conferences, Gould called them "anticlimactical" because the President made all the news with his opening statements and "most of the subsequent questions have been astonishingly drab." A year later, the same critic decided they were still "excellent TV fare," but criticized the President for resorting to "the sticky tactic of trying to be responsive without adding anything to the issue."

Kennedy held fewer press conferences than Roosevelt, Truman or Eisenhower. He averaged roughly one every two weeks, and historian Arthur Schlesinger, Jr., who was a Kennedy aide, called them "the central forum of Presidential contact." Schlesinger believed that Kennedy's "success was the product of study as well as art. Salinger organized a meticulous briefing process, drawing in predicted questions and recommended responses from information offices across the government."[8]

Kennedy continued to worry about overexposure and, according to Robert Kintner, "was immensely conscious of the significance of television. Whenever he appeared on the screen he wanted to know what his ratings were. He worried about timing his appearances and those of his family."[9] Kintner said that when he was President of NBC, Kennedy called him after Jacqueline Kennedy's televised tour of the White House and they had a long discussion about whether she was in danger of overexposure. The President of the United States decided that she was.

There were many critics of his press conference technique. It was felt that Kennedy, by the virtuosity of his performance, often disguised the fact that he was passing over important points. No one doubted that he enjoyed these performances in the State Department Auditorium. He made two women reporters, May Craig and Sarah McLendon, who represented newspapers in Maine and Texas respectively, into national celebrities by calling for their questions whenever the going began to get heavy. He had mastered the difficult art of delivering a funny twist when ending a reply. Gore Vidal, writing after Kennedy's death, described him as "a natural for this time and place, largely because of his obsession with the appearance of things." Vidal said it was not the fault of President Kennedy if his televised press conferences "were not very informative."[10] It was also noticed that the press conferences tended to gloss over weaknesses and play up strengths and that reporters found "their role was largely one of audience participation in a show."[11]

The Presidential press conference has often been compared to the period of searching questions the British Prime Minister is subjected to at "question time" in the House of Commons, but there are important differences. The President himself controls the occasion because he recognizes the questioners, whereas in the British Parliament members are recognized by an impartial Speaker. Because the President is more than a political figure and receives the respect due a head of state, there is a tradition that reporters do not usually bore in on him with questions. If he does not answer satisfactorily, they have to be unusually diplomatic in their persistence if they wish to follow up.

Especially under the public gaze, reporters tend to compete with one another in asking clever or well-informed questions on a variety of subjects instead of cooperating in following up one subject. The televised press conference, in which personal vanity or professional prestige may motivate a reporter to be recognized, makes it easier to plant questions. Kennedy did this on occasion and President Johnson has done it a great deal.

A TV reporter's physical appearance on the screen is the equivalent of a printed by-line. Competition to get on the screen is therefore as fierce as the competition to get a story on the front page of a newspaper. Unfortunately, the criteria are not always the same. When the TV news departments decide what pieces of the televised Presidential press conference to include in their news programs, whether their own reporter asks a question is a factor in the decision. If he does, he is often used, whatever the news value of the response he elicits from the President. Television news organizations, network and local, have frequently considered that the prestige accruing to them in having their own representative ask the President of the United States a question is more important than what the President said in response. So the pressure on TV reporters to be recognized is even greater than for the print journalists. A White House aide who was closely connected with the press conferences under President Johnson says that while newspaper reporters would sometimes refuse to ask questions planted by the White House staff, television reporters never refused.[12]

The Kennedy specter

Lyndon Johnson came to the Presidency haunted by the Kennedy skill with television. For seventeen months after the assassination, he refused to hold a televised press conference in the State Department Auditorium, which Kennedy used. In his desire to be seen taking hold of the Presidency and to keep the nation on course after the shock of Kennedy's death, LBJ used extensively every instrument of publicity. In his first six months in office, he gave 189 speeches, compared to 105 delivered by Kennedy in a comparable six-month period, the year before. Johnson held sixteen news conferences, compared to nine for Kennedy, but preferred the old style of seeing reporters without the presence of television cameras. Presumably to avoid comparisons with Kennedy that would interfere with his effort to impose his personal style on the Presidency, Johnson delayed holding a televised news conference for over a year. Joseph Laitin, who was Assistant White House Press Secretary, says: "The most logical place to hold the TV press conference is in the State Department Auditorium. But he was so self-conscious that it would invite comparisons that we couldn't get him over there."[13] The first televised conference was, in Laitin's view, a "disaster" of overcrowding in the old White House movie theater. After that, President Johnson had conferences moved into the East Room of the White House. "LBJ will not imitate anybody," Laitin says, "so it evolved into the East Room." Finally, on April 16, 1965, he consented to move into the State Department.

Johnson followed the Kennedy technique, but with his own variations. He frequently used a large portion of the half hour for his own announcements. Sometimes this section would last as long as ten minutes, and brought accusations that he was filibustering to limit the time for questions. In many ways he handled questions as adeptly as Kennedy, often with humor, although his replies sometimes degenerated into long-winded recitations of well-known facts delivered in a tone of self-justification. The *Christian Science Monitor* commented after one Johnson press conference that it "felt the President was conscious of the weight of his words being sent around the world. . . . The result was an impression that some questions were not being so much confronted as explained away."

Johnson was perhaps no more self-conscious about image than Kennedy, but showed it more. With a background in the art of manipulating men that makes for success in the congressional leadership, he wanted to arrange and manage. Whereas Kennedy's aides would, with his knowledge, plant one or two questions for a press conference, Johnson often tried to plant a great many. The practice rankled some members of his staff because they felt it was being overdone.

Between his televised news conferences, which never generated the excitement of Kennedy's, Johnson continued to hold meetings with reporters out of the range of the cameras. He felt more comfortable in these sessions because they were more in his control. Often they would be called at very short notice on weekends, and only a dozen or so regulars would be present. Then the President would relax, adopt the highly colorful, pungent language that he preferred, and give candid opinions about people and events. Sometimes Lady Bird would sit in on these sessions, modestly not hearing the President's riper remarks. On this more intimate basis, with the ground rule that his remarks could not be quoted, the reporters as well felt more at ease and would press the President to be more specific when he was vague. Many reporters and members of his staff felt that if something of the personality the President revealed in such informal briefings could be transferred to the public occasions, the image trouble that was constantly being discussed would partly evaporate.

Late in 1967, LBJ did attempt a more informal television press conference. Instead of being anchored to a lectern, he wore a small microphone with a long cable. It let him move around and gesture as he answered the questions. The effect was widely praised as appearing more natural.

How the networks control Presidential appearances

The ambivalence network news departments feel about the President's access to their medium is well summed up by one news executive: "I've had the feeling at times that we should tell the White House to go to hell. Sometimes we just ought not to run the guy. But I feel the medium has some obligation to be fairly open to Presidential use."[14]

The conflict here runs very deep. The White House tends to assume that when the President of the United States has something he thinks important to say to the nation, his wish should be a command. The network news departments, ideally, would like to treat the President journalistically as news, to have the privilege newspapers have of hearing what the President has to say, then of deciding whether to carry a few lines or the full text. TV journalists, like newspapermen, are constantly aware that the President is a political figure as well as the head of state, out for favorable publicity. At the higher levels of the television networks, other considerations complicate the decision of whether to grant the time the White House wants or to refuse. Too often, perhaps, from a journalistic point of view, they have given in. But journalistic considerations are often last in the minds of top network executives, who cannot afford such purity of vision. One consideration is the cost of preempting valuable commercial programs in prime time in response to Presidential whim, which may be prompted by mere political motives. More important is the question of the fundamental relations between the television industry and government, particularly the White House. No American President ever needs to be crude enough to remind the networks in so many words of their responsibility for public service. A Presidential request for a segment of prime time, however gently presented, cannot help but stimulate uneasy emotions in the network headquarters.

There is yet another side to this, which became particularly important with the accession of Lyndon Johnson. The networks were suddenly faced with a President himself intimately connected with the television industry. He had personal and business relations with two network heads, Frank Stanton of CBS and Robert Kintner of NBC. The Johnson family fortune had come from shrewd management of television properties in Texas, notably station KTBC-TV in Austin, which had enjoyed a monopoly for fifteen years. In 1964, the family business (put in trust when he became President) was valued at $7 million. While the common belief in the industry is that the fortune resulted from normal smart business conducted by a man prominent in public life with good connections, there have been uncorroborated charges of more sinister use of political influence.[15]

Thus the networks, already burdened by their normal sensitivity to Washington opinion, confronted a President who had closer ties with their own business than any previous occupant of the White House. When he did not get his way, he could ring them up and complain—and he did.

What happens when the President wants to go on network television? First let us look at the mechanism that has evolved. Each of the television networks maintains a news bureau in Washington with a bureau chief, or Washington news director. These men form a committee which has the responsibility of maintaining liaison with the White House. On each of their office telephones there is a special button which can tie them into a conference call with the White House Press Secretary. They can all be on the line very quickly when the White House wants to discuss something and they can be reached at home through the White House switchboard after office hours.

The chairmanship of the committee rotates every three months. When the President decides he wants to go on the air, the White House Press Secretary calls the Chairman of the Washington Bureau Chiefs Committee and says that the President has an address to make on a certain evening. The Chairman then talks with other members of the committee and comes back with an answer.

This is where the situation can become delicate. Each President has had his own style of requesting time. Hagerty and Salinger would tell the networks that the President's address was "important" and literally ask for time. Lyndon Johnson, according to one network executive, has a "thing" about never technically *requesting* time. His Press Secretary may or may not be willing to say that the intended speech is "important," so the White House and the networks play what the same executive calls "this elaborate and silly game in which we are assured that he is not requesting, and it is entirely up to us; but that it is going to be important, &c, &c." If the White House says clearly, "This is a major speech," acceptance by the networks is virtually automatic.

William B. Monroe, Jr., who has been Washington Bureau Chief for a number of years and frequently involved in these negotiations, says that NBC has refused on occasion when the White House could not say, "This is an important speech." Monroe thinks the networks have some obligation to go beyond the journalistic criterion: "Often it is not just deciding whether to have the President or another story. It's LBJ or some game show or *Please Don't Eat the Daisies*. It's not purely like a newspaper."

He thinks the decision should be left to the network executives and that "the President should not be able to reach them if they make a decision he doesn't like."[16]

George Reedy, who handled it from the other end as President Johnson's Press Secretary, believes the networks cannot refuse. He says: "I do not believe that any medium which is used to communicate to the public can in conscience turn down a Presidential request for time. If the request is imprudent, it is the President who will be harmed, not the medium, which only loses some money. There are no dangers in the network's acquiescence to a Presidential request for time. There would, of course, be dangers if the networks should acquiesce to any Presidential request for special treatment of news stories."[17] That is another matter, which we shall come to shortly.

In Reedy's philosophy, he cannot conceive of any Presidential request for television time that would have a low journalistic priority. "If the President uses the time for an unworthy purpose, that in itself becomes a newsworthy event. It is not up to the television networks on such occasions to decide whether the President is appearing for substantial or trivial reasons. As long as the networks do not waive their right to comment on the appearance after it is made or to present adversary material, they should merely acquiesce to the request. Of course it is conceivable that such requests could get out of hand, in which case the whole subject would have to be reexamined."

In one sense, adopting this philosophy would be a total abdication of the network's journalistic role. It is like asking newspapers to print, sight unseen, the full text of a Presidential speech on the front page every time he asks. That is what happens on the front pages of *Pravda* and *Izvestia*. But Reedy's qualifications are interesting. One of the grave weaknesses of the present system is that the networks *do* largely "waive their right to comment" on the President's appearances. They do not do it purposefully to avoid embarrassing the President, although it has that effect. They do it by default. Resumption of the full commercial program schedule has a higher priority than analytic comment by reporters after the President has finished speaking. The usual network practice is to "fill" until the normal time slot is expired, if there are only a few minutes to go. If it is a long period, they will fill briefly and then rejoin normal programs. Knowing this, an astute President will time his appearance so as to fill all or virtually all the time allotted to him. Detailed analysis of what a President has said just after he has finished speaking (when it would be most valuable) is so rare that when National Educational Television devoted an hour to a discussion right after President Johnson's 1967 State of the Union Message, it was considered a remarkable innovation.

Reedy's other qualification, that Presidential requests might "get out of hand," is also not as hypothetical as he makes it sound. To many observers, including some in the White House, President Johnson's requests for television time did get out of hand in 1965 and it was felt that the networks were far too acquiescent in putting him on.

The situation has changed since the Eisenhower years, when the networks behaved in a remarkably cavalier fashion. The context of those early disputes is interesting evidence of how much more sensitive the networks have recently become to considerations of prestige, public service and Presidential pressure.

In early 1958, there was a major row when President Eisenhower delivered an important speech on national security and all three television networks refused to carry it, although independent stations and radio did. The President's Press Secretary, James Hagerty, explained that he had not specifically requested time but had told the network committee that it would be an important and a major speech. The networks responded to the wave of criticism by saying there had been no request stating that it was a major speech. Other important speeches had been carried by the networks. During the Little Rock High School integration crisis the previous September, President Eisenhower had broadcast an appeal to the people of the city to respect the law. Jack Gould commented that it should not be left to the White House Press Secretary to decide whether TV covers the President and that television "must learn to make its own decision at all times."

The system had not changed the next fall, however. On September 11, 1958, President Eisenhower made a speech on the Quemoy crisis, warning the Communist world that the United States would have to fight, if necessary, to prevent the conquest of the offshore island by the Chinese Communists. Only the ABC television network carried the speech. NBC and CBS said that Hagerty had told them he would be satisfied if only one network broadcast the speech; the others gave summaries.

Since then, the system of consultation has remained the same but the networks have fluctuated between periods of total acquiescence, moderate rigidity and selectivity.

During another integration crisis, at the University of Mississippi in the fall of 1962, President Kennedy asked to be allowed to appear simultaneously on all three networks at 8 P.M. Eastern Time in order to reach Mississippians at 6 P.M. That would have broken into prime-time evening entertainment, however, and the networks balked. A compromise was reached eventually and the President appeared at 10 P.M. Eastern Time.

Occasionally the decision has been made at the highest network level in New York without the knowledge of the Bureau Chiefs who are negotiating in Washington.

There was such a case just after the Johnson-Kosygin meeting at Glassboro, New Jersey, in the summer of 1967. The White House contacted NBC to ask whether it would agree to turn its mobile unit into a pool unit (for the use of all three networks) when the President's helicopters landed on the South Lawn. NBC agreed and then, with the President already flying toward Washington, a White House official came through from the helicopter wanting to be sure that all the networks were willing to carry the President's remarks. According to William Monroe, it sounded as if he was looking forward to being on all three networks simultaneously. The President's plane was about to set down and there was not time to find out if all the networks were willing. "I advised the President's plane of the uncertainty," Monroe said. "A minute later he landed, came up to the microphones and spoke. I expected him to come up on NBC but he didn't. The other two networks carried it live but NBC didn't. The decision had been taken in New York. NBC delayed it and put it out at 8 P.M. in the early moments of the Kosygin news conference, which by sheer good luck had been delayed with introductory remarks. . . . The White House was very happy with it."

The system continues to be erratic, with considerations taking precedence that have no basis in journalism or a feeling of obligation to the President and the public good.

On September 29, 1967, President Johnson delivered what the White House had seen fit to describe as a "major speech on Vietnam policy." Only one network, NBC, carried it live at 9:30 P.M., preempting a program called *Accidental Family*. CBS was running the Hitchcock film *North by Northwest*, which had been under way since 9:00 P.M., and taped the LBJ speech for delayed broadcast at 11:40, out of prime time. ABC chose not to preempt the half-hour Western *Guns of Will Sonnett* at 9:30, and instead presented the President on videotape at 11:30. But the NBC decision was not based on journalistic factors alone. The program *Accidental Family* had turned out to be one of the "bombs" of the 1967 new season and was about to be dropped from the schedule. Such an opportunity to preempt was perhaps providential. The speech, delivered in San Antonio, turned out to contain a highly significant change of emphasis in Washington's attitude to Vietnam peace talks.

Frequency of Presidential special reports

The three Presidents who have had full network television available to them have varied considerably in using it to exploit what Theodore Roosevelt called the "bully pulpit" of the White House.

President Eisenhower tended to take to the air only in times of recognizable crisis or national importance—his announcement, to allay concern about his health, that he would run for reelection in 1956; the Little Rock crisis; and the Quemoy threat. He also submitted occasionally to experiments in Presidential television. In October, 1954, there was a special broadcast of a meeting of the Cabinet, with reports by Secretary of State Dulles and others. The session was criticized for appearing too staged. In May, 1955, Eisenhower and Dulles took part in a televised "dialogue" that resulted in the President listening to a long lecture from his Secretary of State with only occasional interjections. Gould said it made the mistake of casting the star as a supporting player and that Eisenhower's presence merely distracted from what Dulles was saying.

Early in his term, President Kennedy ran into a wave of newspaper criticism for not doing enough to educate the public. He was compared invidiously with the two Roosevelts and President Wilson, being criticized, as Arthur Schlesinger, Jr., puts it, for selling "himself and his family rather than his ideas," and being "unwilling to convert personal popularity into political pressure for his program."[18] Pierre Salinger says that from the first he urged the President to use television as FDR had used radio, to take his case directly to the people when he was under strongest attack. But Salinger emphasizes that even when the situation was urgent—during the Cuban Missile crisis, for example—JFK was always sensitive about asking the networks for time. James Reston believes that Kennedy's fear of appearing too often on the screen prevented him from exploiting television fully, although he had a rare ability to do so.

An innovation was an interview President Kennedy gave correspondents of the three networks just before Christmas, 1962. The program, which showed him relaxed and with an opportunity to discuss issues more fully than at his press conferences, was well received. The following year he was interviewed by CBS and later by NBC when their main evening news programs were expanded to thirty minutes.

In general, Kennedy showed restraint in using television to preach to the nation on special occasions. His press conferences gave him every opportunity to do that. He never submitted to the critics who tried to urge him to use television more to bypass an awkward Congress. It may have been that he was feeling his way toward reelection with much bigger Democratic majorities in both houses in 1964 and felt he could afford to wait.

Restraint is not the most obvious of President Johnson's personality traits. During the early months of his Presidency, he limited his television appearances, but in 1965 he wanted to use the medium so much that the television industry was stunned. So were members of his White House staff, one of whom said: "Lots of times I felt that the news was unjustified and the cost to the networks was unfair. The only man who could have told him was Jack Valenti and he was afraid to."[19]

Johnson's attitude, according to the same source, was that "when a President of the United States had a message for the American people, it should go out right away. He used Stanton on a number of occasions when there was balking at the lower echelons. On one occasion, all three networks turned down a suggestion for a remote broadcast. He called Stanton and CBS carried it in full."

Under Johnson, a fully equipped television studio was installed in the White House for the first time, located in the old movie theater. The networks actually agreed to keep a camera "warm" there at all times at a joint cost estimated at one million dollars a year. The studio, which had a director and camera crew constantly on duty, was on a five-minute alert.

The President never understood why he couldn't go down to the studio and go out, live, right away across the country. Sometimes he would want to go on at such short notice that his staff would have time only to notify the director in the studio and not the network committee. During the winter of 1965 and the summer of 1966, the networks did quite often put him on right away.

On one occasion the networks protested. The President wanted to go on immediately at nine-thirty at night, and they asked if he would wait until one minute past ten. He refused and went on at nine-fifty-five, right into *Bonanza*. The President said, "I'm ready to go now," and his staff wouldn't argue with him. One staffer said later: "The networks acted stupidly, instead of putting their collective feet down. Regardless of whether the man is President, there are certain abuses they should not put up with. You have to educate him and do it forcibly."

Eventually, Johnson too began to consider the dangers of overexposure. He also learned that barging into regular entertainment programs could cause anger and alarm in the audience.

There was a constant attempt by his staff to improve the physical mechanics for his performances. He was fitted with contact lenses to improve his appearance and became quite pliable in listening to advice on his delivery. His staff advised him to speak faster, as one put it, "to pick up the slack of his accent, give him a sharper appearance and eliminate some of the cornpone, benign paternalism."

LBJ could be irritable if arrangements were not just right. The "see-through" TelePrompTer (in which the moving script is reflected in glass invisible to the audience) was carefully placed a certain number of feet away for optimum focus on his contact lenses. On one occasion, the television cameraman made an adjustment to a cover on his lens which slightly tipped the glass plate. Instead of reflecting the script on the TelePrompTer, it showed nothing but the Seal of the President on the front of the podium. LBJ strode in and went straight on live. Since all he could see was the Seal, he had to ad-lib the speech and was furious afterward. It happened, however, that Billy Graham, the evangelist, was with him in the studio, and Mr. Johnson had to limit his complaint to: "Why can't the President of the United States get a simple thing like this done?"

Like his own staff, the television networks found President Johnson a hard man to say no to. While his enormous exposure may have been self-defeating because people tired of seeing him so much, the industry's willingness to give him carte blanche must raise serious questions about Presidential access to television. Each time a President appears on nationwide television, the occasion can be viewed from several aspects. It is the head of state dutifully informing the public about important issues of the day. It is a partisan politician, however wrapped in official dignity, scoring points against his opposition. It is the voice of one branch of government engaged in a power struggle with the others. In the last two categories at least, overheavy exposure for the President, in Reston's phrase, unbalances the system. The public is being fed too one-sided a view. This is aggravated by the absence of any penetrating discussion, as is so often the case, after the President has spoken.

In his book *Lyndon B. Johnson and the World,* Philip L. Geylin says: "He and his closest advisers made no bones about their concept of how a President's thinking ought to be conveyed to the public—by Presidential appearance on television, without comment or interpretation or analysis."[20] That is, in effect, what television has given President Johnson.

The television industry may argue that the medium cannot be expected to play its selective journalistic role fully until it is, like the press, free of government regulation. But the regulations which bother the industry (Equal Time and the Fairness Doctrine) do not in any obvious way prevent the networks from establishing sounder criteria for giving the President access to the public ear. At the moment, the criteria are confused, an accidental mixture of commercial canniness, journalistic integrity, hunger for prestige and blind fear of the White House, a fear which threatens to make television a conduit for the propaganda of one branch of government.

It does not stop there. Another of the qualifications mentioned by George Reedy needs to be examined—the danger of the networks acquiescing to any Presidential request for special treatment of news stories.

Presidential news management

Long before the question of news management became a *cause célèbre* in the Kennedy years, people in the White House have wished or tried to control what is said about them in the press. Some have been subtle about it and some crude. The subtlest method of news management is to cooperate very fully with the press, give them a great deal of information, omitting what you think is sensitive. With its back to the wall, an Administration can lie and deceive. Such an attempt to justify the tactical lie was what caused bad feeling between the Kennedy Administration and the press after the Cuban Missile Crisis in 1962. The crudest possible kind of pressure is to attempt to force journalists to bend their stories, to leave out material embarrassing to the Administration or to alter stories once they are written. Because officials believe that television has enormous power to do them harm or good, and because its journalistic foundations are new, the White

House has occasionally been very crude in attempting to manipulate programs.

"People in the White House think of censorship in terms of the printed words," one official said. "They do not think of it in terms of film. It may be the thought that something produced on TV is going to have tremendous impact."

He gave as an example the NBC documentary about Lyndon Johnson's background in Texas, *The LBJ Country*. LBJ had been consulted during the planning of the film and when it was made some parts were changed at his request. His staff felt that if the film had been a feature in a magazine, nobody in the White House would have been interested in reading it before it went to press. But they feel entitled to interfere when a network lets them take part in what they regard as show business, not journalism.

A senior network executive said: "I think it is a shame that what special documentaries he allows to be made about him he insists on controlling. Frankly, I think it is an even worse shame that a network which does such a documentary permits such control."[21]

George Reedy's views are pertinent again. He believes it is possible for television to be as independent journalistically as the other media, but it takes more courage. "The networks are dependent upon government franchises and cannot operate without them," Reedy says. "I have never known of an improper use of federal authority to influence the journalistic operations of the networks and as long as the networks are operated by courageous people, I do not believe there is any danger. But should there be a combination of an overbearing President and fainthearted network executives, there would be a cause for concern."

There are people in the White House and in television who would think that situation existed between President Johnson and the TV networks for a period.

In April, 1965, President Johnson met his first major foreign policy crisis by sending the Marines into the Dominican Republic, ostensibly to protect American lives but, as it later turned out, to prevent a feared Communist takeover. The wisdom of his action was widely questioned in the American press. In his study of

Johnson foreign policy, Philip Geylin says that his "flailing around in search of [consensus], his irrelevant rationalizations and often inaccurate reconstruction of events, conspired to turn an essentially unmanageable and in some ways unavoidable crisis in a fundamentally unstable and crisis-prone Caribbean nation into a crisis of confidence in the President himself."[22] It was, in Geylin's words, "an unreasoned reckless, impulsive piece of jingoism." That was the tone of much of the editorial criticism that flew around the President's ears in the weeks of the crisis. It was not the way he wanted the American people to think about the episode and when NBC News prepared a documentary on the Dominican crisis, LBJ saw his opportunity.

The documentary was produced by Ted Yates, who was killed while covering the 1967 Arab-Israeli war. Yates had a reputation at NBC for independence of mind. He wanted to tell a story as he saw it. His documentary on the Dominican intervention did not turn out totally flattering to the Johnson Administration. In common with many newspapers, Yates and the NBC correspondents raised the question of whether the U.S. intervention was right. When the program was edited, the usual screening was held for network executives, who approve any documentary before it goes on the air. After the screening, there was a curious meeting in Washington between President Johnson and NBC News executives. During the conversation, LBJ strongly made the point that his Dominican action had been badly misinterpreted in the press. Following that meeting, Yates was made to reedit the film. The tendentious parts were replaced by a very long interview with Secretary of State Dean Rusk, who naturally supported the Administration position. Since the end of any TV documentary is what usually leaves the strongest impression, that was the view the audience was left with. The script for the program was rewritten to conform with the new editing and was approved by NBC brass before it went out.

NBC was not the only network which has knuckled under to White House pressure. During the Kennedy Administration, Edward R. Murrow left CBS to become head of the United States Information Agency. He gave the propaganda arm of the American Government a new look, insisting that it tell the truth about this country in the materials it sent overseas. Before Murrow left CBS, he had made a documentary called *Harvest of Shame,* an emotional and critical account of the indignities suffered by migrant harvest labor in the United States. In March, 1961, CBS sold rights to the film to the British Broadcasting Corporation. It is common practice to sell American documentaries all over the world and it helps to recoup some of the production costs. It came out, however, that before the BBC had shown the film, Murrow, now with USIA, had tried to stop its being aired.

The story was widely used in the newspapers of both countries. It seemed uncharacteristic of Murrow to act in a way that belied his enormous reputation for independence and editorial courage. A few days later, Pierre Salinger admitted publicly that the White House had played a role in trying to get CBS to stop the film from being shown in Britain. Salinger's explanation was that the State Department feared, since Murrow was now a government official, that *Harvest of Shame* would be taken abroad as an official American Government document. Salinger said that CBS had assured the White House that it would not be offered to any other foreign countries. Why did CBS give that assurance? The film was valid and powerful journalism and its export overseas was totally in keeping with Murrow's own philosophy about truth in propaganda. And why was the White House involved if the State Department had raised the problem? Jack Gould suggested that the pressures of Congressmen from states shown in the film and whose votes were needed for Administration measures played a big part in the White House's decision to intervene.

There is a general belief among government officials, newspaper critics and network news personnel that the television networks are more susceptible to such pressure than other news media. Their weakness may at times be exaggerated because the suspicion is so rife.

Objective evidence of actual submission does not often see the light of day. It is hidden away in the minds of network executives, who rationalize one surrender by congratulating themselves for pressures they have resisted. But very often it does not require blatant White House intervention to influence TV coverage. Coverage has a way of turning out pro-Administration, or in support of the political establishment unconsciously, through a feeling in the bones of the people involved, by unverbalized anticipation of what is expected.

Just before the midterm elections of 1966, when the Democrats seemed in danger of losing strength in Congress because of general disaffection with the Administration, President Johnson attended a conference on the Vietnam war in Manila. There was press speculation that his reason for going was political, to influence the elections by a display of purposeful activity connected with Vietnam. There was a great deal of television coverage of the event and the President's comings and goings, which also served to divert television attention from the political campaign. One of the special television reports, on NBC as it happened, disturbed Michael Arlen, *The New Yorker*'s very articulate TV critic, for its unquestioning support of the Administration line. "I don't know what gets into a television network news department that makes it think it has got to stand so foursquare behind the government of the United States in all its comings and goings," Arlen wrote. "I wonder if NBC's television news people really understand the degree of complicity with official government policy that they achieve by presenting government statements at face value and then simply *not asking* the questions that intelligent men are bound to be concerned about. . . . At no time did one even hear the intimation of a murmur of a suggestion that President Johnson might have had some political interest in his Asian journey."[23]

At the time of that conference there was a constant stream of advice from the White House to the networks. NBC's White House Correspondent, Ray Scherer, and I shared at the time a Saturday-evening network news program called the *Scherer-MacNeil Report*. On the Saturday of the conference, I included in my script a mild reference to the speculation that the President's trip might be politically motivated. After the program there was a complaint to NBC from a White House official. On that occasion, as on many others, the NBC News Department told the White House official politely to mind his own business, but such a spirit of independence does not always appear when pressure is put on. It depends very much on the individual who is approached in the network and how senior is the official making the approach from the White House. Although the network news departments try to stand by their guns, if the matter is big enough it is often dealt with at a higher level and the newsmen have to do what they are told.

At the reporter's level, such pressure is usually least likely to be effective. President Johnson is very adept at playing on the vanity and ambition of the reporters who cover him, but most of them are hardened to it and not susceptible to crude pressures. But top network executives, whose ultimate concern is the safety of their franchise and the health of their business enterprise, have been susceptible.

A member of President Johnson's White House staff put it this way: "If a network can get scared by fifty letters from outraged citizens, how would you expect it to cope with the outrage of the President of the United States?"[24]

In December, 1967, the President granted one of his rare interviews to the White House Correspondents of the three networks. The networks were happy to oblige, since these occasions have always made good television, but there was considerable uneasiness in the news departments when they discovered the kind of control the President wanted—and got—over the program. During the videotaping, the day before the broadcast, he stopped the interview several times and asked for playbacks of the tape to see how he was "coming across."

The tape was edited in New York by a team drawn from the three networks. While they were editing, a stream of telephoned instructions came from the White House on what they should leave in and what they should take out. The editing was continuing when he took off to fly to Australia for the funeral of Australian Prime Minister Harold Holt. Final instructions were received by the network team in New York from Air Force One in flight. CBS and ABC both protested to White House officials but were told that the remarks the President was concerned about were matters of security. When pressed, they admitted they meant the President considered them politically sensitive.

When the program went on the air, CBS told viewers that the interview had been edited under White House supervision. The other networks did not.

The incident typifies the disturbing editorial subservience the networks are prepared to accept as part of the bargain for a President's willingness to cooperate in such a program.

The fact that on this occasion some of the TV journalists involved were moved to protest to the White House may be a hopeful sign for the future. It would be sounder policy in general, and certainly sounder journalism, for the networks to consult each other the next time such a program is proposed and make it a condition that they, not the White House, control the editing.

If the President refuses, they should not interview him.

13 The Future

In his State of the Union Message for 1967, President Johnson made a strong commitment for his Administration to better television, promising legislative proposals for a Public Broadcasting Corporation. Although he did not directly criticize commercial broadcasting, he did so by implication when he said: "We should insist that the public interest be fully served through the public's airways."

The President pressed for, and succeeded in getting from Congress, legislation setting up the Corporation with an initial operating budget of $9 million.

Considering the impact a viable public broadcast system could have politically, it is interesting to examine the pressures which attended the progress of the bill through Congress.

Educational television had existed in this country for fourteen years on a precarious financial basis. Although government grants made possible the construction of Educational stations, the heavy operating costs had to be met from charity—grants from foundations like Ford, subsidies from universities and commercial broadcasters, donations by private citizens and direct support from lower levels of government. Only on rare occasions, like the 1967 and 1968 State of the Union Messages, had NET been able to afford the luxury of connecting itself into a nationwide network. The charges for land lines operated by AT&T are very high and are a source of constant complaint by the rich commercial networks. For NET they were prohibitive. So were the salaries, equipment and studios taken for granted by commercial television. Not only were Educational stations understaffed, but they often had to make do with television cameras and studio equipment discarded by the networks. Consequently, since even imaginative television costs money, the output of many NET stations did not have the glossy, professional appeal of commercial competitors, although there were stations in Boston, New York, Washington and some western cities that achieved high standards. The impact of Educational TV was also diminished by the frequencies it was allotted in many communities, UHF channels which produced an inferior picture on whatever sets were equipped to receive it. NET had longed for better financing and, as pressure built up for an alternative to commercial fare, Educational broadcasters saw the promised land on the horizon.

Then Fred Friendly quit CBS in a storm over the Fulbright hearings and joined Columbia University. As he has described in *Due to Circumstances Beyond Our Control,* he interested McGeorge Bundy, the new head of the Ford Foundation, in a scheme to produce an experimental series of broadcasts to show the public (and the Congress) what informational television could do when freed of commercial restrictions. The result was the Public Broadcast Laboratory, a two-year series of Sunday evening broadcasts, financed by a $20 million Ford Foundation grant. The money made possible a weekly connection of some 125 NET stations, and the launching of PBL on November 5, 1967, was keenly anticipated by critics hungry for more intelligent broadcasting. Due to shortages of trained staff, PBL's initial impact was less dramatic than the advance publicity had promised. Critics were disappointed and commercial broadcasters tended to sneer, but there were signs that the output of the prestige-minded network news departments was being subtly influenced by PBL's presence. There was every reason to expect that under Av Westin, Friendly's protégé from CBS, the impact of the Public Broadcast Laboratory would grow.

Its presence, however, produced antagonisms among NET educational producers, who had operated on a shoestring for so many years, and who now resented PBL's lavish budget. Many also felt that it was tactically unwise to stake the future prosperity of noncommercial broadcasting on one series of programs which could fail to impress Congress with the need for a permanent public network. Alternatively, there were fears that PBL, which boasted that it would be provocative and irreverent where other broadcasters were timid, would fatally antagonize Congressmen. These uncertainties, and disagreement over precisely what structure a public broadcasting system should have, tended to divide the noncommercial forces in congressional hearings, when a solid front would have been more effective. That may have made it easier for opponents of noncommercial broadcasting to impose restrictive amendments on the bill which did finally pass.

By July, 1967, a composite bill had passed the Senate, and hearings opened in the House Commerce Committee. The bill provided for a Public Broadcasting Corporation with fifteen members appointed by the President. Republican members of the Committee tried unsuccessfully to kill the proposal altogether. In the behind-the-scenes bargaining, they were able to impose the requirement that no more than eight members of the Corporation could be from one party. Thus, to the disappointment of many, public broadcasting was from the beginning given a strong political complexion. The Republicans also succeeded in getting another amendment forbidding any Educational station to editorialize. The bill passed the House in that form. The restrictions constituted a grave infringement of the new television's journalistic independence.

The commercial television networks were reported to be playing a curious role. Overtly, they supported the bill. CBS promised to help launch Public TV with a grant of $1 million. There were indications, however, that the networks were anything but enthusiastic about the prospect of a vigorous Public TV system.

The establishment of a permanent system of Public TV creates the prospect, for the first time in this television generation, of a genuine alternative to the business-oriented television which has dominated our screens. If it succeeds in laying down better standards of television journalism, it will have two overlapping effects. Public TV will gradually build its own following. Frank Stanton of

CBS has estimated that it would eventually attract 10 to 20 percent of television viewers at a particular time, and would "constitute a considerable rating drain." What is hopeful in this prediction is not that commercial broadcasting will be penalized, but that it will provide more satisfying television for the minority who urgently want it now or who do not bother to watch television at all. To bring such people gradually into television's regular audience would greatly enhance the medium's prestige as a cultural force. Secondly, the more prestigious Public TV becomes, the more commercial broadcasters will feel forced to imitate it.

Some critics see a danger that commercial broadcasters for the most part will let Public TV build its own intellectual ghetto while they continue to exploit the mass audience. Jack Gould, for instance, saw the two systems on a path of disturbing mutual accommodation. "Noncommercial TV will hit the high road of culture and information, and commercial TV will sprinkle its schedules with enough periodic specials to keep a polish on its showcase windows," Gould said. Walter Goodman, a journalist writing in the *New York Times Book Review,* suggested that "with educational TV doing its job, NBC will never again have to bear the cost of televising Senate hearings and CBS will never have to bear the embarrassment of not televising them."

Network broadcasters swear it isn't so. Testifying on the Public Broadcasting bill in April, 1967, Julian Goodman of NBC said: "We do not look to the development of noncommercial broadcasting as reducing our responsibility for cultural and informational programming, or our efforts to lead the audience and pursue innovation."

For those whose chief concern in television is that the medium's enormous potential in journalism should be vigorously exploited, the political independence of Public TV will be crucial. Unfortunately, public television has, from the beginning, been steeped in politics. In some ways, as many witnesses at the congressional hearings testified, the dangers of political interference may be greater in noncommercial TV than they are on the existing networks. If the President of the United States can call the head of a commercial network to complain about a broadcast, what could he not do to the head of a corporation all of whose members he appointed?

It will be the job of the first Chairman of Public TV, from the earliest moment of its full operation, to assert real independence. He will have to be adamant, even if it means an occasional dust-up with the White House or Congress, or Public TV will become a pathetic domestic shadow of the Voice of America. Not only will the corporation become a snake pit of political rivalry and recrimination if it is not demonstrably independent of political parties, but the public will rightly have no respect for its journalism. It was unfortunate that the congressional compromise resulted in a ban on editorials. There should be an early effort to have this challenged and amended.

Because commercial TV's other interests have often forced it to be too accommodating to Congress, politicians expect the medium always to bow to their wishes. Both Public and commercial TV have a considerable job of education to do on Capitol Hill and in the state houses, not to mention the White House.

A healthy precedent was set by the existing Educational TV system in January, 1968. The NET *Journal* broadcast a film made by a British producer called *North Vietnam—a Personal Report,* a view of the war effort and bomb devastation in North Vietnam, and largely sympathetic to Hanoi. Thirty-three members of the House of Representatives had tried to stop the film from being shown by issuing a public statement denouncing it and NET. It was shown anyway.

The independence of noncommercial television will be determined not only by courage but by how it is financed. The Ford Foundation suggested that a domestic satellite system be launched to carry, among other communications, the network television signals. This would remove networking from the land lines operated by AT&T and, by Ford's calculation, save the networks millions of dollars a year. The amount saved (some estimates put it as high as $30 million) would go to Public TV. The Carnegie Commission proposed, instead, that the public system be financed through a special tax. Each new television set sold would carry an excise tax of, say, 2 percent. As more revenue was needed, the rate of tax would be increased. A third proposal, regarded by many as most limiting to political independence, is for a direct appropriation by Congress each year.

The new technology

A number of innovations in television technology may, if thoroughly exploited, radically change the face of broadcasting in this country.

The UHF system is already a creeping revolution. Since 1964, each new television set sold has had to be equipped to receive UHF signals. In August, 1966, 32 percent of all television households could receive UHF and the penetration was increasing at the rate of about 1.5 percent a month. By mid-1967, some 50 percent of TV set owners could pick up UHF. The licensing of UHF stations was proceeding as rapidly. In 1966, twenty-two new UHF stations went on the air; in 1967, fifty. In July, 1967, FCC figures showed there were 616 commercial television stations in operation (both UHF and VHF) and 166 Educational. Construction permits had been granted for thirty-three VHF stations and 184 UHF.

One of the obstacles to greater UHF penetration (which brings with it the prospect of many more channels in each community) was that stations needed network affiliation to provide the programs large audiences wanted to watch. They could not get network affiliation easily. It is believed in the industry that as soon as more UHF stations discover a successful programming formula to attract an audience large enough to make operations profitable, there will be hundreds of applications for licenses.

With the existing television audience fractionalized, the networks are not expected to have the preeminence they do now. Recognizing this, perhaps, and fearing some leveling off of the great surge of profits after a generation of expansion, the networks have begun to diversify their interests, buying out car rental companies, book publishers and other businesses.

The other innovation of major significance is cable television, or CATV. This is a system for wiring television signals right into the home. It is particularly welcome in rural areas of fringe reception beyond the reach of desirable stations, and in cities like New York, where there is intolerable interference with good television signals. In 1964, according to the National Cable Television Association, there were 1,200 CATV services. By 1967, the number had risen to 1,817, with over 3 million subscribers. Three major controversies surround CATV, however, and could prevent its fuller exploitation: (1) whether it should or should not be permitted to originate programs; (2) whether the FCC has jurisdiction to regulate these systems; and (3) whether CATV operators should be required to pay copyright fees to broadcasting stations whose signals they pick up and relay into the home.

CATV has enormous political ramifications. One cable system transmitter can carry up to twenty-five channels. For example, a politician with a constituency forming only a small part of an area served by a normal TV station could pay for a broadcast directed only to the homes he wanted to reach in his constituency. It is capable of much greater refinement. If he wanted to reach only Republican voters in his constituency, or to direct a particular message to Negroes or families earning less than $8,000 a year, in theory he could do it.

In September, 1967, the first all-electronic news service designed for cable television was launched by a firm called Television Presentations, Incorporated, in agreement with United Press International and the New York Stock Exchange. Subscribing CATV systems could display news direct from the UPI wire and prices from the Stock Exchanges.

The battle among different groups whose interests are affected by CATV was fought through the courts. The broadcast industry was contesting the right of CATV to originate programs. Broadcasters were also demanding that CATV pay copyright fees retroactively. The United States Circuit Court of Appeals in New York ruled that cable television was totally liable for copyright payments and CATV interests appealed to the Supreme Court. There were predictions that if the Supreme Court fully enforced the liability to copyright, including retroactivity, it would kill the CATV industry. In fact, in June, 1968, the Supreme Court ruled that CATV did not infringe copyright.

As for the right of the FCC to regulate cable television, the U.S. Supreme Court ruled that it did have that power.

The advent of the cable system has upset many preconceptions about the progress of television. Jack Gould reported that "official thinking in Washington has been fundamentally altered by the realization that the revered indispensability of the airwaves faces a rude challenge from the most rudimentary method of connecting points A and B—the old-fashioned hank of wire."

It is envisioned that before many years have passed, the up-to-date home in the United States will be equipped with a communications center combining many services—a television and radio receiver; a telephone with its own picture system, and channels to permit the housewife to dial into a supermarket or department store computerized ordering service, with visual displays of the goods she is buying. The networks predict that such a center will ultimately publish its own newspaper by a facsimile system from information transmitted over television or other circuits. Television news could thus augment its broadcast service by transmitting additional information to appear in print in the home. The rapid development of home videotape recorders has already made possible the storage of programs, like news, which may appear at an inconvenient time, for viewing when people are free to watch.

None of these innovations poses any particular danger to society, if certain values and standards are respected by the people originating the information, journalistic or political. What each new development does increase, however, is the possibility of control over the minds of Americans if those values are not respected. The technology should not be exploited simply for commercial gain or political persuasion. We have seen how the existing technology of television is exploited for those purposes, when journalistic standards are submerged in commercial interests or when the politician's desire to manipulate voters outruns his responsibility to inform them. There is a tendency among both broadcasters and politicians to let their excitement over the power of the technology override their concern for the public they are serving. Rapid technical advances only make it more imperative that they be reminded of that concern.

One hesitates to raise such a hackneyed specter as Big Brother, but he is there all the time. When an elected official as skilled in televisual persuasion as Ronald Reagan can concoct filmed messages that simulate news stories and persuade television stations to run them in legitimate news programs, that is a strong dose of Big Brother. Today's politicians are not different from those of other times. By nature they convince themselves that what serves them serves the public, but it has always been the role and duty of journalists to question every instance of that assumption. If the miracle of television, and its profitability, occasionally blind the electronic journalists to that duty, the health of this democracy suffers.

By the mid-1970's, the innovations we have been discussing may have begun to give this country a new system of television.

Although there are predictions that the importance of the national networks is going to diminish, one assumes that the need for some centralized programming will be felt indefinitely. There may be more networks than exist now. CBS President John Schneider predicts at least a fourth network by 1975. Although they may get a smaller share of the national pie as more unaffiliated local stations bite into the audience, and also a smaller share individually, as competition to originate national programs increases, the networks will probably remain a major influence in American television.

In daily press handouts and lavishly printed editions of speeches by senior executives, the networks constantly assure us that they perform prodigies of public service. But what are these services? Weekends awash with sports commentators who are promoters instead of reporters? Instructional television aired at dawn when even those most dedicated to self-improvement are asleep? A diet of cartoons and violence for children? A news commitment which is the first to suffer when there is even a fractional decline in profits?

Better campaign television

Television could greatly improve the process of political campaigning at all levels of government. It could, as many authorities have pointed out, permit Presidential campaigns to be shortened to reduce the strain on the candidates, lower campaign costs and generally lessen the disruption of the political and Administration system. CBS, for example, has suggested that the campaign be cut to four weeks, with the national conventions held in September. Many politicians apparently would welcome shorter campaigns.

The networks argue that shorter campaigns would be feasible if they could provide time as they wished—if Section 315 were repealed. As we have seen, however, removing that safeguard raises almost as many problems as it solves. Just as important as shortening Presidential campaigns is improving the quality of campaigns. In either case, more extended exposure of the candidates on television would be necessary. That exposure should not all be in the control of the broadcasters, nor entirely controlled by the politicians themselves. Discussion of this problem so far by Congress and the networks has evaded the realities. It is not openly acknowledged by either side that talk of free half hours and freedom to organize TV debates is largely irrelevant today, for, as we have seen, broadcasters and candidates alike find it more convenient and profitable to use television as an advertising medium rather than as a platform.

These facts are also ignored by those, like President Johnson, who are seeking to reduce the burden of cost for candidates. The costs are what they are because politicians and broadcasters have forged a cozy alliance. It serves the broadcasting industry more than it serves the politicians and it serves the public least of all.

Knowledge of the manipulative techniques television offers is only just dawning on most politicians. Because costs will continue to rise while the quality of the political dialogue goes down, there will be a greater tendency to ignore potential candidates who are not rich enough to play the new games. Sooner or later, a major office is going to be filled by some computer-primed and wealthy nonentity put over by commercials as a national savior. The commercials both parties have shown themselves willing to make suggest a return to the nineteenth-century politics of vilification and denigration, but in a medium infinitely more persuasive (and pervasive) than a crude handbill or broadsheet.

A much wider discussion of these trends in political broadcasting is needed than Congress has undertaken so far. Instead of rushing into a scheme to finance campaigns from the Treasury, Congress or the President (or both) should study the whole question more carefully, in a bipartisan spirit, perhaps by a special joint committee and possibly a Presidential study group, with academic backing. Such an examination should include a comparison with practices in other countries, and might well produce a new conception of the role of broadcasting during campaigns. Its conclusions might be to limit commercialization, to require broadcasters to give certain amounts of time and to guarantee all parties access to that time in proportion to their standing in the last elections.

Such reform would enhance the dwindling respect the public now feels for politicians, who cheapen themselves and vulgarize their profession by reducing everything to brash electronic hucksterization.

Rethinking of the uses of political television is necessary before the election process becomes even more closely wedded to the electronic media. Actual voting by television is now being discussed. Edward E. David, Jr., Director of the Computing and Information Research Center of the Bell Telephone Laboratories, proposed in 1965 that telephones keyed into computers might be used to take simultaneous preelection samplings of the opinions of hundreds of thousands of voters in response to questions presented on television. By 1967, there had been a number of experiments with such television polling. In September, 1967, for example, station WFIL-TV in Philadelphia linked itself up with thirteen other stations around the country for a poll about Vietnam. The question—"Should the U.S. stop bombing North Vietnam?"—was presented on television, and viewers telephoned their answers (62 percent No; 38 percent Yes). The idea is capable of great refinement. Frank Stanton has suggested that actual voting could be conducted in this manner, with a device attached to the voter's telephone to identify him.

If a voter were ever thus required actually to cast his ballot on television, his dependence on the medium for information before election day would presumably be even greater than it is at present. The quality of the information he received would therefore be more important.

Better television journalism

The "gaping lack of television," according to Lester Markel of the *New York Times,* "is the effective presentation of news."[1] The pressing need of a better-informed public, he believes, requires more public affairs programming, with an urgent effort to put the news in perspective, and in prime time.

Television has *begun* to earn a respected place in American journalism, but the allegiance of its viewers has given the medium huge responsibilities before it has fully organized to meet them. There are, as we have seen, serious shortcomings in electronic journalism, despite its brilliant performance on special occasions. Most of these faults appear to be due to the subservience of the new journalism to the mass advertising-entertainment industry. There are two ways in which this situation could be improved: voluntary recognition by the industry of its responsibility for factual as well as entertainment programming; or direct government regulation.

In every way, voluntary reform is preferable, but either way will involve somewhat reduced profits for the industry. As Jack Gould pointed out in 1959, the networks must face up to an unpleasant fact: ". . . if they are going to perform a public service within the true meaning of the Federal Communications Act, then at some point there is going to be a limitation on how much profit they can make."[2]

Networks must give their news departments autonomy. Although news is given a separate budget, requested by its own executives and administered by them, there is, as we have seen, constant interference.

Once the networks accept the fact that their duty to inform is as great as their duty to entertain, the restructuring necessary to give news greater autonomy will not be difficult. It could be done gradually and, with imagination, program forms could be devised which remain profitable but do no damage to journalistic values. What is needed is some regular effort to present interesting, informational programming in prime time when a majority of viewers can be there to see it, if they choose. Just as important would be the removal of the news operation from the atmosphere of entertainment. That means not requiring news to compete with entertainment programs for ratings. It means permitting news departments to choose and treat subjects for documentary or special programs without regard for their commercial repercussions. It means standing up to politicians who attempt through improper pressures to influence programming. It means letting the news departments behave with more circumspection and dignity in their own self-promotion to separate them from the exaggerations of the rest of the industry. Perhaps, most important of all, it means treating the news as not just another commodity to be bought and sold at so much per thousand viewers but as an important contribution to democracy. It means putting an end to the casual preemption of news programs.

The networks can claim truthfully their expenditure on news has been rising. It is also true that the large news budgets of the networks (ranging from $40 million a year at ABC to $80 million at NBC) permit the parent networks to appear more generous to news than they are. We have already mentioned the considerable profits earned by the more popular regular news programs, which go a long way toward paying for less profitable ventures. In addition, each network has a complicated system of internal cost accounting which greatly exaggerates the apparent expenditure. Thus, if it cost NBC News $150,000 to make a one-hour documentary, an outside producer might make the same film for one-third to one-half of that amount because he would not be paying certain overhead charges to NBC. In other words, while the news operation does make a loss, as far as one can tell it also comes very close to paying for itself. If to that is added the intangible benefit of audience allegiance and respect which the best news programming brings a network, it could be argued by enlightened people in the industry that news is a bargain.

Also, it is difficult to concoct a convincing hard-luck story for the television networks. It is true that in 1967, as a result of uncertainties about the economy and a bad crop of new programs, profits were lower. In the third quarter of 1967, CBS made a net profit of only $10,451,065 or 43 cents a share, compared with $18,205,519, or 76 cents a share, in the same period in 1966. NBC's profits are embedded in those of the parent corporation, RCA, but ABC, the least profitable of the networks, managed to come through with a net profit of $9,515,000 in the first nine months of 1967, compared with $12,391,000 in the same period of 1966.

Perhaps a more revealing picture of the economic health of television as a whole was given by FCC Commissioner Johnson, who said in 1967 that the industry represented half a billion dollars in tangible assets that produced approximately a 100 percent return in annual gross profits. That was made possible by consumers who paid $2,000 million a year for products to sustain the "free TV" which came to them on approximately $15,000 million worth of equipment they have bought to receive it.[3] It is appropriate to point out that the 100 percent return on tangible property is achieved by using public airwaves granted as a franchise on condition that broadcasters operate in the public interest.

There is only one known cloud on the profitable horizon for broadcasters. A ban on cigarette advertising is anticipated in the industry. In fact, CBS has budgeted for 1969 on the assumption that the 19 percent of its revenues attributable to cigarette advertising would be missing. The network feels that either the government will ban such commercials or the network will feel morally obliged to do so itself.

Otherwise, years of rising profits stretch ahead as long as the economy continues to expand. Revenue from advertising was $420 million in 1952, when there were 15 million TV homes, $3 billion in 1967, with 55 million TV homes (17 percent of them with color TV), and is expected to be $7 billion in 1977, when 82 percent of TV homes have color.

The news budgets of the networks need to be considered in the context of their total business. In the third quarter of 1967, for example, NBC's total revenues were $343,028,100. One-quarter of NBC News's budget for the year was $20 million—6 percent of the company's revenues.

In 1961, Louis L. Jaffe, then a Professor of Law at Harvard, said that "given the fact that the TV industry has perforce a monopoly because of the limited TV channels, it can and should be required to devote some of its monopoly profit to the satisfaction of tastes which are commercially less profitable."[4] While that judgment could be applied to all manner of programming for minority audiences, it is particularly persuasive in the case of news.

How much time the networks should devote to public affairs programming has been a matter of debate for years. Critics have often come up with proposals to require a certain proportion by FCC regulation or by act of Congress. The industry thus far has been strong enough to defeat such attempts to impose a formula for programming on broadcasters.

Broadcasters have always contended that any attempt by the FCC to tell them how much of their programming must be devoted to one subject or another violates the intention and spirit of the 1934 Communications Act. Other authorities think differently. Newton Minow pointed out that Section 303(b) of the Act gives the Commission specific authority to "prescribe the nature of the service to be rendered by each class of licensed station and each station within any class."[5]

Attorney General William Rogers reported to President Eisenhower in 1959 that in every case in which the question had been raised, the courts had upheld the FCC's authority "to concern itself with a licensee's program policies and practices." Rogers added: "No action by the Commission has ever been held by the courts to constitute censorship to violate constitutional protections of freedom of speech or of the press."[6]

The way would seem to be open, if a majority on the FCC at any one time had the nerve, and the backing from Congress, to impose a formula.

In almost every field, private enterprise has at times had to be constrained, corrected, limited in its greed, and steered closer to the public interest. There is no reason why the broadcasting industry should be exempt. If it is absurd that Detroit should have put profit before safety, then it is absurd that an instrument as powerful as broadcasting should be controlled by men who put profit before public service; whose devotion to public service is at best a fluctuating, secondary concern, subject only to occasional crescendos of public outrage and based upon an acute public relations sense of what they can get away with.

The remedy, unfortunately, lies with Congress and the President —unfortunately, because they have a selfish interest in the behavior of broadcasting to them, as politicians.

It is sadly ironic that one should have to look to government to push broadcasters into recognition of their journalistic function, which, when performed well, should itself make government uncomfortable. It would be much better if broadcasters needed no urging.

If broadcasters continue to need urging, and if government remains loath to urge them, we may expect that the most powerful medium of all will continue to make but a small and timid contribution to our public life.

Notes

Introduction: Television—One Generation Old

1. Burns W. Roper, *Emerging Profiles of Television and Other Mass Media: Public Attitudes 1959–1967* (New York: Television Information Office, April, 1967).
2. "How Drastically Has Television Changed Our Politics?" *TV Guide,* October 22, 1966, p. 7.
3. Interview with author, July, 1967.
4. Letter to author, October 6, 1967.
5. *Equal Time, the Private Broadcaster and the Public Interest,* ed., Lawrence Laurent (New York: Atheneum, 1964), p. viii.

Chapter 1: The Audience-Electorate

1. "The Television Debates: A Revolution That Deserves a Future," *Public Opinion Quarterly,* Fall, 1962, p. 337.
2. Figures supplied by Brand Rating Index (1967), courtesy NBC and CBS Research Departments.
3. Nielsen figures, supplied by NBC.
4. Brand Rating Index figures (March, 1965), supplied by NBC.
5. Brand Rating Index estimates (1966), supplied by NBC.
6. Cited by Lester Markel, "A Program for Public-TV," *New York Times Magazine,* March 12, 1967.
7. "Some Changes in American Taste and Their Implications for the Future of Television," in Stanley T. Donner, *The Future of Commercial Television,* Report of the Stanford University Television Seminar, 1965, p. 41.
8. Elmo Roper, "The Politics of Three Decades," *Public Opinion Quarterly,* Fall, 1965, pp. 368 f.
9. Gans: Donner, p. 43.
10. *Ibid.,* p. 37.

336 | NOTES

11. "Popular Culture in America: Social Problem in a Mass Society or Social Asset in a Pluralist Society?" in Howard S. Becker, ed., *Social Problems: A Modern Approach* (New York: John Wiley & Sons, 1966), p. 566.
12. Interview with author, July 6, 1967.
13. "Television and Voting Turnout," *Public Opinion Quarterly,* Spring, 1965, p. 84.
14. Charles Thomson, *Television and Presidential Politics* (Washington: Brookings Institution, 1952), pp. 70–71.
15. *Loc. cit.,* p. 375.
16. Interview with author, May 31, 1967.
17. July 5, 1967.
18. *New York Times,* August 4, 1961.
19. Gans: Becker, p. 560.
20. August 2, 1967.
21. "Reappraisal of the TV Picture," *New York Times Magazine,* January 14, 1962.
22. *The New Yorker,* December 10, 1966.
23. Burns W. Roper, *op. cit.*
24. "Television Loses Its Grip on the Educated Viewer," *New York Post,* January 17, 1967.
25. Nielsen Survey, reported by Television Information Office, January 5, 1967.
26. Herbert E. Krugman, "The Impact of Television Advertising: Learning Without Involvement," *Public Opinion Quarterly,* Fall, 1965, p. 354.
27. *The Occasions of Justice* (New York: Macmillan, 1963), pp. 110–11.

Chapter 2: The Frailties of Television News

1. Speech to Radio-Television News Directors Association annual conference.
2. "TV Journalism—Some Thoughts by the Professional," pamphlet reprinted from *Esprit,* University of Scranton.
3. Interview with author, June 17, 1967.
4. *Loc. cit.*
5. *Equal Time,* p. 118.
6. *Ibid.,* p. 55.
7. Carnegie Report, pp. 229 f.
8. *Loc. cit.*
9. (New York: Harper & Row, 1966), p. 82.
10. Interview with author, July, 1967.
11. Scripts and/or audio tape recordings were supplied by the news departments of the three networks.
12. Interview with author, May 26, 1967.

Chapter 3: Consensus Journalism

1. Interview with author, June 1, 1967.
2. *The New Yorker,* December 10, 1966.
3. Speech to National Association of Broadcasters annual convention in Chicago, quoted by *New York Times,* May 30, 1954.
4. Robert E. Kintner, "Television and the World of Politics," *Harper's* magazine, May, 1965, pp. 129 f.
5. (Garden City: Doubleday, 1963), p. 178.
6. July 6, 1967.
7. Federal Communications Commission, "Opinion and Order on Petition for Reconsideration, ABC-ITT Merger Proceedings," Release 67–743 2055, June 22, 1967, pp. 65 f.
8. Quoted in *Time,* December 1, 1967.
9. *The New Yorker,* October 15, 1966.
10. Quoted by Joan Barthel, "When Will They Say Their Final Goodnights?" *TV Guide,* July 1, 1967, p. 19.
11. *Report of the National Advisory Commission on Civil Disorders,* The New York Times Company (New York: Bantam Books, 1968).
12. *Ibid.,* p. 366.

Chapter 4: Documentaries and Special Events

1. Quoted by former CBS executive in interview with author.
2. *New York Times,* July 13, 1958.
3. *Due to Circumstances Beyond Our Control* (New York: Random House, 1967), Introduction.
4. Quoted by Barthel, *TV Guide,* July 1, 1967, pp. 16 f.
5. *New York Times,* July 12, 1959.
6. Speech in Chicago, August 3, 1961, quoted in *Equal Time,* p. 92.
7. Edith Efron, "The Great Television Myth," *TV Guide,* May 6, 1967, pp. 8–13.
8. Theodore H. White, *The Making of the President, 1964* (New York: Antheneum, 1965), p. 403.
9. Carnegie Report, p. 232.
10. Interview with author.
11. Interview with author, July 21, 1967.
12. Quoted in *Newsweek,* June 20, 1966.
13. Speech in Pittsburgh, November 11, 1966.
14. Letter to author, August 11, 1967.

Chapter 5: Conventions and Election Nights

1. See Herbert Waltzer, "In the Magic Lantern: Television Coverage of the 1964 National Conventions," *Public Opinion Quarterly,* Spring, 1966, pp. 33–53.

2. *Elections 1964* (Silver Springs, Md.: *National Observer*, 1964), p. 80.
3. June 5, 1964.
4. Interview with author.
5. *Loc. cit.*, p. 45.
6. Thomson, *op. cit.*, p. 9.
7. August 23, 1956, quoted in *New York Times*, August 28, 1956.
8. *Op. cit.*, pp. 110–11.
9. Interview with author, June, 1967.
10. Letter previously cited, October 6, 1967.
11. Letter previously cited, August 11, 1967.
12. Quoted by James A. Fixx, "An Anniversary Talk with Huntley and Brinkley," *McCall's,* October, 1966, p. 56.
13. *Loc. cit.*, pp. 51 f.
14. Interview with author, May 23, 1967.
15. *Op. cit.*, p. 201.
16. This and subsequent quotations are from an unpublished manuscript of a speech by Paul Tillett to a meeting of the Republican Committee on Convention Reform, Washington, D.C., September 15, 1966. Tillett died a few weeks later.
17. Interview previously cited, May 23, 1967.
18. "Where the Action Is," *Book Week* (*New York Herald Tribune*), April 30, 1967.
19. *The Making of the President, 1960* (New York: Atheneum, 1961), p. 188.
20. Pierre Salinger, *With Kennedy* (New York: Doubleday, 1966), p. 362.
21. Douglas A. Fuchs, "Election Day Newscasts and Their Effects on Western Voter Turnout," *Journalism Quarterly,* Winter, 1965.
22. Kurt Lang and Gladys Engel Lang, "Ballots and Broadcasts: The Impact of Expectations and Election Day Perceptions on Voting Behavior," paper presented at the 1965 Annual Conference of the American Association for Public Opinion Research, May 14, 1965, p. 10.

Chapter 6: The Televisible Candidate

1. See Samuel L. Becker and Elmer W. Lower, "Broadcasting in Presidential Campaigns," in Kraus, ed., *Great Debates* (Bloomington: Indiana University Press), pp. 27–44. Also Thomson, *op. cit.* Other historical material from 1952 onward from files of *New York Times.*
2. Text of Nixon broadcast, *New York Times,* September 24, 1952.
3. "The Influence of Television in the 1952 Elections," cited by Thomson, *op. cit.*
4. Arthur M. Schlesinger, Jr., *A Thousand Days. John F. Ken-*

nedy in the White House (Boston: Houghton Mifflin, 1965), pp. 714–15.
5. *The Making of the President, 1960*, p. 51.
6. See John R. Owens, *Money and Politics in California: Democratic Senatorial Primary, 1964* (Princeton, N.J.: Citizen's Research Foundation, 1966).
7. Interview with author, June 30, 1967.
8. P. 276.
9. This and all subsequent Napolitan quotations, unless otherwise indicated, come from a series of interviews with the author during the summer of 1967.
10. Interview previously cited, May 23, 1967.
11. "The Future of National Debates," in Kraus, *op. cit.*, p. 168.
12. Interviews with author, June 1 and 16, 1967.
13. Interview with author, June 12, 1967.
14. Interview on BBC-TV, September, 1967.
15. "California: Man vs. Image," October 6, 1966.
16. Interview with author, July 11, 1967.
17. Interview with author, June 12, 1967.
18. "The Case for Political Debates on TV?" *New York Times Magazine*, January 19, 1964.
19. "Were They Great?" in Kraus, *op. cit.*, p. 134.
20. Interview on BBC-TV, September, 1967.
21. Interview previously cited, May 23, 1967.
22. Thomson, pp. 138 f.
23. Murray B. Levin, *Kennedy Campaigning* (Boston: Beacon Press, 1966), p. 289.
24. Bernard Rubin, *Political Television* (Belmont, Cal.: Wadsworth Publishing Company, 1967), p. 11.
25. *Op. cit.*, p. 299.

Chapter 7: Debates

1. Salinger, *op. cit.*, p. 54.
2. *Robert Kennedy in New York* (New York: Random House, 1965), p. 138.
3. Interview previously cited, June 28, 1967.
4. "Production Diary of the Debates," in Kraus, *op. cit.*, p. 78.
5. "Notes from Backstage," *The Reporter*, November 10, 1960, reprinted in Kraus, *op. cit.*, p. 129.
6. *Ibid.*
7. "Personalities vs. Issues," in Kraus, *op. cit.*, pp. 155 f.
8. In Kraus, *op. cit.*, pp. 313–29.
9. *The Making of the President, 1960*, p. 292.
10. Katz and Feldman, in Kraus, *op. cit.*, p. 204.

11. In Kraus, *op. cit.,* p. 132.
12. "A CBS View," in Kraus, *op. cit.,* pp. 68–69.
13. *Op. cit.,* p. 11.
14. In Kraus, *op. cit.,* p. 71.

Chapter 8: Campaigning by Commercial

1. Interview with author, May 23, 1967.
2. Interview with author, June 1, 1967.
3. Interview previously cited, July 21, 1967.
4. *TV Guide,* October 22, 1966, p. 9.
5. "A Candidate Is Not a Product," *Fair Comment,* Quarterly of the Fair Campaign Practices Committee, February, 1965, p. 2.
6. In Kraus, *op. cit.,* p. 50.
7. Interview with author, June 28, 1967.
8. White, p. 294.
9. White, p. 294.
10. Interview with author, February, 1964.
11. Kintner, *loc. cit.,* p. 128.
12. Interview with author, June 6, 1967.
13. Interview with author.
14. "Nelson Rockefeller's Last Hurrah: The Almost Perfect Political Campaign," *The National Observer,* January 9, 1967.
15. Interviews previously cited, June 1 and 16, 1967.
16. Interview previously cited, June 12, 1967.
17. A. C. Nielsen figures.
18. Interview previously cited, July 6, 1967.
19. *Loc. cit.,* p. 353.
20. See Angus Campbell, "Has Television Reshaped Politics?" *Columbia Journalism Review,* Fall, 1962, pp. 10–13.
21. See Fred I. Greenstein, *The American Party System and the American People* (Englewood Cliffs, N.J.: Prentice-Hall, 1963), pp. 22–26.
22. Lawrence W. Lichty, Joseph M. Ripley and Harrison B. Summers, "Political Programs on National Television Networks: 1960 and 1964," *Journal of Broadcasting,* Summer, 1965, pp. 217–30.

Chapter 9: The Cost

1. Based on calculations by Dr. Herbert E. Alexander, Director of the Citizens' Research Foundation of Princeton, N.J., in his study *Financing the 1964 Election,* 1966.
2. Quoted in *The Reporter,* February 16, 1960, p. 20.
3. Cited by Rubin, *op. cit.,* p. 129.

4. Quoted by Roscoe Drummond, "Campaign Costs," *Christian Science Monitor,* April 24, 1967.
5. *Op. cit.* Figures from Alexander Heard, *The Costs of Democracy* (Chapel Hill: University of North Carolina Press, 1960).
6. November 3, 1952, cited by Thomson, *op. cit.,* p. 60.
7. See Herbert E. Alexander, *Financing the 1960 Election* (Princeton, N.J.: Citizens' Research Foundation, 1962).
8. Figures from Alexander, *Financing the 1964 Election.*
9. "Survey of Political Broadcasting, Primary and General Election Campaigns of 1966" (Washington, D.C.: FCC, June, 1967).
10. Cited by Herbert E. Alexander and Harold B. Meyers, "The Switch in Campaign Giving," *Fortune,* November, 1965.
11. Alexander, *Financing the 1964 Election,* p. 26.
12. Quoted by Tom Buckley, "The Three Men Behind Rockefeller," *New York Times Magazine,* October 30, 1966.
13. FCC 1966 Report, Table 4.
14. Interview with author, July 10, 1967.

Chapter 10: The Congressional Image

1. Date p. 31.
2. *Equal Time,* p. 36.
3. Interview previously cited, July 11, 1967.
4. Interview with author, July 10, 1967.
5. *Loc. cit.*
6. *Equal Time,* p. 37.
7. Letter previously cited, October 6, 1967.
8. Interview with author, July 11, 1967.
9. *New York Times,* May 2, 1954.
10. "Goodman—On Record," *Television Digest,* March 13, 1967.
11. See Cleveland Amory's review of *Meet the Press, TV Guide,* March 9, 1968, p. 44.
12. May 9, 1966.

Chapter 11: Government Regulation

1. *New York Times,* March 8, 1967.
2. Interview previously cited, June 17, 1967.
3. *Saturday Review,* May 7, 1966, citing report in *New York Herald Tribune.*
4. Interview previously cited, July 11, 1967.
5. *Loc cit.,* p. 131.
6. FCC, *Applicability of the Fairness Doctrine in the Handling of Controversial Issues of Public Importance,* Public Notice of July 1, 1964, *Federal Register,* July 25, 1964, pp. 10415–27.

7. Reg. G. Howell, "Fairness . . . Fact or Fable?" *Journal of Broadcasting*, Fall, 1964, pp. 321–30.
8. "Access to the Press—A New First Amendment Right," LXXX (1967), 1664.
9. *Ibid.,* 1661.
10. Speech in Chicago, August 3, 1961, quoted in *Equal Time,* p. 62.
11. "The Fairness Doctrine," *Journal of Broadcasting*, Summer, 1965, p. 14.
12. FCC Public Notice of July 1, 1964, Question and Answer section.
13. *Ibid.*
14. "A Statement of the Fairness Doctrine," Spring, 1965, pp. 106–7.
15. *Ibid.,* p. 111.
16. *Report of the Federal Communications Commission in the Matter of Editorializing by Broadcast Licensees,* Public Notice of July 1, 1949, paragraph 18.
17. Speech in Washington, D.C., March, 1962, quoted in *Equal Time,* p. 62.
18. Winter, 1963–64.
19. *Ibid.*
20. *Op. cit.,* p. 122.
21. *Ibid.,* p. 102.
22. June 28, 1967.
23. "Broadcasters and Editorializing, A Study of Management Attitudes and Station Practices," summary of report by the Research Department of the National Association of Broadcasters, July, 1967.
24. FCC Public Notice of October 9, 1962.
25. "Statement Before the Subcommittee on Communications, House Interstate and Foreign Commerce Committee, March 4, 1963," CBS press release.
26. "Testimony Before Senate Communications Subcommittee, July 10, 1962," CBS press release.
27. Herbert E. Alexander, Stimson Bullitt, Hyman H. Goldin, "The High Cost of TV Campaigns," *Television Quarterly,* Winter, 1966, p. 50.
28. *Loc. cit.,* p. 343.
29. Speech to NBC-TV Affiliates Convention, March 13, 1967, Los Angeles, NBC press release.
30. Alexander, *Financing the 1964 Election,* p. 51.
31. In Kraus, *op. cit.,* pp. 139 f.
32. Interview with author, July 7, 1967.
33. Interview with author, July 11, 1967.

Chapter 12: Presidential Access to Television

1. In Kraus, *op. cit.*, p. 156.
2. P. 50.
3. *Op. cit.*, p. 119.
4. *Op. cit.*, pp. 50 f.
5. Letter previously cited, October 6, 1967.
6. *Op. cit.*, p. 51.
7. *Op. cit.*, p. 54.
8. *Op. cit.*, p. 716.
9. *Loc. cit.*, p. 123.
10. "The Holy Family," *Esquire,* April, 1967.
11. Rubin, *op. cit.*, p. 86.
12. Interview previously cited.
13. Interview with author.
14. Interview with author.
15. See J. Evetts Haley, *A Texan Looks at Lyndon* (Canyon, Texas: Palo Duro Press, 1964), especially Chapter 3.
16. Interview previously cited, July 11, 1967.
17. Letter previously cited, August 11, 1967.
18. *Op. cit.*
19. Interview with author.
20. (New York: Frederick A. Praeger, 1966), p. 154.
21. Interview with author.
22. *Op. cit.*, p. 237.
23. "The National Broadcasting Company Views the Manila Conference and Finds It Pleasing," *The New Yorker,* November 12, 1966.
24. Interview previously cited.

Chapter 13: The Future

1. *Loc. cit.*
2. "Forgotten Clues to the TV Crisis," *New York Times Magazine,* December 13, 1959.
3. Quoted in *Variety,* September 13, 1967.
4. Letter to *New York Times,* August 5, 1961.
5. *Equal Time,* p. 79.
6. *Ibid.,* p. 85.

INDEX

ABC, 306, 307, 316
  Army-McCarthy hearings on, 251–52
  merger with ITT, 63–64
  news budget, 330
  profit, 331
  selling time to candidates, 235
  See also ABC News; *individual programs*
ABC News
  and affiliate stations, 29
  breakdown of content, 41
  expansion from 15 to 30 minutes, 29
  one evening compared with CBS and NBC, 42–54
  See also Smith, Howard K.
ABC Scope (documentary series), 29, 67–68
Accidental Family, 307
advertising, TV, xv
  cost of, 228–39
  impact of, 16, 224
  political, ix, 134–35
    impact of, 224
    used by Shapp in 1966 campaign, 149–57
  See also commercials
advertising agencies, 228
  used by JFK in 1960, 231
  used by Johnson in 1964, 204–209

advertising agencies (*Continued*)
  used by RFK in 1964, 202–203
  used by Rockefeller in 1966, 209–19
  used by Taft in 1950, 127
  See also individual agencies
AFTRA strike in 1967, 31
Agnew, Spiros, 124
Agriculture, Department of, 249
Agronsky, Martin, 257
Alexander, Herbert E., xi, 178, 229–30, 231, 237, 283, 285
Ally, Carl, on political commercials, 195–96
Alsop, Joseph, on Reagan, 143
American Broadcasting Corp., *see* ABC
American Federation of Television and Radio Artists, *see* AFTRA
American Political Science Association, 177
American Research Bureau (Arbitron), 297
American Revolution of 1963, The (NBC documentary), 8
Anti-Defamation League of B'nai B'rith, 273–74
Arbitron, 297
Arlen, Michael,
  quoted, 60

Arlen, Michael (*Continued*)
quoted (*Continued*)
on TV coverage of LBJ's trip to Manila, 315
on TV coverage of Vietnam War, 66–67
on TV voices, 14
Army-McCarthy hearings, 251–52
Associated Press, 45
and Goldwater, 190–91
used by network news, 22, 30, 33, 53
Atlantic, The, 243
AT&T, 259, 318, 322
audience, TV, 222–25
audience-electorate, 3–7
characteristics of, 15, 222–25
of sports programs, 24

Barron, Jerome A., 266–67
on Fairness Doctrine, 291
Battle of Newburgh, The, 272
Baus and Ross, management of Pat Brown's campaign by, 145–46
BBC, x, xi, 314
BBDO, 197
Becker, Samuel L., 196
Berlin, effect of JFK-Nixon debate in, 167
Berlin Wall, NBC film of tunnel under, 62
Beyond the Sky (NBC documentary), 80
Binns, Edward, 214
Biography of a Bookie Joint, 272
Black, Charles L., Jr., quoted, 17
Blondes Have More Fun (ABC documentary), 80
B'nai B'rith, 274
Bonanza, 309
Brechner, Joseph L., 274
Brinkley, David, 3, 34, 107, 251
and Administration policy, 69
with Huntley as convention anchor team, 98, 106–107

Brinkley, David (*Continued*)
quoted
on convention coverage, 69
on documentaries, 77
on Vietnam, 69
salary of, 32
on use of computers for election returns, 120
See also David Brinkley's Journal; Huntley-Brinkley Report
British Broadcasting Corporation, *see* BBC
Broadcasting magazine, on conventions, 100
Brocaw, Tom, 44
Brookings Institution, 98, 160
Brown, Pat
debate with Nixon, 176
1966 defeat by Reagan, 141–48
Bucci, E. John, 154–55
Bundy, McGeorge, 319
Burch, Dean, 208
and 1964 election, 121, 206
Butler, Paul, 113

Campaign Associates, 197–98, 231
Campaign Consultants, 225
Campbell, Angus, 224
Carnegie Commission, 37, 86, 322
Carson, Johnny, 192
Castro, Fidel, 293
Cater, Douglass, 166
on JFK-Nixon debates, 168
CATV, 323–25
CBS, 316, 317
Army-McCarthy hearings on 251–52
control of news broadcasts, 27
and Fulbright hearings, 253
policy on coverage of special events, 90–91
on presidential campaigns, 327
profit, 331
public relations, 25–26
and Public TV, 320

CBS (*Continued*)
  and resignation of Fred Friendly, 25, 319
  See also CBS News; *CBS Evening News with Walter Cronkite*; individual programs; Salant, Richard S.
CBS Evening News with Walter Cronkite, 3, 29, 39, 40, 66, 184
  breakdown of content, 41
  expansion from 15 to 30 minutes, 27, 77
  and Goldwater, 96–97
  one evening compared with ABC and NBC, 42–54
CBS News
  and affiliate stations, 29
  boycott of Emmys for news programs, 26
  Richard Salant on, 91
  See also CBS Evening News with Walter Cronkite; Cronkite, Walter; Salant, Richard S.
CBS News Hour, 223
CBS Reports (documentary series), 77, 85, 272
Chambers, Whittaker, Nixon and, 130
Chancellor, John, 101
Chet Huntley Reporting (NBC program), 27
Chicago Daily News, on JFK-Nixon debate, 169
Choice (film), 207–208
Christian Science Monitor, 300
Citizens' Research Foundation, 229
civil rights movement
  influence of TV on, 7–8
  TV coverage of demonstrations, 70–72
  TV coverage of riots, 72–74
Clark, Joseph, 239
Collingwood, Charles, 42–43
Collins, Leroy, 76, 276
Columbia Broadcasting System, *see* CBS
Commercials
  effect on audience, 16–17
  higher volume of, 16
  political, xviii, 182, 193–227
    Daisy commercial, 205, 208
    effect of, 196, 239
    Ice Cream commercial, 206, 208
    JFK's use of, 204
    Johnson's use of, 182, 204–209
    Nixon's use of, 204
    perversion of political role by, 195
    used by Rockefeller in 1966, 209–19
Commission on Campaign Costs, 178
Commission on Civil Disorders, 72
Committee on Convention Reform, 116, 118
Communications Subcommittee, 256
Computers
  used in elections, 119–22, 220–22, 228
  See also People Machine, The
Conventions, TV coverage of, xvii, 95–119
  Broadcasting magazine on, 100
  Charles Thomson on, 100
  Clif White on, 115, 117
  David Brinkley on, 106
  Edwin Roberts on, 100
  George Reedy on, 106
  Herbert Waltzer on, 97, 108
  John Galbraith on, 115–16
  1956 Democratic, 113, 117
  1948 Democratic & Republican, 99
  1964 Democratic, 99, 101, 110, 113
  1964 Republican, 101–104, 112–13
  Paul Tillett on, 114, 116, 118

Conventions (*Continued*)
  Richard Salant on, 105–106
  Theodore White on, 116
  Vance Hartke on, 113
Congressional Campaign Committee, 247
Coolidge, Calvin, 126–27
Cowan, Louis, 261
  quoted, on TV news, 19
Cox, Kenneth A., 274
Craig, May, 298
Cranston, Alan, 203
Cronkite, Walter, 3, 26, 108
  salary of, 32
  See also CBS Evening News with Walter Cronkite
Cuban missile crisis, 308, 311

Daley, Richard J., 116
Daly, Lar, 284
David, Edward E., Jr., 328
David Brinkley's Journal (NBC program), 27
Davis, Elmer, 37
Davis, John W., 127
Deardorff, John, 225
debates, 163–81
  art of avoiding, 174–81
  Brown-Nixon, 176
  Brown-Reagan, 145
  Dewey-Stassen, 127, 165
  Goldwater-Johnson, proposed, 178–80, 285
  Humphrey-JFK, 165
  involving incumbent President, 177–78
  Javits-Wagner, 165
  JFK-Nixon, 148, 163, 164, 165–72, 175, 199, 284
    chief criticism of, 171
  Keating-RFK, proposed, 163, 175–76
  Kefauver-Stevenson, 165
  Lincoln-Douglas, 164
  Romney-Swainson, 176

debates (*Continued*)
  Ted Kennedy–McCormack, 172–74, 175
Dewey, Thomas E., 99, 128, 129
  debate with Stassen, 127, 165
Dilworth, Richardson, 176
Dimension (CBS series), 37
Dingell, John D., 269
Dirksen, Everett, 193, 250n., 251
documentaries, 75–88
  ABC survey of, 81
  on Arab-Israeli war, 83
  David Brinkley quoted on, 77
  Jack Gould quoted on, 76, 76–77, 80
  N.Y. Times comments on, 84
  on politicians, 191–92
  and ratings, 80–81
  TV Guide on, 81, 82
  Variety comments on, 83, 84
Doerfer, John, 262, 284
Douglas, Paul, 136
Downs, Hugh, 60
Doyle Dane Bernbach
  used by Johnson, 204–209
Drew, Elizabeth, 243
Dr. Kildare, 236
Due to Circumstances Beyond Our Control (Friendly), 319
Dulles, John Foster, 307–308
Dumont network, 251–52
Dunphy, Jerry, 32

Edwards, Lee, 248
Eisenhower, Dwight, 209, 261, 305–306, 307–308, 332
  and 1956 campaign, 132–33, 228
  and 1952 campaign, 192–230
  and 1952 election, 128–29, 130–31
  and JFK-Nixon debates, 166
  personality of, 159–60
  and TV press conferences, 295–297
election nights, TV coverage of, 119–25

election nights (*Continued*)
  David Brinkley on, 120
  Eric Sevareid on, 120
  effect of early returns on outcome, 120–22
  John O. Pastore on, 122
  Kurt and Gladys Lang on, 121–22
  Pierre Salinger on, 121
  prediction of result, 122–24
  role of computers in, 119–20
Eleventh Hour News (NBC program), 22
Emphasis (NBC series), 37
Engle, Clair, 136–37
Equal Time provision, 183–84, 192, 231, 264, 281–87, 311, 327
  See also Fairness Doctrine
Evans, Mark, 225
Experiment in Television (NBC series), 23, 74
Eyewitness to History (CBS program), 27

Face the Nation (CBS program), 189, 255, 256
Fair Campaign Practices Committee, 206, 286
Fairness Doctrine, 184, 264–65, 270, 275–81, 291, 311
Farley, James A., 131
FCC, 46, 86, 155, 239, 243–45, 249, 259–91, 332
  and corporation control of broadcasting, 63–64
  and cost of political broadcasting, 230, 231–32, 234–35
  direct control of networks by, 76
  Equal Time provision, 183–84, 264, 281–87, 311
  Fairness Doctrine, 81, 184, 264–65, 270, 275–81, 291, 311
  regulations, 61, 259–91
  See also Minow, Newton
Federal Communications Commission, *see* FCC

Federal Corrupt Practices Act, 238–39
Felknor, Bruce, 102, 286
film, political, 146, 151–53, 228
  proposed use by Goldwater, 207–208
  used by JFK, 200–202
  used by RFK, 202
Folliard, Edward T., 297
Ford, Frederick W., 267
Ford Foundation, 319, 322
Foreman, Robert L., 78
Frank, Reuven, 103–104
Frank McGee Saturday Report (NBC program), 23
Frank McGee Sunday Report (NBC program), 23
Frankel, Max, 37
Frederick, Pauline, 60
Freed, Fred, 268, 269
Freeman, Orville, 87
Friendly, Fred, 75, 97
  and *CBS Reports,* 77
  resignation from CBS, 19, 25, 90, 253, 319
  and *See It Now* series, 75
Friendly, Henry J., 260
Fulbright hearings, 90–91, 188, 252–54

Galbraith, John Kenneth, quoted on conventions, 115–16
Gallup, George, 44
  poll on firearms control, 269
  poll of JFK vs. Nixon, 169
Gans, Herbert J.,
  quoted, 7, 8, 16
  on TV audience
  on TV's emphasis on visual, 50
Gardner, Gerald, 163, 176
Garrison, Jim, NBC program on, 85–86
Gaston, Robert, 249
Geylin, Philip, 313
Glaser, William A., 9

Goldwater, Barry, 135–36
    and CBS, 96–97
    commercials used by Johnson against, 204–209
    debate with Johnson, proposed, 178–80, 285
    delegates, 101, 112–13
    on *Issues and Answers,* 190–91
    newspapers' opposition to, 131–32
    and 1964 California primary, 120, 190–91
    and 1964 campaign, 231, 232, 237
    and 1964 convention, 101, 103–104, 112–13, 114, 115, 116, 117–18, 161, 233
    and 1964 election, 121
    upstaged by Howard K. Smith, 34
    use of Interpublic, 204
    use of TV by, 131–32
    and West German right-wing groups, 96–97
Goodman, Julian, 103
    quoted, 253
        on documentaries, 83
        on free time for candidates, 283
        on noncommercial broadcasting, 321
        on special events, 91
Goodman, Walter, 321
Gould, Jack, x, 308
    quoted
        on Army-McCarthy hearings, 252
        on CATV, 325
        on coverage of special events, 90
        on David Brinkley, 107
        on documentaries, 76, 76–77, 80, 84, 85
        on editorializing by station owners, 276
        on Eisenhower's TV press conference, 296

Gould, Jack (*Continued*)
    quoted (*Continued*)
        on equal time for fringe candidates, 283
        on fairness, 287
        on government pressure on TV, 63
        on *Harvest of Shame* documentary, 314
        on Pay Television, 262–63
        on public service vs. profit, 329
        on Public TV, 321
        on reorganization of FCC, 244–45
        on TV as time-killer, 14
        on TV awards, 26
        on TV coverage of President, 305
Graham, Billy, 310
Gray, Barry, 176
Guggenheim, Charles, 146, 151, 155, 202
Guild, Bascom and Bonfigli, 231
Guns of Will Sonnett, 307
Gunsmoke (CBS program), 12

Hagerty, James, 102, 296, 303, 305
Hall, Leonard, 137, 165
Halleck, Charles, 110, 250
Hard Day's Night, A, 223
Harriman, W. Averell, 234
Harris, Louis, 44, 124
    on loss of TV popularity among affluent, 15
    used by JFK in 1958, 135, 200–202
Hartke, Vance, on conventions, 113
Hartz, Jim, 22
Harvest of Shame (CBS documentary), 77, 314
Hatfield, Mark, 110
Hayden, Carl, 136
Health, Education and Welfare, Department of, 249

Henry, E. William, 261
Herblock, xiv
Hiss, Alger, Nixon and investigation of, 128
Holt, Harold, 316
Hoover, Herbert, 228, 259
House Commerce Committee, 282
House Committee on Interstate and Foreign Commerce, 269
Howe, Quincy, 37
Howell, Reg G., 266
Hughes, H. Stuart, 174
Humphrey, Hubert H., 192
 and convention reform, 110
 on debates involving incumbent President, 180
 debate with JFK, 165
 and Milton Shapp, 150
 on TV costs, 229, 236
 use of TV by, 201, 255–56
 and West Virginia primary, 200–201
Huntley, Chet, 3, 31, 33, 43, 107
 and Administration policy, 69
 with Brinkley as convention anchor team, 98, 106–107
 salary of, 32
 See also Chet Huntley Reporting; Huntley-Brinkley Report
Huntley-Brinkley Report, 3, 7, 29, 33, 35, 38–39, 57, 236
 breakdown of content, 41
 Dirksen on, 251
 expansion from 15 to 30 minutes, 27, 77
 one evening compared with ABC and CBS, 42–54
 preempted by sports, 24
 revenues from, 40
 See also Brinkley, David; Huntley, Chet
Hyde, Rosel, 261

Interpublic Group, used by Goldwater, 204

Issues and Answers (ABC program), 145, 180, 189, 255
Izvestia, 304

Jack Denove Productions, Inc., 231
Jack Tinker Associates, and 1966 Rockefeller campaign, xv, 210–19, 226–27, 234
Jaffe, Louis L. quoted, 13, 332
Janowitz, Morris, on TV coverage of Vietnam War, 65
Javits, Jacob, debate with Wagner, 165
Jennings, Peter, 41
 See also ABC News
Johnson, Lyndon B., 145, 184, 295, 307, 309–16, 318
 and debates, 178–80
 debate with Goldwater, proposed, 178–80, 285
 and firearms control, 268
 and Fulbright hearings, 253
 meeting with Kosygin, 306
 and 1964 campaign, 231, 237
 and 1964 Democratic Convention, 101, 110, 113–14
 and 1964 election, 120, 121
 1967 State of the Union Message, 305
 1966 flight to Honolulu, 188, 253, 294
 and public financing of campaigns, 184, 195, 238, 239, 284, 327
 relations with broadcasting industry, xix, 302, 316–17
 speech on Vietnam, 307
 TV's inhibiting effect on, 158
 TV press conferences, 299, 300–301, 303, 304
 use of commercials by, 182, 204–209, 226
 use of Joe Napolitan, 150
 walking press conferences, 193

Johnson, Mrs. Lyndon B., 193, 301
Johnson, Nicholas, 244, 260, 286, 331
Journal of Broadcasting, 274, 276, 277, 281
journalism, TV, *see* news, TV
Journals of Lewis and Clark, The (documentary), 81
Junior Press Conference of the Air, 192
Justice for All, 223

Kalber, Floyd, 32
Kate Smith Show, 192
Keating, Kenneth
  debate with RFK, proposed, 163, 175–76
  and 1964 campaign, 203, 237
  at 1964 convention, 104–105
Kefauver, Estes, 161
  debate with Stevenson, 165
  and 1952 convention, 117
Kendrick, Alexander, 37
Kennedy, Edward, 159, 251
  debate with McCormack, 172–74, 175
  on *Meet the Press,* 189
  1962 Senate campaign, 161–62, 202, 236
Kennedy, Jacqueline, 298
Kennedy, John F., 99, 113, 161, 177, 178
  on cost of TV, 228–29, 308
  debate with Humphrey, 165
  debate with Nixon, xiii–xiv, 148, 163, 164, 165–72, 175, 199, 284
  and Federal support of campaigns, 238
  and Milton Shapp, 150
  1960 campaign, 135, 221–22, 228, 231, 236
  1960 nomination, 116
  televised press conferences, 131, 296–99, 300, 301

Kennedy, John F. (*Continued*)
  TV appearance of, 139
  and TV appearances, 193, 306
  TV coverage of assassination and funeral, 88
  use of commercials in 1960, 204
  use of Guild, Bascom and Bonfigli, 231
  use of Joe Napolitan, 150
  use of Louis Harris, 135, 200–202
  and West Virginia primary, 200–202
Kennedy, Robert F., 87, 150, 188, 192, 216, 217, 239, 247, 251, 294
  assassination of, 272
  debate with Keating, proposed, 163, 175–76
  debate with McCarthy, 180
  on *Meet the Press,* 189–90
  and Milton Shapp, 150
  and 1968 California primary, 124
  and 1964 convention, 113–14
  and 1964 Senate campaign, 202–203, 237
  with Ronald Reagan on TV, 148–49
  TV coverage of assassination and funeral, 89
  TV impression on viewers of, 140–41
Kennedy Administration, 244, 311
Key, V. O., on TV news, 60
Khrushchev in Exile (NBC documentary), 28
King, Martin Luther, Jr., 271–72
  TV coverage of assassination and funeral, 89
Kintner, Robert E., 62, 103, 206, 207–208, 251–52, 261, 262, 298, 302
Kismet, 223
Kitchel, Denison, 117
Klein, Herb, 165, 166

Kleindienst, Richard, 204
KNXT-TV (Los Angeles), 32
Kosygin, Alexei, meeting with Johnson, 306
Kraft, Joseph, 143, 192
Kraus, Sidney, 166, 167, 168
Kravetz, Walter, 103–104
KREX, 266
Krugman, Herbert E., quoted, on impact of television advertising, 16, 224
KTBC-TV (Austin), 302
KTLA-TV (Los Angeles), 273
KTYM, 273
Kuchel, Thomas, 142
Kunzig, Robert, 153

Lafferty, Paul, on TV as escapism, 13–14
Laitin, Joseph, on Johnson's press conferences, 300
Landis, James M., 260
Lang, Kurt and Gladys,
  on early election returns, 121–22
  on JFK-Nixon debates, 168
Lawrence, Bill, 102
Lawrence, David, 152
LBJ Country, The, 312
Lee, Robert E., 155, 244
Legend of Marilyn Monroe, The (documentary), 81
Leonard, Bill, 97
Levin, Murray, xv, 160, 162, 172, 173
Lindsay, John V., 138, 187
  and police Review Board, 215
Lippmann, Walter, 192
Little Rock High School, 305
Lodge, George, 174
Lower, Elmer, 196
Lubell, Samuel
  quoted, 170
    on debates, 164, 168
    on Presidential image, 292

Lundberg, Ferdinand, on government pressure on TV, 63
Lyndon B. Johnson and the World (Geylin), 310
Lynn, Jack, 247

McAndrew, William R., 103, 270
  quoted
    on news image of network, 96
    on TV journalism, 18
McCarthy, Eugene, 124, 182, 190, 251
  debate with RFK, 180
  use of advertising by, 226
McCarthy, Joseph, 161, 226
McCormack, Edward
  cost of campaign against Kennedy, 236
  debate with Ted Kennedy, 172–74, 175
McDonald, Myron, 210, 211, 212, 214, 234–35
McGee, Frank, 23, 87, 160
McLendon, Sarah, 298
McLuhan, Marshall, 59–60
Maddox, Lester, 124
Magnuson, Warren, 256
Mahoney, George P., 124
Man Against the Machine, The (film), 146, 151, 153
Man from U.N.C.L.E., The, 256
Markel, Lester, 37
  quoted
    on evening news programs, 37
    on TV as entertainment, 19
    on TV lobby, 244
    on TV news presentation, 329
Marketing techniques, applied to political campaigns, 134–35, 200–202
Mass Communications Research Center, 168–69
Meet the Press (NBC program), 28, 60, 189–90, 255
  Brown and Reagan on, 145

Meet the Press (Continued)
　Robert Vaughn invited to appear on, 256
　Ted Kennedy on, 162
Merv Griffin Show, 192
Minow, Newton, 14, 76, 244
　quoted, xix–xx, 267
　　on advertisers, 78
　　on Communications Act of 1934, 332
　　on Congressmen and broadcasters, 243–44
　　on documentaries, 78
　　on editorializing, 276
　　on growing power of broadcasting, 245
　　and regulation of networks, 76, 288
　　"vast wasteland" speech, 28–29, 76
Mitgang, Herbert, 87–88
　on political documentaries, 191–92
Monroe, William B., Jr., 289, 306
　on granting the President TV time, 303
Montgomery, Robert, 296
Morgan, Edward P., 107–108
Morgenthau, Robert M., 138, 234
Morton, Thruston, 110, 111, 200, 208
Mr. Novak, 236
Mudd, Roger, 46, 51
Murphy, George, 147, 203
Murrow, Edward R., 37, 313, 314
　and *Harvest of Shame* program, 77
　McCarthy broadcast, 61
　quoted
　　on broadcast news, 18
　　and *See It Now* series, 75

Napolitan, Joseph
　on campaigns, 233

Napolitan, Joseph (*Continued*)
　Johnson's use of, 150
　Kennedy's use of, 150
　management of 1966 Shapp campaign, 149–57, 210
　and People Machine, 220–22
　quoted, xv, 139, 159
　　on debates, 174–75
　　on RFK, 140
National Association of Broadcasters, 245, 260, 263, 280
National Broadcasting Corp., *see* NBC
National Cable Television Association, 324
National Educational Television (NET), 37, 305, 318, 319
National Observer
　on campaign financing, 234
　on conventions, 96
National Rifle Association, 268, 271
NBC, 251, 306, 313, 315
　control of news broadcasts, 27
　on editorializing, 277–78
　and Fulbright hearings, 253–54
　granting President TV time, 303
　news budget, 330
　profits, 331
　public relations, 25–26
　revenues from *Huntley-Brinkley Report*, 40
　selling time to candidates, 235
　See also Huntley-Brinkley Report; individual programs; NBC News; Sarnoff, Robert
NBC News, 22
　and affiliate stations, 29
　use of news services by, 30
　See also Huntley-Brinkley Report
NET *Journal*, 322
networks
　control of news broadcasts by, 19, 20, 26–27
　prestige programs of, 20–21, 23, 25

INDEX | 357

networks (*Continued*)
  prestige provided by news broadcasts, 20–21, 23
  See also ABC; CBS; NBC
New York Stock Exchange
  and formation of all-electronic news service, 324
New York Times, 37, 233
  compared with TV news, 40, 43, 51–53
  NBC advertisement in, 22
  quoted
    on documentaries, 84
    on JFK press conference, 297
    on radio, 127
    on Reagan, 142
    on TV, 147
  used by networks, 30
  See also Gould, Jack; Markel, Lester; Mitgang, Herbert; Reston, James
New York Times Book Review, 321
New Yorker, The, see Arlen, Michael
Newman, Edwin, quoted, 89
news, TV, 18–55
  amount of material covered, 40–42
  audience of, 3–7
  candidates' use of, 184–93
  effect on public awareness, 56
  expansion from 15 to 30 minutes, 27, 77, 185–86
  glorification of commentators by, 32–34
  government pressure on, 61–64
  lack of background information in, 36
  lack of opinion and ideas in, 60–61
  neglect of reporting function, 32–35
  network control of, 19, 20, 26–27
  preempted by sports programs, 22–24

news, TV (*Continued*)
  preoccupation with visual effects, 35, 50, 54, 188
  as prestige for network, 20–21, 23, 27
  as "reassurer" of public, 58
  removed from Equal Time restriction, 184
  role of commentator in, 33
  role of reporter in, 30–33
  timeless features in, 50
  Vietnam War coverage by, 35, 65–70
  weekend, 22–24
  weekly reviews, possibility of, 37, 50
  See also ABC News, CBS News, NBC News
News in Perspective (NET program), 37
news services, used by networks, 30, 33, 53
newspapers, xvi
Newsweek, quoted, 88, 89
  on Reagan, 149
  on *Today* show interviews, 257
Newton, Carroll, 134, 165, 166, 196–99, 220
  on electorate, 223–24
Nielson Company, A. C., 209
  on convention audience, 99
  on public service broadcasts, 76
Nixon, Richard M., 203
  adaptation to TV, 126
  Checkers speech, 128–30
  debate with Brown, 176
  debate with JFK, xiii–xiv, 148, 163, 164, 165–172, 175, 199, 284
  on debates involving incumbent President, 180
  and investigation of Alger Hiss, 128
  Kitchen Debate, 61, 197
  1956 campaign, 230–31

Nixon, Richard M. (*Continued*)
  1952 campaign, 192
  1960 campaign, 135, 157, 196–99, 221, 228
  1960 convention, 116
  on *Open End,* 192
  refusal to debate with Rockefeller, 180
  TV appearance of, 138–39
  use of advertising, 196–99, 204, 226
Nofziger, Lyn, 158
North by Northwest, 307
Northshield, Shad, 103–104
North Vietnam—a Personal Report, 322
Nurses—Crisis in Medicine (ABC documentary), 78

O'Brien, Lawrence, 149–50
O'Connor, Frank, 141, 157
  1966 campaign, 187, 229, 237
  Rockefeller's use of commercials against, 215–18
O'Donnell, Harry, 140, 238
Open End, 192
Opinion Research Corporation, 170–71
Orth, Franklin, 269–71

Paley, William S., 83, 97, 176
  quoted, 75
  on fairness in controversy, 61
Panorama (BBC-TV program), xi
Papert Koenig Lois, 202
Pastore, John O., 122
Pay Television (PTV), 262
Peabody, Endicott, 159
Pearson, James B., 238–39
People Machine, the, definition of, ix, 219
  Napolitan's idea of, 220–22
Percy, Charles, 136, 185, 251
Perry, James M., 215, 234

Pettit, Tom, 30
Pfeiffer, William J., 210–12, 233–34, 236
Please Don't Eat the Daisies (Kerr), 303
Pravda, 304
President's Club, 230, 237–38
President's Commission on Civil Disorders, 8
Presley, Elvis, 99
Price, Bob, 138, 187
Public Broadcast Laboratory (PBL), 319
Public Broadcasting Corporation, President Johnson's commitment to, 318
Public Opinion Surveys, Inc., 155
public relations firms, use of, by candidates, 141–42
Public TV, 318–23
Pursuit of Happiness, The (film), 113
Pursuit of Pleasure, The (NBC documentary), 78–79, 84

Quayle, Oliver, 216, 217
Quemoy crisis, 305–307

ratings
  of documentaries, 80–81
  of news shows, 40
  as reason for CBS expansion of news time, 27
  See also Nielson
Rayburn, Sam, 255
RCA, and NBC, 331
Reagan, Ronald, 326
  KTLA editorial endorsing, 273
  1966 campaign, 232
  with RFK on TV, 148–49
  on TV, 158
  use of Spencer-Roberts, 141–42, 144
  victory over Pat Brown, 141–48

INDEX | 359

Real West, The (documentary), 81
Reedy, George, 91, 304, 311
  on convention coverage, 106
  on granting the President TV time, 304–305
  on TV's journalistic independence, 312
Republican Campaign Committee, 248–49
Republican National Committee, 232
Reston, James, 191, 292, 293, 310
  on JFK and TV, 308
  on Presidential press conferences, 296
  on weekly news reviews, 37
Reuters, 35
  used by network news, 22
Rich, John, 43
riots, TV coverage of, 72–74
Roberts, Bill, 142, 144
Roberts, Edwin A., Jr., on conventions, 96
Rockefeller, Nelson, 137–38, 207
  1960 convention, 116
  1964 California primary, 120, 190–91
  1964 convention, 112–13, 114, 117–18
  1966 gubernatorial campaign, 209–19, 229, 232, 233–34, 235, 236
  1966 gubernatorial reelection, xiv, 187–88
  request for debate with Nixon, 180
  upstaged by David Brinkley, 34
  use of commercials, 226–27
  use of Spencer-Roberts, 141–42
Rogers, William, on FCC and censorship, 332
Rogers, Ted, 197
Romney, George, 176, 186–87, 225, 226

Ronan, James A., 116
Ronan, William J., 211
Roosevelt, Franklin D., 127, 297, 308
  "fireside chats," 131
  newspapers' opposition to, 131
Roosevelt, Franklin D., Jr., 200, 217
Roosevelt, Theodore, 308
Roper, Burns W., xvi, 14–15, 276
Roper, Elmo, 7
  quoted, 9–10
Rousselot, John, 142
Rubin, Bernard
  on debates involving incumbent President, 177
  on Kefauver, 161
  on relations between broadcasting and Congress, 243
  on TV coverage of President, 292
Rusk, Dean, 254, 313

Safer, Morley, 68
Salant, Richard S., 40
  quoted, xix, 3
  on CBS News, 91
  on convention coverage, 105–106
  on threat of Congressional control of TV, 245
  on TV coverage of President, 293
Salinger, Pierre, 163, 303
  on *Harvest of Shame,* 314
  on JFK, 169
  on JFK and use of TV time, 296, 308
  and 1964 campaign, 203
  on 1964 election coverage, 121
Sarnoff, Robert, 165
  on Fairness Doctrine, 264
  on journalistic freedom for TV, 287, 290
  and Kitchen Debate film, 62
  opinion of TV, 14

Scammon, Richard
  quoted, 8–9, 224
Scherer, Ray, 315
Scherer-MacNeil Report, 315
Schlesinger, Arthur M., Jr., 190
  on criticism of JFK, 308
  on Fulbright hearings, 253
  on JFK's TV press conferences, 297
  on LBJ, 180
  on political commercials, 195
Schneider, John, 90, 326
Schorr, Dan, 96–97
Schulberg, Stuart, 74
Scott, Hugh, 167
Scott, Walter, 35
Scranton, William, 102, 153, 176
  and 1964 convention, 114, 161, 232–33
Section 315 of Communications Act, *see* Equal Time provision
See It Now (CBS documentary series), 75–76
Seldes, Gilbert, 140
Seltz, Herbert A., 166
Senate Commerce Committee, 285
Senate Foreign Relations Committee, 253, 254
Sevareid, Eric, 37, 42, 48, 108, 160, 279
  on use of computers for election returns, 120
Shafer, Raymond P., 153, 154
Shapp, Milton, 146, 232
  use of TV in 1966 campaign, 149–57, 210, 219
Sheridan, Walter, 85–86, 269
Siepmann, Charles A., 157–58
  on JFK-Nixon debates, 170
  on suspension of Equal Time provision, 285
Sixth Hour News (NBC program), 24
Slote, Leslie, 187

Slote, Leslie (*Continued*)
  on 1966 Rockefeller campaign, 187–88
  on TV news, 57
Smith, Alfred E., 127, 228
Smith, Howard K., 34, 107–108, 191, 279
Smith, Stephen, 217
special events, TV coverage of, 88–91
  Elizabeth II, coronation of, 89
  Jack Gould on, 90
  Julian Goodman on, 91
  Kennedy assassinations, 88
  King assassination, 89
  Kosygin's press conference, 90
  U.N. deliberations on Arab-Israeli war, 89
  Variety on, 90
Spencer-Roberts, public relations firm
  use of by Reagan and Rockefeller, 141–42, 144
Spivak, Lawrence E., 256
Spock, Dr. Benjamin, 256
Sponsor magazine, 230
Stanton, Frank, 122, 128, 167, 302, 309
  and polling by TV, 328
  quoted, 157
    on debates, 181
    on Equal Time provision, 282
    on JFK-Nixon debates, 171
    on public TV, 321
Stassen, Harold E., debate with Dewey, 127, 165
State of the Union Message, 1967, 305, 318
Stevenson, Adlai
  adaptation to TV, 126
  debate with Kefauver, 165
  "fireside chat" of 1952, 130
  1952 campaign, 128, 130–31, 230
  1956 campaign, 132–33

Stevenson, Adlai (*Continued*)
  1952 convention, 117
  TV impression, 199
Straus, Peter, 286
Sullivan, Ed, 99
Susskind, David, 192
Swainson, John, 176

Taft, Robert, 127
TelePrompTer, 310
television
  as "audience-deliverer" to advertisers, 12–13
  aversion to controversy in, 38
  candidates' use of, 126, 149–57, 184–93
  creation of candidate by, 161–62
  as depiction of real world, 10
  and escalation of campaign costs, 228–32
  as escape, 13–15
  government control of, 245
  influence on public opinion, 7
  influence on voter turnout, 8–10
  personality revealed by, 157–60, 162
  as reassurance, 13
  relationship with government, xviii–xix
  See also ABC; CBS; NBC; networks; news, TV
Television Code, 11, 12
Thomson, Charles
  quoted, 160
  on conventions, 100
  on political television, 279
Tillett, Paul, on conventions, 114–15, 116, 118
Time, 96
  on Milton Shapp, 152
Tinker, Jack, *see* Jack Tinker Associates
Today (NBC program), 60, 256, 257

Tonight (NBC program), 192
Town Meeting of the World (CBS program), 148–49
Truman, Harry S., 99, 199, 295, 297
  and 1952 convention, 117
TV Guide
  breakdown of ABC survey on documentaries, 81, 82
  quoting David Brinkley on Vietnam, 69

UHF channels, 288
  and NET, 319
United Press International (UPI)
  and formation of all-electronic news service, 324
  used by network news, 22, 33, 53
United States Information Agency (USIA), 313, 314
University of Mississippi, 306
Unruh, Jesse, 143

Valenti, Jack, 309
Vanocur, Sander, 104
Variety
  quoted, 279
    on coverage of special events, 90
    on documentaries, 83, 84
    on Fulbright hearings, 254
    on Lafferty's speech about TV as escapism, 13–14
    on low estimation of TV, 10–11
    on Robert Vaughn, Dr. Spock appearance on *Meet the Press*, 256
    on *Whose Right to Bear Arms?*, 271
Vaughn, Robert, 256
Vidal, Gore, 298
Vietnam War, 315
  as campaign issue, 226
  David Brinkley on, 69
  Fulbright hearings, 90–91, 188, 252–54

362 | INDEX

Vietnam War (*Continued*)
  peace talks, 307
  RFK on, 294
  TV coverage of
    Michael Arlen on, 66–67
    Morris Janowitz on, 65
    speech by Romney on, 225
    by TV news, 35, 65–70
Vietnam Weekly Review (NBC program), 67
Vietnam: Where We Stand, 223
Vision Associates, 159
Wagner, Robert, 138, 190
  debate with Javits, 165
Wallace, George, 30
Waltzer, Herbert, on conventions, 97, 108
Warren Commission, CBS serialized study of findings, 28
WBZ-TV, 226
WDSU, 277
Westin, Av, 39, 319
WFIL-TV, 328
White, F. Clifton, 112, 115, 204
  quoted, 139–40, 159
    on conventions, 117
White, Theodore H., x–xi

White, Theodore H. (*Continued*)
  quoted, 83, 113, 200
    on conventions, 116
    on JFK-Nixon debates, 168
    on JFK's use of Louis Harris, 135
    on Nixon's TV appearance, 138
    on Nixon's use of BBDO, 198–99
    on TV coverage of Negro Revolution, 72
Whose Right to Bear Arms?, 217
Wicker, Tom, 37, 191
Wilson, Woodrow, 228, 308
Winchell, Walter, 38
WMAQ-TV (Chicago), 29, 32
WMCA, 277, 286
WNDT (New York), 29
World of Jacqueline Kennedy, The (documentary), 81
World of James Bond, The (documentary), 81
Wolper, David, 154
Wright, James C., 229

Yates, Ted, 313
Yoakam, Richard D., 166
Yorty, Sam, 143–44

ABOUT THE AUTHOR

Born in 1931 in Montreal, Robert MacNeil received his A.B. from Carleton University. From 1955 to 1960 he was with Reuters News Agency in London and also worked in television for the CBC.

The author joined NBC News as a correspondent based in London in 1960. Among the major stories he covered were the wars in the Congo and Algeria, the building of the Berlin Wall and the Cuban Missile Crisis. In East Berlin and Cuba he was arrested and briefly held on spy charges. In 1963 Mr. MacNeil was transferred to Washington and covered the racial disturbances in Birmingham, Alabama, and Cambridge, Maryland, the assassination of President Kennedy from Dallas, Barry Goldwater's Presidential campaign, the Brazilian Revolution, and Sir Winston Churchill's death and funeral.

Moving to New York in 1965, the author was "Co-Anchorman" of the *Scherer-MacNeil Report,* covered the 1966 gubernatorial campaigns, and reported, wrote and narrated a number of news specials. In 1967 he was invited to join the BBC. Among his assignments have been the 1968 American Presidential campaign, the funerals of Martin Luther King, Jr., and Senator Robert F. Kennedy and the French Crisis of May, 1968.

Mr. MacNeil now lives with his wife, Jane, and three children in London.

Design by Sidney Feinberg
Set in Linotype Times Roman
Composed, printed and bound by American Book–Stratford Press
HARPER & ROW, PUBLISHERS, INCORPORATED